P9-CPW-923

3. 60

Friend of Life

ELIZABETH GRAY VINING

Friend of Life

THE BIOGRAPHY OF

Rufus M. Jones

J. B. LIPPINCOTT COMPANY

PHILADELPHIA   *NEW YORK*

Printed in the United States of America

To

Mary Hoxie Jones

Preface

To have lived for three years so close to the mind and spirit of Rufus M. Jones has been a rare privilege and an experience both stimulating and satisfying. It has also brought me into contact with many other persons, to whom I wish to express my warm appreciation of their generous aid and advice.

My thanks go first of all to Rufus Jones's daughter, Mary Hoxie Jones, who has given me unstinted help and encouragement. She has, in the first place, put at my disposal the wealth of manuscript material which came to light after her father's death. This includes letters, both to and from Rufus Jones, family correspondence over a long span of years, notebooks, calendars, photographs, manuscripts of articles, addresses and books, and the unpublished Journal of his first trip to the Orient. This material, which was assembled and classified, first by Mary Hoxie Jones and her mother, Elizabeth B. Jones, and then, after Mrs. Jones's death at Haverford in 1952, by Miss Ruth Hays Smith, is now housed in the Library of Haverford College, for restricted use. It includes also notes taken by Mary Hoxie Jones on conversations with her father during the years 1939 to 1948, and after her father's death with friends who remembered him, some of whom are no longer living. I am grateful also to Mary Hoxie Jones for permission to quote copiously from her invaluable brief biography, RUFUS M. JONES, published in England in pamphlet form by the Friends Home Service Committee, London, 1955. And not least of all I am indebted to her for her tireless willingness to answer questions of all kinds and to check points of fact.

To Henry J. Cadbury I am grateful for a sympathetic and careful reading of the whole manuscript and to Lydia C. Cadbury for her translation from the German of the letters of Theodor Sippell to Rufus Jones.

The Honorable Herbert Hoover was kind enough not only to see me and talk with me about his associations with Rufus Jones,

but also to lend me the file of correspondence between himself
and Rufus Jones from the Hoover Collection in Palo Alto, which
supplemented those of the Rufus Jones Collection at Haverford
and the A.F.S.C. files there. Mr. Hoover also read the chapter entitled "Herbert Hoover and Friend Jones" and made valuable suggestions for the amplification and clarification of the complicated
story of the negotiations described in it.

To Clarence E. Pickett, who has read the three chapters concerning
the American Friends Service Committee, and Douglas V. Steere,
who read the chapter on "The Mysticism of Rufus Jones," I wish to
express my appreciation, and to say that they are in no way responsible for any discrepancies that may appear in those chapters.

D. Robert Yarnall and George A. Walton, who accompanied
Rufus Jones to Germany in 1938, most generously made available
to me their diaries, notes, and personal letters written during that
momentous expedition, on which I have drawn heavily for fact and
background.

To the Honorable Francis B. Sayre, for allowing me to quote
his letter to Rufus Jones on the Truce of God, and to the many
correspondents who wrote me about their memories of Rufus Jones,
as well as friends and Friends in personal interviews who told me
revealing incidents, I am profoundly grateful.

During the month that I spent in England in 1957 the cordial
welcome of English Friends and their varied assistance helped me to
recover the atmosphere which surrounded Rufus Jones in his long and
close association with English Quakerism. To Eric D. Cleaver,
secretary of the Rowntree Trust, to the Wardens and Faculty of
Woodbrooke College, with which Rufus Jones had an especial tie,
to Miss Jean Rowntree and Mrs. George Crossley, daughters of John
Wilhelm Rowntree, and to the late Barrow Cadbury and the late
John S. Hoyland, I am especially grateful. In Marburg, Germany, I
was fortunate enough to have illuminating conversations with Herr
Theodor Sippell and Fräulein Hanna Happich.

Miss Anna B. Hewitt, in charge of the Quaker Collection, Haverford College Library, has been a constant source of cheerful and
able assistance, and Miss Muriel A. Hicks of the Library of Friends
House, London, was helpful to me during my time there.

To The Macmillan Company, New York, I am indebted for permission to make numerous quotations from the following books by
Rufus Jones: FINDING THE TRAIL OF LIFE, 1926; PATHWAYS TO THE

REALITY OF GOD, 1931; THE ETERNAL GOSPEL, 1938; THE FLOWERING OF MYSTICISM, 1939; A SMALL-TOWN BOY, 1941; NEW EYES FOR INVISIBLES, 1943; THE RADIANT LIFE, 1944; THE LUMINOUS TRAIL, 1947; A CALL TO WHAT IS VITAL, 1948.

E. G. V.

Contents

Illustrations

Friend of Life

I

South China, Maine

On THE night of January 25, 1863, the village of South China, Maine, lay blanketed in snow. It was a beautiful village with its avenue of elms, its large, well-built houses, its violin-shaped lake, and it was remote and self-sustaining as no hamlet in the country is today.

A light burned in the front parlor of Edwin Jones's house at the edge of the village facing the lake. A baby wailed his first cry. The village doctor delivered the child into the arms of his Aunt Peace, who, holding him, uttered words of prophecy:

"This child will one day bear the message of the Gospel to distant lands and to peoples across the sea."

"It was spoken," wrote Rufus Jones many years later, "solemnly and with a calm assurance as though she saw the little thing suddenly rising out of her lap to go."

The baby was named Rufus Matthew; Rufus for a paternal uncle who had died the previous year, and Matthew for his mother's father. He came into a family that consisted of six persons: a sister, Alice, four years old; a brother, Walter, ten; his father, mother, grandmother, and Aunt Peace.

On both sides his forebears had been Quakers for generations. Thomas Jones and his wife Thankful, who had come from Wales to Massachusetts in 1690, were probably Friends. Rufus Jones took

satisfaction in the fact that "by a series of happy marriages" he
inherited also the blood of four colonial governors of Rhode Island.
Abel Jones, great-grandson of Thomas and Thankful, born in Brunswick and a member of the nearby Durham Friends Meeting, came
to China Lake in 1803, when Maine was still a part of Massachusetts
and China was called Harlem. The region around the lake had been
sparsely settled by Quakers and Baptists thirty years earlier. Two
years after Abel began to clear his first farm, Jedediah Jepson, a
Friend of Irish descent, came from Berwick with his son and his
young daughter Susannah. Abel and Susannah were married in 1806.
First and last they cleared seven farms out of the wilderness, enough
to endow each of their seven sons. To their youngest son, Edwin,
came the house, built in 1815, in which Rufus Jones was born.

Susannah Jepson Jones, through her mother, Peace Robinson, was
descended from the great John Robinson of Leyden, who said to
the Pilgrims as they left Holland, "God has yet more light and truth
to break forth from His word." "Grandmother Susie" was one of the
pioneer women to whom the United States owes much of its character and spirit. She bore eleven children and reared nine of them.
She was cook, dairymaid, weaver, tailor, gardener, soapmaker and
laundress, as well as mother, nurse, and, for many years, elder in
the Friends Meeting. She smoked her long clay pipe three times
a day—and she must have needed it. To her practical ability, her
grandson testifies, was added "breadth of mind and depth of heart,
and a culture whose source and origin nobody could explain."

In addition she could remember in her old age the wilderness
adventures of her girlhood and regale an enthralled small boy with
stories of Indians, of moose, of herring-runs so thick you could
walks across the lake on their backs, and the shooting of the only
cow in the settlement by mistake for a deer. Born in the last year
of the Revolutionary War, she was seventy-nine at the time of
Rufus's birth, and she lived until he was fourteen.

Peace Jones was Susannah's second daughter, Edwin's sister. She
was forty-eight in 1863, and unmarried. A photograph of that time
shows dark hair parted in the middle, under a white cap, beautiful
eyes, full of wisdom and clarity, a sweet, controlled mouth, a serious,
serene, strong face. Again and again in his books and articles Rufus
Jones paid tribute to Aunt Peace and to the influence she had upon
him, not merely through her words but through her radiant presence in the household, her extraordinary understanding of him, her

rare gift of insight. Long before he ever heard the word *mystic* he recognized its quality in Aunt Peace. He never ceased to marvel at the grace of manner, the wisdom, the cultivated mind of this woman who grew up in surroundings that were simple sometimes to the point of crudity. In 1900 he wrote of her to a friend, "She is a very finegrained soul, a pure exotic, quite unlike the native growth."

Into this household dominated by two unusually strong women had come nineteen-year-old, red-haired Mary Hoxie—and had held her own. Rufus's mother was thirty in 1863, pretty in an honest, unaffected way, with a wide mouth, humorous, sweet, and sensitive, and big luminous eyes, a slightly turned-up nose. She was the daughter of Matthew Hoxie, a Quaker cabinet-maker of Albion, a village fifteen miles away. It was from him that Rufus got his blue eyes and light hair, and his humor. The Hoxies were of English descent, with possibly a French origin in the mists of time. There never was any question that Mary Jones was the mistress of the house, or that the reverence which her son gave to his Aunt Peace took nothing at all from his love and need of his mother.

Of Edwin, his father, Rufus Jones wrote always with loyal affection. "He was a straight, honest, faithful, rugged man who in his small round did his plain duty day by day and somehow managed to support our large family with his hands." Undoubtedly he had his peculiarities. He wore his overcoat all year round, in winter to keep the heat in, in summer to keep it out. His granddaughter, Walter's daughter, reports that he was "difficult." He would postpone necessary work until it was almost too late, and then would do it all at once in a prodigious burst of energy. The report that he was epileptic seems not to have been true; in his youth he was subject to some sort of "fits," from which in later years he entirely recovered. Like Jess Birdwell, in Jessamyn West's THE FRIENDLY PERSUASION, he had a keen eye for horseflesh and was a skillful driver, though it was on his annual visit to the County Fair, rather than in going to Meeting, that he urged his Morgan mare Fannie to pass all other carriages.

Rufus Jones himself has told the story of his boyhood—"that marvelous epoch between five and fifteen"—in two little books which are classics of their kind. FINDING THE TRAIL OF LIFE covers the adventures of his spirit, A SMALL-TOWN BOY the environment in which he grew up. His literary style had reached a kind of perfection; clear, simple, flexible, warm, lighted by his inimitable humor and penetrating shafts of insight. He saw his childhood not sentimentally but lovingly; his

memory was faithful to homely details as well as to the reaches of
the spirit; and the picture that results is not of one family and one
village alone, but a way of life in a vanished age.

Out of such a wealth of material it is not possible to include all the
threads that were woven into the fabric of his life, or even to summarize the whole. One can only select what seem to be the enduring
influences, and attempt to trace, as he himself said an illuminating
biography should do, "the springs and motives, the sentiments and
loyalties which build character."

The home into which he was born was unquestionably the determining factor in the kind of man he became. Some men of genius are
sports in their families, startling variations from the parent stock, but
not Rufus Jones. One could not imagine him springing from any
other plant.

Outwardly, it was quite normal and ordinary, even a little limiting.
The house was a large, plain, two-story frame house with a long ell
stretching behind it to the barn. The farm which supported it was a
small one, worked by Edwin Jones with such assistance as his growing
sons could give him: there was no hired man. From the time Rufus
was big enough to wield a small ax he helped cut wood for the
winter supply; he drove the cows to and from pasture, and milked
them; he helped with the hoeing, weeding, threshing, and haying;
when it came time to work out the family road-tax, he was one of
the troop with the plow and scraper.

It was necessarily a hard-working, frugal household of busy people.
There were others in the village who had more possessions and more
leisure, but none who were more generous in hospitality. It was to the
Jones house that a constant stream of Quaker visitors came—an average
of one or more a week—and were made welcome in the spare room,
regaled with the simple, abundant farm fare, which in winter consisted
of carrots, potatoes, beets, and turnips from the cellar, salt pork from
the barrel, cheese, baked beans, and pies made of dried apples.

All of the family were deeply religious in the Quaker way. "I was
not 'christened' in a church," wrote Rufus Jones in FINDING THE
TRAIL OF LIFE, "but I was sprinkled from morning till night with the
dew of religion. We never ate a meal which did not begin with a hush
of thanksgiving; we never began a day without 'a family gathering' at
which Mother read a chapter of the Bible, after which there would
follow a weighty silence."

In 1945 Theodore Dreiser lifted this passage bodily from FINDING
THE TRAIL OF LIFE and incorporated it in his novel about Quakers,

THE BULWARK: "Solon and Cynthia Barnes, the children [of Rufus Barnes] never ate a meal which did not begin with the hush of thanksgiving, and apart from that, no day was ever begun without a family gathering at which Mrs. Barnes read a chapter of the Bible, which was followed by a weighty silence." Two other incidents from Rufus's childhood, which will be described later, were appropriated in the same way.

Whereas Dreiser stopped with the "weighty silence," Rufus Jones went on to explain the meaning of that silence and its effect on the child he was. The fact that there was work pressing to be done on the farm, and yet, even so, time was invariably taken for this daily practice, impressed upon the boy the importance which the grown-ups attached to it. When occasionally the silence was broken by one or another speaking simply and quietly to God, he realized both the reason for the silence and the communion that was sought and experienced in it. Unconsciously he early acquired a conviction of the reality of the "unseen world impinging on his world of things" that he never lost and which became the basis of his mature faith.

Twice a week the whole family went to Meeting. On Sunday and Thursday mornings the four-wheeled wagon with the buggy seat would be hitched up. The parents and Alice sat on the seat, the boys on the floor with their legs dangling over the side. After Walter, the eldest, was old enough to go away to become a carpenter, Rufus had Herbert, four years younger than himself, to sit beside him. In winter there was a warm soapstone under the buffalo robes. The road led three miles through deep woods to Dirigo Meeting, which stood on a hill from which the Kenebago Mountains, eighty miles away, could be seen on clear days.

Meeting lasted two hours and was mainly silent. Even when he was so small that his feet did not touch the floor, Rufus understood the silence and fed on it. The spoken messages, when they came, varied widely. His father's message was always the same, something about "making a little heaven on the way to Heaven." That he expected and respected, but it must have been difficult to keep his bubbling laughter under control when an earnest Friend would rise week after week and declare solemnly, "The question isn't whether or no or not we darsent, no, not by no means." When Eli and Sybil Jones were there, however, it was quite different. Rufus was fired by Uncle Eli's gospel of valiant action and awed by Aunt Sybil's spiritual power. But they were recognized everywhere as two of the greatest living Friends and were often away from their Dirigo farm.

Eli Jones was Abel's eldest son, twenty-one years older than his brother Edwin. He had married Sybil Jones of Brunswick, and in 1840 they began the series of religious journeys which took them first to Nova Scotia and later to England, Liberia and Sierra Leone, Europe, Greece, and the Holy Land, and resulted in the establishment of Friends schools in Syria and Palestine. They had five children, and the leaving them behind, in school or in the care of relatives, was fraught with anguish.

Sybil Jones was considered the greater of the two. The "concerns" arose with her, and in the beginning Eli went along as her traveling companion. She had a beautiful voice, "like wind in the pine trees," and a rare gift for speaking; her message was always the overwhelming and penetrating love of God. Though she was never in robust health, her courage and determination carried her through the most strenuous travels. To her small nephew, as to countless others, she was a saint and a seer, but the modern observer studying her photograph—the intense brooding face within the frame of the Quaker cap—wonders if a gifted woman, restless with the pressure of unused talents, did not find in religious missions a glorious escape from the narrow confines of a small farm in the backwoods.

Her husband Eli, strikingly handsome in a patriarchal way, compelled a respect and admiration perhaps less immediately obvious but more soundly based. To English Friends he was the ideal of an American Quaker, a forthright, simple farmer, whose natural dignity made him at ease and self-forgetful in any company, a self-taught man of intellectual stature and moral force, whose messages brought conviction. John Bright recorded in his diary that Eli Jones had preached the greatest sermon that he had ever heard. At home, he carried his religious insights into practical action, laboring unceasingly for the cause of temperance, a better system of taxation for the town, and the support of the town library—or going to visit a sick neighbor.

Sometimes there were visiting Friends from distant parts of the United States or even from England. The itinerant ministry was part of the genius of nineteenth century Quakerism. By this method, which had sprung up and been developed through two centuries, a religious society of scattered members without a central authority, a presbytery or a priesthood, was held together, instructed, and reinvigorated. A member of a Meeting, perhaps a recognized leader, or perhaps one of the obscurer Friends, would feel a concern to travel in the ministry. He, or frequently she, would bring this concern to the Monthly

Meeting, which, after deliberation, would liberate the Friend to go, usually with an appointed traveling companion. It was all immensely serious, done with a profound sense of mission and often at considerable personal sacrifice of time, money and strength. Aunt Peace had once gone on such a journey to Iowa and Kansas—very far away in the 1860's—and her return was one of Rufus's most exciting early experiences.

In addition to the semi-weekly meetings for worship, there was also a monthly meeting. The purpose of this was to deal with the business affairs of the meeting, but since it is a fundamental part of the Quaker belief that religion and life are bound together and that nothing is really secular, the monthly meetings had nearly as much silence and fully as much moral and spiritual exhortation as the meetings for worship. Monthly Meeting, however, took place in the afternoon, and afterwards Friends were invited to farmhouses in the neighborhood for a bountiful supper. To the small boy, weary and hungry and stiff from two hours on an uncushioned bench, this was the high point of the day. It was moreover a cherished opportunity to play with Charlie Jacob, a beloved cousin of his own age, who lived at Dirigo and whom, ordinarily, he saw only at meetings for worship.

There were few books in the home in which Rufus Jones grew up. "The Bible was our one book," he wrote, "and we used it as a scholar uses his library." This is not to be taken literally, however, for we find twelve-year-old Rufus paying his way into membership in the village library with a copy of J. G. Holland's LIFE OF ABRAHAM LINCOLN which his father gave him for the purpose. Two other publications competed for second place in literary importance, the indispensable *Farmer's Almanac*, and *The Friends Review*, a weekly "religious literary and miscellaneous journal." One would think that there was little in this sober sheet for a boy, but the man remembered, "In my boyhood home it came next to the Bible and was eagerly waited for by young and old." As one leafs through the bound volume for the year 1873, the year that Rufus was ten and laid up with an injured foot for many months, doubtless willing to vary the Bible with news from the outside world, one comes on articles that would appeal to the eager and intelligent boy; articles on Meteor Showers and the Transit of Venus, on the sea (that still fascinating subject), on storms, or the past and future of Niagara, and other scientific plums amid the dough of religious discussion. Each week there was a summary of Foreign News. The King of Spain abdicated and a republic was proclaimed.

Those in Alsace and Lorraine who decided to remain French were emigrating in great numbers. Britain declared her intention to protect Afghanistan against attack in case Russia annexed Khiva. The railway between Tokyo and Yokohama, the first in Japan, was formally opened by the Emperor. Quaker news also found its place, and Rufus could read here of "our valued Friend, J. Bevan Braithwaite of London," of Haverford College, and of John Greenleaf Whittier years before he was to meet all three in the life. *The Friends Review* was to play an important part in Rufus's career, and some of the threads of his later interests run through those volumes of the 1870's.

It was a home of great moral earnestness. Once when small Rufus said something hurt "like the devil," his father said slowly, "Thee is never to use that expression again in thy whole life"—and he didn't. Duty was one of the foundation stones of existence. Aunt Peace defended the cause of truth by making Rufus return without reading the copy of GULLIVER'S TRAVELS which he had borrowed from the library—he considered it, when he was sixty-three, the only mistake she ever made, though he accepted the ruling unquestioningly at the time. And yet in spite of occasional austerity it was a moral earnestness so natural, so inevitable, so attractive that all his life the effort to be good was to seem a beautiful thing to him. When he was thirty-seven he wrote to Elizabeth Cadbury, "I think there is nothing more beautiful in this world than a soul all aglow with the fire of resolve to be *good* at all costs and hazards."

So many boys who have grown up in religious homes have later rebelled bitterly against religion—"I got enough of church when I was a boy to last me all my life"—that it is perhaps worth while to inquire why this did not happen to Rufus Jones. There was never any rejection of what he received at home, only a deepening of the roots, and a flowering of the seeds planted and nurtured in that early home.

It was, for one thing, never in any sense professional religion, with all that that term implies of a front maintained with thought and effort and a relaxation behind the scenes. What was true in Meeting was true for every day. There was little talk about worship. "It was a religion which we *did* together. Almost nothing was *said* in the way of instructing me." It was not a narrow, rigid set of dogmas from which the developing mind reacts. God was an indwelling Spirit, not a "sky God." Above all it was a religion of love, "The life in our home was saturated with the reality and the practice of love. We spoke to each other as though love were ruling and guiding us."

Rufus Jones records an instance of his mother's discipline that not only reveals his own normal boyish sins but sheds light on the quality of his mother and her sureness of touch. Though the story is told in FINDING THE TRAIL OF LIFE, a more detailed account is given in a chapter he wrote in the year of his death for a book of "spiritual autobiographies."

In this chapter he described the hot summer day, the turnip patch choked with weeds, and the task which his parents set him before they drove off to Augusta for the day. Along came a band of his young friends, carrying tackle and bait, urging him to go fishing with them on the lake in a boat. They promised to help him with the weeding— after they came back. It was late when he returned and with a pang he saw his mother watching his approach.

"Mother in silence took me by the hand," he wrote, "and led me to my room. I knew what I deserved and expected to get it in full measure. But a miracle happened instead. Mother put me in a chair, kneeled down, put her hands on me and told God all about me. She interpreted her dream of what my life was to be. She portrayed the boy and the man of her hopes. She told God what she had always expected me to be. And then how I had disappointed her hopes. 'O God,' she said, 'take this boy of mine and make him the boy and man he is divinely designed to be.' Then she bent over and kissed me and went out and left me alone in the silence with God. That was an epoch. I discovered then and there the meaning of grace—*agape*—not only in a wonderful mother but in the Heart of God."

Such a Quaker home, enclosed, tender, guided, while not universal, was not singular or perhaps even very unusual, in its day. A number of Quaker journals of the eighteenth and early nineteenth centuries give similar pictures. But its day was passing as the world changed after the Civil War. "The Quakerism which was the atmosphere of this boy's life," wrote Rufus Jones, "has in a large measure already ceased from the earth. It was a unique type of religious life, and it kept its peculiar form only as long as it existed apart from the currents of the larger social whole."

Outside of the home and all around it, was the village. Before the fire of 1872, which destroyed some twenty-two buildings as well as the avenue of glorious elms, it had been a beautiful village. Though rebuilt after the fire, it was never again so prosperous or so comely. The new houses belonged to a less happy period of architecture than those they replaced; maples grew where the elms had been. Though the Jones house was spared, they had some anxious hours while the waves of flames rolled closer and closer, and the small boy learned of the black squares on the checkerboard of life, and pondered the problem of evil. He knew that the fire was set by an evil man; for the first time he knew that good people had to suffer.

Four roads met in the center of South China: the roads to Augusta, to Belfast, to Bangor, and to Damariscotta. But the highways of those days were narrow, hilly, and rough, and even the twelve miles to Augusta were formidable. The village was self-contained; it made its own shoes; there was a carriage shop as well as a smithy; before the fire there was a bank. Town meeting twice a year was a great event, and the issues were thrashed out for months before and after by the cracker-barrel philosophers in the grocery store. Rufus, going daily for the mail, lingered to hear them talk. He liked their salty humor, and he gathered up their stories. Sometimes the way home in the dark afterwards was made fearful by the tales he had heard of supernatural lights followed by sudden deaths.

Still more interesting to Rufus was the band of village boys, of whom he was the acknowledged leader. More carefree than he, they waited for him to finish his chores, or would go with him to fetch the cattle from the pasture. A playground of infinite variety and adventure lay all around them: the lake for swimming, fishing, and boating in the summer, for skating and coasting in the winter—"No one who has not experienced it can appreciate the worth of a lake to a boy"—the woods, where they visited Indian camps still inhabited by actual woods Indians, the village itself, where they played "guard's clear," "truck," and other games in the back yards and barns. Play, he wrote, "is one of the greatest of the nurturing forces of group-life, and it contributes to health and sanity and joy to an almost unparalleled degree."

When he was past eighty, I heard him preach a Lenten mid-day sermon on the text that had been a favorite of his all his life. "They that wait upon the Lord shall renew their strength; they shall mount up with wings as eagles; they shall run and not be weary; and they shall walk and not faint." "When I was a boy," he said, "I never walked if I could help it. I always ran—and usually along the tops of the fences." One can see him still, barefoot, thin and wiry, his yellow hair ruffled in the wind, his blue eyes alight, flying along the tops of the stone walls, followed by his yelling gang. "My group of boys, as we played together and did daring things together, helped me to build secretly and silently the hidden inner self which they very little suspected."

It was an inner self immensely receptive to beauty. The stars, the lake in all its varied moods, the distant mountains, the migrating wild geese, the call of the loons at night, the swish of his scythe in wet grass, the sound of his ax in the snowy woods: all fell on his heart and filled it with delight. It was an inner world of imaginative fears, fear of the creatures that lived in the cellar and the attic, of strange lights and portents, fears never acknowledged outwardly, and overcome in the end by bold investigation. It was a hidden battleground of moral issues.

When he was ten, he had one of the experiences that he termed "epoch." A stone bruise on his foot had turned into a painful abscess, and the doctor was summoned. Finding his lancet dull, the good man sent for the whetstone from the barn, and sharpened the blade before he opened the abscess. The foot promptly became infected and the infection spread up the leg. For nine months the active boy lay on a couch in the living-room, in danger of losing his leg, and, at first, in great pain and in danger of his life.

Now he came to know the depth and tenderness of his mother's love, as she sat up all night with him that first week, holding the swollen and agonizingly painful leg in her hands, whispering words of comfort and encouragement.

As time went on and some way of amusing him had to be found, he and his eighty-eight-year-old grandmother entertained each other, she by telling him stories of pioneer days, he by reading the Bible aloud to her while she knitted. They ploughed without skipping through the Begat chapters, Rufus dealing as best he could with names like Chedorlaomer; they delighted in the hero stories, and bogged down at length in Jeremiah.

There was one time when the fear of death came close indeed. Rufus awoke to find the bone of his foot actually protruding through the flesh; he saw himself in rapid disintegration, and he wept aloud. Then Aunt Peace came to him. Acknowledging the dark moment, she assured him that it was only a tunnel in his earthly journey, from which he would soon emerge into the light. "And then with her prophetess face all lighted up with the warmth and glow of her vision, she said: 'This is not the end; this is the beginning. There are much better things ahead than behind. God is going to make thy coming days thy best days.' My fear vanished. My discouragement disappeared. I was ready to live again. In her faith I found my own."

To this prophecy was added that of a visiting Friend. James E.

Rhoads, "a dear, saintly man, who was as graceful and courtly as though he had been a knight of Arthur's Round Table," was traveling in the ministry with Rufus King of North Carolina. They stayed with the Joneses, as visiting Friends usually did, and one morning when the family sat together in silence, James Rhoads suddenly rose, walked across the room, and laid his hand on Rufus's head. "In this crooked and perverse world," he said, "this boy will be a shining light."

Years later, James Rhoads was President of Bryn Mawr College and Rufus Jones was one of its Trustees. Though they knew each other very well, Rufus Jones never reminded James Rhoads of this "extraordinary utterance," and Rhoads himself never mentioned it. But it had made a deep impression on the sensitive boy. "Nothing seemed more unlikely," Rufus Jones said, seventy-five years later, just before his death, "and yet I could not get over the feeling of that prophetic hand on my head." Together with Aunt Peace's prophecy and her earlier one at his birth, it gave him the conviction that his life had been spared for a purpose, that he had been chosen for a destiny which for many years remained hidden from him.

This whole episode of the injury, the doctor's methods and Aunt Peace's prophecy appears in THE BULWARK. The injury is described as having come not from a stone bruise but from a cut from his ax when the boy was helping his father with the wood-cutting. Here Dreiser borrows from another passage in FINDING THE TRAIL OF LIFE. Rufus Jones wrote: "I began my trips to the woods in winter very early in life, going with father at first to ride on the sled loads of fire wood; then as soon as I could handle a small ax, I trimmed off the branches of the big trees which he felled, and I rapidly reached the stage when I could join in the splendid work of bringing the trees down. I still pride myself on being a skilled wood chopper with some of the craft of the expert woodsman. Here in the winter woods of Maine was beauty enough to feed any young soul and mine was full of joy over it." This appears in THE BULWARK as: "He very early began to take trips with his father to the woods in winter to obtain an ample supply of firewood. At the very first, Solon went merely for the ride and to explore the woods. A little later, when he was old enough to handle a small ax given him by his father he was allowed to trim off the branches of the big trees which his father felled. However, his growth in body and strength being considerable, before long he was allowed by Rufus to join in the, to him, splendid work of felling the beautiful evergreens of the snowy forests."

In Dreiser's story, the boy's ax slipped and he cut his leg above his left ankle. The doctor came. "Having first opened and looked at the wound, which Solon's father had bound with his handkerchief and some strips of rags, he proceeded to grind his lancet, with which he proposed to trim and cleanse the wound, on a scythe stone from the family barn!" The result, as in the case of Rufus Jones, was infection, long illness, and the moment of despair. Instead of Aunt Peace, as in the passage quoted above, it was the boy's mother who came to prophesy over him. "Do not cry, Solon, my son, thy life and health have only now been given into thy keeping. This is not an end for thee—it is just the beginning. God is going to make thy coming days thy best. Thee will live to serve him in love and truth."

The third incident which Rufus Jones noted that Dreiser had borrowed from him was that of the schoolboy fight. Here, however, the parallel is much less obvious. It is true, Rufus Jones did engage in two fights, under provocation, and in both cases he held his own and became friends with the boys afterwards. Dreiser evidently held fighting to be too un-Quakerly an activity for his hero, and, though he allowed him to wrestle successfully, he made him decline further combat with the words, "I do not wish to fight thee. Besides, thee knows I have no quarrel with thee."

Rufus Jones himself enumerated these incidents without comment in a talk that he made on the subject of THE BULWARK to the Library Associates on May 19, 1946, in the Quaker Room of the Haverford College Library. Theodore Dreiser had written to him, three years earlier, saying that he was writing a novel that involved Quakers, and asking for the names of educational institutions within a hundred miles of Philadelphia which were influenced or controlled by Friends between 1885 and 1890, and he had replied with a list of colleges and schools but with no description of "the inward life of any of these institutions." The only identifiable one that turned up in the book was Llewellyn College for Women, which was plainly intended to be Bryn Mawr.

Rufus Jones's considered judgment on THE BULWARK was that it was not a successful novel. "The author is interpreting a theory of life and action rather than creating persons who live and breathe and have authentic being," he said in part. "He never gets inside of this Quaker family or of a Quaker Meeting, and his characters remain too much like constructed frames for presenting the author's theories."

The experience of this ten-year-old brush with death, though it brought Rufus a deeper thoughtfulness, by no means made a saint of him. As soon as he was well again—and he did recover completely —he was out skylarking with the boys or hanging about the grocery store. His companions were often rough-tongued and earthy both in language and point of view, but he considered always that he got from them an essential part of his education, for he learned much about human nature that he had no later opportunities for learning and he discovered through them the value of friendship with people of different ideals from his own.

Rufus's formal education began when at four and a half, holding tight to Alice's hand, he walked down the road to the one-room village school. During the next few years, with a succession of teachers, some effective and some not, he progressed through Sanders's five Readers and reached the heights of the Grammar Class, which stayed on after the lower orders had left, to parse—pronounced pass —long passages from PARADISE LOST. Having at thirteen got all there was to get from that school, he pursued learning at three other schools in neighboring districts. The last of these, the Weeks Mill School, involved a three-mile walk each way. Here he encountered a really inspiring teacher, with whom he began to study Physics and Physiology and who opened up to him the glories of Mathematics. However primitive these district schools may seem now, they must have offered a sound foundation, for no fewer than twenty-five men and women, mostly Joneses, went out from South China to teach in schools and colleges across the nation.

The following autumn, when Rufus was fifteen, he went to Oak Grove Seminary. This was a Quaker boarding school in Vassalboro, on the other side of China Lake, of which his Uncle Eli and two of his cousins had been principal at one time and another. Rufus spent eleven weeks there, and he financed this enterprise himself. The proceeds of the sale of a sheep he had raised, plus her lamb, paid for his tuition and room; his food he took from home. With another boy, Herbert Goddard, who became a well-known doctor and started the hospital at Vineland, N. J., he brought enough supplies from home on Sunday to last till the following Friday, when they went home again. In their room they had an air-tight stove, and once they boiled some eggs in a saucepan with a tight cover. When the power of steam disclosed itself and both eggs and cover hit the ceiling, the boys gave up cooked food and relied on cold pies and doughnuts. It seems incredible now that no scholarships were available for two boys who wanted an education badly enough to eat stale cold food in their bed-room while the rest of the school enjoyed hot meals in the dining-hall, or that a school administration could countenance such an arrangement, but consciences have evidently become tenderer since 1878, and education has changed.

Rufus began to study Latin at Oak Grove, continued with his Mathematics, and embarked on the study of Astronomy with a teacher so competent that, without telescope or instrument, she gave him enough knowledge later to pass the Astronomy examination at Haverford, without taking the course, with a mark of 95. The teacher no doubt deserves all the credit he gave her, but one thinks also of the astonished joy she must have felt at discovering a boy with Rufus's mind among her pupils.

When he left Oak Grove Rufus took with him not only a formal certificate testifying to his completion of the prescribed course of the Philosophy Department and his "honorable character for scholarship and deportment," but a secret determination to aim still higher—at the Friends School in Providence, Rhode Island.

That winter he returned to the South China School, where his cousin Frank E. Jones was now teacher, and struggled on with his Latin, partly with Frank's slender help but mostly by himself.

In the summer of 1879, Rufus and his father were working together in the pond field, hoeing parallel rows of potatoes, keeping along side by side. Suddenly Rufus leaned on his hoe and said, "Father, I've made up my mind I've got to go away to school."

The story of this conversation as told in A SMALL-TOWN BOY differs slightly from the account which Rufus Jones gave to his daughter in 1939 and which she recorded. Since the second account is more intimate, more vivid, more human, I give it here in its entirety.

Father: Why, thee's got all the education thee needs.

RMJ: No, I feel as though I'd hardly begun.

Father: Well, thee knows there isn't any money for thee to use.

RMJ: Yes, I know that well enough, but I guess if an American boy really wants an education enough, nothing's going to stop him.

Father: If thee feels that way, thee's free to go ahead. I've said all I can.

In a sermon at South China, July 29, 1939, Rufus Jones said that this decision marked a turning point in his life and that he dated his life from that moment.

II

Into the Quaker Stream

W HEN the Committee of the Providence Friends School met to consider applications for scholarships, they found the name of Rufus M. Jones among the candidates. "Why," said one of the members, "I know that boy's mother, and if he is like her he deserves all the help he can get."

So it was that in September 1879 a tall, thin, eager country boy who had never before ridden on railroad train, steam boat or horse car, traveled by all three of those conveyances and arrived at the school which is now known as the Moses Brown School. It was then a co-educational boarding-school, one of the best of that distinctive type of school developed by Friends during the nineteenth century; and the scholarship which he was given covered all expenses.

The large buildings set at the head of a sweep of well-kept lawns on a hill overlooking Narragansett Bay seemed at first a little over-powering to the boy from South China, Maine, even though he found among the students five cousins whom he had never met before, and though his best friend and dearest cousin, Charles Jacob of Dirigo, was his classmate. "You know I came to Prov. a green, backward, awkward boy, extremely rustic in all my ways," he wrote years later to his friend Edward Farr. "I had very little to recommend me, but from the first you were a friend to me, and your encouragement has done much to spur me on."

The strain of the early days soon disappeared, as he made friends. He was in demand for athletic teams; he liked girls and was at ease with them; he was delighted with this new world.

Also new to the school that autumn was its principal, Augustine Jones, who was Rufus's first cousin, twenty-eight years older than he. A lawyer in Lynn before he was called to head up the school, he had been still earlier principal of Oak Grove Seminary. A tall, handsome, dignified man, was held in respect and some awe by the boy who for some years had been wearing his cast-off suits, cut down to fit. He brought to the school his own enthusiasm for art, and under his rule more pianos were added. Rufus became very fond of him and enjoyed his classes in the Bible, which were of a broader type than any he had yet experienced.

In spite of his somewhat haphazard preparation in rural schools Rufus was well able to take his place with others of his age. He joined the Latin class reading Caesar, took up Geometry enthusiastically, began Greek with Seth K. Gifford, an exacting, exciting teacher. Weakest in science, he entered the class in Natural Sciences—and was astonished to discover that the world was not made in six days and that man did not begin with Adam. Through the guidance of a wise teacher, Thomas Battey, who had studied with Gray and Agassiz at Harvard, Rufus made this hurdle without difficulty, and found his religious faith all the more secure when it marched with facts.

The first Christmas he went home, because neither he nor his mother could endure the separation any longer. Mary Jones had been growing steadily frailer since a severe attack of rheumatic fever four years earlier, and Rufus felt an uneasiness about her which he scarcely admitted even to himself. With Charlie Jacob and two girls who were going to Vassalboro, he came up from Boston in a blizzard, and was touched to find his father at Augusta to meet him with the sleigh. The ceilings of the old house looked low and primitive to him now, after the spacious rooms of the school, but he was happy to be at home.

In April he went home again, this time to attend his mother's funeral. It was that dismal season known as mud time, and the stage from Augusta sank hub-deep in the mire, so that it took about five hours to cover the twelve miles to South China.

The death of his adored mother was a far more serious test of his faith than Geology or the theory of evolution could offer. Before the shocking fact of the body in the coffin, his trust in the goodness of God and the immortality of the soul was all but shattered, but memories of his mother's faith and the love of God as it had been manifested in her life came flooding in to restore his spirit, and the crisis passed, leaving him its blessing of new strength and maturity.

Summer vacations he seems to have spent in Lynn, working in a shoe factory, and staying with his aunt Lizzie Hoxie, who kept a small boarding house, and who was a friend of Whittier's.

Various distinguished people came to the Friends School to speak to the students while Rufus was there. Clara Winslow, his classmate, mentioned Susan B. Anthony, Frances E. Willard, Julia Ward Howe, and others. It may be that it was in this way he first heard Phillips Brooks. "I heard Phillips Brooks preach twice in my youth," he wrote, "and I knew instantly that the man I had been waiting for had come." It was from Phillips Brooks he got one of the figures that he was often to use, that the checkerboard of life was made up of black squares on a white background, not white squares on fundamental black.

Some of their visitors were dimmer lights, however. One of these provided Rufus Jones with a story which served him well whenever he in his turn talked to a group of school children. "He got up on the high platform," he would say, "somewhat higher than this, and he got badly scared, the way I am now, and he looked down in the faces of the children, and he said, 'When I look down into the faces of these dear boys and these dear girls, it makes me think of the time when I was a little boy and a little girl.'"

In 1881 he graduated, in the largest graduating class in the history of the school: ten boys and fifteen girls. His essay, read at Commencement, was entitled, "North America in the Age of Ice." Others dealt confidently with subjects ranging from "Characteristics of Pre-Historic Man" to "Modern Superficiality."

He came back to school the following September for a post-graduate year to pull up his Greek to meet college requirements. It was a wonderfully pleasant and stimulating year for him. Five of the girls in his class, whom he called "the puellae" in his letters to Ed Farr, were also back, and there were sleighing parties, reading groups, and debates on historical and literary subjects. "I tell you, Ed," he wrote, "you can't imagine what a good time I have been having."

Rufus, who had grown up in a household dominated by three remarkable women, was always at ease with women and well liked by them. More than that, he was to be all his life very dependent upon women for companionship, sympathy, and encouragement. His friendships were all natural, spontaneous, open, and based upon the high ideal of women which was the natural outcome of his upbringing. "A noble, lovely woman seems to me," he wrote to Ed Farr, "the highest thing in the world, and what a power she can have."

When the post-graduate year was finished, he had the problem of what college to choose. Brown University in Providence attracted him in many ways, but in the end he decided on Haverford. Uncle Eli, two of whose sons had gone there, was strongly in favor of Haverford, and so was Aunt Peace. Charles Jacob had gone there in the fall of 1881 and wrote urging Rufus to come and be his roommate, a powerful inducement. Haverford moreover offered him a full scholarship for board and tuition, which he accepted and later repaid. The choice of a college he was later to count as one of life's three major events, the other two being the involuntary one of "getting born in the right place, of the right parents, at the right moment in time" and the choice of a wife.

When he left for college, to enter the Sophomore class, he considered himself a man; he had attained his full height of six feet and he had a Prince Albert coat. But the photographs of college groups show a tall, thin, gangling boy with protruding teeth, which for years, until they were replaced by artificial ones, were to cause him mortification. Among the other students, who had a look of city and of means, he was a country boy still, but there was something unmistakable in his open, ardent, vulnerable face that won him immediate and lasting friends.

Haverford was a small college, minuscule by today's standards. When Rufus Jones entered it in 1882 the student body numbered seventy-one, chiefly Quakers from perhaps a dozen different states. It had been founded forty-nine years earlier by a group of earnest, far-sighted Orthodox Friends who, ascribing the tragic Separation of 1827 to the general ignorance prevailing among the membership, sought to repair the long Quaker neglect of higher education.

Their first step was to select a farm with a dependable spring of pure water, situated on the "main line" of the Pennsylvania railroad. Then, with the flair for beauty and the recognition of its worth which is a rather unexpected trait of the old time plain Friend, they imported a famous landscape gardener from England to design the campus. He brought with him as an additional gift the game of cricket, which became Haverford's chief sport. The first building, Founders' Hall, a wide-winged, ample building of simple lines, with a high porch and a belfry, was in the good taste of its period. By the time that Rufus Jones got there, Barclay Hall and Alumni Hall, one wing of which housed the library, had been added, in the less fortunate, dressed-stone and top-heavy gable architecture of the '70's.

The founding fathers selected their faculty with care, and though the college, cautious and paternalistic, kept for long years some of the qualities of a boarding-school, a governor to preside over conduct persisting even into Rufus Jones's day, still there were men of intellectual stature and high character to fire the imaginations (if at all combustible) of the students and to provide them with substantial, invigorating intellectual fare.

Logan Pearsall Smith, who was for a time a classmate of Rufus's before he departed for Oxford, via Harvard, experienced "no stirring of the mind" at Haverford, though he conceded that the scheme of teaching in this Quaker college was rather sounder than in some of the large universities, which dispensed what he stigmatized as a "vague, diffused kind of intellectual varnishing and plastering over."

To the boy from Maine, however, who, from the moment when he first passed between the stone pillars at the entrance and saw the long roll of lawns, the pond, the stately trees planted in "quincunxes"—an oak, an ash, an elm, a locust, a tulip-poplar—gave his heart to it, Haverford was a place of vital study and growth and discovery, where the lines for his future life and work were laid, his potentialities for leadership explored. He brought to it the qualities of deeply springing energy, originality, imagination, and penetration which are associated with genius. His was a genius already attuned to spiritual ends, but without the psychic imbalance that marks many religious geniuses, from George Fox backward and forward.

He met nothing that did not become grist to his mill. The ability to experience vividly is a talent like any other, though not always recognized as such, and Rufus Jones had it in unusual measure. His zest for life and learning was unquenchable. He liked food, fun, and jokes. His friendships included people of all ages and many types. Among his friends was an attractive girl who, in spite of her charm, suffered from the nickname "Goat" because she wore a goatskin fur; because of her he taught Sunday School in the Methodist Church all the time he was in college. He delighted in long walks with the president of the college, Thomas Chase, and learned to match his gigantic stride, a habit which continued with him all his life. He spent fourteen continuous hours one day mastering Kant's "transcendental deduction of the categories" and when a mathematical truth broke upon him in a blaze of illumination like a religious conversion, he worked off his elation in a cross-country run, leaping all the fences that lay in his path. He entered a non-credit course in Italian and felt "great gratifi-

cation, even pride, in thinking that we are reading Dante." He enjoyed swimming, long hikes, sledding and ice-skating; he loved cricket
and savored its "subtle values." He threw his energy into the Y.M.C.A.,
then only ten years old and a fresh and exciting cause, and in his
Senior year he was its president. He was president of the Senior Class
and editor-in-chief of the *Haverfordian*. He was the upper classman
to whom the younger men went for help when they got into trouble.

Above all, at Haverford he encountered Pliny Earle Chase. Philosopher, mathematician, linguist, meteorologist, Professor Chase was
most remarkable for the quality of his personality, for his radiance,
his gentleness and humility, his gift for inspiring youth. "My whole
life would have been different if I had gone to Brown University in
Providence as I expected to," Rufus Jones said in 1938. "By coming
to Haverford I came under the influence of Pliny Chase and that made
all the difference. He sat on the lower bench of Haverford Meeting
because he never was recorded as a minister. He had a piano. But we
knew he was recorded in Heaven and that was all that mattered . . .
not a day goes by but I remember him." He was the one person, not
even excepting Uncle Eli and Aunt Sybil, whom Rufus had found
to put on a level with Aunt Peace for saintliness and wisdom of the
heart.

To his tribute to his beloved professor in THE TRAIL OF LIFE IN
COLLEGE, Rufus Jones adds the cautionary word: "I do not claim that
he was all that I am saying he was. I am only insisting that this is what
we believed about him. That is what he was for us." It is perhaps
well to add a few objective facts. He was a half brother of Thomas
Chase, the president of the college, born in Worcester, Massachusetts,
in 1820, educated at the Providence Friends School and at Harvard,
where he took his M.A. in 1844. He came to Haverford in 1871 as
Professor of Natural Science and Philosophy and in 1875 became
Professor of Philosophy and Logic. He contributed many papers to the
Proceedings of the American Philosophical Society, and he won its
seldom awarded Magellanic Gold Medal in 1864. Best known, perhaps,
as the author of the standard text, CHASE'S ARITHMETIC, he was highly
respected for his character even by those who considered him too
versatile for his intellectual good or too liberal for his spiritual welfare.

For his part Pliny Chase was obviously drawn to Rufus, recognizing
no doubt the rare promise in the boy. Rufus went to the Chases' house
for supper every Thursday throughout his three years at Haverford.
Mrs. Chase was a superb housekeeper; there were three gay and

friendly daughters: Maria, who was older than Rufus, Harriet, just his
own age, who most resembled their father, and Eliza. All the family
loved music, and the piano which kept Pliny from being a "recorded"
minister, was well used. Maria and Rufus went together to see the
famous Italian actress, Maria Stuart. It was Rufus's first venture into
a theatre and in later years, when Maria Chase had become the
conservative Mrs. Thomas Scattergood, he enjoyed teasing her by declaring that she had "wrecked" him by leading him into a theatre.

Professor Chase's courses in Philosophy were probably less effective
than the man himself. Certainly time spent on Paley's EVIDENCES OF
CHRISTIANITY and Dymond's MORAL PHILOSOPHY was time largely lost,
but there was also a historical review of Philosophy, with emphasis on
Berkeley's Idealism, which provided a sketch map for the student
who was ready to do his own exploring.

Rufus's real meeting with Plato took place in the Greek classes
where he read the APOLOGY and CRITO and found a life-long companion
and guide. "I can hardly imagine," he wrote, "what it would mean to
live and to try to solve the problems and mysteries of life without the
help of Plato!" Greek and Latin he studied first with Seth Gifford,
who had come to Haverford from Providence the same year that Rufus
himself did, and later with President Chase, whose massive head and
benevolent expression won for him the title Zeus from the students.

Next to Pliny Chase as a midwife to the soul, to use the phrase that
Rufus Jones loved to borrow from Socrates, was Isaac Sharpless, the
professor of Mathematics. Under him Rufus studied Trigonometry,
Solid Geometry, Analytical Geometry, and Calculus, and got a mark
of 100 in Analytical Geometry. He found in the study of Mathematics
an immense stimulation of the imagination and a training in habits
of exactness.

In 1884 Isaac Sharpless, then thirty-six years of age, was made dean
of the college. With his string tie, his Sunday shave, his high boots with
his trousers tucked inside, his conservative Quakerism and his still
youthful awkwardness, he was a figure of some amusement as well as
affection to the students, but his knowledge of character, his "subtle
and marvelous humor," his regard for truth, and his undeniable scholarship won their unqualified respect.

Mysticism broke upon Rufus Jones with the same shock that the
man experienced who had been speaking prose all his life without
knowing it. He found the word in Emerson's ESSAYS, and he found
there also mention of George Fox, whom he had supposed to be a

strictly Quaker prophet unknown to the outside world. To discover that Fox was one of a great historical succession of mystics and that the religion practised at home, in the family silences and in the little meeting at Dirigo, was mystical religion, was exciting and enlightening. Looking back, more than fifty years later, on this moment, he wrote: "It was a turning point in my life when I discovered that I belonged to a mighty spiritual movement rather than to a peculiar and provincial sect. I saw honest and self-sacrificing leaders in the Society of Friends devoting their precious lives to the task of preserving peculiarities and scruples and narrow conventions, when to me it seemed absolutely certain that our one hope of becoming a vital instrument in the hand of God lay in realizing the passion of our great founders to be the living seed of a world wide and ever growing spiritual movement."

It was Pliny Chase who suggested that Rufus write his graduation thesis on the subject of "Mysticism and Its Exponents." Drawing chiefly on Vaughan's undependable *Hours with the Mystics* and on Karl Schmidt's French and German studies on John Tauler and fourteenth century mysticism, Rufus emphasized Tauler and Fox as examples of the purest mystics. The original manuscript is in the library of Haverford. Written in a somewhat flowery manner that resembled his later style as little as the Spenserian penmanship resembled his later large, open, inimitable hand, still it reveals something of the future Rufus Jones: the dislike of the abnormal, the self-torturing, the negative; the insistence upon the real, the living, the useful. "Mysticism," he wrote, "does not have to do with creeds and dogmas: Christianity is broader than any creed. It leaves religious problems and deals with life and motives."

"I had here found the field of my life work," he wrote in 1929. He had discovered the field that contained the treasure, but he had not yet seen how he was to go about digging for it. That would not come for several years.

The usual pace of study in college was too slow for Rufus, with his eagerness and his capacity. He carried more than the regular load of courses and by the end of his Junior year was practically ready to graduate. Accordingly he asked and received permission to use his spare time in his Senior year to do work that would lead to a master's degree. Rather surprisingly he chose not philosophy but history as his subject. He was at that time intending to become a lawyer, perhaps because cousin Augustine Jones had been a lawyer before he went to Providence, and he thought that a knowledge of American History would be of use to him in the law. He read systematically and copiously under the direction of Allen Thomas, Professor of History, and though his research dealt with secondary rather than primary sources, he felt that he gained a familiarity with the historical method and the historical point of view that were of great value to him throughout his life both in his teaching and in his writing. Though most of the reading was done during this final year in college, his thesis and the last of three searching examinations were not accomplished until the year following his graduation.

Another experience of future value was his work on the *Haverfordian*. He began in his first year in the lowly position of assistant business manager, and suffered the usual initiation of being sent unsuspectingly to ask for an advertisement from the bad-tempered avowed enemy of the paper—and returned triumphantly with a large subscription and a promise of more. By his Senior year he was editor-in-chief, with his friend Gus Murray as one of his assistants. When Rufus took office the paper was in the black books of the faculty and the Board of Managers. It was characteristic of him that his endeavor to "promote good feeling" took the form not of appeasement and caution but of open and at that time rather daring discussion of college policy and the proposal of a system of self-government then revolutionary. "Where petty rules are reduced to the minimum," he wrote in one of several articles, "broad principles laid down as guiding points, and the good common sense of the students trusted, the most satisfaction and the least amount of jarring between ruled and ruling is secured."

Among the items of contemporary interest noted by the *Haverfordian* that year was the building of Taylor and Merion Halls on the campus of the new Friends college for women in nearby Bryn Mawr, which was to open in the autumn of 1885. Rufus often walked over there to visit the Garretts, who were living in a small house, later to be the Deanery, on the campus, watching over the erection of the buildings. John B. Garrett was vice-president of the Lehigh Valley Railroad, a manager of Haverford, a trustee of the new Bryn Mawr College, and a "weighty Friend" of Twelfth Street Meeting. He had two attractive daughters. After noting the bell tower on Taylor Hall, Rufus remarked, "But let us not dwell on clocks and bells, for how soon one tires of their musical sounds except at three particular occasions during the day." Going on to more serious topics he reported that Pliny Chase was to fill the chair of Mental and Moral Philosophy

in the new college. "It was Dr. Taylor's desire that Haverford and
Bryn Mawr should mutually assist and strengthen each other and so
we hope and trust it may be. Each doing its work in its particular
sphere but each laboring for the same end, may they stand like two
watch-towers to catch the earliest glimmerings of truth."

Like the other students Rufus Jones went to meeting at Haverford
every Thursday and Sunday morning. He heard Pliny Chase's
mystical yet practical messages, delivered in a conversational, medi-
tative way far more impressive than oratorical display. Quaker
neighbors attended these meetings also and sometimes distinguished
visitors to the college. But Haverford Meeting was then only a preparative meeting, a subsidiary of Twelfth Street Meeting in Philadelphia, a mere trout pool in the powerful stream of Philadelphia
Quakerism.

A fingerling from South China, Maine, might be expected not to
venture out of the pool, but young Rufus Jones, the nephew of Uncle
Eli and Aunt Sybil, had friends who introduced him to the larger
waters. Through a complicated series of second marriages in the
family of Augustine Jones, he had acquired an "aunt" and "uncle,"
Lydia and Mark Balderston, who opened to him their house on
Marshall Street, in Philadelphia, at Yearly Meeting time, and there
he met many other Friends who came from nearby meetings in
Pennsylvania, New Jersey and Delaware to attend the sessions of the
Orthodox group at Arch Street. His cousin Richard Jones, Uncle
Eli's son, was headmaster of William Penn Charter School, then
situated at Market and Twelfth Streets, next door to the Meeting
house. The weighty Friend described but not named in THE TRAIL OF
LIFE IN COLLEGE who invited Rufus to spend his first Christmas holidays with him and took him to Twelfth Street and to Germantown
Meetings, where he was kindly received and launched on several life-
long friendships, was possibly T. Wistar Brown.

At Twelfth Street Meeting he found a spacious, well-proportioned
room with unpainted walls and benches of natural wood where between four and five hundred Friends, "nearly all of them city-bred,
many of them persons of business success, of wealth, of culture, and
of prominence," sat in a profound and living silence. On the high
benches facing the body of the meeting were the ministers and elders,
all wearing the traditional costume, collarless coats for the men, gray
or drab silk shawls and bonnets for the women. Occasionally there was
a message, delivered in that quavery Quaker chant which has been

likened to the medieval plain-song, but it was the depth and vitality of the silence that made a deep impression upon Rufus.

In the spring he went to Yearly Meeting, and attended every session of the week-long series, as he did also in 1884 and 1885. Quaker schools and colleges had their spring holiday during Yearly Meeting week, but few of the students can have been as assiduous in attendance as Rufus Jones. He went, he worshiped, and he observed.

Philadelphia Quakerism, it seemed to him, had congealed in outworn molds. The form of speech, the cape on the bonnet or the absence of it, the size of a beard had assumed a spurious importance. More than that, the ministry arising out of the silence seemed to him lacking in thought content—just a series of texts strung together and delivered in that unnatural voice. In his little country meeting he had heard Uncle Eli preach far better sermons.

His own studies in mysticism and his historical perspective made him feel that an eighteenth century Quakerism, impregnated with Quietism, had superseded the "freedom and marching power" of the original movement which Fox had set on foot in the seventeenth century. He did not yet see all the currents involved nor his own role, but he "resolved even then that I would throw in my lot with the discoverer and creator and not with the conformist."

In June, 1885, he received his diploma, his A.B. degree, and the large wooden spoon traditionally given to the man who best exemplified the ideals of the college and was most loved by the class; he had his picture taken with the other seventeen members of the class, all in frock coats and derby hats and five of them with moustaches; and then he was out in the world, faced with the question of what to do next.

A prominent citizen of Wenonah, N.J., whom he had met when visiting his school friend, Ed Farr, had offered to see him through law school and to help him get started in life, This offer, which came some time before Commencement, he had, after deep and searching thought, refused. He wrote his friend that his mind "was unexpectedly moving in a different direction" for his career in life, though at that time he could not have said definitely what that direction was.

He returned to his home in South China and waited for further light. Before the hay was harvested, the answer came, in the form of a choice between two divergent lines, a veritable fork in the road. He was offered a graduate fellowship in History by the University of Pennsylvania, with the prospect of working with Edmund James in

Political Science and the widely-known John Bach McMaster in American History—surely an opportunity for the young man who had already spent most of a year in historical research.

Before he could reply to this offer, the following morning in fact, a woman drove up to the door and set the alternative before him. She was associate principal of Oakwood Seminary, a Quaker boarding-school at Union Springs, New York, on Lake Cayuga, about twenty-five miles from Cornell. She had come to offer him a position as teacher in the school. The salary was three hundred dollars and she must have an answer the next day.

It was a difficult, a crucial decision. One path would lead him into the academic world, the other deeper into Quakerism. One wonders what the choice would have been had Aunt Peace not been right at hand to be consulted—and very sure that the way was clear. Rufus Jones acknowledged the weight of her influence, but he felt also as he pondered late into the night that he knew the guidance of an invisible hand. He came finally to see it as a question of the kind of person he wanted to be, and in that insight he turned down the university and took the school.

"*A Grip on the Base of the World*"

OAKWOOD SEMINARY, which had been established in 1796 at Nine Partners, in Dutchess County, New York, and later moved to Union Springs, was one of the oldest of the Friends boarding-schools. Elijah Cook was its principal in 1885, and the students numbered fewer than a hundred, the oldest of them being very little younger than the new teacher, fresh from Haverford.

He taught Greek, Latin, German, Surveying, Astronomy, and Zoology, but though the schedule sounds formidable the actual teaching time was no more than three and a half hours a day. "I enjoy teaching ever so much," he wrote Ed Farr. "I do not have very much Government to look after, but just enough to try myself. We have good food and that has taken a big burden off my mind. The great trouble has been that I have no one who is congenial for me to ally myself to, so I have to flock alone to a large extent, but the older scholar(s) have entertained me nicely . . . On the whole I think I am in the right place."

He went to the Union Springs Meeting and soon found messages pressing against his lips. Among the meeting members he made friends. John and Susannah Howland opened their fine private library to him, and he read widely during his spare time, not only American history and the mystical writers, but Goethe, Carlyle, Lowell and Browning, who became his favorite and most quoted poet. *Saul* he encountered for the first time at the house of Elizabeth Comstock, a venerable English Friend who lived in Union Springs, and her sister, Lydia Rouse, who for some years had been governness to John Bright's children and later headmistress of the Mount, a Friends school for girls in York, England. He was invited every Sunday evening for supper by these ladies, and after supper he read aloud to them.

Perhaps he read too much. He had begun to have trouble with his eyes in college, but now he suffered seriously from inflamed lids and aching eyes. A visit to an oculist brought no relief.

This weakness of the eyes was for a long time a burden, and a threat always. It was one of the thorns of the flesh that he learned to carry so quietly that few people noticed or remembered them. Though he had a tall, muscular, limber body, he was often physically under par, made miserable by hay fever, asthma, and indigestion. He was subject also to periods of depression. "My body and spirits are closely connected," he wrote to Sarah Coutant in 1886, "and go to the heights and depths together." More than most people he was affected by the weather. Cold, gray, rainy days so lowered his spirits that he said of himself, "The weather molds me like wax." Rufus Jones's lifelong optimism, which was so integral a part of him, was hard won and deeply based. He had to learn "to live above the level of moods," in the phrase which he used in a talk at Pendle Hill in 1936.

It was not long before he found someone at Oakwood to ally himself to. Sarah Hawkeshurst Coutant, herself a graduate of the school, had returned to teach there the previous year. They read together, and when his eyes began to hurt, she read to him. There is a notebook extant, dated 1885-86 in which she copied out quotations from a variety of writers, including Lowell (A FABLE FOR CRITICS, BIGLOW PAPERS), George Eliot and George Macdonald (two of Rufus's favorite novelists), AURORA LEIGH, Whittier's TAULER, and, possibly significant, ROMEO AND JULIET.

Sallie, who was nearly a year older than Rufus, was a fine-looking girl with clear-cut, regular features, dark hair and eyes, and a look of fire and intensity. She had a dry sense of humor, a keen mind, a flair for style, and an immense capability in practical affairs. Her mother was Elizabeth Griggs and her father was James Hawkeshurst Coutant, a Quaker farmer of Huguenot descent, who lived in Ardonia, New York, across the Hudson from Poughkeepsie. After her mother's death, when Sallie was quite small, James Coutant married Clementine Heaton, to whom Sallie was devoted and whom she called Mother. There were three children of the second marriage, Emma, Lydia and Peter.

Rufus and Sallie "were both filled with a passionate love for truth, for education, for making their lives pure and good. They both came from small, country, Quaker homes where poverty was a reality but where a homespun culture and dignity were equally real. They both had lost their mothers and yearned for an understanding soul with whom to share the gropings which all young people have."

When school was over at the end of June, Rufus traveled with Sallie to the big old house in Ardonia, where Clementine Coutant, a famous housewife, "took in boarders." Rufus spent the night there and went on the next day to New York and then to Maine.

Lucy Hawkes Meader, a close friend of both Sallie and Rufus, tells the story, which she had from both of them, that after he had said good-by and left that morning, he turned back, unhappy in the parting—to find Sallie in tears on the sofa. He impulsively proposed to her.

It was unpremeditated; it was inevitable. Rufus was not one to see a woman's tears unmoved, and his heart was already engaged. But it was not what he had intended at this time.

He wrote her from South China a week later. He had had an "inward fog." As the climax of a year's struggle, he had resolved, before that momentous morning, to leave the matter as it was, to keep everything to himself, and wait for Time to give the decision. But after all, he had spoken, and he thought it was right, if they were sure. "Until we feel sure, unmistakably sure, we should keep all our thoughts from the outside world . . . What I have said does not in the least imply faithlessness or change of opinion." He concluded the letter, "Faithfully thy friend, and more."

Sallie's letters of this period have unfortunately not survived, but it seems clear from Rufus's that though she herself was "sure" she was willing to follow his lead.

He was doubtful about his plans for the next year. Even though he had been offered a higher salary he was reluctant to return to Oakwood. His eyes were still troublesome and needed rest. He turned to his family for guidance. Aunt Peace, his father and Herbert, "the rosebud of the family," were still in the old homestead, though Alice, his sister, had married and gone to live in South Durham, Maine. Aunt Sybil had died thirteen years earlier, but Uncle Eli was at hand. Rufus also consulted his cousin Richard Jones, headmaster of the Penn Charter School, who spent his summers in South China, and who, Rufus wrote to Sallie," is somewhat my style of a man; he is full of life and activity, understands boys, can see a joke if it has a point, 'knows a few things,' has known of a 'digging deep,' and has an opinion on nearly everything."

Cousin Richard was in favor of a year abroad, such as he himself had had, for study and experience. Augustine Jones, whom Rufus had seen in Providence, had talked to him seriously on the subject of early marriage and advised a trip to Europe. Aunt Peace and Uncle Eli gave warm approval to the project. The only difficulty was the financial one. Rufus still had most of the $300 that he had earned at Oakwood, but no more, until Hannah J. Bailey, a well-to-do and philanthropic Friend who lived in nearby Winthrop, offered to lend him whatever he needed.

He wrote to Sallie on the seventh of August that his "Bunyan's load" was beginning to roll off a little, for one important question had been settled. "My European blossom has become a seed, which is fast ripening. I propose to go to Europe for a year, spending most of the time getting the French and German languages. I am arranging to go by the State Line from New York two weeks from Thursday (the 26th). My plan is to visit for about two months in England and Scotland. Uncle Eli is going to give me letters to his old friends there and he is doing all he can to make my visit a big success. The remainder of the year will be divided between France and Germany . . . I never felt so much in my life before that I had reached the dividing line between past and future, boyhood and manhood as I have this summer. Sometimes when I stop and listen I can almost hear the infinite sea of life roar and rumble and I know that everything is shouting in my ear, 'embark on it,' and I mean to obey the voice."

In a postscript he reported the offer of the position of principal of Damascus Academy, a Friends school in Ohio. "But having put my hands on the plow handles and having the horses nearly harnessed and furthermore feeling that I am in the right furrow I do not think it best to turn back."

His joy was complete when Charles Jacob, who since graduation from Haverford had been principal of the Friends School in Oxford, Pennsylvania, arranged to follow him to London and spend the rest of the year with him.

No passport was necessary in those innocent days, and passage was quickly obtained on the *Pennsylvania*, a one-class ship of eight thousand tons, for forty dollars. The day before he sailed Rufus took the *Mary Powell* up the Hudson to pay a final visit to Sallie.

He wrote her afterwards from the ship: "I never went at anything with better courage than I now feel, and had [I] an assurance of a continuation of the spirit I had in me coming down the Hudson I should surely do something. I had as it were in the language of Lowell 'a grip on the base of the world.' "

On the 26th of July he was seen off at the dock by Ed Farr and another boy, and set forth in the highest of spirits on the first of many voyages across the Atlantic. During the ten days that it took this small vessel "using sails as well as steam" to cross the ocean, he wrote a journal letter to Sallie, full of the minutiae of a first voyage.

His cabin mates were a Scotch Presbyterian minister and a Jamaican planter. He sat at the Captain's table. He played deck games, and played to win.

"You know I make it a point always to beat," he wrote, "no matter how insignificant the game, for if one gets used to coming out ahead in little things it is easier in larger things. I have not been beaten so far although the games were new to me. I hate croquet but it breaks me all up to get beaten at it, and I have felt so in all my games since I was a little boy. To me it is important to seem to have fortune on your side, and it does seem so if you generally beat."

His reading included, besides the Bible, Scott (*Lord of the Isles* and *Marmion*), Tennyson (*In Memoriam*), and Holmes (*The Poet at the Breakfast Table*). He was throughout his life an omnivorous reader, often keeping three or four books going at a time.

This section of the letter ended, "With best wishes of thy sea tos't friend who has a heart full of love."

Then with the innocent clumsiness of the inexperienced, he remarked, "There is a girl here who makes me think lots of Miss Clark." Edith Clark was another teacher at Oakwood, who had also taken a turn at reading to Rufus when his eyes were bad, and of whom Sallie would doubtless have preferred him not to be thinking "lots." "She is from Glasgow and she sits where I can watch her though I have not talked with her. She smiled an encouraging smile when I got off my first poor pun at the table. The ladies are not attractive, with this exception."

Later, possibly after some roughness in the sea, though he was usually a good sailor, he wrote, "I am not feeling as well tonight as I would like to feel and I shall continually need something to cheer me. I should be glad if I were not so variable in my feelings but I am so constituted and unless I can be remodeled I shall always be more or less so. I am generally buoyant enough to float and if all is well I can get on with the aid of a 'life preserver' on the voyage of life."

After landing in Glasgow, he went on to Edinburgh. He spent a

week in Scotland, visiting friends of Uncle Eli's, and having tea with
the Scottish minister who had been his cabin mate, but the constant
rain and the sense of being among strangers was depressing to him.
When he went on to Wilmslow, in Cheshire, however, and was warmly
welcomed at the house of Ellen Clare Pearson, who had accompanied
Uncle Eli and Aunt Sybil to Palestine, he felt as if he had reached his
own home. From there he was passed on to a succession of Friendly
homes. "Uncle Eli's name is like 'Open Sesame' at every Friend's
house." He visited Fielden Thorp, headmaster of Bootham School in
York, and with him saw York Minster for the first time, a tremendous
experience for which Lowell's poem, *The Cathedral,* had somewhat
prepared him.

He went to "One Ash," Rochdale, to see John Bright. The 'great
commoner' was at his brother's house nearby, and so Rufus read Gray's
Elegy while awaiting his return. "Very soon the door opened and in
came—a cat, followed by two dogs, and the dogs by the real John
Bright, who looked just as his pictures do. A grand, good face,
crowned with snow white hair. He is short and shows by his step that
he has quite a load of years on his back. He took hold of my hand with
his soft hand and asked me to come into his room, where we sat down,
and he began the battle by asking me why I had come to England,
which question I answered. Then we talked of Lydia Rouse, whom
he admires, Blaine, whom he does not admire. I told him about the
Maine liquor law and its success. He said he had heard Eli Jones preach
some remarkable sermons and that Sybil Jones was a true poet in her
thoughts and expression. He blew up Gladstone, spoke of free trade
and some other things." Rufus stayed for tea, but not overnight,
though invited to do so. He continued his letter to Sallie, expressing
some concern over the mental barrenness of Oakwood and urging
her to read Milton "and Shakespeare somewhat, especially *Hamlet,
Othello, Lear,* and *Merchant of Venice.* John Bright told me there
was nothing in poetry to compare with Milton, and he has great admiration of Whittier."

At Birmingham he visited Richard Barrow, a well-to-do Friend, and
in his house met two of Pliny Chase's sisters, who were also traveling
in England. He went to meeting at Bull Street on Sunday, a great,
solemn gathering like the Orthodox meetings in Philadelphia. "Trembling," he rose to speak, and began with the phrase now so familiar
in Friends meetings, "Since sitting in this meeting I have been thinking—" At the rise of the meeting, an elderly Friend in the plain dress,

William Graham, the uncle of John William Graham, the writer, took him aside and said, "I was grieved at what thou said in meeting. Thou said that since sitting in the meeting thou hadst been thinking. Thou shouldst not have been thinking."

It was a story that he loved to tell in later years, to illustrate the point of view of the old-time Friend who held that the mind should be swept clear of all thought as well as sense impressions, so that the divine light might shine the more purely through it, but at the time it must have been a somewhat daunting experience.

He spent ten days in London, where he was entertained by a number of Friends. In fact, during all of the six weeks that he spent in Scotland and England, he passed but one night in a hotel, and that in Edinburgh during the first week. He saw all the sights from Westminster Abbey to Madame Tussaud's. For part of the time William Charles Braithwaite, like Rufus twenty-three years old, was his guide in London, and a friendship began which was of great future importance to both of them.

William Charles Braithwaite was the son of Joseph Bevan Braithwaite, whose home in Camden Road was always open to visiting Friends. Born in 1818, he had been a recorded minister from the age of twenty-seven. His wife, Martha Gillett, had had her gifts thus recognized at the even earlier age of twenty-two. A successful barrister, he had an intense interest in the Bible, which he read in Hebrew and Greek, and in church history. His devotion to Quakerism, his service in its behalf, the depth of his faith, as well as the simplicity and nobility of his character, made him a towering figure in London Yearly Meeting.

This seasoned, important, immensely dignified English Quaker looked upon young Rufus Jones and saw something there that moved him to an extraordinary—and a touching—act. Rufus, in awe, wrote about it to both Uncle Eli and Sallie.

"Bevan Braithwaite, who is the 'Pope of London Friends', kissed my hand when he bade me farewell, which I considered as a Jacob's blessing from an old Patriarch."

Charles Jacob joined him in London and they went together to France. They boarded first with a French Protestant pastor in a village called La Paillette in the foothills of the French Alps, where they spoke French with the family and struggled to maintain it with each other. The pastor himself was a good teacher, but his wife was untidy and talkative, the weather was inclement, Rufus had a "regular *Grendal*

[sic] of a cold" and a toothache, but he was learning a good deal of French and he tried to make the best of the situation. He and Charles laughed together a great deal.

During the month that he was there, he had a mystical experience. He did not write about it to Sallie, but in later years he described it in two of his books, THE TRAIL OF LIFE IN COLLEGE, and A CALL TO WHAT IS VITAL. By that time his knowledge of mysticism was as great as that of anybody in the world, and he had a wide perspective from which to appraise it. He was always, as he wrote in THE TESTIMONY OF THE SOUL, "cautious about expecting secret messages from sociable angels," and he drew a clear distinction between real intercourse with God and purely psychic events. During his years of study of mysticism, he developed criteria by which the objectivity of mystical experience might be verified: The mystic's own intense conviction, "a marked increase in unity and coherence to the personality," and an increase in creative energy.

His own experience at Dieulefit near Le Paillette, though "too fleeting and elusive to catch and hold," would seem to have met all of these tests. The account given in THE TRAIL OF LIFE IN COLLEGE is the most complete:

"I was on a solitary walk, absorbed with my thoughts about the meaning and purpose of my life, wondering whether I should ever get myself organized and brought under the control and direction of some constructive central purpose of life, when I felt the walls between the visible and the invisible suddenly grow thin, and I was conscious of a definite mission of life opening out before me. I saw stretch before me an unfolding of labor in the realm of mystical religion, almost as clearly as Francis heard himself called at St. Damiens to 'repair the Church.' I remember kneeling down alone in a beautiful forest glade and dedicating myself then and there in the quiet and silence, but in the presence of an invading Life, to the work of interpreting the deeper nature of the soul and its relation with God."

The effect of such an experience is not, however, immediately clear. He had during the next few months much discouragement, much questioning and soul searching.

"I am affraid [sic] of myself," he wrote to Sallie from Nîmes, where he went early in November, to stay with Jules Paradon, one of the leading French Friends, "for I know [I] am so made that I am as it were a compromise between good and evil, if I should once get on the *bob-sled* of sin I should go down the hill clear to the bottom while

on the other hand with a light heart and a bright future I can go up
as high as I wish."

The weather was gloomy in Nîmes, an icy wind swept down from
the Alps, and snow fell on houses not equipped for cold; the food
was unappetising, Rufus had an ulcerated tooth, and his eyes were
troubling him. Still, he worked doggedly at his French and he visited
the sixty or so French Friends who lived in four centers in that region.

Sallie evidently sent some of his letters to her Aunt Mary, who had
taken care of her during the period between her mother's death and
her father's second marriage. That old lady's comment was, "I hope
he [got] well of the toothache. I felt real sorry for him, and through
it all he seems to be having a good time seeing the country and the
people."

News of the death of Pliny Chase in January filled Rufus with
sorrow. "To me he was a father and his last talk with me just a year
ago is beautiful to remember."

There were, furthermore, the misunderstandings and hurts that
arise when two ardent and sensitive young people try to clarify their
relationship through long-distance correspondence. Marriage to Rufus
was wholly serious; he saw it not only as a sacred partnership for life
but as the medium in which a soul's growth might be either encouraged
or inhibited. He knew well his own temperament and his needs. He
was young enough to believe that complete honesty between two
people required the expression of every doubt.

"Is Sarah able to infuse joy and courage into me when the world
looks dark," he asked himself—and, unfortunately, Sarah too—"when
everything is discouraging. After a hard day's work can she say something that will roll off my burdens, can she be my high tower against
the thousand arrows of care, loss, discouragement, etc. Will her arm
around my neck make me feel young when old age begins to carve
my vissage [sic]?" He was then approaching his twenty-fourth birthday. "Can I be in close companionship with her day after day and
feel my life strengthened and made better by her love, her gentleness,
will she be mother, sister, wife and friend to me? The answer must be
affirmative. I do not forget on the other hand that it is a two-sided
question and that I must be examined as well. I am not perfect. I am
a specimen of humanity, hence I have faults, but I trust I shall always
see the pole star. I mean to be as faithful as the law of gravitation, and
I have no eyes to see a bad end to the life which I have tried in all
sincerity to commence well, but I must be loved, loved by one whom
I can always love in return."

Another month brought the certainty that he craved, and he was writing, "There is one person in this world whom I want for my wife and thou art that person."

In the middle of February Rufus and Charles said good-by to the French Friends, of whom they had become fond, and went on to Geneva, "the most agreeable city" that he had seen so far. After a week there they parted and Rufus went on alone, via Lausanne, Berne and Lucerne, to Strasbourg, then in Germany, "the city which I have always desired to see."

He had a letter of introduction to Paul Sabatier, who took him to see the great European scholar, Karl Schmidt, then considered the greatest authority on the mystics. Schmidt, whose studies on fourteenth century mysticism he had read in preparing his graduation essay and who reminded him of Pliny Chase, was kind and cordial to him and gave him a list of the best works to read on mysticism. Though Rufus Jones later came to find Karl Schmidt less infallible than he then believed him to be, he remembered always that meeting with him and sometimes spoke of him as one of the important influences in his life. Paul Sabatier, who was at that time studying for a doctor's degree at Strasbourg under Karl Schmidt, later became in Rufus's judgment, "the greatest interpreter of St. Francis of Assisi." Rufus had time during the day also to visit the Cathedral where John Tauler had preached, to admire the clock and to recall Whittier's poem *Tauler*, before he took the train for Heidelberg, where he arrived the same day.

Here he was to remain for four happy months. He stayed in a boarding house on the Unter Neckarstrasse, the old street near the river, running along behind the armory and under the shadow of the Holy Ghost Church. The house was kept by two kindly spinsters, Fräulein Eliza and Fräulein Gretchen; the food was good, everything neat and bright and homelike; he had a stove in his room. Most of the time there were two or three other Americans staying in the house, with whom to chat in the evenings, to go to see the Castle by moonlight—wishing Sallie were there instead—or to stroll on the Philosopher's Walk across the river. "If a pillar of fire had led me, it could hardly have brought me to a better home," he exulted.

Best of all, the university was at hand. There was no campus in the American sense. The buildings were concentrated in the old part of the town, thick with romantic tradition. Rufus made no mention of the Student Prince, or the duelling, or of the prison where it was every German student's pride to spend some time and add his bit to the primitive art on the walls; he did not even mention the lecture hall, panelled and beautiful, to which he went at seven in the morning, but he was well aware of the stature of the men whom he heard there.

He attended ten hours of lectures a week on Greek Philosophy, German Literature, and English Literature of the nineteenth century. Most of his work was with the celebrated German scholar, Kuno Fischer, "the most perfect lecturer in Germany." "He speaks and looks like a conqueror as he really is, for he has stormed many a fort intellectually," he wrote to Sallie.

"These lectures settled for good and all my allegiance to philosophy. I had strayed off into the field of history and for a time I seemed likely to make history my major work, but after I had followed Kuno Fischer for a few weeks I knew that philosophy was to claim me henceforth—'for this I was born.' My interest in mysticism had been steadily growing and deepening, and now I saw that the best approach to an understanding of this great human experience was to be found in philosophy and psychology."

He also heard the celebrated Bunsen lecture—the inventor of the Bunsen burner known to every high school student—then seventy-five years old and greatly honored in his own university and throughout Europe. He read Emerson again and Goethe, congratulating himself on not having read him when he was younger, "for he is full of dangers for a young undecided person." He rejoiced in the glorious unfolding of the spring, the light green of the larches, the tiny leaves of beeches, the blossoms of apricot, almond, peach, cherry, apple. And in Heidelberg the sixth of a line of oculists fitted him with the right glasses and he got relief from the pain and worry of his eyes.

Once more he had to grapple with the problem of "next year." He could not endure the prospect of a return to the "humdrum, carthorse life" of Oakwood. He wrote to his cousin Augustine Jones and asked for a job at Providence Friends School, even though he had almost no hope, for Augustine Jones had gone on record against the practice of employing relatives. During the weeks when he waited for an answer, he wrote to Sallie:

"It is not easy to be good . . . How do great souls decide their all important questions so quickly? Their whole life has been preparing them for the moment. I know how easy it is to talk; I know too how hard it is to act. I have fought—more than one would think. I do not always succeed, but I am in earnest in this business and I do not intend to be a knot in the tail of the devil's kite to help it fly . . . Sallie, thou knows that I aspire to be something and do something. What it shall be

I do not know but this I know, that he who would ease the burdens of the world must himself breathe the 'ampler aether and diviner air.' . . . The day is past when to be good means to wear gray clothes and a long face. If any man is to be loaded with sunshine it is he who feels himself at peace with the world and its Creator."

Late in April the offer came from Providence and was accepted with alacrity. "It is just the work that I want, German, French, and literature, and I am to take the place of Dr. Wells, who is a character. My recompense for the first year will be $900 and all the potatoes I want to eat, which is as much as I ought to expect at the beginning and if I do as well as I hope it will of course in time be better."

When he first wrote to Augustine Jones he' had told his plans for marriage, and Augustine evidently passed the word along, so that soon he was getting congratulatory letters. "It makes me feel strong," he wrote, "when I think how many true, sincere friends are shouting God Speed to me and who wish that our life may be a real success."

"I try more and more to live just what I am," he commented a few weeks later, "so that I may not deceive the world which by the way is very hard to do."

Charles Jacob rejoined him in July, to his delight. They went to Worms, for Luther's sake, sailed down the Rhine ("in no way so grand as our own Hudson") visited Cologne, saw the battlefield of Waterloo with some of Ed Farr's family, and had a fortnight in Paris. There he visited the Louvre, enjoying most Murillo's Assumption of the Virgin and the Venus de Milo, of which he said, "It is the only statue of Venus which makes her anything more than a beautiful woman. Here she has more than human expression and her beauty is full of grandure [sic]. Her lovely face shows the consciousness of power." He also followed the trail of Napoleon, who was, incongruously, a hero of his. "For a deeply convinced Quaker I was strangely enamored of war heroes and battle scenes," he confessed in 1929, "and worst of all I had my money put up on the wrong horse! The years have pretty thoroughly corrected my perspective, though with all my pacifism I still glow over *ancient* battlefields!"

After a few days in London, he sailed for home at the end of July. Immediately on landing in New York he went to Ardonia to see Sallie. It had been a long and difficult year for her. She had had to leave Oakwood and go home to nurse her much loved Aunt Mary through her last illness and death. She had lost twenty pounds.

Fresh Fields

SINCE Rufus and Sallie could not be married until he had earned and saved enough to repay the money he had borrowed for his year in Europe, he went alone to Providence in September. He found there a congenial group of young teachers, among whom was George A. Barton, Haverford '82, who was to become one of his closest friends and associates.

Sallie was in Ardonia, teaching in the one-room district school everything, she said, "from primer to physiology." She began with twenty-three pupils, but by the time she resigned in March she had seventy. Besides the work in the school, which was heavy, though she wrote of it lightly enough, she had to do a great deal of housework at home, when her stepmother was ill. Rufus was troubled. "I love to think of thee as a strong, well woman," he wrote, "who can walk, row and study with me. It would change everything if thou should get weak. Thou must think how much is at stake."

Though James Coutant was a Friend, Sallie's own mother, Elizabeth Griggs, had not been one, and Sallie herself was not. In October she wrote to Rufus, "I will gladden thy heart by telling thee that I sent in a request for membership last Wednesday . . . I feel a great deal better now that it is done, and I already have visions of *two* old Friends, jogging along to 'Select Meetin'. I did it for love of thee and because I thought it a good place for me." She had not acted hastily. They had discussed it in their letters the previous April.

About that time there was a great meeting of Friends in Richmond, Indiana, attended by ninety-nine delegates from yearly meetings in the United States, England, Ireland, and Canada. Uncle Eli and Augustine Jones were there to represent New England, and J. Bevan Braithwaite came from London. After the Conference all three stopped at Providence Friends School, where no doubt Rufus heard them discuss issues and problems that were to occupy much of his thought and energy and call forth his powers of leadership in years to come. The Richmond Declaration of Faith, with which he was to wrestle repeatedly, was drawn up by that Conference.

He was enjoying his teaching. He had discovered in himself the power of interpretation of great ideas and the ability to quicken the enthusiasm of the students. He gave freely of himself in the process. "My classes are in fine condition," he wrote, "but they take the life out of me, for I cannot teach in a cold, business way. It comes out of me warm with my life blood."

In the spring he began to plan his first book, which was to be a biography of Eli and Sybil Jones. As Whittier had long been a friend of Uncle Eli, Rufus asked him to write an introduction for the book. The poet refused, but he invited Rufus to come and see him in his house, Oak Knoll, in Danvers, Massachusetts. For most of a day they talked together, a day which Rufus rated on a par with his visit to John Bright. Whittier, then old and frail but luminous and full of insight, urged the young man to stand for the primitive, mystical Quakerism rather than the authoritarian, evangelical doctrines which were then sweeping the Society of Friends. He held, Rufus Jones was to write many years later, the "yeasty doctrine of immanence in sane balance with the equally important fact of transcendence. He is never swept off his feet, or carried into the swirl of an engulfing pantheism ... At the time of my visit to him in 1887 he criticized the tendency to pantheism in Emerson's writings, and he told me that he had more than once expressed this feeling to Emerson himself." To Rufus Jones Whittier was beyond question the wisest and most profound interpreter of Quakerism during the half century between 1830 and 1880.

In April, when Rufus went to visit Sallie during his spring vacation, they set the date of their wedding. Rufus was determined that they should be married in strict accordance with Friends discipline which required that the engaged couple should inform their respective monthly meetings of their intentions. The monthly meetings would then appoint Friends to visit the young people to ascertain their "clearness," after which the couple was said to have "passed meeting" and could proceed with arrangements for the ceremony. At Plattekill Meeting, however, this process had been allowed to fall into neglect and Sallie, a new member, was reluctant to revive it.

"*Thou* can get consent of thy meeting," she wrote persuasively to Rufus, "and *I* will *elope*. I have come over to thy faith and manner of being married and now let us compromise."

Rufus, however, would not yield, and two weeks later she described her capitulation with rueful humor, and incidentally gave a vivid picture of a small rural meeting in the 1880's.

"Well Rufus we have set all Plattekill agog. When thy letter came with that folded paper in it, my heart sank for I did so dislike to have this very prying community gratified by so much preliminary business, so thou will have to love me very much more for yielding to thy wishes . . . Pa went to Preparative Meeting and handed the paper to the clerk, Georgia's father. When he read it a fervent 'praise the Lord' burst from Sammie Birdsall, and all the women Friends who had been thinking about their dinners, opened their eyes and ears. It was the first thing of the kind in twelve years. So many spoke about it and in fact they had a very amusing time. One man said that he had always liked *me* and now he was glad to see that I was not ashamed of my prospects. David Sampson said, 'I feel that I must pray for them' and he knelt down and put up a fervent prayer for the two brave ones who had gone back to the straight Friends' principles, so thou sees what a commotion we are making."

Though Rufus had stood out so firmly for straight Friends prin- ciples, he evidently forgot to do his part in his own meeting and two weeks before the wedding Sallie wrote to him with barely concealed triumph, "Dost know that thou must send a paper *before next Wednes- day* from thy Monthly Meeting showing thy clearness of engage- ments?" In a tender "last letter" to Sallie "as a single sister," written a week before their marriage, Rufus poured out his hopes and resolu- tions for their future. "I hope I shall not be autocratical," he said. "I propose to look up to thee, but I shall often look for graceful yielding on thy part."

The wedding took place at noon on the third of July, 1888, in the front sitting-room of Sallie's home, a spacious old house surrounded by evergreen trees. Three children were present, Rhoda Birdsall and her sister Mary, and William Battey, a nephew of Sallie's stepmother, who grew up to marry Rhoda. Twelve-year-old William remembered especially the wonderful wedding meal, which Sallie must have helped to prepare. Early in June, we know from her letters to Rufus, she was at work on the fruit cake. She was married in her going-away dress of brown or gray, and she took the trousseau over which she had labored all spring on her wedding trip to South China. Rufus wore a new suit with a Prince Albert coat, made for the occasion, and he had now acquired the moustache which he kept for the rest of his life.

They spent the summer at the Providence Friends School, which Augustine Jones had asked Rufus to hold down for him while he went to Europe. "Beautiful grounds, fine sky, water not far off," Rufus had set forth its attractions when the proposal first came up, "trees as old as this century, and good people, what more do you want, except books, of which there would be nearly 9,000."

During this first summer of their married life, Rufus wrote his book about Eli and Sybil Jones, which was published by Porter and Coates of Philadelphia the following year. It was an act of love and piety as well as his first real venture in writing. His style was still unformed; he used well-worn evangelical terms instead of the fresh-minted vivid phrases that marked his later manner, and he had not yet mastered the art of simplicity; but it was a milestone for him and he was glad that Uncle Eli was still there to read it.

In February of 1890, Eli Jones died. He had had pneumonia and Rufus had gone to South China to be with him. He asked to be lifted up to see the lake, and so, in Rufus's arms, he died. "No one else can affect me as he did," wrote Rufus to Ellen Clare Pearson.

By that time Rufus and Sallie Jones were living in Vassalboro, only ten miles from South China.

At the end of his second year at Friends School, Rufus had intended to go to Harvard for graduate study in philosophy. "This is not to be my future home," he had written to Sallie during his first year at Providence, "and I hope some time to be ready for higher work." But when an offer came, in the spring of 1889, of the principalship of Oak Grove Seminary, Sallie urged him to take it and postpone his graduate year. "She felt," he wrote in The Trail of Life in College, "that it would give us both opportunity and scope for the development of capacities and powers in us which so far had not been drawn upon."

Howard H. Brinton, in his illuminating book, Friends for 300 Years, has written: "The co-educational Quaker Boarding School was a unique institution carried on like a large family. The heads of such a school were, as in the case of a family, a man and wife, who divided executive responsibilities." Such a school was Oak Grove Seminary, founded in 1850 "for the guarded and religious education of the children of Friends." New England Yearly Meeting owned the property, and a committee managed the school, which included a Primary Department, as well as the equivalent of a modern Secondary School.

The buildings were not those which Rufus had known during his term there in 1878, for the school had burned down in 1887 and had been entirely rebuilt. The new school was "modern," with steam heat, bathrooms with hot and cold water, and "Rochester burners" for lighting. The boys and girls had separate wings, each with its own sitting room; the central part, topped by an elegant cupola, held the dining-room, the library of 350 volumes, the mineral collection donated by Eli Jones, the classrooms and administrative offices and the living quarters of the principal and his wife. A square front porch looked down over the school's six acres to the Kennebec River and the stretch of country lying beyond. A windmill supplied the water and broke down at inconvenient moments.

Running the school, with its six or seven teachers and 118 pupils, one of whom was Sallie's half-sister Emma, called forth all the energy and ability of the young pair. Sallie, whom one of the pupils remembers as "an outstanding beauty and very capable," was matron and teacher of Botany. She kept hens to insure an ample supply of fresh eggs, and it is certain that under her rule no hungry boy ate cold pie in his bedroom when there was a hot meal in the dining-room downstairs. She was passionately fond of flowers and she collected specimens for her Botany classes from the woods and fields round about.

At first Herbert Jones acted as business manager for his brother, but this arrangement was only temporary, and soon Rufus included among his duties that of driving around the countryside behind a white horse named Napoleon buying firewood and other supplies for the school. He taught. He carried the responsibility for the meeting.

Meeting was attended twice a week by both the school and local Friends, and Rufus Jones, who was now recorded as a minister by China Monthly Meeting and Vassalboro Quarterly Meeting, found that most of the speaking devolved upon him. It was a burden for a young man whose mind must have been cumbered with many practical problems and necessities, but it was also a training for him and a preparation.

To the pupils these four years were wonderful ones. They were hostile to their new principal at first, for they had liked the former one and resented his dismissal. They tried Rufus out with exploding matches and other forms of deviltry, but he soon had them in the hollow of his hand. "He was always just, radiant, interesting, inspiring," said one of them, Nettie Burleigh, who graduated in 1892 and went on to Mt. Holyoke College. Guy B. Healey, a lawyer in Boston, wrote to Rufus Jones in 1934, "I think the turning point in my life was when at the end of the evening study hour as the boys filed out of the room you motioned me to come to your desk. When I did so, you merely said, 'Guy, I would like to have you go to college. Good night.' That was all. Up to that time, I had never seriously thought of going to college, but from that moment I decided that if you felt that there was anything in me, perhaps there was."

If the winters were breathless, the summers at any rate were times of comparative leisure, when the springs could fill up again. Colby College was only five miles away and Rufus Jones found in its library the books he needed to go on with his study of Philosophy. Josiah Royce's SPIRIT OF MODERN PHILOSOPHY and William James's two-volume PSYCHOLOGY were "epochs" for him and their authors would be "major influences" in shaping his later thought.

The greatest event of those four hard-working valuable years, indeed one of the greatest events of his life, was the "divine miracle" of the birth of his son on January 23, 1892. The experience of hearing this child's first cry and holding him in his arms was indescribably thrilling, and the wonder of it never faded. "We fell in love with each other from the start."

The baby was named Lowell, after the poet, and Coutant, for his mother's family. Both Rufus and Sallie ardently admired the poet. Rufus had made him the subject of his "junior oration" in college; his letters bristled with quotations from Lowell, one of his favorites being, "Nothing is safe from thought that keeps thought out." "It isn't that I regard Lowell as so much greater than many others," he had written to Sallie from Nîmes, "but only that he says just what I would have said if I had thought of it before he did."

In 1893, as the fourth year at Oak Grove was drawing to an end, he again arranged to go to Harvard for his graduate work, and again his plan was broken into by a call to service. He was offered the editorship of *The Friends Review*, that same Quaker weekly which had come to his house when he was a child.

It is necessary at this point to sketch rapidly the Quaker separations of the nineteenth century and to attempt to trace some of the currents that made up the whirlpool of Quakerism at the time when Rufus Jones first began to emerge as a leader. "Sallie, I love the Society of Friends," he had written six years earlier, "and I believe the good part will triumph." He saw it always as a movement rather than a sect and related its problems to universal questions of religion, but he knew it also in its pettiest and most thorny aspects.

The bitter separation of 1827 left Philadelphia Quakers, together with some in Maryland, Ohio and New York, divided between the Hicksites and the Orthodox. There was more social and organizational division and less doctrinal difference between the two than anyone was willing to recognize at the time, but broadly speaking the Hicksites were the more liberal group, the Orthodox the more conservative, believing themselves to be a "remnant" guarding the precious heritage of Quakerism. The periodical of the Hicksites was the *Friends Intelligencer*, that of the Orthodox, *The Friend*, popularly called "The Square Friend," because of its shape.

Eighteen years later a second controversy took place, known as the Wilbur-Gurney Separation of 1845, after the names of the two leaders around whom the issues clustered. Joseph John Gurney had come over from England a, handsome, scholarly, and magnetic figure, brother of the famous Elizabeth Fry, and had preached a powerful, evangelical doctrine, basically Calvinistic in its teachings in regard to the Bible, the nature of man, and salvation. When John Wilbur in New England Yearly Meeting opposed this much-admired English Friend, the Yearly Meeting as a whole supported Gurney and disowned Wilbur who, with his followers, set up a second organization in New England and other parts of the country.

In Philadelphia the Hicksite group went on its way unaffected. The Orthodox body was not actually divided but it felt the tug of the two currents throughout its meetings. *The Friends Review* was founded in 1848 by sympathizers of the Gurneyites; it supported the cause of Bible schools and foreign missions, and it was widely read in both east and west.

Howard H. Brinton sums up the situation in the second half of the nineteenth century in these words: "The Hicksites represented the more mystical, liberal, non-creedal branch; the Gurneyites the more evangelical, authoritative and theologically conservative branch; and the Wilburites a branch whose position was between the two." But, he goes on to say, although the Wilburites were closest to the original Quakerism, "there was an important difference. The code of behavior which the first Friends arrived at through immediate experience of the Inward Light, the Wilburites, with many exceptions, tended to accept in large measure on the basis of tradition." What complicated the situation still further was that the Gurneyites, whose theology is by present standards conservative, were called the Progressives, while the Wilburites, whose theology is more liberal, were the conservatives.

Meanwhile another division was gathering in the Middle West and South. The revivalist movement, which swept the country in the sixties and seventies with its Moody and Sankey hymns, its emotional fervor, its ecstatic conversions, influenced the Society of Friends in those regions that had been somewhat prepared for it by the doctrine of Joseph John Gurney. Where the Quaker silence had grown static and empty, the new "awakening" seemed to bring in a fresh power and vitality. Furthermore in the mid-Western Quaker communities, many who were touched by revivalist preaching joined the Society of Friends because there was no other place locally to go. Knowing little or nothing of Quaker history and thought, they had no understanding of the silent meeting and no inherited love for it. They wanted hymns, Bible reading and prepared sermons. Pastors and programmed services of the Presbyterian or Methodist type followed naturally, though in theory a spirit-led worship was maintained. The organ of this group was *The Christian Worker*, started in Ohio in 1871.

In 1893 *The Friends Review* was in a critical condition. Owing to the competition of *The Christian Worker*, itself in none too healthy a condition, its subscriptions had fallen off disastrously. Dr. Henry Hartshorne, its editor, was discouraged and wished to resign. The publication committee, which consisted of several rich and influential Friends, decided to reorganize the paper "under vigorous editorial management" and give it greater financial backing. At the suggestion of Isaac Sharpless, who remembered Rufus's conduct of the *Haverfordian*, Rufus Jones was offered the position of managing editor and publisher, "clothed with ample powers," at a salary of $2000 a year and a possible opportunity to teach Philosophy at Haverford.

Rufus Jones wrapped up his dream of graduate study at Harvard and put it back on the shelf. He would consider this assignment, he replied, if the teaching at Haverford became a certainty. Isaac Sharpless, since 1887 President of the college, offered him a course in Philosophy and two rooms on the third floor of Founders' Hall. The school committee at Oak Grove was reluctant to release him, but by the 22nd of May it was all settled.

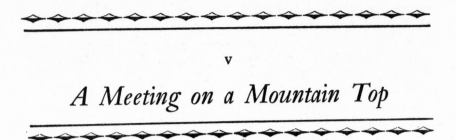

A Meeting on a Mountain Top

Rufus Jones preceded Sallie and nineteen-months-old Lowell to Haverford in August, in order to get out his first issue of *The Friends Review* on the twenty-fourth. The first thing in it was a poem, "Godminster Chimes," by James Russell Lowell. Then the young editor stated his policy.

"It [*The Friends Review*] is not designed to be the organ of a party or section, and it knows nothing of divisions but aims to advocate and proclaim safe, sound, consistent methods and policies in individual life, in public action and in the Church, seeking as ever before to maintain and honor *spiritual realities* rather than *forms* and *traditions*."

In succeeding numbers he set forth his ideas of salvation as a transformation of life rather than a theological transaction; of divine immanence; of the nature of the Inner Light; of truth as a personal experience instead of a statement to which the mind gives assent; of the place of mysticism in the history of Christian thought. A new voice was speaking in the Society of Friends, fresh, fearless, compelling. Not many heard it at this stage, but to those who were listening it bore the authentic note of prophecy.

The men who were backing this new enterprise financially, with moral support and counsel, and by the contribution of articles, knew well the quality of the man they had discovered. Isaac Sharpless, now forty-five, past his early awkwardness and maturing into a wise and gifted leader and scholar; David Scull, trustee of Bryn Mawr, manager of Haverford, practical business man and saintly character; James E.

Wood of Mt. Kisco, N.Y., also on the boards of both colleges, probably at the time the best-known Friend in the United States; James E.
Rhoads, president of Bryn Mawr and a former editor of *The Friends
Review*; James Carey Thomas, leading Friend and physician of Baltimore and father of M. Carey Thomas, dean of Bryn Mawr; T. Wistar
Brown, president of the Haverford Board, businessman and philan-
thropist: John B. Garrett of Rosemont, vice-president of the Lehigh
Valley Railroad, member of the Bryn Mawr and Haverford Boards:
these were some of the men who stood behind Rufus Jones, men of
influence who had a wide knowledge of Friends of all kinds. Starting,
most of them, with the Gurneyite point of view, they were ready to
modify it with the findings of modern science and historical study.
They gave to the young editor their friendship as well as their encouragement and assistance. The seasoned wisdom of their minds, their
affection and their faith in him, the quiet elegance of their hospitable
homes gave him a new kind of social experience and helped to develop
his self-confidence.

These were all prominent Quakers, but most of them were not
members of the inner councils of the Orthodox Philadelphia Yearly
Meeting. This citadel was not yet breached. To at least one of the
Yearly Meeting elders the young prophet was "that man Jones." They
did not like his emphasis on a thinking ministry; they distrusted equally
his tolerant attitude toward Quaker pastors and programmed meetings
and his adoption of modern thought and the so-called Higher Criticism; they looked askance at his moustache. Perhaps most distasteful
of all was his hardihood in commenting on the occasional flaws that
he found in Philadelphia Yearly Meeting itself.

He reported in *The Friends Review* on the sessions of Philadelphia
Yearly Meeting in 1894. After praising its continuity, its sincerity, its
"spirit of broad charity," he went on to say that he saw in it too much
stress on specific observances and minor details, too little utterance
of great general principles, no new messages of truth, no encouragement of the young to dedicate themselves to the advance of truth and
the service of mankind. It was the criticism of a young man, but there
was enough truth in it to sting.

It would have seemed the natural thing for Rufus Jones to move his
membership from China Monthly Meeting to Philadelphia, and some
urged him to do so. T. Wistar Brown, knowing well the scene and the
climate, advised him not to: there was a very good chance that he
might not have been accepted.

Believing that he should know more, personally and individually, of the constituency of *The Friends Review* and give them a chance to know him in the flesh, he made that autumn and winter the first of innumerable trips into the region of western Quakerism. This beginning was somewhat tentative and limited. He met the leading Friends of Cincinnati, of Richmond, Indiana, and of the surrounding districts. At Earlham College in Richmond, he lectured to the students on Dante and thus made his first contact with a Quaker college not his own. Through it all, he was seeking primarily to understand.

Even on this first trip he saw that the pastoral system had come to stay and that it would have to be accepted by Friends in the east who tended to think that it was not Quakerism at all but something quite different and inferior when meetings were programmed and a "hireling minister" preached. The realization of this fact spurred him on to seek the deeper meaning of Quakerism and to find the essentials on which all could unite.

The Friends Review, though it appeared in an attractive new format and though it contained in addition to the excellent editorials good articles by leading Friends, still gained no new subscribers. Some remedy was necessary and Rufus Jones characteristically found a daring answer. Why not combine it with its rival, *The Christian Worker*, to form a new paper altogether?

The Christian Worker also was in a fainting condition and its editor was tired and disposed to welcome the proposition. In May, 1894, Rufus Jones, Isaac Sharpless, Allen Thomas and James Wood met in conference with representatives of *The Christian Worker* and they came to a decision. The two papers were to merge under the title *The American Friend*, to be edited by Rufus Jones. The new editor told the western Friends frankly that he could not adopt the position of *The Christian Worker*, but that he was ready to widen his interests and broaden his sympathies, to try to understand western Friends and to interpret for them and others "a fresh and vital type of Christianity inwardly mystical and outwardly socially constructive." The first issue of the new paper was to appear on July 19, 1894, not quite a year since Rufus Jones had come to Philadelphia.

During this decisive year he had also been an instructor at Haverford, teaching Psychology, which was then still a new subject. The University of Pennsylvania had established the first chair in the United States exclusively assigned to Psychology only five years earlier, to be followed the next year by Harvard, when William James became Professor of Psychology. Rufus Jones's study of the two volumes

of James's massive PRINCIPLES OF PSYCHOLOGY, published in 1890, constituted his preparation for his task. The following year he added
a course in the History of Philosophy and the year after that one on
English History and a seminar on Constitutional History. To meet
these new responsibilities his Haverford salary mounted in 1896 to
$700.

In 1893 when Rufus Jones came to Haverford, three other young
men also joined the faculty as instructors: Wilfred P. Mustard of
Toronto, Henry S. Pratt, from Harvard, and James A. Babbitt from
Yale. Henry Pratt and Rufus Jones, who became lifelong friends,
read together the *Purgatorio* and the *Paradiso* in Italian during that
first winter. W. P. Mustard, Dr. Francis Gummere and Rufus Jones
inaugurated golf on the campus. James A. Babbitt was to be active
with Rufus Jones twenty years later in the early work of the American Friends Service Committee.

It was the largest addition to the faculty that had ever been made at
one time, and housing was a problem. Like most newcomers, they had
a term in "the elastic quarters of Founders' Hall." Rufus and Sallie and
the baby occupied two rooms on the third floor until they found more
comfortable lodging in the house of their friends George and Carrie
Barton. George Barton had come from Providence to Bryn Mawr
as professor of Biblical Literature, and for many years the two families
were the closest friends. In 1896 Rufus Jones was able to rent a
house, number seven College Lane, on the Haverford campus.

Whatever else his interests and concerns, the students, now and
for many years to come, were primary. The purpose of education, as
he saw it, was not the stuffing of the mind with information, but the
development of life and character. Besides his classroom work he felt a
deep responsibility for the meetings for worship on Sundays and
Thursdays, and he was determined to give the students messages that
should have real meaning for them and direct bearing on their lives. It
was at this time that he developed his own characteristic way of speaking, simply, conversationally, as if he were talking to a single person,
using homely illustrations and not being afraid of a humorous story
if it illumined his point. Generations of Haverford students have
testified to the inspiration which those talks of Rufus Jones gave them.
"It has always been a matter of amazement to me," wrote one, "and
I am sure to many others, to recall that during the four years when I
would attend those Fifth Day meetings you never repeated yourself
and always gave us something that was worth while."

The American Friend aroused immediate interest. Its subscription list grew week by week. Each issue contained two or three editorials by Rufus Jones, articles by leading eastern and western Friends, presenting varied points of view, and regular departments of Bible study, missions, and news notes about Friends sent in by correspondents from different sections. It sought to maintain the precarious balance between staying open to discussion of different aspects of a subject and slipping into acrimonious controversy. Always the editor strove to find the fundamental thought and the basis of underlying unity, to place ideas in their historical perspective, to interpret Quakerism as George Fox conceived it, to persuade his readers that religious truth and scientific truth need not be enemies, that the Bible studied in the light of historical knowledge gained rather than lost in power and illumination.

"Quakerism was . . . a return to the simple, every-day, Christ-like life of the early Christians at Antioch and Jerusalem," he wrote. "As to this company Christ was always present, directing all their work and inspiring them, so with the Friends of those first years."

And again, "The kernel of his [George Fox's] mission was to bring men to Christ Himself and to leave them with Him, to show that a religion which does not make new creatures is only a sham religion, and to prove that genuine religion, embodied in genuine lives, is an irresistible, transforming force."

The mail was full of response to this new periodical, letters of praise, letters of judicious comment, letters of criticism, written some of them in that intemperate language people use who have no imagination to see the face at the other end. "Several of thy articles in *The American Friend* lately have seemed to me most timely and most valuable as expositions of the real spirit of Quakerism," wrote a Philadelphia Friend, while from Indiana came the charge, "You have refused to print some pieces that some of our true ones have sent you. You failed to print them because you are afraid of your reputation." "I have grown to love you and our paper," a Friend wrote from Brooklyn. A western Friend found the paper full of "good sense, literary ability and religious fervor," while a Philadelphian, objecting to the tolerant attitude toward pastors, angrily desired his name to be removed from the subscription list. Both eastern and western Friends complained that the other side was given the advantage in the paper. It won the "warm sympathy" of M. Carey Thomas, now president of Bryn Mawr. Cousin Augustine Jones waited three months after the first issue and then delivered his judgment to his former pupil. While the editorials "state many true and beautiful features of the society," came the word from the headmaster's office, they did not "put in original, native, clear, irresistible, red-hot logic that which distinguishes the Society of Friends from everything else in history."

Even if the logic was not red-hot, still the subscription list grew steadily, and English Friends took notice of the new periodical and its editor and found good in both.

There was a great stirring in the mulberry trees in England. In 1895 English Friends held a conference at Manchester, which Elbert Russell declared to be "a turning point in Quaker history." Whereas the Richmond Conference in 1887, seeking for unity, had produced a conservative Declaration of Faith, the Manchester Conference met with a clear realization of the demands of the age and a determination that Friends should be ready to meet them and to take their place in the work of the world. Friends must know much more about their Quaker heritage, must meet squarely the questions posed by science and modern study of the Bible, and they must deal with social questions and social needs. The first obvious result was the establishment of summer schools to study religious and social questions on modern lines.

This conference threw up, as such gatherings sometimes do, a young leader of real potentialities, John Wilhelm Rowntree, who said in effect just what Rufus Jones was saying in the United States: "Let us in our message offer that which is beyond all creeds—the evidence in our lives of communion with the spirit of God."

During these early years of *The American Friend*, Rufus Jones was extending his knowledge and understanding of all types of Quakers in the United States. He attended yearly meetings and spoke at Quaker colleges in Kansas, Indiana, and North Carolina, writing his editorials on trains and hurrying from the station to his classrooms after a restless night on a sleeper.

Now it occurred to one of the "elder statesmen" of *The American Friend* board that Rufus Jones ought to know something of English Friends also. Lying awake one night he remembered his own joy in Switzerland and wanted his young friend to have that experience of beauty also. Accordingly David Scull proposed to send Rufus Jones abroad in May 1897 to attend London Yearly Meeting and to travel afterwards in Italy and Switzerland.

It was a great opportunity, but it meant leaving Sallie behind with burdens. Though there was an office assistant for *The American Friend* and Rufus himself would send home editorials, still Sallie would have to oversee the getting out of the paper. She had three or four students boarding in their house, to supplement their small income, and until Commencement was over they must be cared for. Then she must get the house ready to rent for the summer, and as she was a meticulous housekeeper, this meant an immense amount of work to meet her exacting standards. When that was done she and Lowell, who was now five, were to go to Wernersville in the Pennsylvania mountains, where, it was hoped, Sallie could get rid of a cough that had been troubling her ever since an attack of bronchitis the previous fall.

One after another the pieces fell into place and early in May Rufus sailed on the *Lucania*. He was troubled about leaving Sallie, and the editorials he wrote on shipboard did not suit him. "It just escapes being idiotic," he complained of one. But when he reached Liverpool, after a short visit to Ireland, he found a welcoming letter from his friend Rendel Harris. Harris, foremost New Testament scholar at that time, who, after teaching six years at Haverford, had returned to England and Clare College, Cambridge, was one of the group of young English Friends who were moving forward into the new age with a spirit of confidence. John Wilhelm Rowntree said of him, "He is Puck turned saint and now and then Puck gets so much the upper hand." It was no doubt Puck who sent the message which contained a single sentence: "Are thee there, Rufus?"

Jubilantly Rufus replied, "I are."

London Yearly Meeting, which was held in Devonshire House, in Bishopsgate, London, the central headquarters for English Friends, was very impressive to the young American, who confessed to finding it something of a strain to be almost the only visiting Friend. As he went from meeting to meeting, attending plenary sessions, committees, and executive groups, he was filled with admiration for English Friends, for their social concern, their ability to think clearly and to express themselves competently without fumbling for words, for their fidelity to the principles of Quakerism, and for the numbers of them who were qualified to take responsibility for the work of the Society of Friends.

"I believe there is no other body in the world which represents original Quakerism so nearly as does this one," he wrote to *The American Friend* ... "They have as the early Friends had in their time an open heart for the needs of society in this age." He found things also to criticize: too much speaking, a "waste of words," and "a lack of warmth and heartiness,—I do not mean shouting or fervid enthusiasm —but warm heart love which flows over many of our meetings and binds us into one."

There was certainly no lack of personal warmth to him. This time English Friends welcomed him, not for Uncle Eli's sake, but for his own. After going to a London tailor and ordering a suit and an overcoat, revisiting Westminster Abbey and standing with one foot on Tennyson's grave and one on Browning's, "a deeply affecting experience," as he wrote to Sallie, he went to Oxford with Thomas Hodgkin ("the ablest and most noted man in the Y.M.") for the boat races and dined at Balliol, to Ludlow with Henry S. Newman, editor of the *Friend* (London), to Birmingham to visit the Cadburys, to see their famous chocolate works and the model town which they were building for their 2200 workers, to Swarthmore Hall and the Lake Country, to Bamborough Castle, where the Hodgkins lived in the Keep, and to Cambridge to stay with Rendel Harris. Everywhere he went he picked flowers for Lowell, which he pressed and sent home in his letters. Lowell, a slender, ardent, sensitive child, had a passionate love of flowers, learning the Latin botanical names along with his nursery rhymes.

In the middle of June Rufus Jones and Rendel Harris went together to Switzerland on a walking trip. They planned their day's marches so as to arrive at Mürren on a week end, when they could meet a party of English Friends from York who were staying there. Though Rendel Harris was a delightful companion, full of amusing talk on all kinds of topics from folklore to the church fathers, Rufus Jones was low in his mind. He had not heard from Sallie in some time; the weather was bad; rain and snow blotted out the Jungfrau, the Eiger and the Monk. But at Mürren everything changed. There was a letter from Sallie; and John Wilhelm Rowntree, who had not been at London Y.M., was here in Switzerland. He was the son of one of England's three great chocolate families. Five years younger than Rufus Jones, he was, like him, immensely concerned for Quakerism, seeing it faced with the possibility either of withering into a tiny sect interesting only to antiquarians, or of expanding into a spiritual force adequate to the needs of the day and the future. A young man with thick, wavy hair, deep-set eyes, clear features, brown moustache, he had a magnetic personality in which gentleness and heroism were combined, and there was about him that luminous quality that comes from suffering courageously met and from the experiential knowledge of God. Five or six years earlier he had developed an obscure kidney disease which was slowly but irrevocably destroying his hearing and his eyesight and threatening his memory. With darkness and silence ahead of him, but upheld by an extraordinary experience in which he knew beyond any doubt the power of the love of God, he was seeking to devote the years that remained to him to "making the Society of Friends a real and living force in the world."

The group of fifteen Friends, five of whom were recorded ministers, as a matter of course held a meeting for worship in the hotel on Sunday morning.

"It was a heavenly meeting," wrote Rufus to Sallie, "and at the close thy letter came. I had been praying most earnestly in my heart for thee and the *burden* of our little meeting was love. I have solemnly resolved to love more deeply and more truly and to be a sweeter man."

The rest of the day, while the rain dashed against the window panes and the great mountains were hidden behind clouds, Rufus Jones and John Wilhelm Rowntree talked the hours away. They agreed on the problems of Quakerism, they shared a vision of its future, they planned the means for bringing it about. They should both take part in the summer schools projected by the Manchester Conference. They should write a history and interpretation of the Society of Friends, and Rufus's part would be to relate it to the other mystical movements in the Christian Church. There should be a magazine for the modern Quaker point of view, thoughtful, fearless, open. There should be, in addition to summer schools, a permanent "settlement" where Friends could study religious and social questions.

Their imaginations kindled each other; their enthusiasms matched. They gave each other strength. They decided that once a year they would meet, whether in England or America—a plan which was actually followed out as long as John Wilhelm Rowntree lived, for though Rufus did not go again to England until 1901, John Wilhelm Rowntree came regularly to the United States to consult a doctor in Chicago who helped him.

The next day the mountains emerged in snow-topped glory after the storm. After an uncomfortable night—"we [Rendel Harris and Rufus] occupy the same room always avec deux lits. I am all bitten up with bugs de lits"—they saw the sunrise over the Jüngfrau, and walked together all day, talking, talking. "We both knew before the day was over that we were to be comrades for the rest of life."

At Grindelwald they parted, and Rufus Jones and Rendel Harris went on to Meiringen and Lugano, where it was warm enough to swim in the lake, and to Axenstern, as David Scull had planned. July fourth found Rufus Jones in Dresden, planted before the Sistine Madonna. "I am almost afraid I am not going to be able to enter fully into the greatness," he wrote in some bewilderment. "It is a tremendous test of a man and I came home dreadfully humiliated. I felt like a pygmy trying to comprehend the world and I knew my life was too shallow and unripe to fathom such a miracle of conception. I am going again tomorrow."

At first Sallie wrote cheerfully from the boarding house in Wernersville, where the other guests were all old and doddering. "This place is as beautiful as the garden of Eden," she commented with dry humor, "and there is much less chance of sinning." But very soon, the tone changed. She was not feeling well and her fellow boarders depressed her. She had decided to leave Wernersville and take Lowell home to Ardonia. She was tired of staying alone "night after night for months."

Her husband's quick sympathy penetrated the slightly querulous surface to the real trouble beneath. He wrote in great distress from Berlin: "It was a serious mistake for me ever to come and leave thee and I have deeply and bitterly condemned myself for allowing myself to be led astray, but that is now of the past and I shall try to make up to thee in some true way for the long and lonely period of separation."

The *Koenigen Luise* docked in New York on July 16th. He had been away only a little over two months. During that time he had entered on a friendship that was to be of immense importance both to him and to the Society of Friends. Through his contact with English Quaker thought, he had come to a new vision of the social as well as the spiritual task of Quakerism. The trip was essential for the architecture of his life.

But at home tragedy awaited him. A letter from Sallie met him at the dock.

"I feel that it is not right," she had written, "for thee to come up here without knowing that for a little time more we must be separated. God give me grace and strength to write so that thou may get just the right idea of the situation. I have learned today that it is necessary for me to go to the Adirondacks and place myself under the care of Dr. Trudeau the great lung specialist if I ever hope to be in my dear little home again with my darling husband and child . . . The Dr. says that he can *almost assure* me of recovery but it is *vital* that I get away at once . . . All is hopeful, dear, but the shock has been great to us all . . . With more love than ever and a prayer that thou may see only hope. Come to me very quickly."

A Time of Digging Deep

A WEEK later Sallie was at Saranac Lake, installed in Conklin Cottage, where, under a doctor's supervision, she could have the air and the regime of life then considered so beneficial. Rufus boarded with a Friends' family in Haverford—"all rather interesting people," he wrote Sallie, "when they don't have the current turned off for religious purposes"—and spent as many weekends as possible in Saranac.

Everything was done for her that the medical skill of the time could provide, including an experimental serum to which she was evidently allergic and which only increased her bodily misery. Their almost daily letters to each other during the year and a half of her illness make poignant reading. The fluctuations of determination and despondency, the tacit recognition of the steady encroachments of the disease, the inevitable regrets over the overwork and fatigue of the previous years, the problem of what was best for Lowell, the effort to be bright and cheerful in recounting the small daily happenings, the anguish of love and pity on the one hand and the cry of the young heart for life on the other, are recurrent themes in somber counterpoint. The weeks during the summer of 1898 which the little family spent together on an Adirondack farm were a brief sunlit time on which Rufus looked back with gratitude. He never admitted that he had lost hope. "It is encouraging to hear of any improvement though it may be slight," he was to write only two months before her death, "and I always feel so happy when I strike thy vein of humor which is so rich."

For a time Lowell was with Sallie at Saranac, but before long he was taken to his grandparents at Ardonia and she was writing sadly, "Not a somersault has been turned on my bed today." Later Rufus had Lowell with him in Haverford and struggled to fit baby-sitting into the crowded program of a college professor and the editor of a religious paper. "I have had a time of it writing editorials and entertaining Lowell at the same time," he wrote ruefully. "It is not easy to have two consecutive thoughts when he is awake and active."

To the weight of sorrow and anxiety and the stress of trying to be in two places at once was added the pressure of mounting expenses on a small income. The eleven biographical sketches of American writers from Marion Crawford to Hamilton Wright Mabie which he wrote for a book published by Winston are a comment on his need to supplement his meager salary. In the autumn of 1898 Sallie moved to her father's home in Ardonia, in an attempt to lighten the burden.

On January 13, 1899, Rufus wrote his last tender letter to her. "My darling, thy two lovers send much love to thee." The next day her valiant struggle came to an end.

For all the warm outpouring of sympathy and understanding which he received from devoted and numerous friends, Rufus Jones was now very much alone. He had "nobody at home to brace up" his heart when things went hard. His father and Aunt Peace were still living in the old house in South China, but Edwin Jones had never been very close to his son and Aunt Peace was now nearly ninety and both physically and mentally fragile. Walter, the elder brother, had died four years earlier; Alice was married and living in Brunswick; Herbert, the much loved younger brother, was an optician in Waterville, Maine, and busy with his own family. Sallie's father and stepmother, her half-brother and two half-sisters, were still at the house in Ardonia; they were able from time to time to relieve him of the care of Lowell, but they were neither geographically nor temperamentally available for support in his loneliness.

Lowell was just seven when his mother died. Rufus's loneliness and the fact that he had no one near at hand to help him with the little boy, intensified the "mystic union" which already existed between him and the child. Intelligent, eager, lively, sensitive beyond the average, passionately fond of flowers, endowed with big, wide-set gray eyes and a pointed chin, he was a child to arouse the inevitable adoration of a tender and heart-hungry father. Though, according to a playmate of those early years, he knew the Bible from back to front, he was, fortunately, a normally naughty little boy, a fact which his father forgot in later years but the neighbors remembered. The violet which Lowell found on the first of March became an almost sacred symbol in the Jones family; the handsful of sand tossed into the ladies' tea-cups at a decorous porch party survived only as scuttlebutt. To Rufus Jones, then and to the very end of his life, when he included a chapter on Lowell in a book about the great spiritual torchbearers of the ages (THE LUMINOUS TRAIL) this little son was evidence of the love of God made manifest in human life.

To the tribal Society of Friends of Philadelphia Rufus Jones for all his prominence and his five years' sojourn in their midst, was still an outsider. His roots were in New England, the Maine twang was in his voice. He criticized Philadelphia Yearly Meeting for arid traditionalism, and he dared to say that a meeting could have a paid pastor and still remain Quaker. Many loved him for the warmth and clarity of his personality, and the vitality of his message, but still the conservative portals were guarded against him. His letters to Sallie betrayed his awareness of his position. "George Vaux and his whole family including the Bartletts are coming to supper tonight. I must be a very good boy and say nothing unfortunate." And again, referring to a Friend whom they both knew, "I never saw such family satisfaction. It is limitless. I have grown rather sulky under it and I meet her talk with a cold vacant stare. Common sense is worth all the pedigree in the world." Looking back in his old age on that period, he wrote, "I was never invited into the Arch Street Meeting House Ministers' Gallery during the entire period of my Editorship [of *The American Friend*] ... and I do not remember ever having spoken in Arch St. Yearly Meeting during that time." Then he adds with satisfaction, "All the time at Haverford College I was happily teaching the sons of the pillar Friends of Arch Street Yearly Meeting."

He was teaching three courses now, Psychology, History of Philosophy, and the History of Christian Thought. Besides teaching the sons of the pillar Friends, he began at this time to take some responsibility for the education of their daughters also. In February of 1898 he was elected to the Board of Trustees of Bryn Mawr College, to fill the vacancy left by the death of Dr. James Carey Thomas, and within a year was put on the Executive Committee.

At the same time another Quaker college, Earlham in Richmond, Indiana, approached him with a view to offering him its presidency, but he declined. First and last over the years all the Quaker colleges in turn cherished the dream of having Rufus Jones for president, but college administration never tempted him.

If the Arch Street pillars remained reserved, Rufus Jones still had wise and powerful older Friends who gave him support and guidance during this period.

T. Wistar Brown, then past seventy, lived at Villanova, four or five miles from Haverford, devoting his time and thought and much of his money to a quiet, deep and generous interest in Haverford College and the Pennsylvania Hospital. On the board of the College for nearly fifty years, he had been for nine years president of the board. His grandfather had come from New England, his father had married a Philadelphia Wistar, and he himself had been brought up according to the strictest old-fashioned Quaker principles. Thrust at sixteen into the family dry-goods business, he had accumulated what was said to be one of the largest Quaker fortunes in the United States. While rebelling against the narrowness and illiberalism of his upbringing and therefore arousing some alarm among the old guard, he remained a member of the Twelfth Street Meeting and his religious life was deep and spiritual. When Rufus Jones returned to Haverford in 1893 T. Wistar Brown was immediately drawn to him, recognizing his brilliance, his originality and his fire; he defended him against criticism, gave him friendship and advice, and bided his time for decisive action. Once or twice a week during these years Rufus Jones went to the Browns' house for supper.

Another influential friend, also many years older than himself, was James Wood, with whom he worked closely on the Bryn Mawr Board, *The American Friend*, and, increasingly, on a plan for the uniting of the Yearly Meetings. "Braewold," the Wood estate at Mt. Kisco, N. Y., was a large, comfortable, hospitable place where James and Emily Wood, their son Hollingsworth and their daughters Ellen and Carolena, welcomed a large circle of Friends, American and English.

The editorship of *The American Friend*, like the teaching at Haverford, continued to be a full-time job on a part-time salary. Though the steadily increasing number of subscribers testified to the success of the paper and though it was read and quoted in England, Rufus Jones's mail was full of critical and somewhat hostile letters. He was accused of having "gone over to the Higher Criticism," of being unspiritual, of not appreciating Philadelphia Yearly Meeting, and of theological unsoundness. "It seems as though everybody wanted my scalp," he remarked. "I think they will soon get most of my hair." He was wondering whether it was actually worth all it cost him when in October, 1897, soon after Sallie had gone to Saranac, he went to the Quinquennial Conference in Indianapolis.

It was the second of such meetings held since the Richmond Conference of 1887, and to it all the Orthodox Yearly Meetings in the United States, Canada and Great Britain sent delegates—all but Philadelphia, though a Philadelphia Friend, Edward Wistar, was present in an unofficial capacity. Rufus Jones attended as a delegate of New England Yearly Meeting, to which he still belonged.

He was aware that the Conference would be a crucial time for him, and that on its outcome would depend in large measure the future direction of his life. He was troubled not only about *The American Friend* but about the state of American Quakerism in general. At Dieulefit, ten years earlier, he had dedicated his life to the work of interpreting the deeper nature of the soul and its relationship to God, and in Switzerland four months before the Conference he and John Wilhelm Rowntree had shared their vision of a Society of Friends, united and alive, which offered in Rowntree's words "that which is beyond all creeds, the evidence in our lives of communion with the Spirit of God." The problem before him now was the channel through which he should carry out his purpose. "I have expected all summer that this conference would determine very largely whether I cared to go ahead with the paper or whether I should throw the whole thing up," he had written to Sallie. "It is strange how we have drifted into a type of Quakerism totally different from that which our fathers knew and I regret to realize that it is very unlike what I long to see prevail."

He went to the meeting in Indianapolis prepared to make a bold movement toward the reawakening of the kind of Quakerism to which he could give his life and loyalty. He was to propose an organic union of all the Yearly Meetings of America, through a meeting every five years of delegates with legislative powers.

The idea did not originate with him, nor was he without the support and advice of other Friends in presenting it now. At the conference of 1892 a Kansas Friend, Dr. William Nicholson, had suggested as a remote possibility the formation of a single yearly meeting in America. This thought had been regarded as visionary at the time, but in 1897 four yearly meetings came to the conference prepared to ask for the establishment of a conference with delegated powers and binding authority. It was Rufus Jones's part to present the plan as an immediate, practical, and desirable move.

"Shall There Be a Central Body?" was the title of the paper which he read to the assembled delegates. He based his argument upon two primary considerations, the danger of disintegration of a Quakerism composed of "fourteen absolutely independent and ever fluctuating bodies," and upon the more cogent fact that the causes which Friends had at heart—foreign missions, work for Indians, and for temperance —could not be carried on effectually without an organizing and directing center.

His purpose in proposing this union went far beyond the coordinating of good works and the halting of disintegration; he sought a genuine drawing together of the different kinds of Friends in a spirit of love and a unity based upon the essentials of the Quaker faith, but he understood very well, with the genius that was his for the practical and the immediate, that the unifying power of shared work for the benefit of others was far greater than theoretical statements. "If one does expect to change states of mind, habits of thought and attitudes of will," he wrote in 1934 in his account of the conference, "he will hardly begin by announcing that that is what he is doing! He will set about attaining some goal which will arouse group loyalty and create teamwork for the common end in view and in the process new mental states get formed."

He had felt, as he moved about among the delegates the day before he was to present his plan, that there was opposition to it. "I do not, however," he wrote to Sallie, "have any desire to see the thing go through unless it is best." Whatever opposition there was, however, was swept away on the tide of enthusiasm aroused by his paper—and no doubt by his own personality—when he put it before them. "My Address 'took' the conference beyond my expectation," he wrote two days later in relief and joy. "People rose to grasp my hand as I came down from the platform and James Wood said he never saw an audience more impressed by an address which was read."

The next morning reaction came with a discussion of the proposal and the airing of unfavorable opinions, but in the afternoon Rufus Jones spoke again, supported by Edmund Stanley, clerk of Kansas Yearly Meeting, and the pendulum swung back. "A quiet and apparently unanimous feeling marked the conclusion to appoint a committee," wrote Harriet Green, one of the English delegates.

"To appoint a committee"—the decisive Quaker action! Two

members of each yearly meeting were named to the body which was to draft the plan of union and a statement of theological basis, with a subcommittee consisting of Rufus M. Jones and James Wood to do the actual work.

The American Friend also came in for discussion and the approval of the conference. "The afternoon session was the greatest triumph *The American Friend* ever had," wrote Rufus jubilantly—though in sober fact the previous triumphs of that three-year-old publication could have been but few and modest. "This has been a great experience for me," he summed it all up. "I think it has increased my faith in the future. It is a great conference and even surpassed London Y.M. in interest."

The writing of the document called the Uniform Discipline, setting forth the arrangements for union, harmonizing the diverse procedures of the different yearly meetings, and, most thorny of all, composing a simple statement of belief upon which all could agree, occupied much of Rufus Jones's time and thought during the ensuing two and a half years. He and James Wood corresponded about it, they worked over it together on Rufus Jones's successive visits to Braewold, they submitted drafts to members of the larger committee for "examination, criticism and suggestion." A complete draft was published as a supplement to *The American Friend* in December, 1899, and revised in accordance with the comments of the readers. At a final conference at Braewold in May, 1900, it was finished and a printed version made ready to present to the yearly meetings for ratification.

The plan included three notable departures from historic Quakerism: birthright membership was discontinued, the employment of pastors was provided for, though not enjoined, and decisions of the delegates were taken on the basis of a vote and not by "the sense of the meeting." The greatest struggle came over the theological basis.

Rufus Jones wrote a simple and brief historical statement of the belief of Friends. He was wholly convicted of the validity of the Quaker position about creeds, which holds that "while truth is eternal our apprehension of it enlarges and our expression of it changes and Friends do not feel prepared to pin their adhesion to a form of words which at best embody a sincere attempt to define that measure of truth which has so far been apprehended in words appropriate to the age in which they are spoken." Many of the more strictly evangelical yearly meetings, however, wanted a more definite, more binding statement. They wished to include both George Fox's Letter to the

Governor of Barbados, 1671, and the Declaration of Faith adopted by the Richmond Conference of 1887. To both of these statements Rufus Jones was strongly opposed. "It has been a solemn resolve with me to have nothing to do with a discipline that put in the Richmond Declaration," he declared. He considered it a "poor thin mediocre expression of vital Quaker faith," which showed no awareness of modern problems, no recognition of intellectual difficulties over questions of science and history, and preserved the air of infallibility characteristic of creeds. He was afraid, moreover, that intolerant elements in some of the meetings might seek to use it as a yardstick against which members might be measured for heresy. Fox's Letter he considered uncharacteristic of Fox's real thought, narrowly orthodox, flat and dull, without any specific Quaker insights. As late as 1924 he brought down a hornet's nest about his ears by suggesting in the London *Friend* that Fox was ill and confused at the time that he wrote it.

In the end a compromise was reached; the statement of belief as written by Rufus Jones stood, and those who would like "more explicit and extended statements of belief" were referred in a footnote to the two disputed documents.

The first yearly meeting to act upon the plan of union was New England Yearly Meeting, in session at Newport in June 1900. When that body adopted the Uniform Discipline, Rufus Jones, foreseeing that others would follow, wrote to James Wood, "American Quakerism now must stand or fall together. The next few years will settle which it is to be."

Immediately after the meeting at Newport Rufus Jones returned to Haverford for the second great venture of this period, the Summer School of Religious History, which was held on the college campus from June nineteenth to the thirtieth. One of the means to revitalize Quakerism, and especially to nurture the lay ministry, which he and John Wilhelm Rowntree had agreed upon in Switzerland was a series of summer schools on religious and social questions. The first one had been held successfully in England in 1897. Now Rufus Jones, with the help of a committee that included Isaac Sharpless, chairman, George Barton, David Scull, James Wood and T. Wistar Brown, had arranged this first one in America. Three of his English friends came to uphold him and to lecture on the Bible and Church and Quaker History: Rendel Harris, William C. Braithwaite, and John Wilhelm Rowntree.

J. W. Rowntree had come to see his doctor in Chicago, who was

attempting to arrest the progress of his fatal disease, and to gather
material for the history of Quakerism, to which he was now applying
himself, as the second of his means for promoting Quakerism. Another
project, the quarterly magazine called *Present Day Papers*, had been
launched the year before. "I want a tremendous big talk with thee!"
he wrote to Rufus on May nineteenth.

The summer school was attended by six hundred registered students,
with two hundred more visitors, most of whom were Friends, though
thirteen denominations in all were represented.

In addition to the three Englishmen, there was an impressive list
of lecturers, including, besides Rufus Jones himself, who gave a series
of five lectures, a young Quaker prophet from the mid-west, Elbert
Russell, professor of Biblical Literature at Earlham College, George A.
Barton, Isaac Sharpless, Allen Thomas and others. The response of the
students was enthusiastic, and the impact of the whole experience
was so lasting that Howard Brinton has pronounced it to be for
American Friends a "turning-point" comparable to the Manchester
Conference of 1895 for English Friends. Succeeding summer schools
were held in America approximately every two years thereafter until
1923.

This summer of 1900 also initiated a brief but poignant episode
in Rufus Jones's personal life. Early in the ten days he became engaged
to James Wood's daughter Ellen.

He had been thrown with her much during the past two years
when he had gone often to Braewold to work on the Discipline with
her father, and they had been corresponding regularly for nearly
a year, but that they had not reached the decision to marry until they
were together at the summer school is made plain by the contrast
between previous letters and a scribbled, pencilled, undated note
in Ellen's handwriting: "Please do not sit beside me nor talk to me
except casually before 5:30 this evening. Talk to Lena or anybody else,
but unless everybody is to know we must not be together."

She was thirty-one years old, fair, slender, pleasant-looking, though
her face was too long and narrow for conventional prettiness. Delicate
coloring and vivid change of expression might have given her beauty
at times. Despite the ease of her family circumstances she had a fervent
desire to do something to help the world. She had not only prepared
herself by training at the Johns Hopkins Hospital to become a nurse,
but had actually put her training to use in nursing soldiers at Camp
Hamilton at the time of the Spanish-American War. Her letters re-

veal a warm-hearted, impulsive, sensitive, idealistic personality, very much in love. Rufus Jones himself described her in THE TRAIL OF LIFE IN THE MIDDLE YEARS in the following words: "She was a rare and wonderful person, sensitive in her spirit, broad in her sympathies, extremely tender of heart, a dedicated soul, with a rich life before her."

In July she went abroad with her father and her sister, Carolena, intending to visit Denmark, Sweden, St. Petersburg, and Moscow, and to stop in England on the way home. On her return the engagement was to be announced and they would be married the following spring, when Rufus Jones should have completed the long postponed year of graduate study which he had decided at last to take at Harvard.

On the voyage out Ellen Wood was taken ill with a high fever. It was thought at first that it was the result of overtaxing herself in the care of a seaman on the ship who was stricken with pneumonia and to whom, in the absence of medical help, she was both doctor and nurse, but at the hospital in Copenhagen to which she was taken her illness was diagnosed as typhoid fever. On the ninth of August she died.

When the sorrowing father and sister returned, Rufus Jones went to Mt. Kisco to be with them for the memorial service. His own grief was not declared to the world, but his summer school lectures, published that winter in England by Headley Bros. under the title "A DYNAMIC FAITH," bore the dedication:

"To the sweet and shining memory of a friend, now in the heavenlies, whose inspiration touched these pages."

This was the second book in which he spoke not only to Friends but to the world beyond. The first, PRACTICAL CHRISTIANITY, which had appeared in the summer of 1899, was made up largely of editorials from *The American Friend*, setting forth the principle that truth is ever-changing and developing, modifying its form but keeping its essence. It had been generally well received and the London *Friend* patted it on the head as "a bracing and helpful book."

A DYNAMIC FAITH was a bolder and more sustained work. In it one sees Rufus Jones coming to his full stature as a religious thinker, setting forth in the direct, natural, vigorous, luminous style that was so characteristically his, some of the enduring ideas on which his life and thought were founded. Beginning with the basis of religious faith, considered in the light of modern scientific discoveries, he traced the life history of Quakerism from its sources in the Bible and the writings of the mystics through the message of its first creative years, to its modern position.

"The essential fact of religion is love," he wrote, "and love is impossible apart from relationships."

Of Christ he said: "We find at length one single Personality, who was sinless, who lived entirely open to God, who had a sole purpose —to do His will, and from it this truth emerges that this Personality is a complete expression of Divinity and Humanity."

Of mysticism: "Religious mysticism is an attempt to realize the presence of God in the soul. It is grounded in the fact that a direct intercourse between the human soul and God *is* possible; and its ultimate goal is the attainment of a state in which God shall cease to be an external object and shall become known by experience of the heart."

But mysticism to Rufus Jones was never passivism: "The great mystics who must be our types have learned that every new truth, every new vision, involves a new duty and leads to activity."

Of George Fox's message: "His [Fox's] next step is the discovery that Christ is no dead Christ but a living one still present and able to 'speak to one's condition' . . . We have the glorious fact announced, 'Behold He is here now and I have found Him' and this is the key to the whole Quaker message."

Of salvation: "Salvation is an actual change in the man's life."

Of religion today: "Revelation is a continuous process."

He was to probe further, to amplify and restate again and again all these ideas as the years went on, but never to abandon them. Forty-one years later he wrote in an introduction to a French translation of A DYNAMIC FAITH: "In spite of the passage of the years the book in the main represents my present religious outlook . . . It was my first serious attempt to interpret mysticism and to get at the heart of Quakerism."

The Golden Age at Harvard

RUFUS JONES went to Harvard in what has been called the Golden Age of American Philosophy, when George Herbert Palmer, chairman of the Department, William James, Josiah Royce, Hugo Münsterberg, and George Santayana wrote and taught and sharpened their minds on one another in an atmosphere of intellectual disagreement and personal loyalty immensely invigorating both to themselves and to their students. "In our lectures," wrote Palmer, "we were accustomed to attack each other by name, James forever exposing the folly of the idealists, particularly of Royce and me, Royce in turn showing how baseless all empiricism is, lacking a metaphysical background." And James, writing to Royce, declared, "When I compose my Gifford lectures mentally, 'tis with the design exclusively of overthrowing your system and ruining your peace . . . Different as our minds are," he added, "yours has nourished mine as no other social influence ever has, and in converse with you I have always felt that my life was being lived importantly." Even Santayana, who felt that both Royce and James were hampered in their task of describing things as they are by the responsibility which they felt to find them "propitious to certain preconceived ideas," described that period at Harvard as "a fresh morning in the life of reason, cloudy but brightening."

It must have been a serious disappointment to Rufus Jones when he learned that William James, that "fascinating and captivating" man was not to be there in 1900-01. He had studied and taught James's

PRINCIPLES OF PSYCHOLOGY, had had some personal contact and correspondence with him, and was to consider himself all his life a debtor to James's thought. This year, however, William James was in Europe, convalescing from an illness and working on his Gifford Lectures, which were to be delivered in Edinburgh in the spring of 1901 and 1902 under the title, "Varieties of Religious Experience."

Rufus Jones took four courses at Harvard: Ethics, with George Herbert Palmer; The Ethics of Idealism, also with Palmer; Problems of Comparative and Social Psychology, with Hugo Münsterberg, and New Testament Interpretation with Joseph Henry Thayer. He got A in all of them.

Santayana in his brilliant if not wholly sympathetic essays on philosophy at Harvard did not so much as mention Palmer, but he was to Rufus Jones a major influence. "A year's work in that Phil. 4 course came nearer being a 'complete education' than any other course of study I have ever known," he wrote thirty years later. Kant, Fichte, Hegel, Green's PROLEGOMENA TO ETHICS were the subject of that year, illumined by Palmer's interpretation and his understanding of "the deep-lying springs of moral action." Rufus Jones had earlier come under the spell of Edward Caird, Master of Balliol. Palmer too was a devotee of Caird's, having spent six consecutive summers in England sharing a house with him, walking daily with Professor Caird and Ding-an-Sich, the dog, and discussing philosophy for hours at a time. It was from Palmer that Rufus Jones borrowed the term, the *conjunct self*, which appeared frequently in his books and lectures after this year, especially in SOCIAL LAW IN THE SPIRITUAL WORD. To Palmer it was the *conjunct self* in terms of which the nature of morality might be explained. "Wherever we trace iniquity," he wrote, "it will always be seen to amount to this, the setting-up of the abstract or unitary self against the conjunct." To Rufus Jones, however, it had a mystical connotation, the *conjunct life*, in which the human and the divine were conjoined. "Its [i.e. science's] latest word is that *God and man are conjunct*." Palmer, however, was no mystic, and indeed, frequently warned his students against mysticism, as a will o' the wisp and wandering fire.

Even more than by Palmer, Rufus Jones was influenced by Josiah Royce. Though he did not take any of Royce's courses for credit that year, he seems to have audited the course in Metaphysics. He bracketed Royce with Palmer as one of his teachers at Harvard, and he wrote: "Professor Josiah Royce had a larger influence on my intellectual development, I think, than any other one person . . . He took a group of us through his Aberdeen Gifford lectures, the World and the Individual, and in that process we came to grips with his profound treatment of mysticism as one of the major pathways to reality."

There is general agreement that Royce eminently looked the part of the philosopher. "He was one of the oddest-looking men since Socrates," wrote Rufus Jones, "whom as has been often noted, he somewhat resembled." "His great head," according to Santayana, "seemed too heavy for his small body, and his portentous brow, crowned with thick red hair, seemed to crush the lower part of his face." He had come out of California, studied at Leipzig and Göttingen, had gone to Johns Hopkins as one of its first fellows, where he worked with William James, and through James he had come to Harvard. "His effect as a teacher and writer was profound," wrote William Ernest Hocking. "No previous American thinker had so united moral energy with wide historical learning, command of scientific method and intense interest in logical technique." He was a brilliant and effortless lecturer, of whom Dickinson Miller said, "Royce finds lecturing the easiest form of breathing." He taught a monistic idealism and he laid especial stress upon the "beloved community" in which all lives were part of the divine life. His treatment of Meister Eckhart in *Studies of Good and Evil* impressed Rufus Jones deeply and he considered Royce's study of the psychology of George Fox the best ever written. But though stimulated and influenced by Royce, Rufus Jones did not become his disciple, as he never was a disciple of William James. He believed that monistic idealism came perilously close to pantheism, and he sought to find "the line between a defeative dualism of a two-world theory and an equally dangerous pantheism, which blurs all moral distinctions and which names the All 'God.' "

Of Münsterberg, by whom some of his theories on the vision of children "got pretty badly slaughtered," Rufus Jones wrote, "Dr. Münsterberg can cut one's head off before he knows it."

One other course Rufus Jones must have audited at least in part: Santayana's Greek Philosophy with especial reference to Plato. His copy of the Harvard catalogue shows a check mark beside Santayana's Phil. 12 and on the blank page at the end is written in Rufus's handwriting a list of "Subjects for Reports in Greek Philos." and another list of "Readings." He made, he said, his first systematic study of Plato and Platonism under Santayana. "There may be better lecturers

than he was then and there may be wiser guides for the journey
through that spiritual realm, Plato's demesne, but I have never seen any
person whom I should prefer to have as a pilot for that difficult crossing. There was a fine mystical quality in the Santayana of that period
which made him an admirable interpreter of Platonic love and beauty
and which splendidly fitted him to appreciate the important contribution of Plotinus. Plato, Plotinus, Dante and Goethe have been throughout my life four personalities of outstanding importance." This
appreciation of Santayana is the more interesting in view of the wide
differences of background and outlook that separated the two men,
who were born in the same year. To Rufus Jones moral fervor was
beautiful; to Santayana it was more than faintly ridiculous. The Quaker
from South China and Haverford looked on Harvard and its sages
with love and reverence; the Spanish-born, non-practising Catholic
Santayana found it a place that smelled slightly of brimstone, with
an atmosphere not so much of intelligence or science as of duty, a
place to endure until his inheritance should set him free to return to
Europe.

Of Joseph Henry Thayer Rufus Jones had little to say, though he
spoke of him warmly as "that remarkable New Testament scholar,"
and it was under him that he wrote his thesis on the mysticism of St.
Paul and St. John, which he later used as the basis for lectures, essays
and an important chapter in his book, SOCIAL LAW IN THE SPIRITUAL
WORLD.

With Dr. Francis G. Peabody, college preacher and professor of
Christian Sociology, Rufus Jones took no work, but a lasting friendship between the two was begun. "He is about as near perfect as any
man I have ever seen," wrote Rufus, "and a remarkable speaker."

During this momentous year Rufus Jones lived at the house of a
Friend in Cambridge. Lowell had been installed at Friends School,
Providence, possibly at nine the youngest boarder there. The little boy
was happy in the school which had meant so much to his father; he
spent occasional weekends in Cambridge, and Rufus went every other
week to Providence to be with him and to lead a "Philosophical Club"
for the teachers at Friends School, the meetings of which everybody
attended, "from Augustine Jones to the laundress."

The work of taking four graduate courses and auditing two more,
the trips to Providence, and the writing of two or three editorials a
week for *The American Friend*, by no means occupied all of Rufus's
time. He was in constant demand for talks by local groups, chiefly

Friends, who are beyond all other denominations—perhaps as a reaction from their avowed love of silence—addicted to the spoken word in the form of lectures, addresses, talks and discussions. In a single week, for example, he made talks on "The Subconscious Mind," "Greek Philosophy," and "The Mystics."

In February the decision about his future course was made. T. Wistar Brown, who had been quietly waiting to do something effective both for Haverford and for Rufus Jones, created a chair in Philosophy especially for him. It consisted of an associate professorship with a salary of $2000, which, though it seems little enough today, was a sizable advance over the $800 he had previously received, and furthermore, as Isaac Sharpless assured him, was "quite on a par with the other members of the Faculty of equal, and in some cases more, experience and title." He was to teach a Freshman course in the Old Testament, History of Philosophy, Psychology, which was required of all Juniors, and Senior Ethics.

At the end of the year he received the degree of Master of Arts from Harvard. He already had an M.A. from Haverford and an honorary Litt. D. from Penn College, Oskaloosa, Iowa. During the years to come the honorary degrees would flood in upon him, including a Doctorate of Divinity from Harvard itself, but the Ph.D., which is the meal ticket of today's most pedestrian college instructor, was never his.

From Cambridge in June he went to Longport, N. J., where he worked on a series of lectures to be given at Scarborough Summer School in England in August. Lowell was in Ardonia where he had expected to leave him for the summer, but at the last minute, concerned about the child's health, he scooped him up and carried him off to England with him.

They stayed at Scalby, where John Wilhelm Rowntree and his lovely wife Connie and their children took Lowell to their hearts. Rufus went every day to nearby Scarborough, to lecture at the summer school, and in the evenings the two friends talked about the Quaker History and their plans for it.

The Summer School, which lasted from August third to September seventh, was attended by 280 persons, nearly half of whom were under thirty. It was a memorable gathering, and letters afterwards testified to the inspiration which Rufus Jones brought to the students through his lectures, his Browning readings under the trees near George Fox's dungeon at Scarborough Castle, his talks with the young people about their spiritual problems and yearnings. Besides the association with those tried old friends, J. W. Rowntree, William Charles Braithwaite and Rendel Harris, Rufus Jones made new friendships which were to be lifelong, notably with Joan M. Fry, Arnold Rowntree, John Wilhelm's cousin, and L. Violet Hodgkin, daughter of the famous Quaker leader Thomas Hodgkin, herself a writer and Quaker historian.

When Rufus Jones returned to Haverford in September he came as one who has crossed a great divide in his life. The years of apprenticeship and preparation were over; the years of anxiety and sorrow were behind him and they had given him their incomparable gift. He had returned to a new and dignified position at Haverford. His living arrangements were once more comfortable: he was back in his house at 7 College Lane and Anna Comfort, a responsible Quaker woman, was to run the household and take care of Lowell. He was bringing home the sheaves of his intellectual harvest at Harvard and he glowed with the knowledge of the affection and respect of English Friends.

Stanley R. Yarnall, for many years the distinguished and beloved headmaster of the Germantown Friends School, remembers seeing him at this time. Stanley Yarnall, then a young man, not quite thirty, was going with his Aunt Phoebe to a party at Clovercroft, the Garrett house in Rosemont, and they were met at the station by an omnibus. Rufus Jones, just back from his year away, was also on the bus; he was full of his experience at Harvard, aglow with enthusiasm for the men with whom he had worked there. Afterwards Aunt Phoebe said impressively, "Stanley, that is a perfectly wonderful man!"

Openings

"I LIKE to be with persons who see what life means," wrote Rufus Jones in September, 1900, "and who like to talk over its meaning and its problems. I always *want* to make its meaning clearer, though I know I do not always succeed."

He had had a visit to the Cadbury family which was a "blessing" to him. They were a large, lively, warmhearted family, actively concerned with the affairs of Philadelphia Orthodox Quakerism. Joel and Anna Kaighn Cadbury, who was descended from John Bartram the botanist, their four sons and two daughters, lived at Fifteenth and Green Streets, then a quiet and substantial, though not fashionable, neighborhood, and had a summer home across the Delaware in the pleasant old Quaker village of Moorestown. Joel's father, also Joel Cadbury, had come from England to visit his aunt and uncle, had fallen in love with their daughter and married her, had survived the storm of disapproval at the marriage of first cousins, and lived his life out in the United States. Joel himself was a successful business man and clerk of his Monthly and Quarterly Meetings. Two of his sons had gone into business, one was studying medicine with a view to missionary service abroad, and the youngest, Henry, was a student at Haverford.

Elizabeth Bartram was the eldest of the Cadbury children. In 1900 when Rufus Jones first became aware of her she was twenty-nine. She had attended the Friends Select School in Philadelphia, had cherished dreams of serving mankind by becoming a trained nurse but had settled down instead—quelling the longings of her young heart and the restlessness of her bright mind as manifestations of "selfishness"—to living for her family as a daughter at home. When she was twenty-one she had had one glorious year at Bryn Mawr College and then she retired in favor of her younger sister Emma and took up a life of Quaker committees, Sunday School classes, Y.W.C.A. work, reading, sewing, visiting and German-study, in which she attained considerable proficiency. In the spring of 1900 she went with a group of friends on a cruise of the Mediterranean which included a visit to Egypt and the Holy Land and wound up with a sojourn in England with the Cadbury cousins, with whom family relations were warm and close. Some of her letters home, in which she described with enthusiasm what she saw in Athens, were published in *The American Friend* and elicited the comment from Ellen Wood, "Since reading that letter of E. C.'s in *The American Friend* I have thought that thee does not realize how much more she is thy intellectual equal than I am."

Lily, as she was called by her intimates, was a lovely, glowing young woman, dark-haired, fair-skinned, hazel-eyed, with a turned-up nose and long upper lip, and an expression of great sweetness and humor. With a keen and sensitive intelligence she combined a genuine humility and a deep and sometimes hampering reserve. With all her sunny serenity of disposition she found it difficult to open up her deepest thoughts and share her inner feelings. To Rufus Jones, for whom outward expression was easy and natural, this inhibition was both fascinating and troubling. With what he assumed to be his usual interest in helping half-formed souls to fulfil themselves, he sought to help her develop to the full the potentialities which were so evident. During the year that he was at Harvard the letters flew back and forth, with Rufus playing the part of Mentor and Elizabeth the receptive disciple.

In his third letter he was urging her to read Browning's *Paracelsus*, and to give him an opinion on it, an assignment which she sidestepped, feeling it was too large a subject for her to have an opinion about, though she wrote a competent summary of what she understood to be its meaning. As the winter wore on she read and reported on Caird's FUNDAMENTAL IDEAS and Green's PROLEGOMENA TO ETHICS, both of which she declared she "greatly enjoyed" and which she followed up with Dante's *Inferno*, Royce's RELIGIOUS ASPECTS OF PHILOSOPHY and Emerson's "Oversoul." The last she just mentioned in passing and Rufus was quick to write back:

"Now why didn't thee tell me more about the 'Oversoul'? I was interested in thy coup d'état in the kitchen [i.e. the dismissing of an unsatisfactory cook] but I also wanted to know what thee *saw* in Emerson's great essay. It has had so much to do with my life and I wish thee had given me thy glimpse."

"I know it was unkind not to say anything more about Emerson," she wrote penitently by return mail, "but I really had to read it over again to be sure that the first impression was not only a mood of mine. For it seemed to strike down deeper than most anything I have found lately. Even now I hardly know why, because many of the thoughts were not new—only they came freshly—or else reached down into that inner self that so often has to go unfed."

She read and then reread his own book, A DYNAMIC FAITH, especially the chapter on the Mystics. "I had forgotten how wholesome and normal thee made it," she commented. "My impressions about mystics until last summer [i.e., at the Haverford Summer School] were always of the ultra type, which did not very much appeal to my rather matter-of-fact and unemotional way of looking at things, but if Paul is a mystic—well, I suppose one can try."

In return for the guidance he offered her, she gave him comfort when he was "blue," and he did not underestimate the value of the gift. "Too many of us think the great gifts are those of teaching, of exhorting, of working miracles, of speaking with tongues," he wrote. "Not at all! There is a more excellent way. It is just the power of making our lives felt in others' lives, of giving out ourselves, of suffering long and being kind." And when she demurred, he insisted, "Yes, Elizabeth, but thee *must* see!"

Several weeks later he was still elaborating the subject. "You get tired of *bright* people and of society people and rich people and talkative people and artistic people and so on and so on but you can tie forever to a person with a *soul*, the one who is rich in spirit. There are no gettings to get but that."

He went to say good-by to her before he left for England and the Scarborough Summer School and the first thing he did on his return in September was to go to see her. On the sixth of October they became engaged.

Though they lived but a few miles apart the letters continued almost daily between Mein Liebchen and Dearest Rufus, as they explored their relationship and made their plans for the future.

"I believe in thee as I do in the laws of the universe," wrote Rufus.

Two days later he was tired and ruffled. He had had to give up his golf, which had become a great outlet and release for him, to attend a committee meeting. "Please forgive this useless bit of autobiographic detail which can hardly contribute to thy happiness. Isn't it funny that we should care to tell our woes when there are always so many beautiful things waiting to be told. I wish I might rise to the place where I could live above disturbances of every sort and could say to every situation, 'Thank God for you. I know how to use you.' "

He was still concerned about her growth. "I cannot tell thee how much I want thee to *be* what I see in thee. I carry thee on my heart until the true Elizabeth is formed in thee."

"I wonder if thee thought I was very frivolous yesterday," she wrote a little anxiously," but I cannot be serious too long at a time."

"Thee need never be afraid of being frivolous," he was quick to re-assure her. "I love fun and frolic and spontaneous joyousness as well as any man living. I cannot bear morbidness or primness or stilted piety or goodygoodyism. . . . It will always be my lot to impart ideas and to bear messages and that takes one's very life. I have no one to come to me and cheer me back, to make me see that I hit the mark, to inspire me with courage by showing me what I have done, by giving appreciation and loving criticism. I need this as few men ever need it for my nature is sensitive and I am easily exalted or depressed."

What did trouble him was not her frivolity but her humility. "I am afraid it is a virtue I cannot safely commend in thee," he wrote. "Thee rather needs courage and confidence and heart-boldness." Moreover, he found her literary opinions deplorably lukewarm. "I can never understand how thee can be so calm over a great piece of literature. I throb with it and thee says, 'I liked it.' "

His own humility perhaps prevented him from seeing the gap that she felt existed between his spiritual power and her own gropings. Yet she understood with clearer insight even than he did his love for her and hers for him and she had deep confidence in it. Her letters were full of gentle humor, love, and gratitude for her great good fortune in having won his love, and underneath she knew her strength. When they probed deeper into self-knowledge, she could lay a sure and gentle finger on his tendency to depression and anxiety and main-tain her own refusal to be overborne by it.

"As I told thee," she wrote. "I seldom really worry. Perhaps thee would say I had never had any great trouble and that is more or less true. But if one is disposed one can find many occasions to worry over. I cannot explain why it is. Down in the subconscious self there seems to be a source of strength near at hand to help through possible difficulties which will prove availing when they arise . . . Had I given myself up to meditating of possible future troubles I should have had no time to think of present needs. And that night thee was tired and discouraged and anxious. Would it have helped more if I had fallen into the same mood? It did not seem to me the time to lose courage just then."

"It has done me good clear down where I live to have thy letter with its noble quality of womanhood pulsing through it," he answered the next day. "I did not misunderstand thee and never thought thee lacking in love or abiding interest in all that concerned my real welfare but in a way I did need just this revelation of thy true self."

As she grew in assurance she could begin to help him in his work. "I have been thinking of the editorial," she wrote. "Could it be a little more gentle-hearted without losing fire? The first sentence especially haunts me as being a little blunt, though I do believe strictly true."

He agreed with her about it; indeed he had already softened it. "Thee can help me tremendously in my editorials when thee settles down to look at them carefully and critically, as thee has hardly been able to do in the past."

"I am sure you will find Elizabeth a fine soul, wise, solid, level-headed and most loving," he wrote to John Wilhelm Rowntree. "She will be, as she already is, a real daily helper to me."

In November their engagement was announced to their world and evoked universal approval. "What I like about him," Elizabeth's brother Ben had said, "is that he is a *man* and true to the core." M. Carey Thomas's commendation was characteristic of her. "I am truly glad thee is marrying a college woman," she pronounced, "and a Bryn Mawr woman, for I regard Miss Cadbury as both even if she was able to stay with us only one year." Agnes Tierney of Germantown wrote to Elizabeth, "How full of blessing to the world your united strength will be! I count my meeting with Rufus Jones one of the Providences of my life. It was a time when I was very greatly in need of spiritual refreshment and he filled me, as he has hundreds of others, with renewed faith and courage."

Through the winter Elizabeth competently supervised the redecoration of the house on College Lane and Rufus strove to take a suitable interest in the details of paint and varnish on which she consulted him.

They were married on March 11, 1902. It was a beautiful warm day and the old meetinghouse on Twelfth Street was filled. In the balcony Elizabeth's Sunday School class of colored women occupied a long bench. It was a great occasion, for not only were the bridal couple well known and well loved figures in themselves, but Elizabeth Cadbury lived within the ancient citadel of Philadelphia Orthodox Quakerism and Rufus Jones was passing through the guarded gate at last.

The wedding was held in the solemn Quaker manner without music or any sort of festive decorations in the austere old room. Out of the silence the bride and groom rose and spoke their promises without prompting. The certificate was signed by Rufus Matthew and Elizabeth Bartram Jones and read aloud by an elder of the Meeting; out of the renewed silence Friends were moved to speak, and about 11:45 the meeting closed. The bride wore white satin with a knot of white ribbon in her hair instead of a veil; she carried white flowers. Her three bridesmaids and four "aides" were also in white, with pink flowers. Herbert Jones was his brother's best man and Elizabeth's brothers were groomsmen.

Two hundred and eighty friends were invited to the wedding breakfast in the Cadbury house, where everything was simple, a cousin reported, but well served. Mr. and Mrs. Jones drove rapidly away in a carriage decorated with ribbon and festoons of colored papers and took the train to Washington, where they visited Mt. Vernon and sent happy postals home.

Now at thirty-nine, Rufus Jones had found the true companion of his heart and home, a woman whose sunny disposition and deep-rooted serenity would help to stabilize his mercurial temperament, whose flexible and retentive mind would complement his own, whose strength and quiet practical competence would keep their home running smoothly, whose love was like a spring, still and unrippled on the surface but inexhaustible. "Everything has changed since Elizabeth came," he wrote to John Wilhelm Rowntree in May, "and I am working with a new strength."

Even before they were married they had been faced with a momentous decision. One of John Wilhelm Rowntree's dearest dreams for the reawakening of Quakerism and especially for the revitalization of the ministry was a center for study where Friends could explore social and religious questions and prepare themselves for service to the Society. This dream was now about to reach fulfilment through the generosity of George Cadbury, the head of the Cadbury Chocolate Firm and Joel Cadbury's first cousin, who offered to give his house,

Woodbrooke, near Birmingham, for the purpose, to provide for its maintenance and to endow a lectureship. The immediate necessity was to find the right director of studies to start the school off and indeed to take a large part in determining its enduring shape.

The first of February Henry Lloyd Wilson, clerk of the Meeting for Sufferings, the executive body of London Yearly Meeting, came to Haverford with a letter from John Wilhelm Rowntree offering the post of principal of Woodbrooke to Rufus Jones.

The letter referred to "the variety and extent of the hold which you have won over our people through your visit to Scarborough last year and then your book, A Dynamic Faith," and continued, "You would command the confidence of both wings of the Society as no one else could do. You have moreover I am convinced the right message for us and could give it fully without the trammels and limitations which sometimes harass you in America." Other lures were the importance of the position, the freedom to travel, opportunity for working on the book on mysticism of which they had talked so much together, the proximity of Elizabeth's cousins and, altogether, "a wide field of liberty and service." The salary was to be £1000, equivalent then to $5000.

There was no doubt about the attraction. Rufus Jones then "felt in spirit more deeply identified with English Quakerism than with any other branch of organized Christianity in the world." And John Wilhelm Rowntree was there and behind it all. "I hope you know," Rufus had written to him in January, "that your friendship is one of the best things I have in my world."

He talked the question over with his associates. President Sharpless discussed objectively the advantages and disadvantages, the opportunities offered in both fields and refrained then from offering an increase of salary to meet the Woodbrooke proposal. M. Carey Thomas urged him to accept the English offer. "This English scheme," he wrote to Elizabeth, " 'sort of' filters into everything I do. I make believe not to think of it but there is a stratum down below which always knows about it." Elizabeth, after suggesting that the scheme was still "rather a hazy one," declared her readiness to embrace his decision. "As for me thee knows I am part of thyself. Wherever the work is that is our work, there we can live and be happy together and whatever it is I shall want to enter into it and do my share gladly."

"Of course with me," wrote Rufus Jones to John Wilhelm Rowntree, "it is largely a question of where my life will do the most good.

There is hardly anything else involved, but that is a very serious question. Next year Dr. Barton will be away and it would hardly seem right for us both to be away from Haverford Meeting at the same time."

When George Cadbury invited Rufus and Elizabeth to spend three or four weeks in England that summer considering the proposition on the spot, they accepted, with the idea of postponing decision till after their return, in spite of John Wilhelm Rowntree's plea in May, "Come over into Macedonia and help us!"

In July they left Lowell at Ardonia with Anna Comfort and sailed for England, where they visited the Cadburys at the Manor, North-field, near Birmingham, and the Rowntrees at Scalby, and took an active part in weekend conferences about the future of Woodbrooke. It was not until they had been home for two months, however, that the final decision was made.

By that time the first Five Years Meeting was over. Eleven yearly meetings had accepted the new discipline and their delegates met at Indianapolis in October in the first united session. Rufus Jones was appointed to the important Business Committee, and he made one of the key speeches, on "The Theory and Practice of Public Worship." The needs of Indians and Negroes were presented to the meeting. It was an old concern of Friends but the new concept of the "social gospel" then beginning to stir the air made the appeal more moving. "The most remarkable thing about the meeting," wrote Rufus Jones with satisfaction, "was the unity of spirit which was manifested."

The organic union of American Friends, or at least a sizable segment of them, was now a fact, but it was evident that this meeting marked not the end of a process but the beginning. Instead of feeling released to go to England, Rufus Jones evidently felt bound to stay and help the new organization to find its destiny. At any rate early in November he declined the English offer. After the decision was made, but not before, T. Wistar Brown, in consultation with Isaac Sharpless, arranged for Rufus Jones' salary to be increased to $5000 and the following year he was raised to full professorial rank.

"It is idle to pretend that your letter is anything less than a severe blow," wrote John Wilhelm Rowntree on the second of December. But he began to plan for the opening of Woodbrooke the following summer, and Rufus Jones promised to be there to make the inaugural address and to deliver a series of lectures at the summer school. Rendel Harris, who had been doing relief work among the Armenians, was offered the post of Director of Studies in Rufus Jones's place, and he declined an offer of a professorship at the University of Leyden in order to accept it.

During the year Rufus Jones had been publishing in nine installments in *The American Friend* an account of his boyhood which he called A BOY'S RELIGION FROM MEMORY, and before the end of the year this appeared in book form. Some years later, amplified, it was to reappear as FINDING THE TRAIL OF LIFE. Also fruit of this year was a little book called STUDIES IN NEW TESTAMENT MYSTICISM, which was composed of essays written for John Wilhelm Rowntree's magazine, *Present Day Papers*. The following year, 1903, he published a new edition of George Fox's Journal under the title AUTOBIOGRAPHY OF GEORGE FOX, in which the journal of the founder of Quakerism was presented in such a form that people would actually read it. "It is of course milk for babes," he wrote to his friend in England, "but just now the babes are most in evidence."

In May, 1903, Lowell was exposed to diphtheria. He was given antitoxin and his attack was a mild one, soon over. When Rufus and Elizabeth Jones sailed for England and the opening of Woodbrooke on July eleventh, their minds were at ease about the boy, who was to stay at Ardonia as he had done the previous summer, with Anna Comfort in charge.

The voyage was uneventful until the night before they landed. Then Rufus Jones had the second of the invasions from the Beyond which for him proved the validity of the mystical experience. "I suddenly felt myself surrounded by an enfolding Presence and held as though by invisible Arms. My entire being was fortified and I was inwardly prepared to meet the message of sorrow which was awaiting me the next day at the dock."

The cable that reached them on landing said, "Lowell very ill. Come." Close on its heels came a second cable with the word of the little boy's death on July sixteenth.

The details of Lowell's illness did not reach them till later. The child had been acutely sick only two days. His throat had been paralyzed and he had died of suffocation in Anna Comfort's arms, conscious to the last, aware that he was dying, filled with love, not fear. "The dignity, I can truly say the majesty, of that choking child was wonderful to witness," Anna Comfort wrote to a cousin, easing her burdened heart by recording every detail. Unable to make her understand him, he signalled with his fingers in the air until pencil and paper were brought, then he wrote, "Books for Norris and Philip," two of his friends at Haverford. Once he raised his hand and patted her wet cheek in an attempt to comfort her.

In England Rufus Jones knew only that the very core of his heart was gone. He and Elizabeth were with the Cadburys at the Manor that first week end, then Rufus Jones went to Scalby for a day or two with those dearest and closest friends, the Rowntrees. On the 23rd of July, less than a week after the crushing blow had fallen, Woodbrooke opened on schedule and he delivered his first address.

The summer school had been planned in three sessions of two weeks each. Rufus Jones was to have given his series of ten lectures three times, but now his old friend George Barton was secured to substitute for him in the second and third session.

The first two weeks of that summer school were a time of heightened significance for those who were there. To the natural excitement of the students over the beginning of a high emprise was added the poignant emotion of their sympathy for Rufus Jones and their appreciation of his courage in going ahead with the program. The lectures themselves, dealing with Present Day Ideas of God and the Spiritual Life, he considered in later years the most important course he had ever given.

For him in the anguish of his grief it was undoubtedly best that he had this task to occupy him and the support of the love and wisdom of those around him. Philip Wicksteed, authority on Dante and Wordsworth, who was also on the summer school faculty, was, he says, of "unique help in that early darkness" and through his lecture on St. Francis of Assisi opened up new understanding of the meaning of love. Rendel Harris stood by, and John Wilhelm Rowntree came to the Manor to be with his stricken friend for part of the time.

When the students, who came from England, Australia, Dublin, Glasgow and Philadelphia, afterwards sent to Rufus Jones a gift of books, it was Philip Wicksteed who drafted the accompanying letter and summed up the impact of Rufus Jones's service to the summer school. "Every word you have spoken has come to us tried by the fire. It is not only that your heroic effort for our sake deeply moves us. It is the feeling that you yourself cared to give us in sorrow the things you had prepared for us in joy."

An English Friend writing to Elizabeth Jones described the part which Elizabeth herself had taken in this harrowing time. "May I say that I have watched you daily and marvelled at the quiet way in

23537

which you were able to set aside your own feelings and natural anxiety
for your husband and allow him to give his best for our benefit and
I have wondered after all if you have not taught me a more needed
lesson than any of the others."

One morning during those sorrowful days Rufus Jones went out
to take a walk in the neighborhood of Woodbrooke. Passing one of
those houses so typically English with the little front garden enclosed
by a wall and an iron gate, he saw a frightened child struggling to
open the gate, which had swung shut and locked her out. The mother
appeared, opened the gate and gathered up the sobbing child in her
arms, exclaiming, "Didn't you know that Mother would come?" To
Rufus Jones that became a more than once repeated parable of human
life, with God on the other side of the gate. "Why should there be a
gate?" he wrote in an editorial in *The American Friend*. "Because all
our highest blessings and our supremely precious gains come through
faith and not through sight. The whole training and discipline of life
demand some mysteries and some strain and stretch of heart."

By the middle of August Rufus and Elizabeth Jones were back in
Ardonia, realizing to the full the finality of the loss which had sometimes seemed like a bad dream from which they might awake. They
faced the searing question whether, if they had been there, the boy
might have been saved. According to medical opinion it was paralysis
of the diaphragm and respiratory organs, possibly resulting from the
serum with which he had been injected. Today an attack of poliomye-
litis seems more probable. Their conclusion was, as Rufus Jones wrote
to John Wilhelm Rowntree, "We find that it is very unlikely that any
medical skill could have saved him."

After a rest at Eaglesmere they returned to Haverford to take up
work again without the presence of "the bright, keen, intelligent little
lad with his trustful heart and quick appreciation of all about him."

The stone in the Friends burial ground at Plattekill bore the in-
scription, "Transplanted into the heavenly garden," a paraphrase of
a stanza of Tennyson's *In Memoriam* which throughout his life Rufus
Jones liked to quote:

> I know transplanted human worth
> Will bloom to profit otherwhere.

IX

"Social Law in the Spiritual World"

SOCIAL LAW IN THE SPIRITUAL WORLD: *Studies in Divine-Human Interrelationship,* which appeared both in the United States and in England in the autumn of 1904, was Rufus Jones's first systematic statement of his philosophy, in so far as he can be said to have had a "system." Much of the material had been developed in his classes at Haverford, some of it had been the substance of editorials in *The American Friend* and of the essays on the mysticism of Paul and John which he wrote for *Present Day Papers.* It had formed the basis for his lectures at the Scarborough Summer School of 1901, the Woodbrooke Summer School of 1903, and the Haverford Summer School of 1904. It was the fruit of years of thought, study and discussion.

It was not addressed to the fraternity of philosophers; it was intended for the ordinary reader who did not understand technical terms but who was willing to make an effort of thought and to become "something of a co-laborer with the writer." It was written in a style designed to make clear, much as he made philosophical concepts crystal clear to his college students, his insights as to "the nature and meaning of personal life with special emphasis upon their religious implication."

He wrote at a time when the very possibility of a spiritual interpretation of man and the universe was under attack by materialist philosophy and the new psychology. The theologians with their concentration on petty divisions and quarrels seemed to him like men mending the roof when the house was on fire. Amazed "that so few persons seemed to know that the battle was on," he boldly approached the truths of religion through philosophy and psychology, feeling that this was the field where the crucial struggle was taking place.

It is a little difficult now, when that phase of the battle is over and when the years of the first decade of this century blur into each other, to realize how clearly in the forefront of the thought of his time Rufus Jones was. By 1904 William James had published his PRINCIPLES OF PSYCHOLOGY and his VARIETIES OF RELIGIOUS EXPERIENCE, but not PRAGMATISM or A PLURALISTIC UNIVERSE. The first International Congress of Psychoanalists had not yet been held, and Freud's lectures on Psychoanalysis at Worcester, which would set in motion a whole new era, were still in the future. There was a rising interest in mysticism. Dean Inge had given his Bampton Lectures on Christian mysticism in 1899, but von Hügel's more influential work. THE MYSTICAL ELEMENT OF RELIGION, was not to appear for five more years. Walter Rauschenbush's CHRISTIANITY AND THE SOCIAL CRISIS, which was to arouse the conscience of the Christian churches to an extraordinary degree, would not be published till 1907. In 1904 when Rufus Jones flung open the rusty-hinged doors of religious thought and let in fresh gales of philosophical, psychological and social ideas, his action was both courageous and vitalizing.

The title of his book frankly paraphrased Henry Drummond's NATURAL LAW IN THE SPIRITUAL WORLD, which had appeared twenty years earlier, and it was his purpose to answer the challenge of psychology to religious faith as Drummond had met the challenge of geology and biology. "There is no religious view or practice," he wrote, "so sacred that it does not sooner or later find itself summoned into the sanctum of the psychologist, where it is calmly asked by what right it continues to survive and to hold a place in the lives of mankind."

He acknowledged his debt to Palmer and Royce, to the books of William James, to Baldwin's works on "Mental Development," but his chief philosophical undergirdings are to be found in Plato, in Kant, and in Hegel as mediated through T. H. Green and John and Edward Caird, who, he said, had helped him more than any other British thinkers of recent times. He adopted Palmer's term, the *conjunct* self, and James's "the More" or "More yet." "Man," he said, "is not an isolated entity. He is conjunct with his fellow men and conjunct with God." "Every state of consciousness transcends its finitude, goes beyond its limits and *is what it is because of the more yet which will explain and fulfil it.*"

Kant, "that folio edition of a philosophical thinker," was to him the great figure in modern philosophy. He called Kant's "epoch-making" interpretation of the categorical moral imperative "this Copernican revolution in philosophy." He would say to his students, "We shall soon find that in spite of his splendid service we cannot settle down with Kant, we must go on and transcend him"; he would admit "inherent weaknesses" in Kant's system; he would point out that conscience depended on God rather than God on conscience as Kant held; but to the end of his life he built on the foundation that Kant laid, and he saw always in the moral imperative of man's nature a revelation of God.

Following Kant's lead, he set forth in SOCIAL LAW IN THE SPIRITUAL WORLD the futility of attempting to find God through logic, "at the end of a syllogism," or in the empirical world. He pointed to "one true path," that of personality, and listed the questions that must be asked. "Who am I? What do I live by? What does my personality involve? How am I related to my fellows and to nature? What does my sense of worth imply? What do I mean by goodness? Can I draw a finite circle about 'myself'? Do I have any dealings with 'a Beyond'?" The answers to these questions would, he asserted, "bring us to *that which is.*"

The conclusions of the search he mapped out in advance: "We shall see as we proceed that we at least live our lives in a unified spiritual world—that something divine is woven into the texture of our personal lives. We shall steadily find ourselves as we follow facts, moving toward a God who is Spirit, who has been revealed in a Person, and who can be found now because our finite spirits are interrelated with each other and with Him."

The subconscious mind was in 1904 a fairly new discovery, and Rufus Jones wondered whether we might not find there "some real shekinah where we may meet with that Divine Companion, that More of Life in whom we live?" The theories of Freud and Jung, however, caused him to modify his attitude toward the subconscious in later years. "It did not take very long to discover," he wrote in 1936, "that the subliminal zone like subtropical ones had hissing serpents as well as glorious birds of paradise . . . There is undoubted wealth hidden away in the subsoil regions within us, below the threshold of consciousness, but we cannot yet, if ever, leap forthwith to the sound conclusion that

God is assuredly most at home in regions which we cannot at present explore."

In the chapter on "The Testimony of Mysticism" he foreshadowed the study of mysticism which was to become so great a part of his contribution to religious thought and history. The mystics, he pointed out here, do not trouble themselves with arguments about God because, having known Him by experience, they need no further proof. The reality of the mystical experience, the 'testimony of the Soul', was for Rufus Jones always valid, the laboratory test of God's existence.

His examination of the Quaker doctrine of the Inner Light was objective and critical and was considered in some quarters to be controversial. The early Friends, he pointed out, did not discover the Inner Light but they experienced it so freshly and universally, they acted upon its leadings with such uncompromising boldness and devotion, that it has become the distinguishing doctrine of Quakerism. When they wrote about it, however, they evinced some confusion of mind. They used indiscriminately the terms the Light, the Seed, the Christ Within, the Spirit, That of God in man, and by any or all of these terms they meant three things; "a Divine Life resident in the soul, a source of guidance, and a ground of spiritual certitude."

Robert Barclay, the most theologically sophisticated of the early Friends and so well educated that he wrote his famous APOLOGY in Latin first, explained the Inner Light in a way that Rufus Jones considered both "unspiritual and contrary to all the known facts of psychology." Barclay made the Seed something foreign to man's nature, inserted into it, so that man remained forever a duality, "a human man plus a divine Seed or Light. This view placed so vast a gulf between the divine and the human that it left no basis for divine immanence; it made possible visitation by divine light from wholly beyond, but denied the possibility of God as "the indwelling light and life of the soul, permeating all the activities." It had moreover an unfortunate effect on Quaker ministry, making the person believe himself an entirely passive instrument through which the message comes without any thought or preparation of life on his part. The true Quaker principle, based on primitive experience, was that "man's spiritual nature is rooted and grounded in the Divine Life . . . The truth which comes will then be no injected revelation, no foreign irruption, but the genuine fruit and output of a personal life which unites in itself the finite and the infinite in one ever-expanding personality. The

Inner Light, the true Seed, is no foreign substance *added* to an un-
divine human life. It is neither human nor Divine. It is the actual inner
self formed by the union of a Divine *and* a human element in a single
undivided life."

In his desire to emphasize the reality of divine immanence Rufus
Jones came nearer in this passage to omitting the equally essential
element of divine transcendence than he ever would again. "A God
who is immanent, if He is to be thought of as Spirit, is just as certainly
transcendent," he was to write unequivocally in PATHWAYS TO THE
REALITY OF GOD, and similar statements can be found in others of his
books. But this early description of the nature of the Inner Light has
not been acceptable to some elements of Quaker thought, who have
read it by itself, perhaps, without placing later statements beside it,
and have thought it laid him open to charges of humanism. In 1946
when Rufus Jones was nearly eighty-four he wrote to a friend:

"I am profoundly hostile to humanism and do not lean toward it,
for humanism reduces man to a natural being, which I never do. I
take the Genesis statement very seriously, that 'God made man in His
own image' and G.F.'s reiterated phrase 'Something of God in every
man.' I have spent my life studying the great mystics and I follow them
in my interpretation of G.F.'s phrase. The use of 'seed' goes back to
the great passage in I. Peter. Of course I have never implied in any
of my writings that there is anything in man that would be adequate
for spiritual life apart from God. Certainly the candle must be lighted
by God; only the fact is that there is something in us that is kindred
and can feel the Presence and can be set aflame."

The test of spiritual guidance, whether it reaches us through the
Bible, the Church, or the Inner Light, becomes in the end, according
to Rufus Jones, the test of an individual. The Bible may be an infallible Book, but who is the infallible interpreter? Of many organized
churches, which one produces conclusions that are invariably right?
Can every revelation of the Spirit claimed by individuals be accepted
as authentic? What if two revelations conflict? Does each person become "a full tiaraed Pope?"

To this problem, which has always been a troubling one to Quakers,
the early Friends, he felt, had the solution, though they did not formulate it in their writings. He proposed two tests. One was the test of
life-results, the spiritual vitality and effectiveness of personality of the
individual. The other was the measuring of the individual guidance
against the spiritual experience of the group. "The spirit in one man

must be tested by the spirit in many men. The individual must read his inward state in the light of the social spiritual group. He is not, and he cannot be, an independent organ of God. He can have part in the divine life at all only as he is one person in a spiritually organized community.

"He must therefore learn to know God's will not merely in private inward bubblings, but by genuinely sharing in a wider spiritual order through which God is showing Himself."

In the final chapter, "The Divine-Human Life," Rufus Jones re-states in Christian terms the thesis which he has developed through philosophical and psychological concepts. This chapter, in which the writings of St. Paul and St. John and to a lesser extent the Synoptic Gospels are examined for the light they throw on the Divine-Human Life, seems somewhat separated from the rest of the book, not only by the specifically Christian content but by the style in which it is writ-ten. The traces of an earlier and more conventional style and a more theological approach tend to mar the unity of the book as a whole.

Sin he defines in the words of the THEOLOGIA GERMANICA as the turning away of the creature from the unchangeable Good. Man, who has free will, is free to withdraw into separateness, to refuse to seek spiritual goals. Since, however, it is impossible for the rebellious soul to fall out of the organic whole, his sin does not defeat the divine movement towards holiness but "takes its place in the spiritual universe as a thing to be put down and triumphed over."

On the whole, in his writings, Rufus Jones had little to say about sin and evil. If his phrase, "the divine movement towards holiness," quoted above, suggests the belief in inevitable progress which nine-teenth century liberals embraced as the accompaniment of evolution, he abandoned that point of view in later years, when he declared in several places that the "cosmic elevator" was no longer running. Evil, he said in THE ETERNAL GOSPEL, arises as the result of man's freedom. But a few years later he was not sure even of that. "I cannot deny the fact of evil," he wrote in NEW EYES FOR INVISIBLES, "nor can I accept any of the explanations I have heard given of it. It remains an unsolved problem, a huge mystery."

Redemption is not a legalistic device to avoid eternal punishment but the only means of making personality. "Jesus Christ is the supreme channel in human history for the personal communication of God— the revelation of the Divine and the human, united in one personality. By Him God came to humanity and through Him was expressed the

Type toward which personal life should move, and in Him was exhibited the eternal patience and sacrifice and love of God."

In this book Rufus Jones brought to maturity the style that was so distinctly his and so distinctive in itself that the *London Times* would in a few years bracket him and William James as the "two best stylists writing in America today." There is so far no example of his characteristic use of a humorous anecdote to illumine a point, but the clarity, the persuasiveness, the easy pace, the apt example and analogy, the use of quotation to explain, not to adorn, are all in evidence. The variety of his quotations reveals the catholicity of his reading and his love of poetry. Goethe, Whittier, Browning, Tennyson, Arnold, Emerson, Fitzgerald, George Macdonald, Coleridge, Lowell, Shakespeare, George Herbert and Dante are summoned to drive home, with the impact and economy of the poet, the ideas of the philosopher.

When one considers the make-up of the summer schools to which these lectures were originally presented, the large number of young men and women under thirty, the sizable proportion of older Friends eager for renewed inspiration but unaccustomed to disciplined thought (and many of them hard of hearing at that), one salutes Rufus Jones's faith in the intellectual as well as the divine potentialities in every man. It is easy to understand the case of the woman who rose in a meeting after Rufus Jones had delivered an address and said in a voice trembling with feeling, "Our dear Lord said, 'Feed my lambs.' He did not say, 'Feed my giraffes.' "

The reception of Social Law in the Spiritual World by Friends was disappointing. The *Friends Intelligencer*, it is true, the organ of the Hicksite Branch which, from the first days of his arrival in Philadelphia had been cordial to Rufus Jones, praised "this logical, limpid and convincing book" in a prompt and rather long review. The reviewer, however, apparently did not feel competent to do more than summarize the contents, and there was no real evaluation of the ideas or their importance. *The Friend* resolutely ignored it. The London *Friend* reviewed it in a way that dealt a lasting hurt. "Rufus Jones has struck oil in the title to his last book," it began flippantly, and continued, "His exposition of this aspect of modern thought is worthy of most careful elaboration. The world awaits a competent expounder of the theme . . . In discussing 'the Inner Light' on pages 174-5 Rufus Jones throws himself open to question . . . Rufus Jones has started on lines that lead to the discovery of a new gold-mine of thought, if carefully studied. We shall be very glad if his theme takes hold of students."

He wrote of his chagrin to John Wihelm Rowntree, to whom the book was dedicated: "I am considerably tried over the awkward notice of my book in the London *Friend*. It could hardly have been worse. I should have welcomed a criticism which showed insight. But to praise the title and to say that it is a good subject for somebody else to work up is pretty bad!"

John Wilhelm Rowntree wrote back consolingly, "With regard to the review of your book in the *Friend*, I would not for one moment allow it to trouble you . . . Your book has taken great hold here and will not suffer in the least on account of what the *Friend* has said. It is partly because of the deep impression I feel that it is making that I am so anxious to have you over at the Yearly Meeting."

Three years later, George Newman, son of the editor of the London *Friend* and himself editor of the much respected *Friends Quarterly Examiner*, wrote an article praising Rufus Jones's analysis of Barclay's dualism in his SOCIAL LAW IN THE SPIRITUAL WORLD and also in an essay on "The Divine Purpose in Human Life" which he had written subsequently for the *Friends Fellowship Papers*. "Whatever be the effect of Dr. Rufus Jones's book and paper on Quakerism in America —and it cannot be without effect—its influence on Quakerism in England will we trust be to stimulate us and rouse us to our calling. For now 'the time of our peace is past.' We must no longer be backward and slothful in our presentation of the splendid message which has been given us to bear to the world. Slothful and stupid we have been for long enough; self-complacent and snug in our little meeting houses we have allowed the great stream to pass us by; self centered we have forgotten that the inward life can only be revealed in an outward service for others."

The letter which Rufus Jones wrote in reply to George Newman reveals the disappointment which he had felt. "I was beginning to wonder whether there was any use trying to bring any larger points of view to the notice of Friends. All my attempts seemed to fall so flat that I questioned whether I was not wasting my time and ink! The studies on 'Inner Light' in 'Social Law' resulted in getting the book on the 'Index' here in Phila. It was excluded from 'Friends Library.' Elsewhere it has been left largely to the oblivion of silence. This recent study, which I felt was the most important chapter I had yet written was receiving a slender, nagging sort of comment which quite depressed me. Thy study of it was the first word I had had which indicated an appreciation of its significance."

Outside the Quaker fold, however, the book attracted wide notice. It was reviewed in newspapers across the country, from the *Boston Transcript* ("Philosophic insight and restraint combined with a rare gift of expression renders this book an interesting and valuable addition to the science of religion") to the Los Angeles *Times* ("The book lacks that clear conviction that was Drummond's").

The Nation, London, reviewed the second edition published by the Swarthmore Press in 1908, when the first edition of 2500 copies had been exhausted, in somewhat condescending terms, as a "manual on the central mysteries of the soul, brief and untechnical, true so far as it goes, and preserved from error through its author's familiarity with a wider field." Though it found that "some of its rather dashing style is, doubtless, American," it was obliged in the end to succumb to its appeal: "The beautiful and winning description of the way to God by one who has trodden that way may be of untold value to many an inquirer."

It was in the end not the effect upon reviewers but the effect upon the readers that was important and that has made this book live. Dr. Harry Emerson Fosdick can speak for a host of others. In his autobiography, THE LIVING OF THESE DAYS, he writes:

"Along with Walter Rauschenbusch, another personality deeply influenced me—Rufus Jones, the Quaker. His book, SOCIAL LAW IN THE SPIRITUAL WORLD, was published the year I came to Montclair and reading it was a memorable event in my life. After that I devoured everything he wrote." In the introduction to his RUFUS JONES SPEAKS TO OUR TIME, he describes himself and the impact of the book upon him in these words: "A young man, just entering on his ministry, confused by the theological wrangles of his time, and struggling to find a footing for his faith, the editor of this anthology ran upon 'Social Law in the Spiritual World.' That book opened the door to a new era in my thought and life and, re-reading it recently, I perceived afresh how much of my message has been rooted in the rich soil which that book provided."

It was the first of an impressive list of books to find an eager audience outside of the Society of Friends, and it was at least one of the reasons why Seth Gifford could say, and say truly, "Rufus Jones is the most influential Friend in the world."

The publication of this book was not the only—or the most im-

portant—event for Rufus Jones in the year 1904. On July 27th the
much-hoped-for little daughter was born and named Mary Hoxie for
his mother. "I can hardly hold in I am so happy," he wrote to John
Wilhelm Rowntree.

In this year the Providence Friends School was reorganized and
renamed the Moses Brown School, and a new principal was sought.
The position held for twenty-five years by his cousin Augustine Jones
was now offered to Rufus Jones. When he refused, his old teacher and
present colleague, Seth Gifford, accepted it. The Gifford house on
College Circle, then called Cricket Circle because it overlooked the
cricket field, became available and Rufus Jones bought it. In September the three Joneses moved in.

For the next forty-four years this roomy, comfortable, architec-
turally undistinguished house in its beautiful setting of trees and lawns,
was Rufus Jones's home. Here was his study, with the tiled fireplace,
the roll-top desk, the well-used books with underscored passages, the
photographs of his spiritual and philosophical heroes, the shabby couch,
and the charcoal drawing of Lowell made after his death from photographs. Here was the porch with the row of rocking-chairs, where
Rufus Jones loved to sit, watching cricket practice and talking with
the ever-increasing stream of people—faculty children, students, colleagues, Friends, philosophers, world-renowned leaders and unknown
inarticulate seekers—who came to drink at his fountain.

In 1905 Ada Smith came to 2, College Circle, to serve and love the
family as long as Rufus and Elizabeth Jones lived. The daughter of
Virginia slaves, she could neither read nor write, but her native intelligence, her religious faith and her devotion to her Mr. and Mrs.
Jones and her Miss Mary made her the fourth member of the family.
"She knew her 'Mr. Jones' was a great man," writes Mary Hoxie
Jones, "and she did everything possible to make his life comfortable. It
was to Ada that Rufus Jones said his last farewell before leaving the
house on a trip and to Ada that he gave his first joyous shout of greet-
ing when he returned."

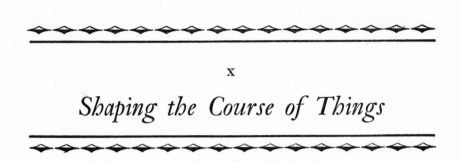

Shaping the Course of Things

"WE ARE still hoping," wrote Rufus Jones to John Wilhelm Rowntree early in 1905, "that the next letter will tell us to 'cool off' one of our rooms for an English visitor from the Yorkshire moors! We will have water in the pitcher duly frozen and the wind shall blow across the bed all night!"

The gaiety was at least in part a cover for very real concern about John Wilhelm's health, which had been steadily deteriorating. It was decided now that he should come for six weeks of rigorous treatments in Chicago, and that he should visit Haverford before and after. With his wife Constance he sailed from England late in February.

On the voyage he caught a cold which developed into pneumonia and affected his kidneys. When Rufus Jones, full of joyous expectation, met the *Caronia* on March fourth he found his friend delirious and unable to recognize him. "Rufus!" he kept saying piteously. "This isn't the real Rufus!"

During the next few hours, as if he moved through a nightmare, Rufus Jones summoned an ambulance and sent his friends off to the hospital while he stayed behind to see their luggage through customs. He had no keys and the customs official, refusing to believe his story, broke the locks and ransacked everything.

During the five days that remained of John Wilhelm Rowntree's life, he did not once recognize Rufus Jones, though he called for him again and again. His mind hovered about his history of Quakerism and he begged to be allowed to finish it. On the ninth of March he died, aged thirty-six.

The funeral was held at Haverford Meeting and he was buried in the corner of the little graveyard there. He had had many friends in America and the meeting house was packed with Quakers of all shades of thought, united in their sorrow and their desire to do honor to the young English Friend whose leadership had been so luminous and so important. For the ten years since the Manchester Conference he had been, as Rufus Jones wrote in *The American Friend*, "the unique inspiring leader of that epoch of our Quaker history."

As soon as the news of John Wilhelm's illness reached England, his cousin Arnold Rowntree sailed for America, arriving after the funeral was over. He took Connie, who was expecting a baby, back to England.

The loss of his great friend was the last of the bitter blows that death dealt to Rufus Jones. His father had died at the age of seventy-eight in a railroad accident the year before. His Aunt Peace, who was not to die in the body until May, 1907, had been for several years mentally so lost that her actual death at the age of ninety-three was only the confirmation of something that had happened some time ago. But John Wilhelm Rowntree, especially since those days after Lowell's death when he had entered so closely into Rufus Jones's grief, had been one of the most important factors in his life. The task which he was left to carry on alone was immeasurably heavier without the support and the faith of his comrade.

Two of John Wilhelm's projects for Quakerism were going forward vigorously: Woodbrooke was well established and the Summer Schools had become a part of the pattern of the period and would continue under their own momentum. A third, the magazine, *Present Day Papers*, which had flourished for a few years, would now have to be laid down. The Quaker History, so much on John Wilhelm's mind at the last, remained a question. Could that be allowed to drop? Evidently Rufus Jones at once wrote to John Wilhelm's father about his concern, for on the 29th of March Joseph Rowntree replied:

"Constance and Arnold reached Plymouth on Monday morning and last night I had a long conversation with the former about the History in which John was so much interested. Before we knew what had been passing in thy mind, some of us here had been feeling strongly about it and seriously hoped that it might not be abandoned or indeed seriously delayed. We very much value thy offer of help and know how valuable it will be. Constance thinks that from thy conversations with John, thou has a clearer view of the proposed scope and general scheme of the work than any one in England, and I think it would be a great help at this stage if thou would kindly have put down thy conception of what this scheme was. With this before us it might be easier to reach the next stage in the work, and to see the divisions into which the History would fall. . . .

"As thou knows John's purpose was not merely to write a History which might be of general interest, but he had the very practical aim of so bringing out the lessons of the past as to throw light upon the problems of the present, both in our own community and in the Church at large. There will need to be some common understanding among the writers so that, as the chapters go on, there may be a concentration of thought in certain directions, and the final chapter in which the threads are gathered together will, I think, be one of very special importance."

He went on to speak of the Rowntree Trust for Charitable Purposes, which he had established a few months earlier, the funds of which would be applicable to this enterprise.

That summer, leaving Elizabeth Jones and Mary at Pocono, Rufus Jones went to England, to lecture at two summer schools and to confer with Joseph Rowntree and others about the History.

It was not a long trip; he was away from home only a little over six weeks in all. He visited Connie Rowntree at Low Hall, the beautiful house started before John Wilhelm's death and only recently finished, he had lunch with George and Elizabeth Cadbury at their summer home in Robin Hood's Bay, where "we ate outdoors— the wind blowing nigh a gale and the warsps [sic] so thick that it was a survival of the fittest," and stopped to "see Woodbrooke and Rendel and other wonders" before he went with Joshua Rowntree, the cousin who was editing John Wilhelm's papers, to Street, near Glastonbury, for the first summer school.

To a group of some two hundred he gave four lectures, on Psychology and Religion, The Historic and the Inward Christ, The Atonement, and Prayer, the last three of which became the basis for one of his most loved books, THE DOUBLE SEARCH, which was published the following year. Parts of the chapter on Prayer he used again in his last book of all, A CALL TO WHAT IS VITAL, written just before his death in 1948.

"Is not the advance of science making prayer impossible?" he asked, and went on to discuss the modern view of the universe, in which there are no uncaused events. "If we met a person who told us that he had seen a train of cars drawn along with no couplings and held together by the mutual affection of the passengers in the different cars we should know that he was an escaped lunatic and we should go on pinning our faith to couplings as before."

He answered his question by showing that what endangered faith was not the advance of science but the "stagnation of religious conceptions." "If religion halts at some primitive level," he said, "and science marches on to new conquests, of course there will be difficulty ... We need to rise to a truer view of God and to a loftier idea of prayer ... On the higher religious plane no collision between prayer and science will be found." "True prayer is immediate spiritual fellowship."

"R. Jones touched all our hearts as usual," wrote Jessie Lloyd to Elizabeth Jones. "I won't dilate! You know how we all love him over here and what he has been to so many. It was lovely to see those who had never seen him or come under his influence feel the goodness and uplift behind the mere words."

Rufus Jones himself felt that the first of the four lectures did not take hold. The hall was a difficult one in which to speak, he was tired, the audience was "sluggish"; but then the tide began to rise, and in the end reached a height which he felt was "extraordinary."

Between this summer school and the next, which was held at Scalby for a much smaller group and which was chiefly a memorial to John Wilhelm Rowntree, the important conference on the History took place at Low Hall, on September fourth and fifth. Besides Joseph Rowntree and Rufus Jones, those who met in John Wilhelm's library were B. Seebohm Rowntree, brother of John Wilhelm, Arnold S. Rowntree, Joshua Rowntree, William Charles Braithwaite, T. Edmund Harvey, and A. Neave Brayshaw. Except for Joseph and Joshua Rowntree, who belonged to the older generation, these were the emerging leaders among the English Friends; their voices would be clearly heard over the twenty or thirty years to come. Having lost John Wilhelm Rowntree, they were disposed to look to his friend Rufus Jones for guidance and inspiration.

Rufus Jones had prepared for this meeting with care. "I rather dread tomorrow for I must more or less shape the course of things and a good deal hangs on our decision," he wrote to Elizabeth Jones on September third. "It will quite settle my future for some years to

come. I have briefly sketched out a plan which I shall present." For
nearly eight years he and John Wilhelm Rowntree had talked over the
plan for the history, had written to each other about it, and he had
John Wilhelm's letter of October 15, 1903, in which he had drawn
up three objectives:

"The object I have in view is not to write an encyclopedic history
of Quakerism nor to collect material which has only an antiquarian
interest but rather to study Quakerism as an evolution . . . The lines
of study would be three-fold: (1) An attempt would be made to
analyse the content of 17th century Quaker thought, to trace its
development through the 18th and 19th centuries in its relation to the
rationalism of the 18th, the modern thought of the 19th and to the
evangelical revival of both centuries . . . (2) An attempt would be
made to trace the changes and development in church organization
and especially in relation to the practical problem of the free
ministry . . . (3) Finally an attempt would be made to trace the relations between Quakerism and the social problem."

It had long been decided between them that Rufus Jones was to
write a preliminary volume or volumes tracing the course of mystical
movements and the place of Quakerism in the stream of mystical
thought.

Rufus Jones presented his plan for the entire history to the group
at Low Hall. They discussed it for a day and a half, drew up a final
outline—and then all went off for a ten-mile walk.

The plan called for a series of volumes, each with an introduction
relating it to the whole study, which was to deal with Quakerism
"as an evolution and as an experiment in spiritual and social Christianity." Authors were tentatively assigned to different volumes, and
Rufus Jones was to be editor of the whole as well as to write several
of the volumes himself. The first volume, which was to be his, should
set forth "the historical development of inward and spiritual Christianity as in contrast to the ecclesiastical and ritualistic types," William
Charles Braithwaite was to write on the formative periods of Quakerism. The Rowntree Trust would supply funds for research, travel,
secretarial help and books, as well as underwriting the expenses of
publication.

When they started on that ten-mile walk, a project had been set in
motion that would occupy much of Rufus Jones's time and thought
and energy for sixteen years to come, the period that was to cover
also the First World War and the founding of the most far-reaching

and absorbing enterprise with which he was ever to be associated, the American Friends Service Committee.

The second summer school was held as Scalby immediately after the conference. Many of the students he had known at Woodbrooke the previous summer. In addition to four lectures at the summer school and numerous individual interviews, he gave a public address on Sunday evening on the lawn near Scarborough Castle, to which two thousand people came, evidence of the drawing power that his name had already won in England. Soon after the middle of September, he was at home again, deep in his book on mysticism.

He had started work on it more than a year earlier. A letter of February 9, 1904, thanked John Wilhelm Rowntree for a gift of books: "The dear old mystics arrived at my door safe and sound. It is a splendid collection and added to what I already had gives me just the tools I need for my magnum opus. There are many precious books in this collection which I never should have owned but for your grace and goodness. Law's Behmen, Henry More's great folios, Görres Christliche Mystik, Everard, the History of Hai Ibn Yokdan, and Poiret's Divine Economy are some of the most prized. But there is not a book in the lot which is not important, in fact indispensable for my purpose. The love, which brought them to me, has through all my months of sorrow been a genuine comfort, and now I must show what I can do with them."

Now the Rowntree Trust made it possible for him to buy all the books he needed and to build up a collection of mystical literature which is one of the most complete of its kind in the United States. He had also started a Haverford graduate of 1904, Howard H. Brinton, on the task of research. For a year he had been reading the mystics, in English, and taking notes on cards. Elizabeth Jones similarly was reading and abstracting the writings of the German mystics. Her disciplined mind and her knowledge of German made her able to give real help to her husband.

Rufus Jones set aside two mornings a week for work on the book, Tuesdays and Thursdays, but as he was always available to the students at any time and as on Thursdays he went to Meeting, the work must have suffered many interruptions.

The problems and divisions of Quakerism continued also to demand his attention, and he traveled far and wide in the United States during those years, speaking to yearly meetings and to Quaker colleges.

The establishment of the Five Years Meeting, successful though it was, had not solved all problems. Among the evangelical group, the Gurneyites, there was an extremist wing which was not satisfied with the moderate stand of the majority. "The history of religion has shown over and over again that creeds do not unite, they tend to divide," writes Howard Brinton in FRIENDS FOR THREE HUNDRED YEARS. "A group held together by a creed is more brittle and more subject to breakage than a more yielding organic group held together by the Spirit." These extremist Friends, who would have liked to use the Letter to the Governor of Barbados and the Richmond Declaration of Faith as a creed, belonged to a strain that had entered Quakerism during the great revival of evangelical religion which took place shortly after the Civil War and which had profoundly affected all religious sects, including the Society of Friends. "Evangelists travelled from place to place, bringing multitudes to their knees crying for mercy and forgiveness. Quakers who had become evangelists or evangelists who had become Quakers held revival meetings in Friends meeting houses . . . They preached a fourfold gospel of Justification, Sanctification, the Second Coming of Christ and Faith Healing." They clung, even in the early 1900's, to revivalist methods, to fundamentalism and a literal reading of the Bible; they recognized no other interpretation than their own as valid.

To this group modern thought was not only dangerous but evil and they looked askance at Rufus Jones's efforts to prevent the "stagnation of religious conceptions."

"The tension between liberal and evangelical wings of the Society increased greatly between 1905 and 1907," wrote Elbert Russell in his HISTORY OF QUAKERISM. ". . . The intolerance of certain evangelical leaders and especially the influence of *The Evangelical Friend* threatened the unity of the Society."

Of this threat Rufus Jones was acutely aware. *The Evangelical Friend* was a weekly periodical set up in June, 1905 by members of this wing. That its editorials pointed directly at him when they called loudly for the removal of all "unsoundness" from the ministry and the rooting out of all "modern thought" from the Quaker colleges did not trouble him for he knew well his own strength, but its emotional impact on the small rural meetings, the lack of confidence among Friends which it engendered, and the resultant division and discord where peace and love should prevail were deeply disturbing. "There seems to be no way to check the movement," he wrote to George Newman, "as it is semi-fanatical and not amenable to rational stearing [sic]. I still hope for better days, but the task of saving Quakerism in America is to say the least gigantic . . . I am, however, not discouraged but I am almost staggered at our problem."

In June, 1905, he made a trip to California to give the commencement address at Whittier College and to attend California Yearly Meeting. On the way he stopped between trains at Kansas City and took a sightseeing tour, of which he wrote: "Kansas City is a wonder. It is the greatest that ever was, according to the man with the megaphone. As a matter of fact it is both fine and horrid. The park side of the city is beautiful and marked by good taste, while the stockyard part of the city was suggestive of Gehenna."

There was among California Friends a strong element of the "narrow wing" and when he first began to speak there he was aware of a tide against him. After the Commencement Address he wrote to Elizabeth Jones, "Hurrah, the ordeal is over and I am still alive. Everybody has been very kind to me and there will be no *row* at all . . . I shall not dread anything else as I did this afternoon."

At the Yearly Meeting he was asked at the last minute to give an address on temperance besides the one on education that he had prepared. He decided to make the additional effort, because, "if I can do it well, it will win over the very element I want to reach."

Both talks went well. Though he had thought that "the meeting did not quite rise to" his talk on education, still the college people were full of praise and gratitude, and on Saturday afternoon, when mention had been made of *The American Friend,* the entire group spontaneously got to its feet and gave him a standing vote of confidence. The temperance address that night was an immense success, and over-stimulated (his own eloquence as heady as alcohol), he was unable to sleep afterwards. The next day he preached to a church congregation of a thousand, "went out to dinner and had to be entertaining but I was pretty limp," and spoke again that evening. The next morning he wrote with understandable jubilation, "Hallelujah! I am through!"

From Pasadena he went to Pacific Grove to visit his old school and college friend, Augustus Murray, by this time professor of Greek at Leland Stanford, and here, after two more sleepless nights and the fatigue of traveling, "struck his first Waterloo." "I had hardly got into bed when an ominous noise was here [heard] in my lungs and

pretty soon I filled up tight full with asthma. It was no worse in
degree than I have had before but it didn't come to any end. It
lasted till the morning . . . About 9 Gus came. I was a t.r. with
bloodshot eyes and a woebegone look but I soon braced up." "T.r."
was a family expression which appears at intervals in his letters to the
end of his life. It stood for "total (w)reck."

After a heart-warming day with his friend, a swim in the bay and
hours of talk lying on the sand in the sunshine, he went on much
refreshed to Oregon, where he expected to address a group of
Friends in Portland. When he got there, however, after a night
on the train, he found that the meeting was scheduled in Newberg,
twenty-six miles away. There were no trains that would get him
to Newberg in time to speak and back again for his train east.
Consternation. Rufus Jones was determined. He hit upon the daring
and expensive plan of hiring an automobile at three dollars an hour.

The road was rough and hilly; part of it was corduroy. It took
nearly three hours to do the twenty-six miles. In the Main Street of
Newberg, which was being repaired, the car stuck fast in loose
gravel. The three passengers got out and shoved—with, Rufus Jones
commented drily, "plenty of spectators looking on."

After supper at Pacific College, they went to the Meeting House
for the program. "It soon filled up with Friends and after an impressive period of worship and devotion I gave the message which
was on my heart. All weariness disappeared and the efforts of the
day were forgotten. It was our one hour together and an hour not
to be forgotten. There are times when heaven seems wonderfully
near and the way of life seems clear." When he left, to take the
bumpy way back in the dark over the corduroy road, the Friends
gathered on the meeting-house porch to see him off, singing "God
be with you till we meet again." "I never felt anything was more
worth doing than this trip," he wrote, "and I never felt more drawn
to a company of people than to these Friends in Newberg."

Whatever barricades people might erect against the figure that they
imagined him to be, they were usually helpless when they came
face to face with the person that he actually was. He told the story
in The American Friend of the little London girl who wrote in a
school essay, "The only place in the city where you can see wild
beasts is in the Theological Garden," but there were no snarls and
growls in Rufus Jones's theology. His letters are full of the friendships
that blossomed along the path of his travels.

In Pasadena the man who had led the opposition against him and who had actually persuaded the Committee of Ministry and Oversight to "condemn" his writings, was John Henry Douglas. Rufus Jones's meeting with him was characteristic. "I got there just as meeting was beginning," he wrote, "and rushed up to J.H.D. with enthusiasm. He was a good deal flustered but he said the right things . . . After Meeting hosts of friends came up to speak to me. The ice was really broken. I have arranged to visit John Henry Douglas. His daughter Mellie, my old classmate at Providence, was there and she was very glad to see me."

The letters are full too of his eager response to the natural beauty that he met along the way. The Grand Canyon, Santa Catalina Island, the snow-topped mountains of northern California and Oregon, the Canadian Rockies filled him with delight, and he described them to his wife with the same fresh joy and awe that the Maine woods and China Lake had aroused in him as a boy.

In 1907 he made a trip to the middle west at the end of January and beginning of February, when the period of mid-year examinations freed him from his college classes, to give lectures on Quakerism at Wilmington College in Ohio, Friends University in Kansas, Penn College in Iowa, and Earlham in Indiana. During the two weeks of this circuit he had a constant struggle with late trains, missed meals, ice, sleet, blizzards, strange beds and other hazards. Styes, colds, and asthma added their misery to the inevitable fatigue.

In Wichita he met real opposition from the old guard, who flocked to the meetings from neighboring towns and villages.

"It was a much tougher proposition than at Wilmington," he wrote. "The Bible Institute complicated the situation. Most of the provincial Friends were red hot anti-modern thought and the issue was raised from the first. Alfred Ware and Prof. Jay were very outspoken in favor of modern thought and finally yesterday afternoon Pres. Stanley got up and delivered a terrible speech—delivered to the gallery. It attacked evolutionists and higher critics. He inflamed and scared all the ignorant and descended almost to the level of ranting. It was one of the worst things I have ever heard. I went to him and told him what I thought of it and I told him I had a mind not to give my last lecture, that I did not propose to spend my breath lecturing if the people wanted the sort of thing he had given them. He was a good deal cut up and promised 'to fix things up,' which he did in a second speech. I resolved to do or die on my final chance at them so I blew off the safety valve and let her go. I hit the audience from the start and the sympathy grew as I went on. When I finished as many as fifty of the young people got up from all over the house and came forward and pledged themselves to help carry out the kind of Quakerism I had been presenting."

His final lecture was "The Message of Quakerism to the Modern World." The text is not extant, but it seems probable that the burden of it was similar to that of an address given to New York Yearly Meeting six months earlier entitled, "Problems of Twentieth Century Quakerism," in which he had said, "It is the duty of every Quaker and every Quaker meeting to study the social conditions of its neighborhood. Nothing less than a great human brotherhood of sympathy and helpfulness will satisfy the demands of Christ." Quaker youth everywhere were eager to respond to a call to service.

These experiences will serve as examples of the numerous speaking trips that he made during these years. In addition he was again in England in the summer of 1906, when he took part in a summer school at Bakewell in Derbyshire, speaking on "The Message of Quakerism to the Needs of Today."

Again this year as before there was a two-day meeting at Scalby about the progress of the History. He worked closely with English Friends on this great project and though the leadership and much of the responsibility was his, there was a complete meeting of minds on the question of policy, scope and approach. After the conference there were a few days for sightseeing and relaxation; Arnold Rowntree drove him to Fountains Abbey, and he visited the Hodgkins in Scotland.

Elizabeth Jones, who was at home taking care of a sick baby, wrote affectionately, "My best way of helping seems to be just to stay behind and not mind . . . So I am going to try to do it as cheerfully as I can—and keep on loving thee more than ever."

Two years later, however, when he was able to take a sabbatical leave during the second semester, in order to finish his book on the mystics, Elizabeth Jones and three-year-old Mary accompanied him to England. They sailed on the 28th of March and went straight to Charlbury, a village thirteen miles from Oxford on a branch of the Thames, where they rented a house for three months.

It was an old gray stone house with its front door directly on the street and a garden behind, where fruit trees were espaliered on sunny walls, a two-hundred-year-old mulberry spread its branches, and asparagus and strawberries ripened for their table. Down the street was a thirteenth century church with a yard where nursemaids and babies still sit on benches in the sun, and up the street and around the corner stood the little Friends Meeting House. They paid a pound a week rent for the house (furnished with canopied bedsteads and other treasures, including an iron bathtub that terrified small Mary) another pound for the wages of gardener and maid, and something more for a nursemaid—halcyon days, indeed.

Every day Rufus Jones went by train to Oxford, where he attended lectures, chiefly at Christ Church and Balliol, and spent long hours working at the Bodleian Library, where, he wrote, he had "indeed entered into a more than royal treasure house without money and without price." Though there were cordial letters from a number of lecturers giving him permission to attend their lectures, it is not possible—and probably not especially significant—to say exactly whom he did hear. It is certain that he heard William James deliver the Hibbert Lectures at Manchester College in May, which were later published under the title A PLURALISTIC UNIVERSE. "His main purpose was to present an alternative to monistic idealism," wrote Ralph Barton Perry, "and thus to consolidate the opposition. This he delighted to do at Oxford—in the very stronghold of monistic idealism."

Though Rufus Jones quoted from A PLURALISTIC UNIVERSE in PATHWAYS TO THE REALITY OF GOD he followed his quotation by the disclaimer, "I am not here endorsing James' well-known conception of God, which I do not share." He admired James and was stimulated by him, but he remained an idealist.

It seems probable that he also heard Hastings Rashdall lecture, as well as William McDougall, J. A. Smith and J. A. Stewart.

Most of the time, however, he spent reading at the Bodleian or writing in the old house at Charlbury. STUDIES IN MYSTICAL RELIGION was finished during the spring and summer and some of the chapters sent to the printer. It was Joseph Rowntree's idea that chapters should be printed separately as pamphlets and sent to various experts to be read and criticized. Hastings Rashdall and Dean Inge were among those who cooperated in the plan, but on the whole Rufus Jones felt it did not justify the expense of money and time and the method was dropped for succeeding volumes. During these months he was in constant demand for addresses at monthly and quarterly meetings, schools, summer schools and like gatherings. In May all three went to Birmingham to attend London Yearly Meeting, staying with the Cadburys at the Manor House.

The evening before the Yearly Meeting began, Rufus Jones gave the first Swarthmore Lecture. Established by the Woodbrooke Extension Committee as "an annual lecture on some subject relating to the message and work of the Society of Friends," this was to become an important Quaker event. The slim green volumes of the printed lectures, beginning with Rufus Jones's QUAKERISM, A RELIGION OF LIFE, now fill a sizable shelf and they provide material for numerous study groups throughout Quakerdom. Among the authors are those friends and colleagues who were closely associated with Rufus Jones in establishing the tone and direction of twentieth century Quakerism: William Charles Braithwaite, Joan Mary Fry, Joshua Rowntree, Edward Grubb, L. Violet Hodgkin, T. Edmund Harvey, A. Neave Brayshaw.

After the three months at Charlbury, there was time to visit English Friends, attend summer school at Kendal, sit again in the twilight at Fountains Abbey, and to talk with men whose minds marched with his own. In August the three Joneses went to Switzerland with Arnold Rowntree and Constance Rowntree and her children and Henry Cadbury, and the energetic members of the party climbed the Faulhorn, the Lauterhorn, the Monk and the Eiger. All of them together read Wilhelm Tell and picked edelweiss and talked and remembered John Wilhelm. "Returning one evening to Grindelwald," his daughter writes, "after climbing the Faulhorn, Constance Rowntree rushed her children to the balcony of the hotel, while Rufus Jones snatched his child from bed and together they saw a double rainbow span the entire valley. It may have seemed a useless effort, for the youngest two in the group were only three and four years old, but the parents hoped that somehow the children might share in the majestic beauty of that moment. Years later, these children grown into women and dear friends, discovered that they all counted that moment of the double rainbow an earliest memory, a flash of beauty from which they dated their beginnings as conscious individuals."

It was a happy and refreshing time, lighted with that special buoyancy that accompanies the accomplishment of a heavy task. STUDIES IN MYSTICAL RELIGION was in the hands of Macmillan in London and by the time that they sailed for home on the tenth of September, a contract had been signed for its publication.

The Quaker History Begun

STUDIES IN MYSTICAL RELIGION was published in London in the spring of 1909.

Though it was a large, solid book of more than five hundred pages, it did not attempt to be a complete history of Christian mysticism. Not only did it not go beyond the rise of Quakerism, but the Spanish mystics were omitted and the English mystical poets of the seventeenth century. Jacob Boehme was explicitly reserved for a later volume. Some of the movements described, such as the Waldensian, the Wyclifite and the Anabaptist movements, were not strictly mystical but were included because they helped to forward religion of an inward type. As it was designed to be an introduction to a series of books on the history of Quakerism, the mystics and the mystical groups chosen for emphasis were those which formed the stream of religious thought and experience out of which Rufus Jones believed Quakerism to have arisen in the seventeenth century.

The three-fold point of view of the philosopher, the psychologist, and the historian, combined with the particular coloration of the Quaker, becomes evident as the story unfolds. The gift for clear and vivid exposition which was Rufus Jones's is manifest even when he deals with material that is difficult, abstruse and confusing. His images, homely and illuminating, his humor, which flickers in a turn of phrase or a realistic observation, his love of poetry and the wide reach of his scholarship, are evident once more in this profound but eminently readable book. "The author is, probably, a heretic himself," commented one reviewer; "but he is, nevertheless, a Christian and a man of culture; and his Studies throw light upon Church history from an unfamiliar standpoint, which is delightfully illuminating!"

To the historian no events, even spiritual insights, are independent of the period in which they occur. They are in some measure shaped by the social or political conditions, the mental climate, the subconscious currents of their time. Rufus Jones's historical perspective on the light that burned in Ireland in the Dark Ages and threw out a spark in John Scotus Erigena to kindle new fires in Europe, on the changing conditions in the Catholic Church that made the Waldensians heretics and found a place of honor for the Franciscans a century later, on the influence of the Babylonish Captivity of the Popes, and of the Great Civil War in the Holy Roman Empire and the Black Death on the formation and nature of the small brotherhood groups of the fourteenth century, on the Civil War in England which released the "noise and flutter of sects and schisms"—to give but a few examples—provides a corrective lens that serves to lessen the distortions in vision inevitable when twentieth century minds examine ninth or twelfth or sixteenth century ideas.

As a psychologist he was aware of the element of abnormality in the mystics and he did not fail to point it out where he saw it. "It is true that the great mystics have often possessed peculiar psychical constitutions. They have sometimes exhibited the phenomena of hysteria, and sometimes they have, beyond question, been pathological, and have experienced abnormal states due to an unstable nervous system. But it is also true that persons possessing such psychical constitutions have in unusual ways, and in heightened degree, been able to correspond with an environing Reality which built up and vitalised their personal lives."

In later years he was to think that he did not give enough weight to this element of abnormality. "I see now," he wrote in 1938, "as I did not see in the early period, what a large pathological factor there has been in the lives of many mystics in the long historical line." Yet it was obvious in STUDIES IN MYSTICAL RELIGION that he was repelled by those psychic phenomena which marked the more extreme types of mystics.

After making allowance for the looser mental organization frequently seen in genius, he stated unequivocally that visions, auditions, automatisms and trances were evidence rather of hysteria than of spiritual power. For all his love of St. Francis of Assisi, that "gentle revolutionist," he regretted the experience of the Stigmata at La Verna. "The modern interpreter, however," he wrote, "unlike the medieval disciple, finds this event, if it is admitted, a point of weakness rather than a point of strength. Instead of proving to be the marks of a saint, the Stigmata are the marks of emotional and physical abnormality. The 'wonder' which moves us in him is the fresh and living fountain of joy and love which Christ opened through him for that age of gloom and superstition; not that he had motor automatisms of this extraordinary sort."

This comment on St. Francis stung Evelyn Underhill, an eminently sane as well as profound writer on mysticism, to retort:

"The modern interpreter, says Rufus Jones, finds in the stigmata of St. Francis of Assisi a point of weakness rather than a point of strength: not the 'marks of a saint' but 'the marks of emotional and physical abnormality.' This is a very moderate statement of the 'rational' position by a writer who is in actual sympathy with certain aspects of mysticism. Yet it may well be doubted whether that flame of living love which could, for one dazzling instant, weld body and soul in one, was really a point of weakness in a saint: whether Blake was quite as mad as some of his interpreters, or the powers of St. Paul and St. Teresa are fully explained on a basis of epilepsy or hysteria: whether, finally, it is as scientific as it looks, to lump together all visions and voices—from Wandering Willy to the Apocalypse of St. John—as examples of unhealthy cerebral activity."

On the other hand, he declared, the evidence of an element of autosuggestion in a mystical experience did not prove it to be merely psychic. "When we have named these great spiritual crises, which carry us up to new levels of life and power and service 'autosuggestive experiences' we have only substituted one word for another. We called them 'new births'; we call them 'autosuggestions'! The *fact* remains on our hands, and the fact is a momentous one."

The terrible austerities of some of the mystics, the hair shirts, the self-flagellations, the nail-studded beds, roused in him pity and the sense of bafflement natural to one of his healthy, life-loving, vigorous nature, but he understood its psychological source. "It was felt by the mystic, no doubt, to minister toward the supreme end in view, namely beatific vision, and there almost certainly came to those who practised asceticism states of intoxication or swoon, in which there was a sense of the fulness of life."

The techniques of the mystics, the stages of Purgation, Illumination and Contemplation, the spiritual ladders, which occupy so large a part of many books by and about mystics, held little interest for him, partly because of their emphasis on ecstasy, which he considered a false trail. The "*union* above thought, above states of consciousness, above knowledge," which is ecstasy, is, he says, "the final refuge of all negation mysticism."

Not ecstasy but an enhanced and unified personality and increased energy to carry out God's purposes in the world were to him the hallmarks of the mystical experience. "The supreme task of spiritual religion," he found, "is this positive task of discovering how a man like one of us can go up into a vision of God and come back with power for the transformation of his human desires, his finite will, and his daily activities."

He traced the course of the immanental and the transcendental views of God through the speculative mystics from Plato to Plotinus and through Augustine and Dionysius the Areopagite, who presented "neo-Platonic philosophy slightly sprinkled with baptismal water from a Christian font," to the Catholic mystics of the Middle Ages.

To Plotinus, in this book, he was rather cool. Though he recognized him as "the profoundest thinker between the flowering period of Greek philosophy and the creators of modern philosophy in the sixteenth and seventeenth centuries," he considered the neo-Platonism of which he was "the master mind" "the last great intellectual effort of paganism." His summary of Plotinus's three spheres of being is rather stiff and perfunctory, and he held him responsible, because of his teaching that the highest stage of truth is ecstasy, for the long succession of negative mystics.

Dean Inge, in the letter which he wrote to Rufus Jones on the pre-publication chapter of STUDIES which he read, commented:

"I have read your chapter with much interest and have really hardly anything to suggest. . . . I am less and less inclined to speak contemptuously of the conception of a 'One beyond existence' in spite of the errors of the *via negativa*. If we follow Plotinus carefully up to his κόσμοςνοητὸς we find a sphere in which thought and its content/object [the writer did not indicate his choice between the two words] are absolutely equivalent—a world which is the complete expression of the Divine Nature. But there still remains the subject-object relation which is the condition of all existence and the form of all normal ex-

Rufus Jones's mother, Mary Hoxie Jones, about forty

Rufus M. Jones at twenty-two, in his Prince Albert coat

Peace Jones, about the time of Rufus Jones's birth in 1863

he old homestead in South China, in which Rufus Jones was born
recent picture)

Sarah Coutant Jones, at about thirty, taken during the years at Oak Grove

Rufus Jones in 1901, during his year of study at Harvard

Lowell Coutant Jones, nine years old, at Providence Friends School

perience. Logically the quest of the Absolutely One points us beyond this, to the super-existent One in whose honor Dionysius coins so many strange compounds. Those critics who foolishly talk about Platonic 'dualism' do not perceive how uncompromisingly monistic the system is. And those who talk about 'dreamy cloud-land' etc. etc., do not do justice to the fundamental faith of the Neo-Platonist that every speculative truth of philosophy must have its copy and its justification in human experience. Therefore even the Absolute must somehow fall within the limits of possible human experience though it be only in the rarest moments of ecstasy. One cannot deal with mysticism satisfactorily without doing justice to its philosophy, upon which Plotinus is the classic authority: and alas! no great thinker has been so persistently and almost universally misunderstood."

In 1918 Dean Inge himself published his own two great volumes on the philosophy of Plotinus, and nearly twenty years later Stephen Mackenna's two-volume translation of the works of Plotinus appeared. There is no doubt that Rufus Jones studied both. His chapter on Plotinus in SOME EXPONENTS OF MYSTICAL RELIGION, published in 1930, is markedly warmer, more sympathetic, more complete than the treatment in STUDIES IN MYSTICAL RELIGION. In 1939 in THE FLOWERING OF MYSTICISM, he spoke of Plotinus as "one of the major intellectual and spiritual guides of all human history" and "one of the world's greatest mystics and . . . as Dean Inge called him, 'a prophet saint.'"

The affirmative mysticism which Rufus Jones felt to be the best and soundest type was that which stemmed from the mystical element in the Christianity of John and Paul and the Acts, when the church was "a mystical fellowship, i.e. a fellowship bound together not by external organization but by the power of the experience of the Divine Presence among the members," and when a direct spiritual fellowship with Christ was expressed in a daily life of love and service. In tracing this emphasis through the history of mystical individuals and groups, he notes, where they appear, features which were later to mark the Quaker movement: the attempt to return to primitive Christianity, cases of group mysticism, opposition to ecclesiasticism, refusal of oaths and objection to war, an individual sense of social responsibility, a characteristic concept of the Light Within.

The Friends of God, who lived in small, loosely organized communities that spread from the Low Countries to Bohemia, devoted to the contemplative life and to the production of a remarkable body of mystical literature, belonged to the fellowship of those who knew God directly in their hearts and who carried their love into daily life and service. The father of this movement, Meister Eckhart, with his lofty mysticism, his active life, his warm interest in people, his indifference to forms, rites and ceremonies, who "in a tumultuous age revolting from dry formalism and empty orthodoxy" told his hearers that "the God whom they missed in the church they could find in their own souls" was especially dear to Rufus Jones. That Eckhart was also a source of Hegel's system is not mentioned here but is later brought out in THE FLOWERING OF MYSTICISM.

To this group belonged also the mysterious Friend of God from the Oberland, who was probably Rulman Merswin and of whom Rufus Jones's account was for some twenty-five years the only one in English, and Heinrich Suso and Johannes Tauler. "We cannot expect a devout Catholic of the fourteenth century to enter fully into the spirit of service which is the very breath of our best modern Christianity but Tauler often rises to an insight which carried him far beyond contemplation and joy in inward states however exalted. 'Works of love,' he says, 'are more acceptable than contemplation.' "

The THEOLOGIA GERMANICA, written by an anonymous member of this band, one of the classical books of mystical literature, contains that great statement of consecration to service: "I would fain be to the Eternal Goodness as his own hand is to a man." The author's philosophy was medieval and scholastic and he tended too much toward self-annihilation, but "it is interesting to note that this Friend of God in the fourteenth century used the term 'Light' almost precisely as the Friends of the seventeenth century did."

Jan Ruysbroeck, "one of the rarest souls in the goodly fellowship of mystical teachers," who had "little patience with those who sit idly, 'with introverted eyes' waiting for a formless vision" was the link between the Friends of God and the Brethren of the Common Life, who included also in their number Gerard Groote and Thomas à Kempis. The Brethren were laymen, their way of life was simple and their emphasis was on practice. They lived in brotherhood houses, supporting themselves by copying the Bible and other holy books, they offered free and practical education, aimed at the formation of good lives, to the common people of their communities. They anticipated George Fox in their disregard of theological degrees. Of the *Imitation of Christ*, which Rufus Jones ascribed here to Thomas à Kempis but in his later books to Gerard Groote, he says: "Next to Dante's 'miracle of song' [it] is the most perfect flower of medieval Christianity." "If one is seeking for a monistic view that does full justice to the concrete facts of experience he will not go to à Kempis for it."

In the Lollards of pre-Reformation England Rufus Jones found not only the actual physical ancestors of the Quakers—Fox and other founders were "of the stock of martyrs" (i.e., Lollard martyrs)—but certain convictions which were also Friends testimonies: "that 'God made not priests'; that *man* and not 'stonen houses with glasen windows' is the true divine temple; that the simplest person may go directly to the *Head* of the Church." Possessing also a strong social spirit, they stood for concern for the poor, simple garb, plain speech, refusal of swearing, and avoidance of war.

Other groups yet closer to Quakerism were the Anabaptists, who broke forth simultaneously with the Reformation, "determined to reconstruct Christianity after the New Testament model," and who after appalling persecution in Holland made their way secretly to England; The Family of Love, who opposed oaths, war, and capital punishment and testified to the unimportance of outward forms in comparison with inward experience, and so far as they could put the Sermon on the Mount into practice; and the Seekers, many of whom actually became Quakers. John Saltmarsh, who died in 1647 and whose "Sparkles of Glory" parallels many of Fox's ideas, William Dell, Gerard Winstanley, and others "are of a totally different type from the mystics who follow the negative path in a passionate search for the Divine Dark. They are primarily of the practical temper that belongs to the English character, and they introduce us to the new social spirit which is the very 'hall mark' of the Quaker Fellowship, which will be studied in the succeeding volume."

STUDIES IN MYSTICAL RELIGION appeared at a time when there was a rising interest in the subject. Dean Inge had published three books on Christian mysticism, the third of which, PERSONAL IDEALISM AND MYSTICISM, appeared in 1907. R. H. Benson, A. W. Waite, and Henri Delacroix, whose ÉTUDE D'HISTOIRE ET DE PSYCHOLOGIE DU MYSTICISM Rufus Jones quoted frequently, had all published books in the two previous years. Baron Friedrich von Hügel's monumental MYSTICAL ELEMENT IN RELIGION appeared in 1908, but evidently too late for Rufus Jones to draw upon it. Evelyn Underhill's MYSTICISM was to appear in 1911. With his STUDIES Rufus Jones took his place as one of the foremost writers on mysticism, to be classed in the ensuing years with Dean Inge, Von Hügel, and Evelyn Underhill. "We all three were working independently of one another and without knowing that anyone else was engaged in the undertaking," he wrote in 1943, "we produced our results almost simultaneously . . . We became intimate friends through our work."

Though some reviewers dissented sharply from his point of view on the sacraments and institutional religion, the majority praised the book and all took it seriously as a major contribution to the subject. "No small part of the value of the book is the beautiful spirit of the author that breathes through it," wrote T. Rhondda Williams in the *Christian Commonwealth*, and G. K. Chesterton, in the London *Daily News*, observed with some surprise, "This very valuable book is in substance something like a rebuke of the medieval church, not for being too mystical but for not being mystical enough."

"The Spiritual Reformers"

W ILLIAM JAMES died in August, 1910. Rufus Jones, in England at the time for another conference on the Quaker History, wrote an "Editorial Letter" to *The American Friend*, in which he spoke of his debt to James, his personal affection for him, and the "loss to the entire race" which he felt his death to be. Several weeks later he was deeply touched to receive a letter from Alice James, in which she wrote:

"Many voices have been raised in affectionate memory of a man who truly loved his kind, but no one has spoken more justly or with finer appreciation than yourself. I should like to read it to my dear husband, who counted himself so lightly—and yet *how* he honored his work and loved it!"

Rufus Jones's debt to William James was due in great part to PRINCI-PLES OF PSYCHOLOGY, which "opened a new world" to him when he read it lying on the grass under the trees at Oak Grove in the summer of 1890. "I have read it and reread it," he wrote, "and have taught it to class after class until it has become an indissoluble part of my life. It has illuminated every aspect of the inner life and brought meaning and significance to all the deeper issues of the human spirit . . . I have seen an entire class hushed with a solemn awe under the moral power of his wonderful chapter on *Habit* and I believe that nobody in our time has uttered a more unescapable and unanswerable moral message than his in this chapter."

QUAKERS IN THE AMERICAN COLONIES, published in 1911, was the

work of three people. Amelia M. Gummere, author of A STUDY IN
QUAKER COSTUME and editor of John Woodman's JOURNAL, wrote the
section on New Jersey, with emphasis on John Woolman. The section
on Pennsylvania was written by Isaac Sharpless, who in addition to
being president of Haverford was the author of A QUAKER EXPERI-
MENT IN GOVERNMENT. Of Isaac Sharpless's historical work Rufus
Jones said that it "did not reveal the finished historical scholar though
it was very good amateur work and distinctly worth doing . . . But
wisdom," he added, "is quite another matter. There are many exact
scholars who speak with academic authority but who, nevertheless,
are quite barren of wisdom . . . He emerged with wisdom, with insight." The sections on New England and the Southern Colonies
Rufus Jones wrote himself, as well as a brilliantly perceptive and comprehensive introduction to the whole. For his research he read every
one of the numerous Friends' Journals of the period and he had an
examination made of meeting records.

In spite of his attempt to unify it the book suffered from the fact
that it was the work of three, not one. It lacked the cohesive power
of a single point of view and of a single style. The other two parts
suffered by comparison with Rufus Jones's vivid clarity and ease of
expression. Today it has been rendered incomplete by the mass of
new material which has come to light.

As soon as the 1911 spring term at Haverford was over, Rufus and
Elizabeth Jones and Mary set off for Europe to do research on the
second volume on the forerunners of Quakerism. They went directly
to Italy and spent nearly three weeks in Rome and Florence. In Rome
six-year-old Mary proved to be a well-informed sightseer and an
open-minded Quaker. "Each church has something of which she
knows something," wrote her mother. "and the people are interesting
to watch. She is practising the semi-kneeling as you pass in front of
altars, etc. Also crossing with holy water, etc." She even led her
Quaker parents up the Holy Stairs on their knees.

Rufus Jones wrote from Florence to Violet Hodgkin: "I have just
come from St. Maria Novella where I have been enjoying the Spanish
Chapel in the Cloister, especially the result of the Descent of the
Holy Ghost—namely the mighty march of truth embodied in Thomas
Aquinas; and on other side the work of the church militant and the
glory of the church triumphant. Philosophy is luminous, calm, stately.
The militant work of the church is confused—some are rapturously
praying, while in among them others are setting dogs on heretics and
there is an evident mixture of ecstatic worship and worldy affairs while

the calm, triumphant and luminous faces are only above in the realm of the Urbs Sion Mystica. This is all very true of the militant church in any age and in any branch of its many divisions. It does take endless patience to put up with the bursts and curves, the halts and the bickerings, but somehow God's strange army *does get on* and occasionally at least a small devil gets beaten."

They spent two months in Marburg, where he studied the German Protestants and mystics, especially Jacob Boehme, Hans Denck, Sebastian Franck, Caspar Schwenkfeld.

In February of the previous year Rufus Jones had had an enthusiastic letter from a pastor in the little village of Schweinsberg, Germany, who had read his Studies in Mystical Religion. Herr Theodor Sippell was himself a student of the Quaker forerunners and had come to the same conclusions that Rufus Jones had. Now he found his discoveries about John Saltmarsh, William Dell and Gerald Winstanley anticipated by Rufus Jones. He asked to be taken into the circle of scholars who sought to investigate the origins of Quakerism "as a modest fellow worker."

A stimulating and friendly correspondence ensued between the two scholars, who found themselves explorers in an almost untouched field. Herr Sippell sent Rufus Jones an article of his on the Dutch Collegiants, whom he considered identical with the Seekers. He was eager to go to England and Holland that summer to pursue the subject further. Could he get Rowntree Trust aid?

It was arranged for him to make the trip to London, and the two met there in August, 1910, when Rufus Jones went over for the conference on the Quaker History. Herr Sippell now at eight-five in his study in Marburg likes to recall that meeting. It was after talking to him, he told the present writer, that Rufus Jones came to the conclusion that Boehme was actually not so close to the early Quakers as Caspar Schwenkfeld and Sebastian Franck and decided to broaden his book to take in all the Spiritual Reformers instead of concentrating upon Boehme. His work on the Westmoreland Seekers had convinced Rufus Jones, Pastor Sippell said, that they were imbued with Schwenkfeld ideas and had passed them on to George Fox.

As a result of that meeting Pastor Sippell was employed to collect material for Rufus Jones to use in the prepartion of his next book on the mystics, and a plan was made for them to work together in Marburg in the summer of 1911. Herr Sippell himself would concentrate on Roger Williams and leave the Seekers for Rufus Jones.

When the Joneses reached Marburg, "a pleasant dwelling" awaited them. Herr Sippell's uncle, Herr Happich, the pastor of the Pfaar-kirche and superintendent of all the Lutheran churches of Hesse, lived near the top of the castle hill in what was called the oldest house in Marburg because a part of a twelfth century building, a round tower with small cryptic faces in the wall, had been incorporated with it. Here the Joneses boarded during the months they were in Marburg, occupying two bedrooms and a sitting-room on the second floor. From their windows they had a beautiful view of the city, the valley of the Lahn and the surrounding hills. Above them towered the Castle and the Marienkirche, of which Herr Happich was pastor; a little below was the slender spire of the church of the Kugelherren, the Brethren of the Common Life. The *pfarrerhaus* itself had a small walled garden with apple trees, lilac bushes, old-fashioned flowers, and a tiny sum-mer house perched on a shelf in the steep hill.

Between the Happich family, the pastor and his wife and their fifteen-year-old daughter Hanna, and the Joneses, a friendship de-veloped that survived two wars. "There was a striking saintly quality in this fine scholar and preacher," wrote Rufus Jones, "and his wife possessed a refined and beautiful spirit. Our life with them was an unalloyed satisfaction and has always been a happy memory." There was but one flaw to mar that happiness: Herr Happich saw war coming and his attitude toward it was that of German militarism.

The city of Marburg itself had great interest for Rufus Jones, as-sociated as it was with St. Elizabeth of Hungary, who was buried in the beautiful thirteenth century church built on the site of her hospital; with the Brethren of the Common Life, whose church had become the Roman Catholic parish church; and with Martin Luther. In the fifteenth century castle that dominated the town from the top of the craggy hill, Luther and Zwingli met to discuss and to disagree on the doctrine of transubstantiation and so to cause "the first great split in the Evangelical Christian Church, a habit, which," commented Rufus Jones ruefully, "has ever since gone on growing."

Arrangements had been made through Herr Sippell by which the books which Rufus Jones needed to examine were sent from libraries all over Germany to Marburg, where he could work over them at his leisure. Herr Sippell came often to Marburg to work with him and between visits letters flew back and forth between the two. Elizabeth Jones's knowledge of German was again of great assistance to her husband, and she spent many hours translating the difficult Old German texts.

While in Marburg Rufus Jones also attended lectures on Ethics given by Professor Wilhelm Herrmann in the University of Marburg, which, founded in 1527, was Germany's first Protestant university. In 1925 it would confer upon Rufus Jones the honorary degree of Doctor of Sacred Theology, when the war which Herr Happich had foreseen was over and the children of defeated Germany had been fed by an American Quaker organization of which Rufus Jones was founder and chairman.

Rudolf Otto, the author of THE IDEA OF THE HOLY, who was living in Marburg at that time, also proved to be a congenial friend, and in 1939 Rufus Jones dedicated his FLOWERING OF MYSTICISM to the memory of Rudolf Otto as "friend and helper."

In August Rufus Jones went to Switzerland for a fortnight of climbing, and out of that came an experience which he was to use in talks and books to illustrate a truth of life. "I came once up the Engelberg Valley in Switzerland to a place which the natives call the End of the World—das End der Welt. A huge mountain closes the pass, the road stops abruptly and no one can go on there. It is a terminus. I stayed in a little inn there at the End of the World. How often in life the gateway shuts, a semaphore drops in front of us, the way closes. We have come to a terminus. The next day, however, I found a zigzag path farther down the valley that went up the side of the mountain. I climbed up and up and went on over the End of the World. There is always, if one can find it, a way higher up that goes over these closed ways which confront us."

Elizabeth Jones's fortieth birthday occurred while he was in Engelberg and he wrote to her after the birthday wishes: "I am not easy to live with and there are strange curves in my nature, but the heart and centre are sound, I believe, and I know that beyond all things on earth I want to be good. I am all the time conscious of a much better and more efficient man than has come to light and capable of better things than have been realized. Perhaps the truer person may break through at last. I hope so." The following day, he wrote, "I believe more and more that the greatest single help to a spiritual life is a deep and living human love for another."

On the way home after leaving Marburg, Rufus Jones attended and addressed a "remarkable" Young Friends Conference at Swanwick, England. There he found the Young Friends concerned, like Herr Happich, with the war that they saw looming ahead, and with their attitude toward it. "What struck me most forcibly," he said, "was the almost unanimous resolve of that group that under no circumstances would they have any part in a coming war, nor would they make any compromise with military demands upon them."

One of the young Friends who was there, John Hoyland, looked back in 1957 shortly before his death upon the effect of Rufus Jones's presence in that conference. The illumination and the dedication which they saw in him welded them together, he said, and prepared them for the tests of the war. "To a whole generation of us he was a prophet and a saint and a shining light. We loved him and we venerated him. He was the leader of our lives. His writing was secondary. It was his personality, his outgoing love, his humor, his geniality, his luminousness. The Holy Spirit was in him to his finger tips. He made each one of us feel worth while and that he saw something in us and loved us individually. He had an extraordinary gift for creative friendship. However American Friends felt about him it was nothing to what English Friends felt."

Still another trip, two years later, was necessary before SPIRITUAL REFORMERS was to be ready for publication. He went alone to England for three weeks in the summer of 1913, to make a final check on references at the British Museum. He took with him for ship-board reading, REWARDS AND FAIRIES, SHERLOCK HOLMES, Ward's REALM OF ENDS, and FOLLOWING THE STAR, by the author of THE ROSARY. His reading throughout his life was extensive, continual, and catholic. The last day at sea, he wrote to his wife: "Thee may not know it, but my own love has been steadily growing riper and richer as our years together go by, and I have felt all the voyage how much I missed thee."

While in London, he was lent Arnold Rowntree's suite of rooms in St. James's Court, where he lived in somewhat lonely state, with a manservant in attendance. "I am very comfortable here, only lonesome . . . I have most of my meals in restaurants or in the Authors' Club where at least I can see other eaters eat!" As so many years ago, he and his cousin Charles Jacob were abroad at the same time. "I had Charles and Hattie Jacob for dinner and for the evening. They came at 7 and my elegant slave served us an excellent dinner in the sitting-room."

As soon as he had finished his work at the Museum, he was off to Wales for four days of relaxation at Sir George Newman's "Huts" in Anglesey. His old friend, George Newman, had been knighted two years before for his work as director of the medical department of the Board of Education.

"Here I am," he wrote, "in Sir George's Huts in a perfectly glorious spot, on a sea-bluff looking south into the sweep of the Atlantic, on the east taking in the entire range of Welch [sic] mountains sixty miles long and west across to Holy Island, which rises high over the rather flat fields of Western Anglesey. This is very wild country with beautiful heather, bracken and yellow wild flowers." The group consisted of those well-loved old friends, William Charles Braithwaite, the Newmans, and Arnold Rowntree, with the addition of three or four new acquaintances—"a perfectly jolly crowd." They spent the days swimming, walking, rowing, "living the simple life de luxe," and hearing Rufus Jones read Walt Whitman in the evenings. W. C. Braithwaite wrote a poem every day and a drama in which Rufus Jones figured as "The Prophet—Our Haverfordian Shikar."

The four friends met again at Scalby, with Joseph Rowntree, Edward Grubb and Ernest E. Taylor, for a conference on the History, which became a conference on Quaker periodicals and reached a decision which will be discussed later.

From there Rufus Jones went to Reading for a summer school. "I must say," he wrote to Elizabeth Jones, "I dread Reading. I do not have quite the old time enthusiasm and *abandon* for S.S.'s"—and what could be more natural, after active participation in at least seventeen in thirteen years! At Reading, however, he had the joy of meeting again Philip Wicksteed, who was lecturing on Wordsworth. Rufus Jones himself spoke on the Spiritual Reformers, as he had done earlier in the year at Hartford Theological Seminary, when he gave the Carew Lectures.

He sent the proofs of his new book to Herr Sippell that fall, and the pastor responded warmly, "Your book marks a great scholarly advance over the presentations hitherto." Although as a "pretty rabid Lutheran" he differed from Rufus Jones in fundamental attitudes, he derived keen joy and rich profit from the book. He himself was now turning to the study of Methodism.

Spiritual Reformers of the 16th and 17th Centuries made its appearance in London in 1914, the second of the historical series in chronological order but fourth in the order of publication. W. C. Braithwaite's The Beginnings of Quakerism having appeared in 1912, with a brilliant introduction by Rufus Jones. Four chapters sufficed for Boehme in the finished book, which dealt with a host of others besides, many of whom had been neglected or forgotten or about whom little or nothing was available in English.

He began with Hans Denck, who, influenced both by medieval mysticism and by the new humanism of Erasmus, conceived a fresh and unique type of Christianity, the practicers of which in the early sixteenth century were called "spirituals" or "enthusiasts." He ended with the seventeenth century English poets, Francis Quarles, Thomas Traherne, Henry Vaughan, and George Herbert, because though "poets are not Reformers" they "are always among the first to feel the direction of spiritual currents and they are very sure voices of the deeper hopes and aspirations of their epoch." In between comes a succession of saints, prophets, geniuses and cranks, most of them isolated figures or trailed by small and dwindling bands of followers, who nevertheless had a message of truth to deliver and who faithfully delivered it, often at a cost of pain and danger and sacrifice. They find their place in this book because their ideas were related to the ideas of the early Quakers. "The Quakers of the seventeenth century are obviously one of the great historical results of this slowly maturing spiritual movement, and they first gave the unorganized and inarticulate movement a concrete body and organism to express itself through." The Spiritual Reformers, Rufus Jones called them, because they were in a sense the product of the Reformation, though they were soon disappointed by it and they broke with its theology.

They discarded the prevailing ideas of the Atonement as the sacrifice of Christ to the wrath of God, and looked on salvation instead as a personal relationship with a God of love, followed by a transformation of life. They abandoned the idea of Heaven and Hell as permanent places of reward and punishment, seeing them as "inward conditions, states of the soul, the normal gravitation of the Spirit towards its chosen center." They believed in free will. The Church was for them a fellowship, "the living body of Christ in the world." Divine revelation did not end in the New Testament, but continued. Religion implied also social and economic reforms, so that the common people might develop their potentialities as persons.

The exact connection of the Spiritual Reformers with Quakerism is not easy to spell out definitively. They preceded it, some of them were contemporaneous with its beginnings, their ideas were "in the air" of the seventeenth century, but did the early Friends read their books, is there evidence of a direct and unmistakable line of influence? Rufus Jones thought that there was. Translations of Boehme's books were available in England between 1647 and 1661, the formative years of George Fox. Fox was no reader, but other early Friends and Seekers who became Friends or influenced them, such as Thomas Taylor, were readers and aware of theological literature. Fox in his writings makes no specific mention of "Behmen," as he was called, but there is a significant number of passages in his Journal that parallel or suggest passages in Boehme's writings. William Penn and John Bellers both highly recommended the sermons of John Everard, through whom the writings of Hans Denck, Sebastian Franck and the THEOLOGIA GERMANICA came to England. The similarity of the fundamental Quaker position with that of the Spiritual Reformers is, Rufus Jones says, perfectly clear. "Quakerism is, thus, no isolated or sporadic religious phenomenon. It is deeply rooted and embedded in a far wider movement that had been accumulating depth and power for more than a century before George Fox became a 'prophet' of it to the English people."

More recent scholarship tends to differ with these conclusions. Geoffrey F. Nuttall in his scholarly and interesting book, THE HOLY SPIRIT IN PURITAN FAITH AND EXPERIENCE, which has exerted a strong influence on some of the younger Quaker historians and theologians, declares that early Quakerism was an outgrowth of radical Puritanism rather than of the mystical movements of the continent. He notes that Schwenkfeld, Denck, Franck and Coornhert preceded Puritanism and in some cases anticipated radical Puritanism, but "any direct influence," he says, "is far to seek." He does not, however, make any attempt to trace the influences bearing on Puritanism or to discuss the reasons for the wide differences between radical Puritans and conservative Puritans such as the Presbyterians. The fundamental Quaker doctrine, "that the Holy Spirit indwells all men, the converted completely and the unconverted incompletely"—or, in Fox's familiar words, "that of God in every man"—he sees as wholly outside of Puritan thought. Furthermore, the Quaker stand on the Bible, the lay ministry, the sacraments, oaths and war, which came out of their primary doctrine, was closer to the practice and writings of the Spiritual Reformers than to that of the Puritans and was responsible for much of the Puritan fury against them.

In any case, whether the connection between Quakerism and the Spiritual Reformers was tenuous or strong, there can be no doubt of the service which Rufus Jones rendered to the history of religious thought, both in retelling and reinterpreting the story of long-neglected mystics and spiritual geniuses and in showing that Quakerism was not an isolated phenomenon but part of a religious movement.

The book was published early in 1914. Shailer Mathews, dean of the University of Chicago Divinity School, wrote, "I regard it as one of the best pieces of historical theological work that America has put out for this generation." Thirty-one years later Rufus Jones received a letter from Aldous Huxley which showed that the book had held its place: "May I take this opportunity to thank you for the much profit I have derived from your books—above all the Spiritual Reformers, which introduced me to a world of men and thoughts, about whom and which I was totally ignorant until I read the fruit of your researches."

The End of an Era

It is necessary now to go back two years, to 1912, when the third Five Years Meeting was held at Indianapolis, and Rufus Jones's labor for *The American Friend* came to an end.

During the summer before the meeting two of his best loved English friends, Arnold Rowntree and Sir George Newman, made a visit to Canada to investigate possibilities for emigration for Adult School members. Rufus Jones met them in Montreal and they all went directly to Lake Louise for ten days of climbing, walking, and talking in the Canadian Rockies. There they met by chance Francis Wyle, secretary of the Rhodes Scholarship Commission, and William Adams Brown of the Union Theological Seminary. "On Fairview we met Professor Brown of the N. Y. Theological Seminary," wrote Arnold Rowntree in his journal letter home, "a colleague of Professor Mc-Giffert's, and the meeting between him and Rufus was quite touching. He knew all Rufus's books, had been wanting to come in touch with him for 20 years, so there was great joy in finding each other. The discussions on education amongst the three wise men of the party have been to me most interesting and instructive."

They "walked over the mountains from Field into the Yoho Valley, explored it from end to end and climbed back over the mountains to that glorious spot, Emerald Lake." Rufus Jones described it years later. ". . . We lived thrillingly and dangerously on that memorable journey and we came back with the great Northwest built into our

imaginations and with its air in our lungs and some of its rugged
strength in our fiber."

Back in London afterwards, remembering those days of fellowship,
George Newman wrote nostalgically, "Dear professor and philosopher
and friend, we miss thee greatly."

In October Rufus Jones met William C. Braithwaite and his wife
at Broad Street Station in Philadelphia and they travelled to Indiana
with Isaac Sharpless, "Master Thomas" Brown of Westtown School,
James Wood and his son Hollingsworth, and Henry Scattergood, a
member of the boards of both Bryn Mawr and Haverford, who with
Isaac Sharpless was to attend the Five Years Meeting as a "fraternal
delegate" from Philadelphia Yearly Meeting (Orthodox).

At one of the sessions in the First Friends Church in Indianapolis
Rufus Jones gave the Social Service Report. "It needs no special plead-
ing," he said, "to show that social service is an inherent part of our
heritage from the past, but it is just as obvious . . . that we as a religious people are not awake to the call of this age for spiritual light
and leading in the solution of the great social and economic problems
that confront us . . . For the most part Friends have not yet caught
the vision nor have they prepared themselves for what is to be one
of the most impressive undertakings of the Twentieth Century, the
conquest of unnecessary disease, the banishment of unnecessary poverty, the transformation of environments which breed and foster
disease and sin, the spiritualizing of both capital and labor and the
recovery of faith in the actual coming of the Kingdom of God in
the world." The report fired the enthusiasm of the meeting and
struck a deep note of unity.

The most important action, for Rufus Jones personally, which the
Meeting took, was the releasing of him from all connection with *The
American Friend*. For the last five years his assistant, Herman Newman, had been the actual editor and his own part had been that of
"editorial adviser," which involved the writing of editorials and a
determining voice on policy. Now he was free entirely from a
twenty-year-old burden which had grown too heavy. Henceforth
The American Friend would be an organ of the Five Years Meeting,
published from Richmond, Indiana. *The Evangelical Friend* would
cease to be a rival weekly and would become a monthly.

"I have always thought of Quakerism as essentially a *movement*,"
wrote Rufus Jones in his last "Editorial Letter," "and with that view
I could never have accepted any position in which I was expected

to repeat the pious phrases of the past or merely to restate the safe positions which dead heroes had won. My central purpose—however it may have failed in achievement—has always been to fight the spiritual battles of the present age, to win the new territory that is here and now to be conquered and to widen the area of light."

He had presented over and over fresh interpretations of the old themes of atonement and salvation, had written on the nature of man and the "perfect union of the divine and human nature of Christ," on education, personality, immortality, love, the ministry, temperance, Quakerism new and old. He had delighted the children from time to time with Bible stories bearing such winning titles as, "The Story of a Boy who Became a Great Leader," "The Story of a Great Boat," "The Story of a Great Rain and Rainbow," which were published in book form in 1911 under the title STORIES OF HEBREW HEROES.

He had had much praise but also much misunderstanding and criticism. Only a few months earlier a California reader had written to cancel his subscription, declaring, "I have been a subscriber for your paper and those that have stood in its line almost continuously since 1870. But when you published that scandal on Isaac and Rebekah I thought it was about time for me to quit." Later, looking back on the barrage of criticism, he saw in it not only a discipline for humility, but other values as well: "They taught me how multiform human minds are, how varied are human needs, and how important it is to respect the heart-beat of the man who does not belong to one's own school of thought."

Happy as he was to be relieved of *The American Friend*, he was less than a year later deeply involved in another Friends' journal—the reincarnation of John Wilhelm Rowntree's *Present Day Papers*.

It arose out of the 1913 conference on the Quaker History. Edward Grubb, editor of the monthly *British Friend*, felt that the time had come to lay it down. Many people were dissatisfied with *The American Friend* since Rufus Jones had withdrawn from it. One reader, who represented a body of opinion, had written to him, "We are tired of doing without thy paper already. If thee can't write for the new-fangled paper, why not start another?" Quakerism in America, Rufus Jones, felt, was in a very critical condition. The great spiritual center of Quakerism, he reported to the group at Scalby, was Philadelphia, with four thousand Friends so severed from the larger body of Friends that it was difficult for it to do what needed to be done.

In view of all these considerations, it was decided to start a new,

international Quaker monthly, with the two objects of carrying forward the spiritual concerns of Friends and of "speaking the Quaker
message without denominational label." Rufus Jones would be editor,
with a staff of co-editors in England and Henry J. Cadbury as his
assistant. His wife's younger brother was now an instructor at Haverford College, and his brilliant mind, keen humor and sweet spirit, as
well as his Biblical scholarship and his interest in Quaker history, made
him increasingly congenial to Rufus Jones.

He went to work at once. "I have been overloaded ever since my
return last summer," he wrote to Violet Hodgkin on New Year's
Day, 1914, "having had the work of starting the new paper and of
carrying my new volume [SPIRITUAL REFORMERS], through the press
in addition to my college work."

The first issue, by a prodigious effort, appeared in January, 1914,
bearing the title: *Present Day Papers:* "A monthly Journal for the
Presentation of Vital and Spiritual Christianity." It contained Opening
Words by the editor, an editorial entitled, "Is Belief in the Personality
of God Necessary for Religion?", a section of Notes and Comments
(by the editor), articles by Isaac Sharpless and Joan M. Fry, a long
review of James Royce's THE PROBLEM OF CHRISTIANITY (by the
editor), other reviews by George Barton, and a report on missions
in Africa by Edward Grubb.

Letters from England were prompt in arriving. Some thought the
cover "dull"; some thought the contents too "intellectual," though
Joan Fry wrote that she did not believe in "too much pap." Evelyn
Underhill called it "splendid. . . . exactly what is wanted," but it was
generally agreed that it lacked variety. In the United States it was
received with more enthusiasm.

The difficulties of international publication were obvious, and after
the outbreak of the War in 1914 became insuperable. Publication
ceased with the December issue in 1915, and there was general grief,
even from those who had criticized it. To Violet Hodgkin it had
seemed "increasingly helpful and to fill a growingly useful place."

Though it had been difficult to get enough articles by English and
American Friends of sufficiently broad caliber to supply the variety
which readers desired, Rufus Jones himself had poured some of his
best writing into the editorials. In 1916 a number of them were
gathered into a little volume called THE INNER LIFE, which takes its
place in the long list of Rufus Jones's inspirational books. If Harry
Emerson Fosdick's anthology, RUFUS JONES SPEAKS TO OUR TIME, be

taken as a sort of measuring stick, THE INNER LIFE ranks high on the list, for only one other book, PATHWAYS TO THE REALITY OF GOD, is quoted more frequently. Excerpts from it help to answer the questions: "Where is God?" "How Does God Reveal Himself?" "How Explain Conscience?" "What is Vital Religion?" "What is True Mysticism?" "What Does Prayer Mean?" "What is the Matter with the Church?" and "What is the Christian Way of Life?"

Rufus Jones had his fiftieth birthday on the 25th of January in 1913. It was the only one, he wrote in THE TRAIL OF LIFE IN THE MIDDLE YEARS, that ever depressed him. He felt that time was running out, and that he had not yet begun to do the particular work for which he had come into the world. "I always knew that the goal of life was not talking or thinking or writing, but *being* and *doing*."

A great change was coming into his life, though there were still only surface indications of it. The laying down of the burden of *The American Friend* was part of the preparation, freeing his hands for other tasks. He had begun also to move out into the world beyond Quakerism, to be known and loved by numbers of people who knew little or nothing of the Society of Friends. The Carew Lectures which he had given at Hartford were the first in a succession of such lectureships which he would hold at institutions all over the country. In 1914 he was appointed for the first time to the Board of Preachers to Harvard University. After some hesitation he accepted. He was accustomed to preaching to college students, but in the Quaker way, rising out of a silent meeting to deliver a message but under no compulsion to speak unless he was moved. To commit himself in advance to a sermon at a particular time seemed to violate his Quaker principles. In the end he accepted for one semester.

Each of the Harvard preachers delivered two Sunday sermons and conducted morning prayers for a period of two weeks in each half year. Rufus Jones, with his humor and warmth, his Maine twang, his utter reality and the cogency of his thought, had no difficulty in holding the attention of the students. He was many times invited to be a Harvard preacher, and he always enjoyed the time spent in Cambridge, the interviews with the students and the renewal of friendships with the faculty, but it was twenty-nine years before he could say, "I have to a large extent got over my fear of a Harvard audience."

During this period he was chairman of the Social Service Commission of the Interchurch Federation of Philadelphia, which concerned itself with problems of wages, housing, immigration and so on.

The Overseers of Haverford Meeting in November, 1914, wrote him
a letter expressing the love and appreciation of the Meeting for him
and his services. "As we think of thy unselfish sharing of those
burdens," they wrote, "we look upon thee as our very own and often
wish that thy membership might be where such a large part of thy
life and work are." This was an outer expression of a condition that had
some years ago come to pass: Philadelphia Quakerdom had taken
Rufus Jones to its very heart. He did not, however, accept the implied
invitation to transfer his membership from South China to Haverford
Monthly Meeting. He felt himself still an essential part of the Five
Years Meeting, which he had done so much to create.

The outbreak of World War I brought the end of an era. It cut
Rufus Jones's life into two distinct parts.

It is difficult for generations that have come to maturity since 1914
to realize fully the impact of horror and betrayal which the war made
upon people's minds. A few here and there, it is true, had seen it coming, had realized that, as Rufus Jones wrote, "Beneath all overt acts
and decisions the immense subconscious forces, charged with emotion,
have been slowly pushing toward this event." To most people, however, the world had entered upon a period of inevitable upward
progress and war had been relegated to a dark age of barbarism now
happily past. The only enemies to be slain were poverty and ignorance.
Germany was an enlightened and cultured country immensely to be
admired and so far as possible imitated. The disillusion that resulted
when the German divisions rolled over Belgium and the treaty of
friendship was tossed aside as a "scrap of paper," was swift and bitter.
Not only the goodness of God became a matter for agonizing question
but the very possibility of His existence in a world such as this had
demonstrated itself to be. Theories of the upward march of humanity
were seen as false and flimsy in the lurid light of man's capacity for
evil.

To Rufus Jones the war was not so much of a surprise as it was to
many. He had heard Herr Happich talk in Germany and had listened
to discussions among young Friends in England in 1911. It was nevertheless a shock—a "terrific jolt" he called it in THE TRAIL OF LIFE IN
THE MIDDLE YEARS—and a deep sorrow. The optimism, both innate and
resolute, with which he faced life kept him from despair. "We must
not let our cable slip in this storm," he wrote in *Present Day Papers*.
"The supreme faiths of humanity have always had their births and
their baptisms in baffling mysteries and in the deeps of tragedy and

suffering." He was nevertheless like a man who has received a severe blow and for a time walks on without knowing the gravity of his injury.

The problems that the war brought to English Friends, the poignant and thorny dilemmas of the pacifist whose loyalty is torn between love of country and obedience to his intuition of the will of God, troubled him deeply and he longed to find some way to share and help. He wrote to Violet Hodgkin, "I have intensely wished that I might make some contribution of my life in this hour of need, but I do not yet see anything definite opening for me to do. Perhaps something will come."

What came first, however, was not an opening but a closing, a terminus such as he had encountered in the Engelberg Valley.

Low Gear

THE twenty-fourth of December, 1914, was cold and glittery in Haverford, with a thin coating of snow over ice. Ten-year-old Mary and her friend and next-door neighbor, Anna Pratt, ran to meet Rufus Jones on his way to the station. "See my new cap!" cried Anna. As he turned to look, his foot slipped from under him and he fell heavily.

The injury was diagnosed as concussion of the brain. He was out of bed again—no doubt too soon—when classes began, but the severe headaches continued. When the period of mid-year examinations came he was ordered off to Nassau for a rest.

He went alone, possibly for financial reasons, possibly because Elizabeth Jones did not want either to leave Mary behind or to take her out of school, but probably because nobody realized the seriousness of his condition. There was also the problem of *Present Day Papers*, which must go to press as usual. "I feel that I am running away to Tarshish and leaving many problems for thee and Henry to wrestle with," he wrote to Elizabeth.

It was a wretched voyage. The ship encountered one of the worst hurricanes in years and there was for some hours a question of its survival. He spent sixty hours in his berth, prostrated by headache and nausea.

He did not feel much better at Nassau. He had one swim, but after he discovered that sea-bathing made his head worse he gave it up and found his entertainment in long discussions on mysticism with a

Catholic priest. The weather continued bad and the least exertion made his head ache.

After a dreary week he left Nassau and went to Miami, where he stayed at a modest hotel. On the last day he went to Palm Beach to take a look at the Royal Poinciana, pausing in the lobby to write a letter home: "Here I am at the mecca of all fashion and social ambition. I am not however living in this superb hotel; I am only going through it as a spectator." Having written a second note, to President Sharpless, he was on his way to post his letters when he encountered Isaac Sharpless himself, almost hidden behind the *Philadelphia Record*, with which he was trying to assuage his boredom. They fell into each other's arms and spent the rest of the day together in the kind of deeply satisfying talk for which busy men, even though they are colleagues, seldom have leisure or opportunity.

His head was still hurting when he turned homeward, finding the jolting of the train almost as painful as the tossing of the ship had been, but he wrote hopefully from St. Augustine, "I believe however, that I can run on low gear pretty well when I get back."

It was not easy, however, and at the end of March he felt that improvement, if there was any, was too slow to be noted. "I am still laid aside," he wrote to Violet Hodgkin, "and must for a long time yet sit and wait."

He persisted in meeting his classes, though with difficulty. With Henry Cadbury's assistance he kept *Present Day Papers* going and his editorials were full of hope and insight. But he could not speak in Meeting or fill any outside engagements. The news of the sinking of the *Lusitania* in May struck horror into his soul and gave him "a bad set-back."

"It began to look," writes his daughter, "as if the cloud would never lift."

Toward the end of June he went to the popular Battle Creek Sanatorium for a thorough going-over. He wrote home with rueful humor about the course of "fad" food, electric heat, hot applications, ice-rubs, stomach pumps and X-rays which he endured. "It is an odd place," he commented, and added characteristically, "I quite enjoy the people . . . The Kaffir tea is made of herbs and is just not worse than the minute-brew postum!" Between treatments he played golf.

Ten days of tests revealed nothing more serious than fatigue from over-work. A summer's rest, he was assured, should put him in perfect health.

"Nervous breakdown" was the approved blanket word then current to cover a combination of physical and emotional troubles.
Certainly there was a long history of over-work: the books he wrote,
the lectures he delivered, the incessant, uncomfortable traveling, the
nagging pressure of weekly editorials to be written wherever he was,
in addition to a full schedule of college teaching. There had been also
a previous history of symptoms that would now be considered psycho-
somatic: digestive disturbances, asthma, hay fever, insomnia, depression. Unconsciously, perhaps, he had felt confined by the pattern
of his work, frustrated by the pettiness of much of the criticism he
had met. His impatience with thinking and talking and writing and
his desire to be *being* and *doing*, which he considered two halves of a
single spiritual reality, suggested that he felt the ache of unused potentialities. There can be no doubt, moreover, that the tide of grief
arising from the war tinctured with bitter brine the springs of all
his energies and purposes. The fact that he could continue teaching
and writing but was unable to bring himself to speak in Meeting
or in other religious gatherings implies an emotional block.

Whatever the physical or emotional causes of his condition, it is
evident that this man who has been to whole generations the embodiment of optimism, radiant serenity and unbounded energy, did not
achieve these gifts without enduring deadly discouragements and
dismaying loss of power. To "win and practice an optimistic temper
of mind" was, he declared, one of the real, even if modest, contributions which the children of light might make to the spiritual stock
of the world, but it did not come without effort.

Throughout these troubled months he had the selfless devotion and
support of his wife. Their daughter writes, "Patiently, lovingly, his
dear Elizabeth coped with this visitation. Never hurried, never cross,
she went ahead, trying to minister to the varied needs of a sick
husband and a growing, often fretful child, endeavoring to be all
things to two very different individuals."

The upturn began when they went in July to Southwest Harbor
on Mt. Desert Island off the coast of Maine, where they stayed at
a rambling frame inn with oil lamps in the simple rooms. It was cold
and foggy when they arrived, and Rufus Jones, with his gift for
seeing analogies between the outer event and the inner state, found
an application to his own condition. One of his editorials in *Present
Day Papers* reveals the struggle that was taking place within him.

"Unusual outside weather is only one of our many means of discipline." (He had come a long way since he wrote to Sallie, "The weather molds me like wax," but still he found small joy in gray or rainy days.) "Much harder is the fight with inside weather and more dreary and pitiless are the fogs and east winds of our human spirits . . . The fight with stubborn inward weather, the battle with the devil in us, if you will, is the best kind of fighting there is to be done, and he who has conquered conditions of inner climate has now the best victories which crown men. Not least . . . [is] . . . the further discovery—joyous like that of Columbus sighting a new world—that there are inexhaustible resources of divine grace for those who are resolved to rise above the fog and mist, the sleet and snow of dreary inward weather."

Violet Hodgkin, who herself had known long illness, wrote encouragingly to him, and her image of the starfish was to delight him for many a year. "Isn't it strange how one has to learn to lie like a starfish on the beach high and dry and cut off from all renewing while the tide rises and falls *just out of reach*. That's the most tantalizing part. And then at last, at long last, in 'Gotteszeit' the real spring tide comes and floats even one's tired out starfish of a body out into the full flood of life again. Only those who know the deadly weariness of the beach can quite understand the living joy of the ocean when we get back to it once more."

Perhaps most of all a chance meeting helped him. A schoolmaster from Connecticut staying at the same inn, occupied himself by clearing trails for climbers on the wooded slopes of nearby mountains. The boy who had helped his father to chop down trees in the Maine woods awoke in Rufus Jones; he provided himself with an axe, and he went out with his new friend.

"I have had the rare good fortune to meet during my holidays this summer a real trail-maker . . . He has been taking me along as a companion of his walks and as a helper in the work . . . What we are finding is that any old trail needs a good deal of restoration work done on it . . . and must be remarked so that the wayfarer cannot miss the trail." He drew the analogy between the old forest fires in the mountains healed over by nature, and the blasting fires of war, then moving across the world. "As soon as *life* gets a chance to work again it will in its own way repair the damage and havoc . . . What will be needed most will be the trail-makers, with solid cairns and clear-pointing arrows, to help the souls of men to discover the true way of life and the real sources of spiritual power."

Before the summer was over, his new strength was put to the test. Dr. Francis G. Peabody, his old friend at Harvard, who spent his summers at Northeast Harbor, across Somes Sound, urged him to come and preach one Sunday to the Union Church there. After Rufus Jones had accepted he felt it was an ordeal which he could hardly face. Before the Sunday came he got a rowboat and he rowed Elizabeth Jones and Mary across the Sound to Northeast Harbor to see the church, to try his voice, and to estimate how many people would be there. That night, sick with dread, he could not sleep at all. Afterwards he could not remember how he got there on Sunday morning; he only knew that he preached the sermon, that his voice was clear, and that people were appreciative. He knew also that it marked the end of his illness.

After church the Joneses went to the Peabodys' house for dinner, and so was inaugurated a long and happy association with Northeast Harbor. Summer after summer he went there to preach, missing not more than two or three out of more than thirty. In later years he preached also at the Congregational church in Seal Harbor and visited John D. Rockefeller, Jr., at the Eyrie high above the water.

September in Haverford was muggy and hot, the opening days of college strenuous. "I thought when I came back a month ago," he wrote to Violet Hodgkin, "that I had returned a new man and that, to use thy phrase, the full tide was floating the dry old starfish off the beach for good and all. But I have not stood the test of work very well and find myself pretty flat again." But he added with the old zest, "My classes are splendid this year and I am greatly enjoying my work with the men."

After the stay in Mt. Desert the Joneses had spent a short time in South China, as they had done occasionally in previous summers. Earlier Rufus Jones had built two or three simple cottages on the lake to rent to friends. Now he was able to buy the land that he wanted on the hill top overlooking the lake and adjoining Pine Rock, where his beloved cousins Richard and Virginia Jones, "Cousin Genie," spent their summers, and he decided to build a summer home for himself and his family. In preparation he went to South China at Christmas time and spent his vacation in the snowy woods, chopping down the trees with which the cottage was to be built, drawing up plans so that the local builder could have their house ready for them when they came the following summer. He named it Pendle Hill, after the place of George Fox's vision.

Like Antaeus, who sprang up with renewed energy from contact with the earth, Rufus Jones found that the touch with his native soil and the long strenuous hours under the northern sky restored both body and spirit. Complete health did not come at once, but when the years of his life were finished and the trail could be seen in its entirety, these difficult and apparently barren months were revealed as a sort of watershed, from which new and greater streams flowed.

"A Service of Love in War Time"

"THE alternative to war is not inactivity and cowardice. It is the irresistible and constructive power of good will." These words were part of a "Message from the Society of Friends" which was printed as an advertisement in leading American newspapers and magazines in March, 1917. It was signed by a body called the Friends National Peace Committee, which represented Quakers of all shades of thought.

In the spirit and intention of this statement Friends met the entrance of the United States into the war on April 6, 1917. Among individual Quakers there would be every possible variation of interpretation of duty, from those whose conscience led them into the trenches to those who felt they could not cooperate with the military system even to the extent of reporting to the camp where they might establish their position as conscientious objectors. Many, although not the majority, took the position that they could not engage in military service but desired instead to do some useful work under civilian control through which the irresistible power of good will might operate against war itself. To find activities which would fulfil this purpose and which would be accepted by the government as an alternative to military service became the immediate and pressing concern of leading Friends.

Rufus Jones went to work at once. Close to English Friends as he was, he had watched with sympathy and admiration the solutions to the same problem which they had found during the past three years.

His old friend, Sir George Newman, was chairman of the committee of the Friends Ambulance Unit, in which young men who would not fight were working under fire to bring the wounded from the battlefields. In 1915, in the midst of his illness Rufus Jones had arranged to send four American Friends, one of whom was Felix Morley, later to become President of Haverford, to join this Unit and had raised the money for their expenses. English Friends had also revived the War Victims Relief Committee of 1870, which had done relief work in France in the Franco-Prussian War. Since November 1914 a mission of British Friends under this Committee, one of the officers of which was T. Edmund Harvey, had been working in France, chiefly in the valley of the Upper Marne.

Four days after America entered the war Rufus Jones, with the assistance of Dr. James F. Babbitt, organized an Emergency Unit at Haverford College, to provide the students with a course of physical hardening and a training in mechanical and agricultural skills which should be useful in any kind of volunteer work that might be found for them to do. It was primarily a stop-gap, "to keep the men from rushing into something else of which we disapproved," as Rufus Jones admitted to Violet Hodgkin, but he quickly set about to find ways of putting the Unit to real service.

His first idea of sending young Americans to work with British Friends foundered on the difficulties of obtaining permits from the War Office in London. His next plan, of an American Friends Ambulance Unit, dried up when he learned that our ambulance work would not be under the Red Cross as it was in England but would be part of the military system. He then thought that an American Quaker unit for Relief Work in France, on the lines of the mission under the War Victims Relief Committee and in cooperation with it, might be formed.

The American Red Cross was in the process of being reorganized, and when it was made public that Grayson Mallet-Prevost Murphy had been appointed Chief of the American Red Cross in Paris, Rufus Jones moved swiftly. Grayson Murphy was a graduate of the Penn Charter School in Philadelphia and had been for two years, 1896-1898, a student at Haverford. Rufus Jones had known him well and felt sure of a sympathetic response when he wrote to him about his plan for a Friends Unit. Major Murphy, still in Washington, promptly invited him to come and talk the matter over.

Meanwhile, on the 30th of April a group of twelve Friends, both

men and women, representing the two Philadelphia yearly meetings
and the Five Years Meeting, met in Philadelphia to attack the same
problem. They set forth their purpose and attitude in the following
minute:

"We are united in expressing our love for our country and our desire
to serve her loyally. We offer our services to the Government of the
United States in any constructive work in which we can con-
scientiously serve humanity."

At that first meeting they decided to enlarge their membership, to
arrange for permanent headquarters and to explore avenues of service.
They appointed a temporary chairman. At their second meeting they
decided to ask Rufus Jones and Henry Cadbury to join their de-
liberations.

When Rufus Jones went to Washington early in May to confer
with Grayson Murphy and Henry P. Davison of New York, who had
been appointed chief of all the foreign relief work of the Red Cross,
he took four members of this committee with him. The upshot of this
meeting and a later one in New York was that Rufus Jones's plan for
a Friends Unit for Relief Work in France, under the civilian service of
the Red Cross, was approved, and a small commission of Friends was
asked to go to Paris at once to make definite arrangements on the
scene.

By the time the Committee met on June fourth, it had adopted the
name which was to become known the world over, the American
Friends Service Committee, and it had acquired the address which was
to be almost as famous: Twenty South Twelfth Street, Philadelphia.

Next door to Penn Charter School, which at that time had not yet
moved out to Germantown, stood the old Twelfth Street Meeting
House, where Rufus Jones had first attended meeting in 1882 and
where he had been married in 1902. Built of traditional red brick with
white trimmings and two neat white portices, it sat peacefully in its
old-fashioned yard, surrounded by the bulky banks and department
stores which the city had thrown up around it in the century of its
existence. One change had been made in 1892: an organization called
the Friends Institute had built a wing at the side, with a lounge and
club rooms for Friends who had no suitable place in the city to spend
their time. The Friends Institute made one of their six rooms available
to the newly formed American Friends Service Committee—and the
camel put his head into the tent. Before the first summer was over,
that small office room downstairs was outgrown and two rooms up-

stairs, known as the East and West Rooms, were lost to the Friends Institute. In time the Meeting House itself yielded up its second story and still there was an overflow to wash into the nearby Commonwealth Trust Building.

But on that early June day in 1917 the name and the address no doubt seemed the least important of the things accomplished. Two Friends had already sailed for France with a big contingent of the Red Cross. They were Morris E. Leeds, President of Leeds and Northrup, one of the largest of the Quaker business firms in Philadelphia, and J. Henry Scattergood, a colleague of Rufus Jones on the Bryn Mawr Board. Four young women, to whom two more would later be added, had been appointed to go to Russia to join British Friends who were working with refugees from Poland in the Samara district. Seven Friends, four men and three women, had been offered to the War Victims Relief Committee for work in France and had been accepted. It had been decided to begin to train a hundred workers at Haverford as soon as possible after Commencement, and a committee consisting of Rufus Jones, Henry Cadbury and Vincent Nicholson had been appointed to decide on applicants and organize the training. An important policy decision had been made: the Committee woud pay the expenses of the workers abroad but no salaries. The only salaries would be those of the Executive Secretary and such clerical assistance as he needed. Vincent D. Nicholson had been appointed Executive Secretary.

All these things had been done in previous meetings. On June fourth the budget, which had been tentatively set at $110,000 for work abroad, $5,000 for office expense, was increased to $200,000 for work abroad. The most important action that the Committee took that day was to ask Rufus Jones to serve as its Chairman.

He did not accept immediately, but took a week to consider. His health was still not good, he carried a full schedule at Haverford, he was engaged in writing the weighty final volume of the Quaker history. They assured him that it would not take much of his time, just the lending of counsel and the presiding over meetings, which would be less frequent as the work got under way. He would have liked to think it was as simple as that, but at bottom he knew it must be otherwise, though he did not guess—how could he?—that for the next thirty years there would be scarcely a day in which, first as chairman and then as honorary chairman, he was not somehow involved in its activities, faced with a sudden trip, an important decision, a delicate piece of negotiation, emergencies of every description, and endless speakng and writing on its behalf. Perhaps the least time-consuming of all was the monthly meeting of the Executive Board, of which Mary Hoxie Jones writes:

"He was an excellent chairman of a meeting, bringing in just the right touch of humor at the right moment, easing tensions and guiding discussions so that the important issues were dealt with adequately. He could go through a long difficult agenda and bring the meeting to a close at the proper time."

The Emergency Unit which he and Dr. Babbitt had organized early in April had scattered to the four winds at Commencement, though some of them returned on July 17th to enroll in what became known as the Haverford Reconstruction Unit #1. There were many applications for membership in this unit. In the final choice of the hundred men considered the best available, almost all sections of the Society of Friends were represented and a small number of non-Friends who were sympathetic to Quaker ideals were included.

For a six-week period of training they were housed in Barclay Hall and went to Chase Hall for morning and evening classes in French language and history, world conditions and social service. The French course was planned and directed by William Wistar Comfort, who had recently been appointed president of the college on Isaac Sharpless's retirement. During the afternoons the men were given instruction in carpentry and masonry, road-building, mechanics and agriculture, and had regular periods of physical exercise. Every day included a half-hour worship period.

Rufus Jones, who had taken his family to their "precious retreat" in South China, himself spent much of that summer on the night train between Maine and Washington or Philadelphia. He was often at Haverford to see how things were going and to mingle with the men. The first morning he was on hand to start them off with a talk on the spirit of Quaker service.

"I had breakfast with the men this morning at 6:30," he wrote to his wife, "and I gave them an address at 7:30 on the deeper purposes of the unit. It was an interesting occasion. This was the first united *exercise* since the unit met. They rose splendid[ly] to my talk and seemed to catch the vision which I tried to give them."

The training of the Unit was a bold act of faith. For a time the expected opportunity for service in France seemed to be evading them. Only a few days before the actual opening of the Unit, when

Elizabeth B. Cadbury at the time
of her engagement to Rufus Jones

←

Rufus Jones in his study in Haverford

Elizabeth, Mary Hoxie and Rufus Jones in March, 1909, at 2 College Circle

Mary Hoxie Jones in 1943

Rufus and Elizabeth Jones at South China in 1947, with China Lake in the background

Rufus Jones talking to students on his front porch in Haverford

the men had been selected and all arrangements made, word came from the two commissioners in France that all Red Cross work was likely to be militarized and that there appeared to be no place after all for a Quaker civilian service. The decision to go ahead and prepare a group for opportunity when and if it should arise was one of the crucial decisions of the summer.

Gradually the commissioners developed a plan. The work done by English Friends offered an impressive demonstration of the quality and extent of Quaker service. The English group generously offered to take American Friends into their projects on the same standing as their own, with equal representation on the executive committee. A "triangular merger" was projected, by which English and American Friends were to unite in the "Anglo-American Mission of the Society of Friends"—affectionately known to the workers as the "Mish"—and the Americans were to be also under the auspices of the American Red Cross Commission, which was *not* militarized. The Red Cross would supply the permits and passes so difficult to get in war-time France, as well as agricultural equipment, motor vehicles and 533,000 francs.

Morris E. Leeds returned on August 24th to report the final decisions, while J. Henry Scattergood stayed on a few weeks longer in Paris to welcome the Unit when they should arrive. Four days later the first fourteen men sailed for France, to be followed by the rest in three or four installments as clearance was finished with their draft boards or as space on the crowded ships became available. Four women who had been recruited by the sub-committee for women's service sailed on the 15th of September. All the workers wore the gray uniform designed and worn by English Friends, and in November the American Friends Service Committee adopted as its official emblem the eight-pointed red and black star first used by the War Victims Relief Committee of 1870.

Problems of the draft had arisen early. The Selective Service Act of 1917 exempted members of the historic peace churches from military service but not from non-combatant service, by which was meant service in the medical, commissary, quartermaster and similar departments of the army. Conscientious objectors, when drafted, were obliged to go to a mobilization camp and there establish their right to exemption. To many this sort of non-combatant service was even worse than fighting, for it implied a desire to avoid the risks of war rather than a rooted objection to war itself. Rufus Jones and other members of the A.F.S.C. made many trips to Washington to interview Secretary of War Baker and his assistants in the effort to get voluntary civilian work in France accepted as an alternative to non-combatant military service. President Wilson, while postponing the setting of a definite policy for conscientious objectors, wrote a letter to Rufus Jones in which he gave a useful measure of approval to the Committee's plans.

"In the meantime," he concluded, "I am sure you will permit me to express deep appreciation of the reconstruction work proposed and my happiness that it is being carried out in association with the Red Cross which is already doing a great work in France to express the heart of America."

A number of the members of the Haverford Unit were drawn in the first draft, and the A.F.S.C., while waiting for the slow government wheels to grind out a general ruling, went to work on individual cases. The District Boards had considerable discretion at that time and could issue permits for members of the Unit to leave the country. They were overwhelmed with work, they had quotas to fill, and they found conscientious objectors a troublesome set of people in any case. Decisions were slow in coming, but in the end all but one of the Haverford hundred got off in September.

Later, when the second American unit was on its way and the Red Cross was clamoring for still more Quaker workers, a system was worked out by which the men were "furloughed" from the army to do farm work at home or to serve abroad under the A.F.S.C. For the men who were waiting for their furloughs or their passports to come through, the Committee rented a large fruit farm near Kennett Square, where training continued and a good deal of useful work was done for the community during the waiting period.

"It looks often to the outside observer that A.F.S.C. affairs run so smoothly," Rufus Jones was to write years later in retrospect, "that he has little comprehension of the stress and strain and the patience that are called for behind the scenes. But as a matter of fact every step is beset with difficulties, handicaps, impossibilities, what Hegel called *Die Ohnmacht des Natur*—the innate cussedness of things. Nothing can be accomplished without endless journeys to Washington, New York."

When the Haverford Unit reached France, 145 English Friends, men and women, all volunteers serving without pay, were working in hospitals which they had established, bringing relief to refugees, putting up portable houses in devastated villages, supplying tools and seeds and manpower to help farmers get started again. Each center of work was an almost self-governing unit called an *équipe* with a chief elected by the workers. All was coordinated by a committee in Paris.

The Americans as they arrived were distributed among the various *équipes* in greater or smaller numbers according to needs and abilities. Some went to Dôle and Ornans to build portable wooden houses, others to Sermaize, where many of the houses were set up and where also the English committee maintained a hospital and a district nursing center. In this hospital Dr. Babbitt was to perform more than a thousand operations during the year and a half that he was there. The maternity hospital at Châlons-sur-Marne was the largest of several hospitals for which the group was responsible.

The need was enormous and the Quaker workers turned their hands to everything, from organizing big projects of rebuilding and relief to trying to infuse French peasants with a spirit of cooperation or to teaching a small child the lost art of play. They gave lavishly of their strength, counted no task too menial, put up with uncomfortable quarters and monotonous food. "I slept on a pile of straw by the side of a bed in which six children slept feet to feet, while around me fifteen other little ones slumbered on mattresses and cots," a woman worker described the evacuation of children from Bar-le-Duc in October, 1917. "For the first two days we had to do all the cooking, as the woman who was sent to help us sat in our one arm chair with her feet on the stove and refused to work. It is some job to cook enough food to stuff forty-one young huskies." Altogether, work was done in four main categories, medical, agricultural, relief, and building and reconstruction.

The second unit worked at first directly under the Red Cross, building hospitals, assisting in the relief of prisoners, helping to care for cases of war-induced insanity, and so on. After the signing of the Armistice and the closing of the work of the Red Cross they became part of the Anglo-American Friends Mission. The total number of Americans working under the A.F.S.C. in France grew to six hundred, of whom about five hundred and fifty were men and about fifty were women.

The triangular merger worked out satisfactorily in spite of the obvious difficulties. In the headquarters in Paris, where the directors, both English and American, were mature and able people successful in their life work, conflicts could be handled objectively and policies adjusted to needs. In the *équipes,* where personalities rubbed and clashed in the daily round, it was more difficult.

There is in the A.F.S.C. files a calm and genial report on the points of irritation by Wilfred Shewell, a member of the English Committee. After referring to "differences of language, training, outlook and sense of humor" he went on to point out that the English Friends had been there three years, that they were pacifists who had established their pacifism in searching examinations before military tribunals. Many of them were war-weary, some "even in their own country would be considered cranks." The Americans on the other hand were chiefly college boys between the ages of eighteen and twenty-three, whose pacifism had been won (or so the English thought) by "a stroke of the presidential pen." Their "cheery irresponsibility" was very trying to the English, whose "dogged reserve" was in turn chilling to them. The English had a plainer standard of living than the Americans, who had come from a land of comfort and plenty. The energetic Americans wanted to get things done quickly and see results. They resented the more experienced English workers as "task-masters."

There is no such analysis from the American viewpoint, but any of the Americans who were in France in 1917-18 will now chuckle reminiscently and tell an illustrative anecdote or two. All will agree, however, with Wilfred Shewell's summing up:

"Months of cooperation in work brought about not only understanding and tolerance but a true appreciation of the qualities of both sides . . . The close of the war found a completely unified group."

To this unity Rufus Jones made his own characteristic contribution.

As early as January 1918 word came to the Committee in Philadelphia that there was some strain between the two groups in France and Rufus Jones was encouraged to write a letter to the American unit. "Those of you who were at Haverford last summer," he wrote, "where our common fellowship was of the happiest sort, will remember how often I used to remind you that our reconstruction work must be a spiritual service as well as a manly effort to rebuild and repair what has been devastated and laid waste. You cannot do your full service to France unless you can help restore and refresh the spirit of those who have unspeakably suffered, and exhibit in your lives and in your words and in your work an underlying faith in eternal realities." Nothing at all about being nice to their English co-workers, just the pointing to the task itself and the spirit in which it was to be done. When you want to change attitudes, he had long ago found, you do not say so directly but set about attaining some goal that will arouse group loyalty and create teamwork.

A little over a month after the Armistice was signed, he left his college work in the hands of Dr. Theodore de Laguna of Bryn Mawr and with Henry Scattergood he made a swift trip to France, sailing on the *Chicago,* which was full of relief workers of all kinds and a large number of Polish officers and soldiers. Norman Angell, William Allen White, whom Rufus Jones found "delightful, like a great, happy boy," and "many other good and interesting people" were also on board.

Norman Angell wrote of the trip in his autobiography: "The end of the war found me in America. I left almost immediately for Paris, traveling to Bordeaux in a rat-infested ship with Henry Scattergood ... With him was Rufus Jones, 'the Quaker saint'—a title I am sure he disliked, for his saintliness had nothing of the dehumanized quality we commonly associate with saints. Both were an honor to the Society of Friends."

The crossing was a rough one and the ship did not reach Bordeaux till after Christmas. Rufus Jones and Henry Scattergood were welcomed in Paris by Charles and Lillie Rhoads, who since the previous September had been heads of the American Unit. From the beginning it was characteristic of the A.F.S.C. that at its call mature and successful Friends laid aside their business or professions to go and serve, without pay, for six months, a year, sometimes two years, where they were needed. It has given the work of the Committee extraordinarily able leadership as well as continual fresh insights and varied talents.

The first thing that Rufus Jones did in Paris was to seek out a well-known nose and throat specialist and have several polyps removed from his nose. The operation was performed with a local anesthetic in the doctor's office. Immediately afterwards he rose up and went home with the Rhoadses for one night's coddling. Two days later, his nose still swollen and painful, he sat up on a train all night long on his way to visit the *équipe* at Dôle in the Jura.

The next weeks were full of traveling, of speaking, and of strenuous manual labor. Following his concern to see for himself the morale of the workers and the effect of the experience on their lives, he visited all but two of the *équipes* and talked with almost every member of the Mission, both English and American. He put on overalls and hammered or dug or pushed wheelbarrows by their side. He made speeches almost daily. "I am supposed to be loaded for every occasion," he wrote to Elizabeth Jones. He was pleased with what he found: the evidence of increasing maturity and depth, the absence of self-preoccupation, the seriousness of purpose. It is evident that wherever he went he spread the contagion of his own good humor, his vision, his willingness to give himself.

By the beginning of the second semester at Haverford, he was at home again, disappointed that he had not been able to go to London to see his friends there but satisfied that "the spirit of the Mish" was in good case.

As the first phase of Quaker service was drawing to its close, Isaac Sharpless urged Rufus Jones to write the history of the work in France. After demurring that he was too busy and getting the bracing answer that "a man can always do more than he is doing," Rufus Jones went to work in October, 1919. He finished the book on the last day of the year, but before it was published Isaac Sharpless, that old friend who had been an influence and guide since he first came to Haverford as a country boy in a Prince Albert coat, was dead. He dedicated his book to the memory of "one of the truest, best, and most loved men I have ever known."

The title which he gave to his history was one of the best in a long list of good titles: A SERVICE OF LOVE IN WAR TIME. The power of love, not the accomplishments of individuals or even of a Society, was the theme of the book. "It is written solely to interpret a spirit and a way of life, to convey, if possible, the truth that love will work everywhere and always—*semper et ubique*—even with enemies, vastly better than the way of hate works." He summed up what had been accomplished. Aid had been given to 1666 French villages and to over 46,000 families. 25,000 trees, mostly fruit, had been planted in the Verdun area. Many of the workers were coming home. The French were deeply appreciative, recognizing the gift of friendship and of hope which gave meaning to the material aid.

Though the work in France was finished, new needs were summoning the Friends to other countries. A small group, which included Andrew W. Pearson of Swarthmore, now better known as Drew Pearson, was in Serbia building houses and providing for orphans. American and English Friends together were fighting typhus in Poland and taking milch cows and coal to cold and rickety children in Vienna. The most daring and the most extensive work that the A.F.S.C. ever did, the feeding of a million German children, was in preparation.

The A.F.S.C. no longer belonged solely to Friends. In the autumn of 1918 people outside the Society of Friends began to take an interest in the work and to contribute generously. Among the workers the numbers of those who were not Friends, of members of the Fellowship of Reconciliation, Mennonites and Brethren, pacifists of all kinds, earnest young people from a variety of churches, grew larger over the years.

In addition to what it did for needy people abroad, the A.F.S.C. enormously benefited the Society of Friends itself. Touched by human suffering, all varieties of Friends had worked together and had found a new unity in their common concern. Sewing committees in local meetings drew stay-at-home members into a direct relationship of love and need and work. The Friends papers published Service Committee news instead of articles on theological problems.

Rufus Jones found his own life flooded with new energy and strength. "As I look back over the years during which I have carried the load," he wrote to Violet Hodgkin, "I am inclined to think it the most important thing I have done . . . God has been very good to me and in spite of the fact that this has been the heaviest winter's work I have ever done, I am in the best health I ever can remember to have had. I do not understand where the energy comes from."

Herbert Hoover and Friend Jones

T HE full story of the American Friends Service Committee has been told elsewhere and told, as it should be, with the emphasis on the workers, the work they did and the spirit in which they did it. It could scarcely have been the unique service that it was, however, if the Chairman of the Committee in those formative years had not been the man that he was. Rufus Jones saw always the human faces beyond the deadly statistics of need and he had the gift of making them vivid both to the workers and to the public to whom he appealed for support. He had also a clear vision of the spiritual revitalization which could accompany the bread that is shared in love.

What has not been told is the constant negotiation behind the scenes, the continuing interplay of personal relations in the realm of policy decisions, that required his particular combination of vigorous honesty, good will, vision and courage. Much was done, of course, by the Executive Secretary and by members of the Board, but it was Rufus Jones who in the pinch stepped in and clarified confused situations. After Vincent Nicholson was drafted in 1918 and his furlough delayed, Wilbur K. Thomas, former pastor of the Friends Meeting at Roxbury, Massachusetts, an able, tireless and devoted worker, became secretary and held the post until 1929.

When the armistice had been signed and the work in France was drawing toward its close, there was some thought that the Service Committee's purpose had been fulfilled and that it should be disbanded.

Human suffering, however, did not stop with the silence of the guns, and new demands and new opportunities cried out insistently for the kind of service that Friends had learned to give.

The work that opened up in Germany and Russia after the closing of the work in France offered new problems. The needs were so gigantic that private resources could not cope with them and government help had to be accepted, with the new and sometimes disturbing factors that government brings into any situation.

Throughout this period the man with whom the Committee worked closely was Herbert Hoover.

Not quite eleven years younger than Rufus Jones, Herbert Hoover came out of a similar background. He was born in a farming community in the little village of West Branch, Iowa, of Quaker parents. His father was a blacksmith and his mother a recorded minister, well thought of in the community. Though they both died when he was small and his work as a mining engineer took him into the far corners of the world, he carried with him always certain fundamental Quaker ideals. After the outbreak of the first World War he poured his time and strength and fortune into the alleviation of human suffering, serving the public welfare without salary.

From the beginning of the war in 1914 he had carried on the relief of ten million people in Belgium and nothern France under the auspices of the neutral ambassadors in Europe. With the Armistice in 1918 he was appointed by the Allied governments the Director of Relief and Reconstruction of Europe. This required organization in over thirty countries and was a mammoth undertaking. To manage the American part of this burden he established under congressional authority the American Relief Administration. Drawing on his experience in Belgium, he introduced the system of canteen special feeding of under-nourished children and by the time the treaty was signed in July 1919 over ten million children had been fed. With the signing of the treaty Mr. Hoover brought official action in European relief to an end by transferring his staff to the "voluntary" American Relief Administration to care for about three million debilitated children for a further year.

Herbert Hoover and Rufus Jones had obviously much in common. The friendship that developed was a real and lasting one, based on mutual understanding and respect, but it was not won without strain. In the long series of letters between them, Herbert Hoover's salutations reveal the ups and downs in their relationship. "Friend Jones:"

begins the earliest, in old-fashioned formal Quaker usage. He soon changed to the more comfortable "My dear Mr. Jones," which became his custom for ordinary use. By the 1930's, however, it had become "My dear friend" and finally, "Dear Rufus."

The A.F.S.C. was interested in taking relief to Germany even before Mr. Hoover appeared on its horizon. In October, 1918, Carolena Wood had written to Wilbur Thomas expressing her desire to work in that country under the Committee, and by May, 1919, she was on her way. She went first to France, where she visted the Mission while she waited for the signing of the Peace Treaty. There she met and talked with the head of the American Relief Administration.

"Mr. Hoover . . . seems to have entered wonderfully into the spirit of my concern," she wrote, "and to feel that it is possible thus to meet one of the needs of the hour . . . Hoover will let us use his passports and sell us all the food we can buy."

"We may count food values in calories," he said to her at that time, "but we have no way to measure human misery."

As a matter of fact, Mr. Hoover had already organized a program of relief to Germany. For four months after the Armistice and in violation of a provision in the Armistice agreement of November 11, 1918, the Allied governments had continued the blockade of Germany, against the constant protests of Mr. Hoover and the American Peace Delegation. In March 1919 when the blockade was lifted, Mr. Hoover was hampered in organzing rehabilitation of the Germans by a provision of American law that no government funds should be used for enemy relief. He did, nevertheless, succeed in sending food to Germany which the Germans paid for in gold. The German government conducted its own distribution and on this basis continued until September 1, 1919.

The Peace Treaty was signed on the 28th of June and on the 7th of July Carolena Wood reached Berlin with three others, one of whom was Jane Addams. Jane Addams had declared that the A.F.S.C. work was the best she had seen and that she wanted to go into Germany to represent its spirit and point of view. These women had $30,000 to spend on food and twenty-five tons of clothing to distribute—only a token but still something to show the practical nature of their good will.

Four English Friends had preceded them to Germany by a single day and it was assumed that English and American Friends would work together in Germany as they had done in France.

At the end of September Carolena Wood and Jane Addams returned to Philadelphia to report to the Executive Board of the A.F.S.C., which promptly decided to send workers into Germany.

Mr. Hoover, looking back nearly thirty years later, says that his arrangement with the German government during the period from March to August 1919 was the best that could be made at that time. It was not as efficient as a charitable system of canteens producing an extra meal a day for children independent of government control, such as the American Relief Administration had installed in the other famine countries, and there was considerable undernourishment among the German children. He was able to get funds for this purpose, but he needed more staff. He decided therefore to ask the American Friends Service Committee not only to manage the program in Germany but also to raise as much money as they could for the work.

On November 1, 1919, he sent the following letter to Rufus Jones:

November 1st 1919

Friend Jones:

This is to follow up my conversation Thursday with yourself and the members of your committee in respect to the relief work on behalf of the children suffering from subnormality due to the continued undernourishment in Germany.

As you are aware, the organization under my direction last winter in Europe undertook the feeding of sub-normal children throughout Eastern and Central Europe as a part of its relief functions and we are endeavoring to carry on this service, involving about three million children in the newly established democracies over the forthcoming winter, and to do so from funds provided by charity of citizens of their descent in the United States, together with funds provided by the various governments concerned.

We have not yet organized such a service for Germany. Your committee has been for some months in service in this particular and I have some funds remaining from the operations of last winter under the Supreme Economic Council, which funds are available to this purpose. I have been approached by various societies in the United States, comprising citizens of German descent, who are anxious to be of some service in this matter. I, therefore, would be very glad to know if your society would be willing to undertake the expansion of your activities to the extent of becoming the repository of any funds which may be subscribed for this purpose in the United States, and to the extent of increasing your personnel in Germany to further organize and safeguard the distribution of food to this specific purpose.

I wish to state at the outset that, despite the suffering and losses imposed upon the American people through the German Government in the late war, I do not believe for a moment that the typical American would have any other wish than to see everything possible done in the protection of child life wherever it may be in danger. We have never fought with women and children and our desire must be to see the wounds of war healed through the world. There can be no question of the need of such support over the coming winter, because Europe generally will not recover from the milk famine until next summer and I am convinced by reports received that the child mortality is higher today than during the war.

I suggest that your society undertake this work for Germany for obvious reasons. The first is the experience you have gained in initiating this work. The second is the fact that this effort in sheer humanity should not be allowed to develop into political propaganda in either the United States or Germany and it seems to me, therefore, that some society such as the American Quakers, which is beyond all question of political interest, should become the filter through which such an effort should pass. I see no reason why the citizens of German descent in the United States should not contribute to this service; I know that the vast majority of these citizens have been loyal to the American Government throughout the war and that they themselves will be timorous about undertaking an effort that might lead to misunderstanding, and I believe that they would welcome the opportunity to support your society as being entirely beyond criticism or misunderstanding in such an effort.

With regard to your query as to whether the evangelical propaganda which the Friends Society conducts in Germany and other countries would conflict with this work, my own impression is that the pacifism of the Quakers, which is of centuries standing, would certainly not be amiss if applied to the German population.

In order that there should be every encouragement to undertake such an effort, I am prepared to guarantee from the funds at my disposal the purchasing department expenses, and to pay the entire cost of overseas transport from Atlantic ports into German ports of any foodstuffs thus delivered for child relief and for which your society is to furnish the purchase money. The amount of foodstuffs represented by the actual expenditure without the United States would thus be made available to your organization in Germany, without any shipping or handling charges, and if out of the funds of your society you could undertake to pay the entire overhead expenses of accounting for contributions and of the administration in Germany, it would thus give a great assurance to these contributors as to the full realization of the value of their contributions.

Faithfully yours,

(signed) Herbert Hoover

Rufus Jones called a meeting of the whole Board, which then accepted this proposal.

Immediately the Committee was faced with two tasks: the recruiting of the Unit and the organizing of a campaign for funds. The first was easier than the second. Nineteen Friends, headed by Alfred G. Scattergood, who had been the first, temporary chairman of the A.F.S.C., arrived in Berlin on the second of January, 1920. The raising of the money took more time. The war was still fresh in people's minds and the thought of feeding the enemy, in spite of St. Paul's admonition, was so new as to feel stiff and strange. Other Christian denominations wondered why so large a job should be the exclusive assignment of so small a body as the Society of Friends. Rufus Jones attended many meetings and made many persuasive speeches.

By the third week in June 1920 over a million children a day were being fed a supplementary meal in 1640 German communities. The small Quaker Unit was assisted by 40,000 Germans, who prepared the food in central kitchens and distributed it in feeding centers, usually schools, to undernourished children from the ages of two to fourteen.

In some other projects in Germany, American and English Friends could cooperate, but this mass feeding of the children was wholly an American operation. It was part of the understanding with Mr. Hoover that it should be done "under the American flag."

Although it had been his original idea to end the German feeding with the harvest in 1920, it was soon evident that the need would remain great, and Herbert Hoover continued his aid to the A.F.S.C. until the harvest of 1921, when the German Americans in the United States raised enough money to continue the feeding of 500,000 German children a day for another year.

As soon as his college classes were over in the spring of 1921 Rufus Jones, with Wilbur Thomas, made a trip to Germany to inspect the work and the needs. Between visiting feeding centers and attending staff conferences he took time to go to Marburg and see his old friends there.

"I had telegraphed Frau Happich that I would have breakfast with her on Friday morning. She figured out the trains and came to meet me at the station at 9:15 p.m. I was going to the Europaischen Hof and had not expected to be met. She was overjoyed to see me as though I had been a long-lost son. I left my bag at the hotel and walked home with her considerably over a mile. We went by the old home. We stopped and routed out Fraulein Grotefend who did not know I was coming! I got up early and climbed the old castle hill going up our old stairs from the church 'bei uns.' It was wunderschön. Everything exactly as it was. The old bent spire is still bent, the gardens as fine as ever . . . We had a simple breakfast together . . ." After calling on several old acquaintances—he saw Frau Sippell but Herr Sippell was at Woodbrooke—he continued, "When I got to the station to catch the 11:26 train there was Frau Happich, who had decided to go with me to Geisen [Giessen] so as to get more visit! We had a beautiful visit on the way and we kissed each other goodby as was right and proper. I think my visit touched her more than anything since the war was over—she feels what the Quakers have done so deeply."

From Germany they went into Poland, where English and American Friends were fighting typhus and helping the Polish farmers to get their farms going again. He sent an almost daily bulletin home.

"We have just left Lublin. Thee can locate that on a map. It is a big and famous city. It has a beautiful castle built in 1270 and still in

perfect condition, though many wars have raged around it. We see
the effects of the last war everywhere. We have ridden all afternoon
on top of the train and so have had a great view of the country, which
is very interesting and well-cultivated . . . It is a rural world, a thousand
miles of sandy plain like New Jersey."

"It was a great experience to have the whole Polish group together
yesterday for a general committee meeting of all the workers, then
this day together. We had a remarkable reception yesterday to meet
all the great celebrities of Poland and Warsaw. Harrison Barrow and
I made speeches for Friends and the President of the City and others
responded . . . We leave tomorrow for a two days' tour of the work
in the general direction of Lemberg . . . It will take us into some of the
most devastated areas of Poland and we shall see the hordes of refugees
who form one of the heavy problems of Poland . . .

"We waited over an hour for the mission auto and finally two 'furmankas' came instead. A furmaka is an odd Polish or Russian cart,
very long and very narrow, a bit like a Maine haywagon. We drove
4 miles to the mission home, run by Hilda Holme of Balt. Here we
had breakfast. The mission is in a fine old manor house. We spent the
day visiting the Quaker agricultural work in the section, going to the
various places on foot or in furmankas as all of the three mission cars
were *hors de combat* . . . We found the mission home infested with
fleas and I as usual got more than my share of their attention . . . The
next morning we had breakfast at 6:30 and started about 7 for Werb-
kowice where we have worked for over a year. This section was completely wrecked by the war and the refugees are slowly straggling
back from Russia. Friends give them their rations, look after their
children, plow their fields and assist them to build their cottages . . .
It is a thrilling piece of work and one of the best we have ever done
. . . Five hundred children, mostly babies and little tiny children, were
brought that day to our dispensary for examination—all refugees."

Along with the traveling there were important decisions to make
about the future work of the mission, and now and then a speech to
explain it all to grateful but bewildered Poles. From Poland they went
to Austria, where they spent four days.

"It is now Monday night. I have just addressed an audience of over
300 people, Austrian professors, students, and others. I never had a
better meeting. They literally 'fell on my neck.' I was very tired as
we have had two very busy days but I forgot all about my body in the
joy over the meeting."

It was a disappointment not to be able to get into Russia, where two Friends, Arthur Watts, English, and Anna J. Haines, American, who had been working in Moscow for over a year, reported a famine to be on the way. "Watts is having difficulty getting back and it would take us many weeks to get in and out again," Rufus Jones had written from London.

For months the A.F.S.C. had been seeking ways to increase its aid to Russia. On the 24th of January 1921 Rufus Jones had written to Violet Hodgkin, "I must go to New York tomorrow morning for an interview with Herbert Hoover and in the afternoon I must go to Washington for an interview early next morning with the head of the American Red Cross. This is in behalf of little children in Russia." The interview with Herbert Hoover had yielded $100,000 of A.R.A. funds to be spent by the A.F.S.C. for food and medical supplies to be distributed in Moscow. The Jewish Joint Distribution Committee also contributed generously.

By July the famine which had been prophesied was an actuality. Anna Haines, the only foreign member of a group of Russian doctors and teachers who investigated conditions in the Volga Valley, sent a horrifying account of what she had seen. At the same time Herbert Hoover, who was now Secretary of Commerce in the Harding cabinet, sent for Wilbur Thomas to talk about aid to Russian children. Maxim Gorki, leading Russian writer and an official of the Soviet government, had appealed to Mr. Hoover and the American people for aid, and Mr. Hoover had replied setting forth certain conditions under which he would undertake the task. The conditions were accepted in a cabled reply from the Communist minister of Foreign Affairs, suggesting a meeting at Riga to settle an agreement.

On the 18th of August Wilbur Thomas wrote to Rufus Jones in Maine that Mr. Hoover distrusted the Soviets. "He especially wanted us to have our Committee take the position that we would not work in Russia unless the Soviets could agree to the same plans that he had laid down for his work. In other words he wanted us to take his demands and insist upon the Soviet authorities accepting them for our own work before we went any further. We told him this was absolutely impossible; that we had been working in Russia for a year in a very satisfactory way; that we were non-political and that any such action would give political color to our own work. He insisted that Litvinov and the Soviet Authorities were constantly saying to Mr. Brown 'Why don't you work like the Quakers do? Why don't you accept their plans?' It was evident that this was a very irritating factor; and he got so angry about it that he literally pounded the table."

Two days later a contract was signed at Riga between Maxim Litvinov, representing the Soviet government, and Walter Lyman Brown, for Mr. Hoover's American Relief Adminstration. It stipulated for freedom of movement of the American staff and control by them of transport from the ports and detailed distribution to the Russian people by such methods as the Americans might decide upon. It also called for the freeing of Americans in Russian prisons. Instead of eleven American prisoners, of whom the United States had information, they freed over one hundred.

Mr. Hoover at once gave directions to undertake the canteen feeding of some two million children from American Relief Administration funds with Russian assurance that they could provide a sufficient amount for the adult population until the harvest of 1922. He dispatched an experienced staff of some two hundred Americans to set up headquarters in Moscow.

To raise money for this relief program, which later had to be increased because of the drought that developed in the winter of 1922, endangering the following summer's crop, he managed during the next few months, to get an authorization from the Congress to use some $20,000,000 balance in the hands of one of his former Food Administration agencies and an allotment from the War Department in medical supplies and clothing. He procured about $7,000,000 from the American Relief Administration, and from the Russians themselves he got about $18,000,000 of former Czarist gold.

On August 23, Herbert Hoover called to a conference in his office the representatives of several organizations, the American Red Cross, the Joint Distribution Committee, the Federal Council of Churches, the International Y.M.C.A., the Y.W.C.A., the Knights of Columbus, the Catholic Welfare Conference, and the American Friends Service Committee. Rufus Jones came from Maine for this conference.

As the talk unfolded it became evident that private organizations would not be able to work independently in Russia but would have to be affiliated with the A.R.A. and be bound by the terms of its agreement with the Soviet Government. Mr. Hoover proposed that the religious organizations select an area or group in which they would like to work, that the American Relief Administration should deliver supplies to them at cost; that he should secure for them the protections of the Riga agreement and that each religious organization should ap-

point a representative to the American Relief Administration headquarters both in Moscow and in New York.

From today's angle of vision, in view of all the difficulties that would
arise if ten different and possibly competing and overlapping organizations undertook to make separate agreements with the Soviet government, this seems a reasonable arrangement. At the time, however, the
A.F.S.C. felt hampered by the ban against dealing directly with the
Soviet authorities and it was disappointed not to be able to work in
collaboration with English Friends. It was also, though the release of
prisoners was no longer an issue, fearful that some political coloring
might develop in the terms by which the work was to be done.
American liberals, including some elements of labor from whom
financial support was hoped for, had already expressed disapproval of
the Riga agreement.

Rufus Jones, nevertheless, having had good reason in the past to
trust Herbert Hoover and believing that the arrangement was the
best that they could get, accepted the terms for the A.F.S.C. and returned to Maine by the Bar Harbor Express that night.

Evidently along the way, possibly in Washington or Philadelphia
that afternoon, he encountered some doubt or criticism of his decision,
for the next day he sent to James Norton, assistant Secretary of the
A.F.S.C., a telegram from South China, which he followed up with
a letter the same day.

South China, 8/24/21
Dear James: I sent the following telegram to thee this morning on my arrival:
"I stand solidly by settlement made with Hoover yesterday. If it stops labor
contribution we must face it and tell Hoover frankly what has happened. Con-
fident he will use us in district and support with his funds. Prefer not to come
again but can if necessary." There is no other course open to us. The opportunity
to go in and carry forward our work of relief in Russia under our own name
and with our own ideals is all we can expect in this crisis. To stand out and line
up with the radical wing is to end our career of service and to defeat the end
we have in view. If our funds fail, as they very likely will, we must either ask
Hoover to use us as his distributing agents or work quietly with English Friends,
who are evidently securing funds through a nation-wide appeal . . . I greatly
prefer to line up in the emergency period with Hoover. I feel sure it will accomplish most and best open the way for our future work . . . I am more than
ever clear that we took the right course in Washington and I see no way to go
back on it.

The following week he returned to Philadelphia for an Executive
Board meeting on the Hoover agreement. English Friends had cabled,
"Consider Friends direct contact with Soviet of greatest value" and
the discussion in the Committee was vigorous.

On the first of September Rufus Jones received a number of letters and telegrams from individuals and groups urging the A.F.S.C. not to jeopardize the "moral and spiritual values" of Quaker work by joining Hoover. A few days later Lewis Gannett, who had been a member of the first Haverford Unit and was now an associate editor of the *Nation*, wrote to James Norton, "Labor groups profoundly distrust Hoover and will not give money to be expended under his direction."

On September tenth Rufus Jones went again to Washington to see Mr. Hoover, who handed him the following letter to be used in appealing for funds for Russian famine relief:

September 10, 1921

Dear Mr. Jones:

In response to your request I beg to say that the efforts being made by the Friends Service Committee to secure charitable subscriptions for their work of famine relief in Russia has my fullest support.

I know full well the difficulties of our own people but there are still many who can afford support and others who will willingly make sacrifices. The need is pathetic beyond description. The effort being made by all American organizations to mitigate this terrible suffering is free of purpose in political, religious or racial contention. It is not the sentiment of charity to ask who and why.

None of the organizations cooperating under the Riga and European Relief Council agreements, which you have accepted, are in any way losing their identity or supervision of their own distribution, subject only to coordination for the common good of the Russian people. The sole purpose of these arrangements is to assure protection and efficiency in administration, that every cent shall do its utmost in saving life—that the whole effort shall be American in name and ideals.

I trust that you will have the support the cause deserves.

Yours faithfully,
(signed) Herbert Hoover

This letter was widely distributed as the Committee made its appeal for funds. Something, however, had happened to change the free flow of confidence that had marked the whole course of the child feeding in Germany. Rufus Jones felt the chill in the air that day, but he did not know definitely that something was wrong until he received a second letter from Mr. Hoover written on the same day after the interview.

September 10, 1921

Dear Mr. Jones:

Since you left my office it has occurred to me that I should confirm formally the fact that the letter which I handed to you this morning was an entire settlement of the relationship of the Friends Service Committee and the American Relief Administration. I do not want this thing to be constantly turning up because a militant group of red-minded people are trying to undermine the American Relief Administration through the Friends Service Committee.

Yours faithfully,
(signed) Herbert Hoover

Rufus Jones ruminated over this development for four or five days before he wrote his forthright answer:

September 16, 1921

Dear Mr. Hoover:

I have your letter of September 10th, expressing the desire that your arrangement made with us last Saturday and set forth in a letter to me should be considered a final settlement. It is so considered and we are satisfied with your letter. I should not however feel it right to pass over in silence your reference to the attempt of "red-minded people" to "undermine the American Relief Administration through the Friends Service Committee." I have always been a sincere and genuine friend to you and loyal to your great work. I would not tolerate for an instant any action on the part of the Service Committee while I was an officer which would array it against you or tend to undermine your reputation or your efforts. I have no affiliation with or leaning toward reds or pinks and I do not intend to have them or anyone else use me or our committee to injure you. I am concerned solely with human service and with getting as much of it done as possible. I am conscious that something has annoyed or offended you and altered your attitude toward us, but I am convinced that we have been perfectly fair and square and honorable in our relations with you and your great Association and I think you will find that we shall play up like men in this Russian situation.

Sincerely your friend,
Rufus M. Jones

Mr. Hoover replied on September 21:

Dear Mr. Jones:

Many thanks for your letter of September 16th.

I have no reserves about the American Friends Service Committee. If there is anything in which I have implicit confidence it is the right-mindedness of the people with whom I have been born and raised.

I think you will agree wtih me that the propaganda in the New Republic and in the Red press is enough to cause some anxiety lest through such intrigues conflict would be created among American organizations and do infinite harm to the whole cause of saving life in Russia. Now that I know that this does not originate or has no sympathetic support from the Friends themselves, the whole matter is at rest in my mind. No one has a higher appreciation of the single-mindedness of your efforts than I have.

For your confidential information I may tell you that you are now safe from being raided by the Reds as they have a delegate from Moscow purporting to have brought $500,000 to organize the elements of discontent in this country under the cloak of relief. At a recent meeting of this committee they made up their minds to fight with you and all the rest of us, part of the announced program of this delegate being to organize a great American Relief Committee amongst workers that will ultimately replace "religious" and "bourgeoisie" efforts. We are thus all of us to suffer the bitterness of outcasts.

Yours faithfully,
(signed) Herbert Hoover

The reference in Mr. Hoover's letter to the danger of being "raided by the Reds" needs an explanation. The Communists in the United States had engaged an American public relations man to organize their own relief drive, who secured the names of some senators and others for his letter-head and announced that his supplies would be distributed through the "Russian Red Cross." Mr. Hoover was informed by his staff in Russia that this organization was practically non-existent in Russia and by the United States government that the money raised was being used largely for Communist propaganda in the United States. He denounced the organization and many of its sponsors withdrew. At once the radicals and radical labor organizations attacked Mr. Hoover. When he learned that "certain individual Friends were supporting the so-called Russian Red Cross organization" and believed that they had joined in the attack on him, he "naturally disliked it." In consequence a "small cloud" arose between him and the American Friends Service Committee.

Though Mr. Hoover may seem to have been unduly sensitive to criticism, it is well known now that he actually was the target of Communist-instigated attacks which became more barbed and more damaging as time went on and which were taken up and repeated by liberals and others who looked on him as a domestic political threat. It was unfortunate that the liberal weeklies coupled criticism of Hoover with praise of the American Friends Service Committee. The articles to which he referred in the *New Republic*, on August 10, August 31, and September 14, had charged him with a "spirit of autocracy and dictatorship," "implacable hostility to bolshevism," and with having "used the power of food in the past to control revolution and overthrow governments of the Soviet type." In contrast it praised the A.F.S.C. highly for "undiluted integrity and impartiality" and stated that people unwilling to give through Hoover would contribute through the "Friends Relief Organization." On September 28, however, it printed in full Hoover's letter endorsing the A.F.S.C. and after that the invidious comparisons ceased.

Anna Haines returned from Russia in October to report in person on the harrowing conditions in the valley of the Volga, where millions of people faced starvation. Besides the loss of crops due to the unwillingness of many peasants to work under the harsh Soviet collectivization of the farms, there had been a severe drought that spring which destroyed the small amounts of food that were raised. Hungry peasants crowded into the towns. Epidemic disease and starvation clasped hands with transportation break-downs and general inefficiency. The Soviet government desperately needed help from outside and at the same time distrusted the motives of the "capitalists" in offering it.

The A.F.S.C. meanwhile, like other private organizations, was putting on a campaign for funds through bulletins, appeals, mass-meetings and speeches. At a single meeting in Brooklyn in December Rufus Jones raised $21,000. The Quaker workers, who had reached Russia late in October and who were "standing all the time on the desolate frontiers of death," were now feeding 50,000 people a day and crying out for more food, more medical supplies, more clothing.

At this point, when everyone was straining every nerve to increase the flow of aid to Russia, Mr. Hoover burst a small bomb.

On January 2, 1922, he summoned the representatives of the organizations which had met with him the previous August for the purpose of giving them information which he thought they ought to have in forming their plans and policies. Transportation in Russia, he told them, damaged by war and revolution, had broken down almost completely. Despite the efforts of the American railway men he had sent over, Russian harbors were blocked with ships full of food that was not yet unloaded, some of which had already begun to "heat" and which could not be carried to the distribution points for months. Whatever the need, it was no use to ship more food until the situation was improved.

The representatives at that meeting felt as if the rug had been pulled out from under their feet. They knew the serious effect that this news would have upon their campaigns for funds. Wilbur Thomas and no doubt others spoke up with vigor and some heat. Mr. Hoover assured the A.F.S.C. that if their campaign failed he could guarantee them enough support from the A.R.A. funds on hand to continue the present rate of feeding.

When he went home that day Rufus Jones wrote Herbert Hoover a letter, in which, after expressing appreciation for Mr. Hoover's sacrifice of his holiday time and for his "friendly cooperative spirit," he recapitulated his understanding of what had been said, pointed out that the A.F.S.C. wished to add medical and clothing relief and assistance in sowing and planting in the famine area, and asked that Mr. Hoover emphasize the need in these directions in his statement to the public.

Mr. Hoover replied that he was going to make no public statement. He was convinced, he said, that the "available supplies of food will occupy transportation for some months to come . . . I feel a good deal of depression," he continued, "at the hysteria that is being injected into many of the begging programs."

Though no public statement was issued, the news leaked out and caused a furor. Fund raisers in all organizations complained bitterly that people were taking it to mean that no more funds were needed for Russia and some of them accused Mr. Hoover of allowing his dislike of communism to influence his judgment.

On February 13th he wrote again to Rufus Jones, explaining once more the situation and his motives in having informed the relief agencies of it.

> I had the conviction that we should for some months overtax the Russian food transport facilities with the funds already provided, and I had the solicitude for your work to advise you of this in order that you could shape your policies to meet it as the reports of delayed transportation will sooner or later begin to flow from the European news agencies. The suggestion seems to have created resentment as being some sort of plot of mine to defeat relief to Russia. . . .
> From a personal point of view I have every reason to regret that I ever touched a situation that is so pregnant with mud and personal vilification from all sides as this appears to be . . . You are doing a good work and I want you to succeed.

To this Rufus Jones replied sympathetically, informing him that, "We are now feeding 100,000 and feel assured that we can continue at least that number until midsummer . . . We appreciate your great work and are sorry that in doing it you have had to endure criticism and abuse."

Doubt was not a one-way street. While some entertained suspicion of Mr. Hoover's motives, other people were anxious about the A.F.S.C., and Mr. Hoover had to write many letters of reassurance about them. Typical of his answers was this to a club woman who wanted to know if there was any truth in a report that A.F.S.C. money was diverted to other needy people before reaching the Russians: "I have only the highest opinion of their [A.F.S.C.] devotion, their ability and their responsibility. Every penny that goes to them for Russian relief or for any other specified destination gets the most economical and splendid administration."

On the 26th of February an article appeared in the New York *Call* a Socialist paper, headlined: "Hoover Sabotages Russian Relief." After accusing Mr. Hoover with the aid of "an incredibly vile and mendacious campaign carried on by the *New York Times*," of discrediting the radical agencies for Russian relief and maintaining a policy of crushing every organization except his own, it charged him specifically with curtailing the activities of the Society of Friends, with discouraging and rebuffing them in their efforts to make a nationwide drive for funds, and quoted an alleged letter from an unnamed "prominent and responsible Quaker worker" in support of the accusation. This article found its way to Mr. Hoover, who promptly blew up.

March 6, 1922

My dear Jones:

I think the time has come when the Friends could take energetic measures to stop the propaganda constantly gotten out that I have been endeavoring to embarrass them and retard their work. If I or the A.R.A. embarrass them then the Friends should at once divorce themselves from all relation to the American Relief Administration, to which I haven't the slightest objection, or alternatively, they should put a stop to this nonsense.

I call your attention to the type of article appearing in the New York Call of February 26th as the sort of thing that is appearing all over the country, and which bears the imprint of the Friends' organization. You can scarcely expect me to go on re(c)ommending the Friends Service Committee and have propaganda of this sort going on without denial from you. I consider that it would be the honest thing for the Friends to address an energetic denial to the New York Call as to the wholly erroneous character of such statements.

I will go even further and state that it will be no embarrassment to the A.R.A. or myself if your committee thinks it desirable to separate entirely from the A.R.A. If you have any feeling that you could be of greater service in this way pray do what you think best.

In order that there should be no misunderstanding do not think that under any circumstances I withdraw the offer made you in a recent letter. My one anxiety has been to see the Russian people fed and the substanial guarantees that we gave to the Friends Service Committee still remain, in spite of any action that you may think it desirable to undertake.

Yours faithfully,

Herbert Hoover

Rufus Jones's answer is not extant. He was ill when the Executive Board met to consider the matter, and thus his name was missing from the letter to the *Call*, signed by seven members of the Board, in which they called its charges "untrue and unfair" and concluded: "Over the experience of several months our Committee has found that Mr. Hoover has done far more to support our work in the Russian field than any original plan contemplated."

The American Friends Service Committee continued to feed 75,000 a day until the first of April, 1923.

Later Herbert Hoover and Friend Jones were again to work together on raising money to relieve suffering, in 1931 when unemployment and depression bore heavily on the miners of Pennsylvania and West Virginia, and Mr. Hoover turned $225,000 over to the A.F.S.C., and in the 1940's when another war spread its black wings over the world.

"Our Rufus"

THE five years from 1917 to 1922, in which Rufus Jones poured out thought and energy for the American Friends Service Committee and travelled far in its behalf, were also filled with other vital concerns: with the Fellowship of Reconciliation, which he had helped Henry Hodgkin to start in 1915, with the affairs of Bryn Mawr College, in which he became more than ever involved by his election to the chairmanship of the Board in 1916, with the All Friends Conference in London in 1920, and with those perennial and fundamental activities of his life, teaching, writing and speaking.

As early as 1917 Friends in England and America began to plan a world-wide conference to be held in London as soon as the war should end, to discuss and explore fundamental problems of war and peace from the Quaker viewpoint. In August 1920 this dream came to fruition.

Three hundred and fifty delegates from yearly meetings in the United States, others from "our colonial empire," as it was still customary to say in England in 1920, and from small and scattered meetings in China, Japan, Africa, India, Syria, Norway, France, Denmark, Hungary and Switzerland, gathered with English Friends; 936 delegates in all. Wives and children who were not admitted to the actual sessions went along for the marginal experience.

Rufus and Elizabeth Jones and Mary sailed from New York on the seventeenth of July, carrying with them in a special suitcase the precious manuscript of the last volume of the Quaker History to deliver to the English publisher. "The bag was never out of his sight during the voyage," his daughter remembers, "and the family knew that whatever else had to be sacrificed in case of a disaster this must be saved." Rufus Jones had time to make three addresses at Woodbrooke and two at Cambridge before the conference opened. On the conference eve he delivered the Swarthmore lecture, the only Friend ever to have given two Swarthmore lectures. This was an open meeting and more than two thousand people crowded into the Central Hall, Westminster, to hear him. It must have been an "epoch moment" for him; his old friend Edward Grubb presided and on the platform behind him were Elizabeth Cadbury, James Wood and his daughter Carolena, William Charles Braithwaite and others; a sea of eager faces stretched before him, the war was over and hopes were high for a new and better world.

His subject was "The Nature and Authority of Conscience." It was not an easy, popular address; its abstract thought and closely reasoned argument made demands on his listeners. He examined various explanations of conscience and found them inadequate. Barclay's description of it as a natural faculty informed and illumined by the Light Within as a lantern is lit by the candle inside, which was not only the long-accepted Quaker view but also substantially that of the scholastic theologians and the great mystics, Rufus Jones criticized as too sharply dualistic, though he recognized it as a valuable interpretation in its time. The "intuition theory" of conscience as an implanted infallible oracle he found not only unacceptable in the light of modern psychology but also unsatisfactory as it deprives man of moral autonomy. The naturalistic explanation that finds conduct merely the product of education and evolution failed, he said, to account for either its origin or its authority. He himself, acknowledging his indebtedness to his old professor George Herbert Palmer, saw conscience as the point of juncture between the individual self and the large consciousness in which it is embedded, the Beyond that is within. Since in the depth of man's being he is never sundered from God, conscience is both human and divine. While recognizing the element of education and social environment which makes the judgments of conscience subject to great variation in different periods or civilizations, he held it to be nevertheless the "surest authority within our reach," a voice to be implicitly obeyed. He warned against the dangers of a static conscience and urged a "continual transformation of conscience in relation to the growing revelation of God."

The young people in the audience responded with especial enthusiasm, finding his humor, his "freedom from affectation," his recognition of the achievements of science, the authenticity of his own life and experience, immensely convincing.

The following day the sittings of the conference began. In the session devoted to the Character and Basis of our Testimony for Peace Joan Mary Fry and Rufus Jones both presented papers. "This, I take it," said Rufus Jones, "is our main business here as it is the central mission of the Society of Friends in the world, to make faith in the moral and spiritual forces somewhat more real." Whether or not this could be truly said of the Society of Friends as a whole, it was certainly true of Rufus Jones; throughout his life, through his writing and speaking and teaching, his attempts to alleviate the suffering that man inflicts on man, he sought to widen people's recognition of the power of moral forces and to make real to others the God who was reality itself to him. All the rest, peace, social justice, unity in diversity, would follow.

In other sessions the assembled Friends wrestled with fundamental problems of race relations, class distinctions, conditions in industry, questions of capital and labor, searching out the seeds of war in the soil of daily life in a new and determined way. The experience of conscientious objectors, the fresh awareness that had come with the work of reconstruction and relief, the vision of international Quaker centers and the consciousness of social movements in the world had opened minds and sharpened consciences. The London Conference of 1920 was a turning-point in Quaker thought, and to the leadership of Rufus Jones and the group of English Friends with whom he was in such close accord much of this great awakening was due.

During the week of the conference the Joneses stayed at the Great Eastern Hotel, where Barrow Cadbury entertained twenty American and English Friends, including such old friends of Rufus Jones as Violet Hodgkin, in a typical Quaker houseparty in which religion and merriment were intertwined.

The London Conference was followed by a briefer one at Oxford, where it rained and the temperature fell to 38°, and a week-long Conference of four hundred Young Friends at Jordans in Buckinghamshire in which Rufus Jones took an important part. Exhausted when it was all over, he was carried off by his old friends for a holiday in Yorkshire.

"How do prophets occupy themselves when not prophesying? It fell to my happy lot," wrote George Newman, "to travel at pleasure with a distinguished American Professor of Philosophy, the English historian of Quakerism, and a well-known director in a famous firm in the north of England immediately after the termination of the conference. They had exhausted themselves (and possibly others also) at the aforesaid Conference, and I was selected as a victim of their subsequent reaction . . . We began our delightful journey through the North Riding moors, the ostensible purpose of all our action and inaction being to supply a rest-cure for the American Professor."

Conversation, W. C. Braithwaite recorded in his diary, ranged over philosophy, psychology, the Quaker History, dreams, snoring, industrial fatigue, and large families. Rufus Jones told his inimitable stories. He told of the time he was scheduled to deliver an address at the Lowell Institute in Boston and how the day before as he sat at his desk he heard a voice saying, "But thou wilt never give it!" How he was stricken that night with ptomaine poisoning, and was taken to the hospital where he was worked over by the doctors, who thought they could do something temporary; and how at two o'clock he stood up on his shaky legs and lectured to a thousand people. "Don't think I ever did anything better," he told them. "I downed the old voice and collapsed afterwards like a balloon."

He told them too of the prayer of a New York Friend before an address which he was to give on the synoptic gospels: "O Lord, thou knowest we are about to hear many things that are not so."

"This then," George Newman said, "was the Professor's rest-cure. Dear friend and comrade and beloved Professor."

"I was completely done out and wondered whether I should ever be rested again. I was far too tired for Oxford and was only a fragment of myself at Jordans, but the hills, the sea, the heather, the air and the splendid fun have restored my poor old dust wreath of a body and my soul feels better," the Professor himself wrote to Violet Hodgkin from Scalby, where he rejoined his wife and daughter.

They came home first class on the *Aquitania*, of which Rufus Jones, fresh from the social probings of the Conference, commented, "John Woolman would not have stayed aboard a minute! It would have struck at his life."

M. Carey Thomas was also aboard, but probably not entertaining any uncomfortable reflections about John Woolman. She was returning to Bryn Mawr after a year's leave of absence from the college, which she had spent travelling in Europe and the Near East.

Rufus Jones had known M. Carey Thomas from his first arrival in

Haverford in 1893, when she was still dean of Bryn Mawr. She then
sat directly in front of him at Haverford Meeting, and when he rose
to speak he was aware of her "awesome" presence. She was six years
older than he and already a formidable figure.

When he was elected to the Board of Trustees of Bryn Mawr in
1898, he had immediately begun a movement to have her made a
trustee too, an end for which she had been laboring ever since she
became president four years earlier. He knew from his own experience
at Oak Grove the difficulties of the executive who is not a member of
the Board. It took four years more, with the efforts of Carey Thomas
herself and the support of her cousin David Scull to accomplish this
purpose, and she was always grateful to Rufus Jones for his part in it.

The friendship between these two strong, gifted and dedicated
but wholly dissimilar personalities was profound and genuine and re-
markably unshaken by the series of shocks and strains which it suffered.
Rufus Jones was disturbed by the methods which Carey Thomas used
to force the resignation of William Allan Neilson, associate professor
of English, who gave, he said, the best course in Browning that he
knew of. The building program of the college provided the next severe
test. The college was poor and the trustees felt obliged to guard every
penny. The President had a vision of Oxonian beauty and dignity and
she looked toward the future when cost would be forgotten but badly
cut stone and inferior wood would still be there to be lived with. To
her mind nothing less than teakwood was good enough for the pan-
elling of the entrance to the Library and the reading room. Rufus
Jones was one of a committee of three who after a careful investigation brought in a decision against teakwood. When in spite of everything, the finished library was panelled in teakwood, tension resulted.
"This was the hottest thing that ever happened, and it came near
ending her career," said Rufus Jones to his daughter in 1948. One
Friend resigned from the Board. Carey Thomas stayed.

The crisis over faculty government in 1916 was deeper and more
shattering. The story has been told in Edith Finch's biography of
Carey Thomas and in Cornelia Meigs's history of Bryn Mawr, and
need not be treated in detail here. Faculty resentment over the President's arbitrary methods of appointment and dismissal came to a head
at a time when throughout the academic world there was a general
movement toward a more liberal policy of faculty participation in
college government. Thirteen full professors at Bryn Mawr offered
a plan of reformation, and Rufus Jones who by then was chairman of

the Executive Committee of the combined boards of directors and trustees, was one of a committee of five to consider the faculty proposals. Before any conclusions could be reached a series of articles personally attacking the President of the College appeared in the Philadelphia *Public Ledger*, accompanied by critical letters from former faculty members, some of whom had been dismissed. Feeling ran high among the faculty, the alumnae, and the community.

All through April and early May the committee held session after session, meeting with the President and with the faculty, together and separately. Among the thirteen full professors who initiated the movement was Rufus Jones's old and close friend, George Barton, through whom and through his own experience as a Haverford professor he must have been able to understand fully the faculty point of view. Rufus Jones's liberality, his wisdom, his broad spirit doubtless played a large part not only in developing the plan of government adopted in May but in reconciling the passionate differences that might have resulted in permanent cleavages. That Carey Thomas could assimilate this humiliating experience, accept loyally the new plan, which increased the faculty's power as it diminished her own, and give her energy and powers of persuasion to making it successful, is a measure of the greatness of her spirit. It is possible that there was also some contagion from Rufus Jones's steadying wisdom.

Thomas Raeburn White, who with Charles Rhoads was largely responsible for working out the legal aspects of the plan, commenting in 1933 on the varied problems which the Bryn Mawr Board had had to meet over the years, said: "We may now look back on some of these problems with a smile, but when they came upon us the way was not so easy to discern. I know I speak the views of my associates when I say I do not know how we could have solved them without the unflagging zeal for the truth and wise counsel of Rufus Jones. With him at the helm we had faith we should weather the storm."

Cornelia Meigs refers to the debt that Carey Thomas owed to Rufus Jones. "Next to her father, he was probably the man who best understood Carey Thomas and gave her the most of the wisdom and caution that she needed. He was in turn the recipient of her deep regard, and those who knew her well were aware of how strong and deep her affections could be."

James Wood, president of the Board, resigned that autumn, in protest against the Board's action, Edith Finch assumed, but actually, Rufus Jones believed, for reasons of health. In December, 1916, Rufus

Jones was elected President of the combined boards of trustees and directors. The association with Carey Thomas over problems major and minor continued. He went often to the Deanery, which was her home, and she came to his house to consult him there. His daughter has a vivid memory of those formidable interviews. The word would come that she would arrive at a certain hour, and apprehension and gloom would settle over the household. Rufus Jones awaited her in the parlor downstairs, while Elizabeth Jones and Mary withdrew to the study above. The carriage—and later the car—drew up, the sturdy figure, made more impressive by the limp and the cane, alighted and mounted the front steps.

"I formed the habit in all these interviews," wrote Rufus Jones, "of being utterly sincere and honest in my expression of judgment or opinion. She knew that I was never acting capriciously or taking an opposing opinion arbitrarily."

After the visitor had departed, wife and daughter emerged to see how things had gone. It was always immediately evident. If they had gone badly, Rufus Jones was depressed and troubled; if well, he was effervescent with high spirits.

"We came through those years of labor together," he summed up, "in spite of our many points of difference, with mutual respect and personal regard for each other."

Eleanor Little Aldrich, for many years a director of the college, recalls Board meetings when Rufus Jones was in the chair, how he would turn to Carey Thomas, whom everyone else addressed as Miss Thomas, to ask, "Carey, what does thee think?"

He recognized always her great gifts to the college and the courage of her devotion. He recognized also what she gave him personally, the enlargement of his knowledge of the educational world and the opportunities for meeting at her house people of interest whom he enjoyed knowing. He referred with obvious pleasure to two occasions when he heard her discussing the deepest issues of life with Josiah Royce and Rudolf Eucken.

In 1922 Carey Thomas reached the age of sixty-five, and by the regulation which she herself had been instrumental in establishing she was obliged to retire. For nearly two years previously the search for her successor was carried on. Asa Wing, treasurer of the Board, was chairman of the committee which made the choice, but Rufus Jones was ex officio a member and it was he who set the policy that determined the basis of the decision.

The committee received many letters on the subject. It was obvious that it would be difficult for anyone to follow Carey Thomas, especially as she was to continue to live at the Deanery. Many agreed with the professor who declared that it would only be an interim presidency, "for no one could survive more than five or six years with President Thomas living in the Deanery ready to jump out at intervals like a jack-in-the-box and give everyone a 'crisis of nerves'." Others were convinced that only a man could handle the situation, and wanted Rufus Jones to be that man. When asked if he would accept the position if it were offered him, he declined out of hand. Carey Thomas herself and many of the alumnae were certain that to appoint a man would be to declare the bankruptcy of higher education for women. In a letter to Asa Wing Rufus Jones discussed the whole question.

He pointed to the obligation to consider Dr. Taylor's purpose in founding and endowing the college. "He had a certain type of life in mind which he hoped the college would produce—a well-rounded spiritual personality." They should look, he felt, for a president "who will be deeply sympathetic to those aims and who will be positively concerned to have the moral and religious life of the students broadly developed." Bryn Mawr stood, furthermore, for a high type of scholarship, and her president must not lower her standards. "But we must insist upon the equal importance of standards of life and character." He did not, he said, care whether it was a man or woman but he did want "a person that has a very high candle power." Desirable qualities which he cited were, in addition to "the scholarly and ideal sides of life," large practical ability, creative power and leadership, insight, tact, and a "tendency to make right decisions and to judge character." Having delineated this paragon, he added that he thought it would be "rather easier" to find such a man than a woman!

Gradually it became clear that the qualities they sought were to be found in a Bryn Mawr graduate very popular with the alumnae, Marion Edwards Park, Bryn Mawr A.B., M.A., Ph.D., who was at that time Dean of Radcliffe. When approached, however, Miss Park refused categorically.

Rufus Jones went to see her. He went directly from Vassar, where he had been speaking, but he was joined at Cambridge by the redoubtable Miss Thomas, who sat in the dining-room of Marion Park's house and waited while Rufus Jones and the Dean of Radcliffe talked in the living-room. She was grateful to him, Marion Park wrote afterwards, for his long trip in her behalf, and for the freedom with which she could talk to him about college affairs, but it was not till a full month later that "slowly and with many hesitations" she accepted Bryn Mawr's offer.

On the last day before Carey Thomas left Bryn Mawr, she invited Rufus Jones to ride into town with her. Driving with Carey Thomas was a fearful joy. Edith Finch describes it vividly. "Straight and masterful she sat at the wheel, the chauffeur, relegated to the rear, gripping the edge of the seat, apprehensive and unhappy as out of the Deanery driveway, across the campus and through Pembroke arch the car surged, cutting corners, jerking at each change of gear, scattering students from the roadway like frightened rabbits."

On this occasion Rufus Jones sat beside her, fully aware of the danger to which he had committed himself. Suddenly, she pulled to the side of the road, stopped the car, reached over and took his hand and said, "We've had serious difficulties in the years we have worked together, but we have never lost confidence and affection for each other and I want to tell thee on this last occasion that I have great affection for thee."

He was deeply touched by this avowal, and it was perhaps at least partly to this that he was referring when he spoke, some years later, of the tenderness that was as much a part of her character as the fire.

The inauguration of Marion Park took place in October, 1922. Rufus Jones presided and William Allan Neilson, president of Smith College, returned to Bryn Mawr to make one of the principal speeches. Elizabeth Jones described it all to Mary, now a Freshman at Mt. Holyoke. "Thee should have been here yesterday to see father install Miss Park as president. It was a wonderfully fine day and they decided to hold the exercises in the cloister . . . Father wore his Haverford hood. He presided and introduced the speakers, the third of whom was Dr. Comfort, who spoke very well. So did President Neilson. Then father said the fateful words that pronounced Miss Park president—and he did it in a most impressive way. Then Miss Park gave her speech at the beginning of which about a dozen cameras were aimed at her, including one with a winding film." Rufus Jones too had time to send a word to her. "Yesterday," he wrote, "was one of the greatest events of my life—a wonderful show."

During these immensely full and varied years Rufus Jones also wrote the final installment of the Quaker History series, LATER PERIODS OF QUAKERISM, which proved to be so long that at the last minute it was decided to publish it in two volumes of five hundred pages each.

In 1919, when W. C. Braithwaite's Second Period of Quakerism was published, Rufus Jones had thought that his own task was on the edge of being completed. "My volume is practically done," he wrote to Violet Hodgkin, "even the Introduction written, but I hope to put the finishing touches on it next autumn before sending the ms. to the printers . . . I shall feel strange not to be carrying this load and no longer to be under this immense responsibility. Nobody could have been a better co-laborer than WCB. We have worked most happily together."

Two years later, however, it was still not out, though he heard it "peeping in the egg." Elizabeth Jones had been working on the index all through the time that her husband was in Europe visiting the feeding centers, and her difficult and exacting share of the work was almost over. "Thou wilt see when thou reads it," Rufus Jones wrote, "that I have had an Atlas' burden on my poor old back. It is a large and complicated task but now it is done and I shall not do it again. I hope nobody will have to do this same sort of thing again."

It covered the eighteenth and nineteenth centuries in England and America, the period of "quietism," the organization of the Society, the social testimonies, the tragedy of the separations, the effects of the "Great Revival," and it foreshadowed the revitalization and growth that were to come in the twentieth century. His estimate of Philadelphia Quakerism had undergone a change since his first arrival in Haverford, when it seemed to him the seat of rigid traditionalism. The isolation of Philadelphia Yearly Meeting from the rest of the Quaker world he still considered a tragedy, but he saw in it a value that he had not found earlier. "Notwithstanding the isolation, however, and the slow decrease in membership from decade to decade, Philadelphia Yearly Meeting rendered a great service to the Society of Friends at large during the half-century from 1850 by maintaining a type of Quakerism which, though conservative, had within its life the potentiality of later breadth and expansion."

The history which this volume concluded had taken sixteen years to write. It comprised seven volumes, of which five—Studies in Mystical Religion, 1909, Spiritual Reformers of the Sixteenth and Seventeenth Centuries, 1914, The Quakers in the American Colonies, 1911, and the two volumes of Later Periods of Quakerism, 1921—were written by Rufus Jones. He also wrote introductions to the two volumes by William C. Braithwaite, The Beginnings of Quakerism, 1912, and Second Period of Quakerism, 1919. It was the history not only of the Society of Friends but of certain large, hitherto almost unexplored areas of mystical religion.

Some of this edifice is now threatened in the storm of neo-Ortho-doxy which is sweeping the Protestant Churches and coloring much of today's Quaker thought. Rufus Jones's introductions have been omitted from the new edition of W. C. Braithwaite's two volumes published in England in 1955 and 1958. His interpretation of Quaker-ism as part of a wider mystical movement and his criticism of the Calvinistic elements in Barclay's *Apology* and other early Quaker writings are not acceptable to some elements of current thought.

THE QUAKERS IN THE AMERICAN COLONIES suffers from lack of unity in the writing and from the fact that much new material has since been discovered. It contains nevertheless much that cannot be easily found elsewhere and it will continue to occupy a secure niche for students of Quaker history.

The two books on mysticism stand unchallenged as important works of historical scholarship whether or not they establish the Spiritual Reformers as forerunners of the Quaker movement, and the two volumes of the LATER PERIODS will not be supplanted, even though the interpretation of the period of Quietism therein set forth has been questioned by other Quaker historians.

Rufus Jones identified Quietism, which came into Quaker thought through the writings of Madame Guion, Fénelon, and Molinos, with passivism and held it responsible for withdrawal from the world, a distinctive manner of dress, and the condemnation of sustained thought in the meeting for worship as "creaturely activity." While recognizing and honoring the number of saintly lives which blossomed in this walled garden, he considered it wholly outside the original stream of Quakerism. To Howard H. Brinton, however, the period of Quietism was a "period of conservatism and consolidation" which exhibited "no change in intention" from original Quakerism. He finds Robert Bar-clay's position to be half way between the Hegelian idealism which in-fluenced Rufus Jones, John Wilhelm Rowntree, William Charles Braithwaite, Edward Grubb and others, and the neo-Calvinism of the present.

Many histories of Quakerism have been and will be written, but it seems unlikely that anyone again will find it necessary to write one in seven volumes, or will write even a single volume without drawing heavily on this fundamental work of Rufus Jones and William Charles Braithwaite.

With his two later histories—HAVERFORD COLLEGE: A HISTORY AND

AN INTERPRETATION and MYSTICISM AND DEMOCRACY IN THE ENGLISH COMMONWEALTH—these volumes of the Quaker History constitute Rufus Jones's claim to the title of historian which was so frequently given him along with those other titles: philosopher, teacher, mystic, prophet, social reformer. This may then be a good point at which to look at his method and his theory of history.

The qualities which he saw in William Charles Braithwaite, that made him "a historian of a high order," throw light on Rufus Jones's conception of the nature of history. They were: "remarkable insight, patience in research, fidelity to truth, genuine historical imagination and sympathetic understanding of the characters whom he interpreted." It was not by chance that he included that final qualification, possibly as the climax in the series. He wrote his own history very largely in terms of the individual personalities that spoke for their time, or influenced it, or passed on the torch. He did not, however, subscribe to the hero theory of history made famous by Carlyle, that the great men create times and events. Nor did he believe history to be an illustration of economic theory or a series of biographies of civilizations, still less a sterile chronicle of events.

To him history was "an immense human drama of man's progress." "I am convinced that we have not formed the right theory of History," he was to write in 1938, "until we see History itself as a spiritual drama, moving toward a significant denouement and at the same time a process which has meaning and value as it goes on." He did not, especially in his later years, accept the Spencerian theory of progress, which he characterized as the belief that "evolution was a vast cosmic escalator always running and always taking its precious freight in an upward direction," but he did believe that "the slow moral gains of the ages are saved and accumulated and a steady addition is made to the precious store." Though God does not interfere with or interrupt the natural course of events, He is visible in history—and so the study of history can become one of the pathways to a conviction of His reality—as "an Over-Mind working through human minds and revealing Itself in the sifting and selecting processes that make certain ideals victorious."

It is the injection of man's free will into history that makes the drama. "If once we admit that History is the drama of the making of man and the seedplot for the growing of a disciplined freedom, we have at least one clue to the mystery of the imperfection and the evil which dog the upward progress of life."

He was always aware of the interaction between ideas and their social, political and economic environment. He points out that concepts of sin and atonement vary in accordance with the structure of the time. "It was perfectly natural in the period of feudalism to think of sin as a debt which must be paid, just as it was equally natural to the mind of the Reformation period to dwell upon the sovereignty of God and His eternal justice" and so to see sin as disobedience to the sovereign will. Thus the rise of the understanding of personality in the nineteenth century leads to a view of "salvation as the healing of the moral and spiritual diseases of the soul through the communication of the life of God to the soul."

He had no trace of what C. S. Lewis calls "chronological snobbery," i.e., the assumption that yesterday's understanding of truth is ipso facto inferior to today's. Nor did he on the other hand accept yesterday's insights without a careful consideration of the enveloping circumstances in which they came to birth. "History," he wrote in 1904, "is the merciless judgment seat where all ideals have been tested and woe to him who scorns or ignores the judgments of this tribunal."

Other books written during this period included three more of his stories for young people, St. Paul the Hero, The Story of George Fox, and The Boy Jesus; The World Within, which was made up of essays published in The Friend (London) and the Homiletic Review; and Spiritual Energies for Daily Life, largely composed of essays published in The Atlantic Monthly, The Journal of Religion, and others. Somehow he had found time to write these pieces full of salty humor and sage reflection which set forth one of his basic convictions, that out of a conscious relationship with God comes the energy we need for our lives.

Two honorary degrees of LL.D. which especially pleased him came within a week of each other in 1922, from the rival Quaker colleges, Haverford and Swarthmore. That from Haverford was a complete surprise, for it was the first such degree given since 1909 and he had not been told of it ahead of time. The citation which accompanied it is the one of all his thirteen most often quoted: "an impenitent optimist who has discovered the secret of perpetual youth and who has helped numberless young men to find themselves in finding a faith."

His optimism was not entirely a matter of temperament, though it was natural to him to think each successive Haverford class the "best ever," each responsive audience the most significant yet, each moving occasion an epoch. He saw too the failures, the discrepancies, the limitations that he encountered, and he could sum up a situation with devastating candor. "That was a new high in lows", he said of one meeting, and he lamented to Violet Hodgkin Holdsworth (his old friend married John Holdsworth in 1922) "the thinness and inefficiency of our Quakerism" and the "general feeling of ease and content and failure to realize that the vitality is diminishing. I was never meant for a Jeremiah and here I am doing his role."

He discarded "the soft optimism" which says, "Dirt is only earth in the wrong place. You can conquer any situation if you smile enough." In sorrow and frustration he found the "very ground" of his optimism: "This dissatisfaction of ours with what is, this endless vision of a beyond unattained, of a reach beyond our grasp is the supreme mark of our grandeur." His optimism found its roots in his firm belief in the perfectibility of man, in the gradual upward progress of history, in his expectation of immortality, which rested not on arguments but "upon the trustworthy character of the eternal nature of things" and "the conservation of moral values."

The years brought, as years do when one reaches the age when one dislikes "to see a new birthday nosing in," their weight of loss. His beloved cousin, Charles Jacob, with whom he had traveled abroad in 1887, died in 1916, his brother Herbert during the influenza epidemic of 1918, his well-loved cousin Richard M. Jones in 1917. Laurence Rowntree, the only son of John Wilhelm and Connie Rowntree, who had felt it to be his duty to volunteer in the British army, was killed in action in 1918. "Over and over again," he wrote to Connie, "I find myself back in those summer days when Lowell played with Margaret and Laurie by the Silverdale and I learned to love him."

George Barton, his close and almost life-long friend, was also lost to him through the war, though in a different way. To George Barton the Quaker peace testimony became untenable in the face of German aggression. He not only withdrew from membership in the Society of Friends and became a communicant in the Episcopal Church but he became a deacon and then an ordained minister. In 1922 he resigned his professorship of Biblical Literature at Bryn Mawr after thirty-one years of service. There is a draft of an appreciative directors' minute in Rufus Jones's handwriting. His turning away from Friends was accompanied by a bitterness which encompassed also the work of the American Friends Service Committee, and in a letter to the newspapers he made the charge that must have seemed to Rufus Jones the most unjust and uncomprehending one possible, that it was established as a means of draft-dodging. In subsequent years attempts were made from both sides to bridge the gulf that opened between them, but the old confidence and companionship were gone.

During the summers Pendle Hill cottage at South China was a haven to which, however often he might be called away, he always returned with joy. "I have bought a Ford motor car which I propose to drive as soon as I can learn how," he wrote to Violet Hodgkin. "I hope I shall like it, but I do not take kindly to mechanics." It was a relief to all when Mary was old enough to take the wheel of the Model T and its successors.

The story is still told in South China of a professor from Haverford and his wife who drove over from Littleton, N. H. where they were spending the summer, to see Rufus Jones. At the blacksmith shop in the village they stopped and asked where Dr. Jones lived.

"Dr. Jones?" The smith scratched his head. "There ain't no Dr. Jones here."

Puzzled, they repeated their question and got the same answer again. As they started to move away, the man ran after them on the spur of a second thought.

"You don't mean Rufus, do you? He *does* live here!"

For his fifty-seventh birthday in 1920 a number of his friends gave him a party, and Agnes L. Tierney of Germantown, expressed what they all felt in verse so warm and witty that parts of it must be given here.

> Who is the Pep of Quakerdumb
> And only has to twirl his thumb
> To make his mechanism hum?
>   One Rufus!
>
> Who cracks our sides until we moan
> With tales of people he has known
> "Down East" where funny folks are grown?
>   Gay Rufus!
>
> Who never needs to be too late
> To catch a train and make a date
> Because his stride is five feet eight?
>   Fast Rufus! . . .
>
> Who points the way to heedless youth
> And guides to glimmerings of the Truth
> Their cerebrations so uncouth?
>   Prof. Rufus.
>
> Who rummages among the saints
> And pokes into their self-restraints

And all their deadly virtues paints?
    Scribe Rufus . . .

Who hopping round o'er all creation
To preach and pray or feed a nation
Shows forth the fruits of consecration?
    Good Rufus!

Who hath to keep his torch alight
A wife so clever, wise and right
She doth to valorous deed incite?
    Her Rufus!

Who'll take these verses as they're meant
And recognize their real intent
To seal a friendly sacrament?
    Our Rufus!

Athens and the Holy Land

For twenty years Rufus Jones had been planning to go to Greece and Palestine when he reached the age of sixty. Now his sixtieth birthday was approaching, Bryn Mawr's new president was installed, the great A.F.S.C. programs in Germany and Russia were drawing toward an end, the Quaker history was finished, Mary was happy in college. He decided to take a long-due Sabbatical leave as soon as the first semester classes were over in January 1923.

On the last day of November an accident almost put an end to all his plans. He and Elizabeth Jones had been spending Thanksgiving with her parents in Moorestown. As they left, Rufus Jones, hurrying across the road ahead to hold the trolley-car, failed to see an automobile coming toward him on the left. He was struck and thrown twenty feet. Even before his horrified wife and her brothers, expecting never to see him move again, had rushed to his side, he managed to pull himself over to the curb. He was carried into the house. Doctors came and pronounced broken bones but no major injuries. The next day he was writing reassuringly to Mary, "I think there will be no serious results and we can live happily ever after . . . Dearest love from thy battle-scarred father."

X-rays disclosed three broken ribs, a radiating fracture at the top of the tibia, torn ligaments, and water on the knee. In a short time he was ensconced, his leg in a cast, in a high hospital bed in his study, where his students came daily and he taught them, lying flat on his back and though physically a "t.r." feeling "all the time an unusual élan."

The accident had a deep inner meaning for him. Not only did he feel, as he told the Meeting in Moorestown the next time that he spoke there, that God had saved his life because He had more work for him to do, but also he had known a welling up of life and energy akin to a mystical experience. In a remarkable article entitled "Why I Enroll Among the Mystics," written nine years later, he wrote of this time:

"There was no single moment of invasion or of uprush. I discovered that a new life and power *had come* to me without my knowing precisely *when* it came . . . I cannot quite date the discovery. But it began to dawn upon me that a 'restoration' of another sort had gone on. I seemed in a new way to be liberated from fears and anxieties and worries. I had entered into an unexpected tranquility and peace. More than that I had gained an immense increase of vitality and *vis viva*. Life had become a more joyous and radiant affair than I had ever known. I no longer cared anything about arguments to prove the reality of God, any more than I did to prove the incomparable worth of the human love which surrounded my life as I lay quietly recovering . . . It has always seemed to me a case of quiet mystical receptivity. Spiritual energies of a more or less permanent order flowed in and operated, as though God at my fountains far off had been raining."

Only a few days before they were to sail, Elizabeth Jones's father, Joel Cadbury, died after an illness,—a man with a "lovely sense of humor and a fine bloom of joy," Rufus Jones wrote to Mary, "about as good a man as one could be." The next day his wife followed him.

When Rufus and Elizabeth Jones sailed on the cruise ship, *Empress of Scotland*, on the second of February, they must have been, in spite of their happy anticipations, subdued and sorrowful. Rufus Jones, moreover, was still on crutches.

There were stops at Cadiz and Seville, Gibraltar and Algiers, but Rufus Jones did little sightseeing, for he was still too lame to enjoy it. He read a great deal, steeping himself in the history of Greece, preached one Sunday on the boat, "wasted" a day writing an article, and shortly before they reached Athens delivered a lecture on Greece that filled the passengers with excited anticipation.

On a glorious morning late in February the ship steamed into the Bay of Salamis, and because the sea was too rough to land at Piraeus anchored at the very spot where the battle of Salamis was fought in 480 B.C. Because of long and exasperating delays in landing, it was late afternoon before they could go ashore, but Rufus Jones's old friend Augustus Murray, who that year was Director of the American School for Classical Studies in Athens, met the Joneses with a car and carried them off.

They went directly to the Acropolis, where Rufus Jones, lame leg, stick, and all, was pushed and pulled up the steep steps of the Propylea, to stand at last where he had so often stood in imagination. "We saw the Parthenon under perfect conditions," he wrote to Mary. "The light was wonderful and as the sun dropped the colors on the hills, mountains and sea were heavenly. Hymettus was one blaze of glory. After we finished seeing the Acrop. we went over to the Areopagus, which is quite near, and Gus recited Paul's sermon about the Unknown God."

They spent the night with the Murrays and the next day saw the Agora, drove to Kolonos and saw the site of Plato's Academy, visited two museums, and returned to the Acropolis. "I can give thee no idea of my state of mind while I was in Athens."

Elizabeth Jones added a note: "Yes, father has been thrilled and I think he was not disappointed in anything but more thrilled even than he expected. He has found a kindred spirit in a fellow traveller named Mr. Coyne, who has detail maps and can tell what happened on every spot. He and father stand map in hand and identify each spot and then speak as oracles to all inquirers."

From Athens they went on to Constantinople, to Damascus, where their dragoman was the son of one that Uncle Eli had had, to Galilee, Ramallah, and Jerusalem. "There was nothing ever like it in my life. The weather was perfect except for one awful storm on the Sea of Galilee where we came within an inch of being wrecked on the rocks by Capernaum. Nazareth was lovely with its hills and flowers. We liked Mary's fountain best because it was certainly the spot where Mary and Jesus often went to draw water . . . The ride to Ramallah . . . was thrilling. We went through Samaria and sat on Joseph's well and drank from it . . . We had four days in Jerusalem . . . The most uplifting thing is the Mount of Olives. We went there first and saw the city from above. We had tea on the Mount with Sir Herbert Samuel, the governor of Palestine, called 'High Commissioner' and Lady Samuel . . . We were there at sunset. Oh my! We went by motor to the Dead Sea down the Jericho Road where the Good

Samaritan came, then to the Fords of Jordan where the Israelites crossed and where Jesus was baptized, and then to old Jericho. What a trip! We spent a day in Hebron where Abraham lived and where he and Sarah, Isaac and Rebecca, Jacob and Leah are buried."

"Some members of the cruise," his daughter writes, "were surprised at his apparent intimacy with a country he had never seen. One woman remarked, after he had explained that this was due to a lifetime of Bible study, 'Why I'd have brought a Bible too if I had realized it was about Palestine.' "

At Cairo, in Shepheard's Hotel, they ran into Rendel Harris and Herbert G. Wood, had dinner with them and "talked for three hours without a pause for wind." Here also he took time to write an essay, "Death as a Spiritual Fact," for the London *Friend*. "I can only add my personal experience," he wrote, "that much which I have done in the last twenty years has been done in the conviction that I was left here to finish what those dearer to me than life would have been doing if they had remained." They took the trip up the Nile to Luxor, where they struggled with fatigue, bad food, sickness, dust and horses, to which Rufus Jones was still allergic. But he was not to be defeated. He donned his wife's veil as a filter, and drove miles through desert valleys to the tombs of the kings.

The following week they were in Rome. St. Peter's, for all its glory, once more struck him as inferior to the great Gothic cathedrals of York, Chartres, Strasbourg, Westminster. "Mother likes it more than I do," he wrote to Mary, "and she thrills over Rome more than I do, I think. I see over it to Greece!" If as John Buchan maintained, people are either Greek or Roman (and he declared himself to be a Roman) Rufus Jones was unquestionably Greek.

His letters to his daughter, who had grown to be a most satisfactory friend and companion, are vivid and enthusiastic, with now and then a gem of fatherly advice and concern gleaming among the monuments and landscapes. He took great satisfaction in the poems that she was writing, and some of them he learned by heart. "If you expect to write good poetry you must sound the deeps of the human heart and feel the great emotions that make us men. Then you must tell it *clearly*." He followed with interest her doings during the holidays, commenting, "I thought Y.M. got skimped. Don't slight thy contact with Quaker things. That has made my life more than anything else has." He compared the "flappers" on the cruise unfavorably with Mary. "We are thrown all the time with American girls who know

nothing, have no ideas, no historical background and no interests. They
are certainly pitiable objects—just pegs to hang good clothes on . . .
Dear Mary, don't forget that *sense* is a big asset for life—just plain
sense."

They left the cruise at Southampton and went to Oxford, where
they rented a house on Walton Street. "It is not very elegant or
swagger but it is comfortable and we are well fed and taken care of
by a trained butler and his wife, who is an expert cook." Here they
were joined by Elizabeth's younger sister Emma Cadbury. For the
next month or six weeks Rufus Jones and his wife worked in the
Bodleian and Radcliffe Camera libraries on the research for his next
book, THE CHURCH'S DEBT TO HERETICS. While in Oxford, too, he
found a masseur who was able to take the pain and stiffness out of
his troublesome knee.

There were many interruptions. "I am so loaded with engagements,
dinners, teas, walks and other forms of wickedness that I have no
time to write and to make matters worse I am overwhelmed with
letters, cables, telegrams which must be answered."

It was perhaps at this time that an incident occurred which has
been related by John Wilhelm Rowntree's daughter, Jean. Friends
in Oxford had arranged a public meeting at which Rufus Jones would
speak and tea would be served afterwards. In making their plans they
had underestimated the drawing power of his name. As more and
more chairs were brought into the room and still people were standing
at the back, those responsible for supplying the tea began to look
anxious. Rufus Jones, with his characteristic combination of the
spiritual and the practical, broke off in the middle of a sentence to
lean over and say in a low voice to the members of the tea committee
on the front row, "You can cut the cakes in half," and then resumed
his discourse without a pause.

He found time also to see Canterbury for the first time, to attend
London Yearly Meeting, and to visit old friends at Jordans, York and
Scalby. In York he was lunching with another of John Wilhelm
Rowntree's daughters and her husband—Margaret and George
Crossley—in a restaurant filled with clergymen there for a conference.
In one of those silences that sometimes occur in crowded places his
voice rang out: "Well, after you've been in a storm on the Sea of
Galilee, you begin to understand why people want to get out of small
boats and walk!"

Wherever he went he had speeches to make. "I don't believe anybody could have thought of another address for me to give, as I spoke on almost every occasion and every topic," he wrote to Mary.

One of the high points of this time in England was his meeting with Friedrich von Hügel, with whom he had corresponded and whose books on mysticism had meant so much to him. "It was a momentous event in my life," he wrote many years later, "to talk freely with this extraordinary man of the matters that meant the most to me of anything in the universe, but the most memorable feature of the visit came as I was saying good-by. He said to me, 'Before you go I want to tell you of the four conditions of life which must be fulfilled before anyone can be canonized a saint in my Church.' " The four conditions he cited were loyalty to the Faith, heroism, endowment with powers beyond ordinary human capacities, and radiance. "The old philosopher and mystic stood up in front of me, half a head taller than I was, and he raised his hands as high in the air as they could reach and said: 'They may possibly be wrong about those first three conditions, but they are gloriously right about that fourth condition—a saint must be *radiant*.' "

Much as Rufus Jones enjoyed England, it could not hold him when it was haying time in South China, and by the end of June the three Joneses were back at their beloved Pendle Hill. There Rufus Jones worked three hours a day in his log-cabin study on a series of lectures which he was to give at Yale and Oberlin the following spring. As usual there was the Fourth of July picnic, of which eggs scrambled by Rufus Jones and the hilarious tale that he told about Brother Jucundus were traditional features for an ever-widening circle of small fry whose adored "Cousin Rufus" he was. The story, which he learned from William Charles Braithwaite, as summarized by Mary Hoxie Jones, was about a "monk from St. Mary's Abbey in York, who was a model Brother for 364 days in the year but on Lady Day slipped away from the Abbey to York Fair. Here temptations beset him and he could not refuse. Getting thoroughly drunk, Brother Jucundus would clamber into a swing-boat and shout at the top of his lungs, 'In dulce jubilo! Up, *Up*, UP we go!' For this serious offense poor Brother Jucundus was taken down to the Abbey cellar and walled in, with a jug of water, a loaf of bread, and, to bring the Middle Ages closer to the Twentieth Century an electric toaster was included. How Brother Jucundus weathered this desperate punishment and ended the tale as an Abbot, Rufus Jones gave with tremendous flourishes, bringing in as often as he could the magic refrain, 'In dulce jubilo! Up, *Up*,

UP we go!' If he varied so much as a jot or tittle in the telling, a child would instantly demand the correct version. Sleepy children went home across the fields chanting 'In dulce jubilo' as they went, not knowing the meaning of the words but feeling the happiness of the moment."

In his regular sermons at the Friends Meeting House in South China, he never failed to remember the children who sat together on the front rows under the pulpit. "I don't suppose you children have ever heard a sermon about *grasshoppers*, have you?" he once began, and having captured their attention with the story of Joshua and Caleb and the ten spies who had a "grasshopper complex," he went on to interpret deeper meanings for the grownups. Or he would explain the mysterious word Selah, found in the Psalms. "Selah means, It's wonderful! Think of that! Think of what has been said!"

THE CHURCH'S DEBT TO HERETICS, written largely that autumn and published the following year, was an examination of the contributions made by heretics to the Christian Church, in stirring it up to sharper definitions and in opening up new insights. Among his heretical heroes were Pelagius, Abelard, Wyclif, Joan of Arc, Luther, Calvin, and George Fox. The book had, Rufus Jones noted, "a very favorable reception."

The lectures given at the Yale Divinity School and Oberlin School of Theology formed the basis for another book published in 1924, FUNDAMENTAL ENDS OF LIFE. Most people, he wrote, are concerned chiefly with secondary ends, like service and pleasure and profit, instead of the values which are good in themselves, beauty, love, goodness, truth. He went to Plato, Plotinus, the Gospels, Kant, and mystical experience for answers to the question, Why were we born? What are we here for?

The pressure for lectures and articles continued unabated. "I live like falling leaves in a constant whirl," he wrote to Mary. "Hither and yon I go, always talking like a gab-machine." And again, "I talk of quiet and hush and I praise concentration, but I rush about like a dervish and act as though the life here below were a mad dash from x to y—two unknown points." He traveled from Virginia to Vermont, from Boston to California, speaking on mysticism, on George Fox, whose tercentenary was celebrated in 1924, on Quakerism. Mt. Holyoke was now one of the colleges, like Harvard and Bryn Mawr, that considered itself entitled to annual talks by him.

Dean and Mrs. Inge came to visit the Joneses in Haverford, and the two mystics spoke on the same program at the Bellevue-Stratford Hotel in Philadelphia. The story has been widely told—as it has been told of many others—that at night the English visitor put his boots outside his bedroom door to be blacked and that the American host quietly polished them and put them back, but Rufus Jones declared it apochryphal. "The true story of Dean Inge's visit may interest you," he wrote years later to an inquiring correspondent. "We were hunting for our hats and coats in the mazes of a great hotel in Philadelphia after his lecture, and he stopped and said with a smile, 'Don't you think we had better get a non-mystical person to guide us?'"

"New Noises, New Calls"

"THE lectures I am asked to give are the quadrennial lectures of the National Council," wrote Rufus Jones to Mary in March, 1926, "and they would be before a group of the leading Christians in China (mostly natives). They could not have an Englishman or a clergyman or a Y.M.C.A. leader. They are all taboo this year. So they turned to me . . . I should hope if we go that thee would go too."

That year in China was a more critical one than most people realized at the time. The Kuomintang, the creation of Sun Yat-sen, was experiencing a rebirth after the death of Sun in 1925. Russian Communists under Borodin were helping to train Chiang K'ai-shek's armies and were shaping Kuomintang policy, stirring up resentment against foreign merchants and against Christian schools, churches and hospitals, which they branded as agents of imperialism. Because of the Shanghai Incident of May 30, 1925, when British-commanded police fired into a crowd of students demanding release of comrades arrested in connection with a strike at a Japanese-owned factory, feeling ran especially high against the British. The Y.M.C.A., wishing to celebrate its fortieth anniversary in China with a series of lectures such as it had been giving every four years, decided that only a Quaker would be neutral enough under existing conditions to be acceptable to the Chinese.

President Comfort urged Rufus Jones to accept the invitation, even though it would require his absence from the college during the fall semester. The A.F.S.C. and the two Philadelphia Yearly Meetings supported the proposal enthusiastically. The churches of Philadelphia united in giving him a farewell luncheon. "It was amazing to hear the things they said," he wrote to Mary, "and I felt as though I was at my own funeral listening to it all through a hole in the coffin!" He had "an interesting interview" with President Coolidge and received his "personal encouragement," though as he admitted candidly to his daughter, he felt that "not much came of it. Anyway I got him to talk a lot and we did not sit silent like two woodchucks looking at each other."

After he had delivered the commencement address at Bryn Mawr and the baccalaureate sermon at Mt. Holyoke, and had attended Mary's graduation ceremonies, the three Joneses sailed from Vancouver on the 24th of June. For the only time in his life he kept a more or less regular journal, and the account of his experiences, his observations and reflections on the changing scene in Asia make fascinating and somewhat wry reading, now that it is too late to profit by his insights.

"This is our first day on the Pacific," he wrote on the first page of his leather-bound notebook. "It is a new situation with new noises, new calls. We must meet the unusual and speak to the age, to the eastern mind in fresh and creative ways . . . I have seldom ever been so penetrated with a deep happiness."

The long days at sea gave time for reading—Whitehead's SCIENCE AND THE MODERN WORLD, Scott's VOYAGE OF THE DISCOVERY and a biography of Robert Louis Stevenson—and for reflection. He thought it a pity that the missionaries had brought rationalistic burdens into a foreign land. "Instead of putting a constructed system of thought down upon them ready made, we ought to give them inspiration and spiritual help to build their own faith in conformity with their own religious genius. There is no *one* sacred pattern system of Christianity to be imposed or adopted outright. Christianity is all the time being built. It needs the genius of Japan, China, and India as much as it needed and used the genius of the Hebrews or the Greeks or the Romans."

They spent sixteen days in Japan, crowded days full of interest and of beauty, meeting with the small but active group of Japanese Quakers in Tokyo and in Ibaragi Prefecture, visiting Nikko, Kamakura, Karuizawa, Kyoto, and Nara, conferring with some of the Japanese leaders. They saw the little group of houses erected by the A.F.S.C. after the earthquake of 1923, and marvelled at the vitality of the nation which could pull itself together after so sweeping a disaster and rebuild so swiftly. A nation can recover from destruction of its external wealth, he reflected, and rebuild. "But if you destroy their fundamental sources of life, the fertility of the soil, the vitality of the climate, the nation suffers a hopeless collapse, as occurred to Greece in the fourth century." He then made the application from the outward to the inward, as he was so fond of doing, "Its deepest life, its truest vitality are to be found in the moral subsoil of a people, in the moral and spiritual ideals of the rank and file." These words, little changed, he incorporated later in his lectures in China.

One of the most interesting experiences that he had in Japan was the dinner given for him by Viscount Shibusawa. "He is 87 years old, a type of man like Charles W. Eliot, interested in the best constructive lines of thought and action," he wrote to Wilbur Thomas. "The banquet was attended by some of the foremost scholars and leaders in the country. The topic for the occasion was on international relations and I spoke of the fundamental basis of a new and better civilization. My reception was generous and hearty and I had about an hour of personal and intimate conversation with the Viscount on the future relations between Japan and America." In his Journal, he recorded some of that personal conversation: "He talked with utmost frankness of the deep wound which our exclusion laws had given him, the discouragement it had brought to his hopes, but of his strong faith in the fairness and ideal spirit of the American people."

"I have quite lost my heart to Japan," he wrote as they left, "and want very much to have a longer visit there sometime."

Sailing from Kobe on a small Japanese ship, the only foreign passengers, they made their way through the fairy-like beauty of the Inland Sea and across the Yellow Sea to Tsing-tao on the southern side of the Shantung Peninsula.

Here they encountered a serious problem, an epidemic of cholera spreading from Shanghai. Should they all be inoculated with the new serum? It was an agonizing decision for Rufus Jones, who remembered only too vividly the aftermath of the anti-diphtheria serum which had been given to Lowell, but he decided in favor of the inoculation and they all remained well.

Elizabeth Jones and Mary stayed with friends in a summer colony of missionaries on a point of land jutting into Kiaochow Bay near Tsing-tao, while Rufus Jones went on to the Y.M.C.A. Conference at

Tsinan, the Capital of Shantung Province, twelve hours distant by express train.

Five hundred Chinese Christians and about thirty American and English Y.M.C.A. secretaries and missionaries met in the University of Shantung, one of the largest of the union universities in China. The August days were stiflingly hot and the nights even worse. Rufus Jones found lecturing with an interpreter difficult at first, tripped up as he was at every paragraph to wait for the halting delivery of unintelligible Chinese words, but after the second lecture he got a more fluent interpreter and things went better. In his six lectures he presented Christianity not as a set of dogmas at war with modern scientific thought, but as "a way of life and a religion of the spirit," and he met here as throughout China a warm and even eager response. The lectures were later published by the Association Press in Shanghai in a little book entitled RELIGION AND LIFE, which contains in brief and simple form most of the basic ideas upon which the whole structure of his philosophy was built.

On the day of his final lecture they gave him a great dinner party, planned without any reference to the fact that he had been on a restricted diet for years. "We had more than 30 different dishes of food, including the famous sea-slugs, bird's nest, shantung duck, lotus seeds and all the rest of Chinese delicacies. It was immense and amazing! I ate something of each thing, all with chop-sticks—and I lived through the night."

After the Conference he had expected to have his wife and daughter join him, but a storm had washed out the railroad tracks between Tsing-tao and Tsinan, and so he had to go on alone, greatly disappointed, to his next engagement.

The Nationalist armies under Chiang K'ai-shek were marching northward against the northern leader Wu P'ei-fu, but news was vague and indefinite. "As to the fighting," Elizabeth Jones wrote to her brothers at home, "I can make nothing out of the reports and most persons seem to regard it chiefly as an inconvenience. In the papers here however we read of the N.Y. subway strikes and difficulties in Mexico, the prolonged coal strike in England and the revolt in South Russia."

Of the forty Chinese Christian leaders who had been expected to take part in the Retreat on Tai-shan, only eight actually got there. With eight Westerners, it was a party of sixteen who started up the long climb on August 12th. Tai-shan was the oldest and most famous

of the five "sacred mountains" of China—a five-thousand foot peak
with a Gate of Hell at the bottom and a Gate of Heaven at the top,
and six thousand ancient granite steps in between. The members of
the party were carried in chairs by coolies to the houses half way
up, where the Retreat was to be held, but Rufus Jones, not liking to
be carried by his fellow human beings, walked most of the way on his
own feet.

He rejoiced in the presence of Henry T. Hodgkin, a cousin of
Violet Hodgkin, and one of the founders of the Fellowship of Reconciliation, now in China as Secretary of the National Christian
Council. Of the entire group only Rufus Jones and Mrs. Wilmot D.
Boone of the Presbyterian Mission were able to milk the goats which
were their entire source of milk, and for the rest of his life he would
laugh about it reminiscently, with pride in the accomplishment.

They studied fundamental Christian problems in the mornings—
Rufus Jones guided the group through the five great historical conceptions of Christ—and practical Christian problems in China in the
evenings, and in the afternoons they explored the mountain, to which
pilgrims had been coming for more than five thousand years. One day
they made the climb to the top, and in the temple of Confucius there
Rufus Jones discussed the nature of authority in religion.

"We are having a happy time and it is a good group," he wrote to
his wife, "but I hardly see how the conference can prove to be an
epoch. There is not enough unity and coherence to it and no one has
quite clear enough vision of what Chinese Christianity ought to be
or do." Later, however, he recorded in his Journal that he felt it
was even more important than the big Conference in Tsinan.

After the Retreat was over he had to make a three-and-a-half hour
train journey from the foot of Tai-shan to Tsinan, where he was
eagerly looking forward to being reunited with his family. It was a
very hot day. Hungry and thirsty after his descent of the mountain,
he was aghast to find the train crowded to the steps. Down the track
he saw an open freight-car, and with William Hung, dean of Yenching
University, he hurried to it and climbed in. Also in the car were a
hundred coolies in loin cloths and three soldiers with guns.

As the train toiled over the plain in the broiling sun, Rufus Jones
set about making friends with his fellow passengers. Opening his
umbrella, he shared its shade with one coolie after another, nodding
and smiling to show his good will. After a while, one of the soldiers
gave him a bowl of bean soup from a thermos and another a cup of

tea, and he drank them for the fellowship, trusting that the heat would kill the germs. Later he learned that the coolies were taking fifty boxes each containing a thousand silver dollars to their war lord and the soldiers were guarding them.

The next three weeks the three Joneses spent in Peking, where they were lodged in the Yenching School of Christian Studies. Martial law was declared while they were there and plans changed from day to day because of troop movements, but they suffered no inconvenience except being obliged to abandon their hope of seeing the Great Wall. The first week, while the university was still having vacation, was given up to sightseeing; after that Rufus Jones had sixteen long discussion meetings in fourteen days with a variety of groups, as well as many luncheon and dinner parties and personal conferences. Wellington Koo gave a luncheon for him, at which he met most of the members of the Chinese cabinet and three ex-premiers.

He found the neglect of the great Temple of Heaven sad, but, he wrote in his Journal, "still sadder is the political collapse everywhere apparent in this vast empire-republic. The functions of government are in large measure suspended. I have had most important conversations with our U S. Minister McMurray, our Commissioner, Silas Strawn, and the first secretary of the legation, Mr. Peck. They all began their labors over here with idealism and with a sympathetic desire to serve China, but they seem at the moment extremely pessimistic. They see no hope of a stable, dependable government being formed, they find no existing courts or system of legal procedure that would insure fairness and justice either for Chinese or foreigners. They have told me tales of corruptions and of the perversion of justice which discourage the most loyal friends of China . . . This deep pessimism has been bred in this generous and fairspirited American citizen (Strawn) by nine months of contact with politicians and grafters. My dealings have been with scholars and broad-minded Christian leaders who are among the best men I have ever met."

Four days later, after he had had a long talk with Dr. W. W. Yen, ex-Premier, sound scholar, and public man of distinction, he recorded the Oriental point of view. After paying tribute to Americans, W. W. Yen complained that the diplomats wanted to see immediate results. "They do not understand the oriental habits of mind. They bring the atmosphere of Wall St. and American hurry. They are not willing to wait for slow developments, for postponements, for the leisurely and evasive methods. They lose their idealism and are im-

patient and grow critical . . . Dr. Yen is very fearful of the economic
encroachment of Japan . . . I asked Dr. Yen what he thought would
be the effect of Russian influence, he said the Russian emissaries had
roused the students to their pitch of opposition to foreign influence
and to a revolt against capitalism and that they had trained the armies
but he believed there was no likelihood that China would ever adopt
Communism . . . The young and irresponsible students might shout
for it and the factory labor unions might call for it but that the
movement would collapse as soon as it struck the stone wall of rural
China."

Because of fighting in Hankow, they went from Tientsin, where
Rufus Jones had ten meetings in four days, to Nanking and thence
to Shanghai, where Elizabeth Jones read proof on the forthcoming
book, FAITH AND PRACTICE OF THE QUAKERS, and Rufus Jones addressed
twenty-three meetings and conferences, answering the questions of
non-Christian and anti-Christian as well as Christian students, including such challenges as: "Do you believe that Jesus Christ was born
of Miss Mary without any husband?"

"Most of the Chinese students expect science to answer all their
problems. Where they are anti-religious it is usually because they
identify religion and superstition and believe both to be incompatible
with science. They have almost no conception of the deeper issues
of life. They have little training in Aesthetics, Ethics, Philosophy or
the philosophical basis of religion. Science is for them the one way
to truth and reality . . . The same old difficulty turns up here that
meets one at home. The class-room presents a materialistic universe
and the religious teacher is supposed to correct the picture in some
tour-de-force lectures or sermons. . . . The missionairies have unfortunately too often presented a type of Christianity at sharp variance with modern science and when *that* is rejected, as it is by most
students, there is no one to interpret the deeper and truer aspects of
Christian faith . . . China desperately needs a *live* religion, dynamic
enough to control personal character and to rebuild the moral and
social habits of the people. This is what Christianity should be doing."

In Hong Kong, to which they went by boat from Shanghai, he
talked with the British Colonial Secretary, who asked him questions
about what he had learned from his contacts with the Chinese. In
regard to the general hostility to Great Britain, Rufus Jones said, "I
often asked them why they were so deeply antagonistic to the British
and the answer usually given was the superior attitude of the English

and their exclusive manners. They never recognize us in the street. They never remember us after they are introduced to us, was the comment. High-handed ways of dealing with the Chinese throughout the entire imperial period was almost [always] referred to, with especial emphasis on the opium policy past and present and above all upon the shooting in Shanghai and Canton and just now the Wanshien incident."

The Englishman defended British action, saying that "the Chinese were cruel, unreasonable, inefficient and only partially civilized and therefore not to be treated as on the same plain [sic] as those who came among them from Europe. I told him that whatever might be the impartial facts about the status of civilization we must all realize that we are confronted in China with a very significant state of mind that must now be faced squarely and be dealt with adequately. The Chinese believe that they have a superior type of civilization, far more ancient than that of any existent nation. They are proud and self-conscious. They feel the outrage of being treated as below the dignity and standing of any other nation. They are forced to have their tariff dictated by other powers. Their rivers and inland waters are patrolled by the gunboats of other powers. They are forced to grant humiliating concessions and they are subjected daily to attitudes and manners that are designed to keep them humble and subject. I concluded by saying that it was my impression that there would never be peace and settled order in China until that mental state was altered and a new psychological state created. I told him that gunboats would not change that. He took full notes and said, 'This is all very important. I want you to go with me and tell the Governor General what you have told me.' Unfortunately I had no free time before sailing."

After a little more than a week in Canton, visiting Elizabeth Jones's brother, Dr. William Cadbury, who was at Lingnan University Hospital, they sailed for Colombo. They had been in China for three months and a day, Rufus Jones had given one hundred and fifteen addresses, he had attended many forty-course dinners, and had lost ten pounds. In a time when anti-foreign and anti-Christian feeling had reached a peak, he had been welcomed and heard everywhere. "Talk about open doors!" he wrote. "The hinges were off and the doors gone. I could have kept up my meetings at the same pace for six months more."

To Wilbur Thomas he summed up his experience in these words: "With all the upsets, military battles, floods, bandits, strikes and other obstacles I have never missed an engagement or failed to be at an appointed meeting. I have not been ill for a single hour and that seems nearly miraculous. I am overwhelmed with thanksgiving that it could all have happened and I feel that an invisible Divine Hand has all the time opened the way and led me on."

The three weeks spent mostly at sea between Hongkong and Madras gave him time for a much needed rest. He prepared for India by reading Pratt's FAITHS OF INDIA and Mukerji's MY BROTHER'S FACE, and for Manila by reading Frank Laubach's THE PEOPLE OF THE PHILIPPINES. During the very crowded day and a half which they spent in Manila, he had time to meet and talk with students and to form an impression of them. After meeting Dr. Laubach's class in Sociology at the University, he wrote in his Journal that the students were "intense patriots and to a person are heart and soul for independence. I have never seen, not even in Canton, such passion for self-government and national independence . . . At 9:30 I addressed the students of the Elementary and the High School jointly. There were about 400, half women. They were quick as a flash to catch my points and any touches of humor. It was another world from China. Every face was alert and full of life. They are much more wide awake and immensely quicker and much more religious in nature and spirit." Talks not only with the students but with faculty members and Y.M.C.A. leaders, led him to the conclusion: "I profoundly hope we shall not triffle [sic] with these remarkable people, that we shall not embitter them or spoil our own chance of doing one of the finest deeds in history."

Penang, Singapore, and four wonderful days in Ceylon were beads on the string that led to Madras. There he went to a Meeting for Worship with about twenty-five Friends, and had his first encounters with Indian students, whom also he found very different from the Chinese. The Indian student was "speculative, idealistic, mystic-minded and often a religious devotee." Caring less for science than for language and literature, he was eagerly patriotic and nationalistic, and thirsting for independence. "They are touchy, easily offended and move in an inner world quite unlike that of the American student. It is not easy to talk to them on religion for religion means something entirely different from what it means to me. The chasm between classes (casts) [sic] makes it hard to deal with my familiar ideas of fellowship and friendliness."

Travelling in India they found different from any previous experience, and they made an unusual concession to the difficulties. "I took a 'servant' in India," Rufus Jones confessed to Wilbur Thomas, "and now I am forever spoiled for travelling without one. We had a perfect jewel of a servant who did everything for us both on trains and in hotels. Neither trains nor hotels have any bedding or any 'service.'"

In Calcutta, Benares, Allahabad, Delhi, Rufus Jones met Friends and misisonaries and university people; he studied India and the Indians. The poverty of the people, the ignorance of the priests, the low level of temple religion, the "fixed" and "set" minds of the audiences he met, troubled and depressed him. He was deeply stirred by the sight of the Ganges and its crowds, and his spirits were lifted by the visit to Sarnath, near Benares, where they saw the Stupa, the Asoka pillar and the excavated ruins of the monastery on the spot where Buddha began his preaching. "He seems to me," he wrote, "with all the errors of his thinking and his practices the person next to Christ among the great revealers and the one who besides the Galilean most clearly reveals and *lives* love and tenderness as a way of life."

Of the Taj Mahal he wrote, "Only a few times in one's earthly life is [one] given to see absolute perfection and when one of these experiences comes it is well to be moved . . . Never, except in the Parthenon, have I felt in the same way the marvelous power of form . . . The Parthenon in its full glory had the advantage of *movement* and *action* in the life-like friezes and consequently it expressed the joy and power of Greek life. Here there is the calm that fits Indian life. It is perfect beauty in repose."

But the high point of his visit to India was his meeting with Gandhi. Soon after he knew that he was going to make the trip to the East, he had written to Gandhi asking if he might see him. The letter, in its largeness of spirit, its combination of humility and confidence, is one of his most characteristic writings. After explaining his misson to China he went on to say:

"I deeply desire to see you. It has been on my mind long before the opportunity for this visit to India came. I know that you want to be quiet and that you ought not to be disturbed. But I am not coming as a tourist or out of curiosity. I am coming as a friend and as one who will be greatly helped by a contact with you at this crucial time when our main business is building a real spiritual civilization." He told the story of St. Louis and Brother Giles, from the *Little Flowers of St. Francis*, how they had met and embraced and Louis had gone away again without saying anything, and how the brothers had protested afterwards. " 'We did not need to talk,' Giles replied. 'I read his heart and he read mine.' I feel sure that you and I could have a visit like that, though I hope that we should talk a little too." He had enclosed with his letter a letter of introduction from John Haynes Holmes. At Tientsin a postal from Gandhi had caught up with him, inviting him to come to Sabarmati.

The Ashram
Sabarmati, 28-5-26

"Dear Friend," was the typewritten message, signed in pencil, "I have your letter enclosing Dr. Holmes' letter. I shall be pleased to meet you whenever you come. However busy I may be, I know that I am by no means so much rushed as people in America are. I have therefore always time to meet friends like you.

Yours sincerely,
M. K. Gandhi."

Gandhi was at this time fifty-seven years old. It was for him a time of quiet and retirement between two periods of intense activity. Behind him were the great campaign of non-violent civil disobedience which he had led, twenty-two months of imprisoment served out of a six-year sentence, and a three-week fast for the purpose of fostering Hindu-Moslem unity, which was recognized to have been a failure. Before him were the Great Salt March of 1929 and the Round Table Conference of 1931. He had withdrawn to his ashram at Sabarmati, on the opposite side of the Sabarmati River from the city of Ahmedabad. Some said that his influence was waning, that the students were disillusioned because he could not show practical results, but to the mass of the Indian population he was already Bapu, father, and to many he was a god. In his retirement he was besieged by inquiring, seeking, adoring visitors from all over the world.

Louis Fischer in his GANDHI: HIS LIFE AND MESSAGE FOR THE WORLD, describes the ashram in these words: "The ashram consisted of a group of low, white-washed huts in a grove of spreading trees. Below the compound is the river in which women pound their laundry on the flat stones and cows and buffaloes wade. All around, the scene is gently pastoral but near by are twisted masses of closely packed slum dwellings huddling under the ugly smokestacks of the Ahmedabad textile factories whose owners financed the ashram . . . The population of the settlement fluctuated from 30 at the start to 230 at its maximum. They tended the fruit trees, spun, wove, planted grain, prayed, studied, and taught in the surrounding villages."

When the three Joneses arrived at the ashram, by car from Ahmedabad, on the morning of December first, they were met by one of the
"brothers," who, explaining that Gandhi was busy at the moment,
took them on a tour of the settlement. At ten they were escorted to
Gandhi's simple hut. Rufus Jones's unpublished Journal tells the story
from there:

"A large number of native guests from the other parts of India
were having an interview to discuss the problems of their sections with
their chief. They all withdrew as we came in and we had our simple
introduction. Gandhi was sitting on a small matrass [sic] with a pillow
at his back. He does all his work sitting on the floor this way with a
little table in front of him. He wore a simple one piece cotton cloth
draped over his body but much of the body showed through and revealed his tiny, thin, physical structure in which the wonderful spirit
has its habitation. His feet were in sight and he played with his toes
with his pencil, somewhat as one plays with a watchchain as he talks.

"He went on for a few minutes talking with his secretary and asked
us to excuse him while he finished some business which had to be attended to. It gave me a good chance to study his face and head. His
hair is closely cut and is turning iron gray. He has lost his lower front
teeth and the gap is a good deal in evidence. The face is full of light
and his smile which comes often is very fine and full of charm and
gentleness. In fact, his face well fits his character and his life history
. . . He has consumed his smoke and translated his struggles into quiet
strength of character and inward depth. A child would instantly feel
at home with him and would run to him with perfect trust and confidence.

"He made us feel at ease at once when he turned and began to welcome our visit . . . I asked him whether after all his experiences of
the difficulties of life and the complications of society he still felt
that the way of love and gentleness would work. Yes, he said, it
works better than anything else will. It has become the deepest faith
of my being. It is built all through me—and he waved his hand grace-
fully over his little body—and nothing now can happen that will
destroy my faith in that principle . . .

"I asked how much he owed his way of life to the influence of
Christ and especially to the crucifixion. He replied very simply that
so far as he was *positively conscious* there was very little direct Christian influence but that the indirect and unconscious influence might
well be an important factor. He went on then to relate his contacts
with Christianity. He began with a hostile attitude toward it, for he

supposed that to be a Christian meant to drink whiskey, to smoke a
big black cigar and to eat beef. At the time he went to England he
still held these crude views of Christianity. He made friends who were
Christians and slowly discovered some of the deeper aspects of the
Christian life. A friend gave him a Bible to read and he began at
Genesis reading straight on but much confused about what it all
meant, until he got to Leviticus where he revolted and gave up his
reading, quite disillusioned in regard to the Bible. It was only in 1893
that he came upon the N.T. and learned to love the Sermon on the
Mount and the story of [the] Cross. His reading of the N.T. has been
frequent ever since and he reads it aloud and interprets it every Sat.
to the students of Ahmedabad University which is his creation. The
dear 'brother' who took us about said, We all read the N.T. and we
all love the Sermon on the Mount.

"I asked Gandhi if he knew much about Quakerism and he said
that he knew little about it except what he got from his intimate
friend Coates who was a Quaker. He has apparently read almost
nothing of our Quaker books and seemed to know little of Geo. Fox
or John Woolman. I told him about our child-feeding in Germany
after the war and he was interested in the expression of love and good
will but he asked no questions and did not show much keenness of
interest in it, I thought.

"I asked him if he had read the Little Flowers of St. Francis and he
said he had not. I reminded him that in my first letter to him I had
told the story of Brother Giles and St. Louis and he smiled beautifully
and said that he remembered the story. He said that Hindu religion
and literature was quite full of the principle of love and sacrifice and
that his own faith in love as a way of life was born out of native
sources rather than foreign sources, though he admitted the unconscious influences might have been much greater than he knew. He told
me that a friend of mine had come to see him the day before and was
still there, someone named Harrison. He sent out for him and I found
that it was Tom Harrison who was spending two days in the brotherhood and speaking in the University."

Thomas Q. Harrison was a young man who had been a part-time
Field Secretary for the Peace Section of the A.F.S.C. and in 1925
and the early part of 1926 had visited many American schools and
colleges to speak on peace. Now on a trip around the world he was
continuing his talks to students wherever he went.

"Gandhi's supreme interest is the reformation of India," the Journal continues, "the building of the new India. His ideals are all for practical ends. I felt throughout our conversation that he was profoundly *Hindu*. His interests are not very keen beyond this boundary line. His religion is saturated with Hindu color and he clings even to the outgrown superstition of his racial religion. The Gita is his sacred book. I expressed my regret to the brother who was my guide that the temple worship seemed so low and poor, expressing the feeling that it seemed too bad to encourage these types of religion. He said there are many rivers and all carry refreshing waters . . ."

Summing up the impression that Gandhi made upon him, he wrote: "Gandhi's simplicity is as natural as everything else about his life. There is no *pose* in his nature. He is thoroughly unspoiled and the most satisfactory thing about my visit was the conviction I brought away that here was a man who had attracted the attention of the whole world, a man who had controlled the thoughts of millions and influenced the destiny of an empire and who was still sincere and simple and unspoiled. It is the last test of greatness and nobility of soul. I was sorry to discover that Gandhi lacked the wider universal interests which are obviously lacking in him. He is first, last, and always Hindu. He has very little of that universal mystical experience which is the ground and basis of a really universal spiritual religion. He is not quite the prophet type. In that respect he seems to me to belong to a lower type than St. Francis. In his own sphere, however, he is an extraordinarly great man and a beautiful character—a lover of men and an unselfish spirit. It is fine to have seen him just after the Taj Mahal. They are the greatest sights to see in India!"

He had also a practical matter to discuss with Gandhi. At the Retreat on Tai-shan he had suggested that it would be a wonderful thing if Gandhi could visit China, believing that the Chinese mind would respond more easily to another Oriental than to a westerner, and the idea had been eagerly taken up. Rufus Jones was therefore the bearer of a definite invitation, and Gandhi expressed real interest in the proposal.

"Gandhi discussed at considerable length with me his proposed visit to China next summer and asked me in detail about my visit, my lectures, and my impression of China. He was especially keen to know about interpreters and the necessity of translation. I spent considerable time telling him the general situation and the state of religion in China. He seemed greatly interested in the prospect of a visit to China and he will go if the way opens for his journey."

The way never opened, evidently, for the visit never came about. It is interesting to speculate what might have been the effect on both China and India, if it had.

When the talk with Gandhi was over, the Brother who had been their guide earlier, "a most lovable and spiritual man," escorted them back to the car, and with Thomas Harrison they stopped for a few minutes at the University.

The memory of his visit to Gandhi stayed always green in Rufus Jones's heart. His later writings, books, articles, speeches, and sermons contain references to the Hindu saint, and always in terms of his personality. In 1944, Rufus Jones wrote in the *Friends Intelligencer* that he considered Gandhi "the greatest person now living on our planet," and two years later, in his LUMINOUS TRAIL, he gave him the highest praise that he had to give: "When I talked with Mahatma Gandhi he made me think of Lowell [i.e. his son] It was the same simple, naturally loving spirit in both of them."

There were ten more days in India after the visit to Gandhi, days in which he visited Quaker projects and gave lectures to some large groups, one a lecture on Mysticism before the Philosophical Society in Nagpur. He left India, he wrote, "with a certain sense of depression." After paying tribute to the many fine people whom he had met, "well-rounded and spiritually organized," he went on to say that he did not find "the inward depth of life I expected to find in India nor do I discover as much moral and spiritual earnestness as I looked for. The Hindu popular religion shocks me and revolts me . . . The mystical religion which I assumed to be an inherent part of Indian life and thought is not much in evidence and has little to commend it. India possesses methods of meditation and a technique of concentration which are worthy of careful consideration but they do not appear to produce much spiritual fruit in the way of enhanced personal quality or social constructive energy . . . They claim that India's contribution has been metaphysical and rational and not intuitive and in the way of vision. They call for speculative work not mystical experience . . . I see nowhere any sign of a *live* mystical interest or a present mystical *movement* in India, using the word mysticism in the western sense of an immediate personal discovery of God . . . The doctrine of Karma expressed through transmigration is a view that *blights* everything it touches. It counts the universe to be *just*, but it makes life in a world of pitiless justice a dark and hopeless affair. It is a land of shadows as compared with the geniality of China and the gaiety of Japan."

After 1926, nevertheless, one sees ideas that stem from his Indian experience entering into his books, and perhaps he himself would consider that his truest summing up of Indian religious and philosophic thought was not what he wrote in his Journal while he was still in that country, but what he said at the end of his book, NEW STUDIES IN MYSTICAL RELIGION, published in 1927:

"Perhaps some day we in the west will learn the secret which India has always possessed—that the soul is the eternally important fact and its testimony the ground of all truth."

Christmas that year they spent in Ramallah at the Friends School, where the library in memory of Lowell still sheltered happy children. They went to the Shepherds' Field near Bethlehem on Christmas Eve, an experience which became a wonderful memory. Rufus Jones described it later in his Christmas story called "The Shepherd Who Missed the Manger."

"Here on this memorable night we ate our modern sandwiches and drank hot coffee out of thermos bottles, which Moses with his manna and quails never dreamed of. We sat under rustling olive trees and watched the sun sink over the Plains of Sharon and seem to fall into the Mediterranean beyond . . . In a little while the entire sky from the Mount of Olives in the East to the Great Sea in the West was filled with what looked like Seraphim, with outspread wings; for as everybody, I hope, knows the Seraphim, which are the highest order of angelic beings, are red—burning with love. And in between the red Seraphim were blue spaces which it was easy to imagine were Cherubim, for, as everybody knows, I am sure, Cherubim are always blue, and are the supreme knowers, 'the great Intelligences', beholding the truth with their minds. Here just above our heads, on the Shepherds' Field, on Christmas Eve, was a sky full of what looked to us like Seraphim and Cherubim. We beheld it with awe and wonder, and though we heard no words from above, we said in our hearts 'Glory to God in the highest.' And under the spell of what we had seen, we silently climbed the hill to hear the midnight Christmas Service in the Church of the Nativity. Perhaps not twice in a thousand years would there come a sky like that—and we were there the night it came!"

The Orient Again

In 1928, as a step in the reorganization of the A.F.S.C. Rufus Jones retired from the Chairmanship of the Board. The reorganization had been started late in 1924, when the work of relief following World War I seemed to have come to an end, and the Committee held a special meeting to make the vital decision whether, as a temporary emergency committee, to disband, or to continue as a permanent organization. At that time, Rufus Jones had said:

"For somewhat over seven years this Committee has been laboring to relieve human suffering, to open avenues of service for our Young Friends and to interpret Christ's way of life to the world today. God has enabled us to accomplish far more than our hearts dreamed of in those agonizing days when we began our work. We have often felt, I am sure, a strange sense of awe as we have seen the way the hand of God has led us forth and opened doors before us. The past is secure.

"It is extremely important that we should make no mistake about our future course. We should not go on unless we are sure that we have a vital mission to perform nor unless we can speak and act for the corporate membership of the Society of Friends. I do not want to see us go out and *hunt* for tasks to keep our machinery going; but if there are tasks lying clearly at our door—God-given tasks which we can do better than anybody else can—let us then once more say, 'Yes, send us to the work, and anoint us for it.' "

Among the tasks that immediately revealed themselves were con-

cern for better interracial relationships, "not by conferences and resolution, not by starting new institutions or managing old ones, but by
quietly forming new contacts, bringing peoples together in friendly
groups and practising the spirit and ideals of our way of life," and the
work of interpreting "our peace ideals and spirit to our own membership and to those who are near and kindred to us in spirit."

The decision having been made to continue the Committee, it was
set up in four sections: Foreign, Interracial, Peace, and Home Service.
The Home Service Section continued the work for miners already
begun in 1922 when the mining industry suffered from economic depression and labor strife.

Though Rufus Jones, three months after his resignation, was made
Honorary Chairman and was never out of the councils of the Committee, he turned the reins of actual leadership over to Henry J. Cadbury, who had succeeded him. In 1929 Wilbur Thomas also resigned,
and with the appointment of Clarence E. Pickett as executive secretary, the A.F.S.C. started on a new phase of work.

Forty-one years old in 1929, Clarence Pickett brought to the Service Committee a gentle, purposive and shining personality and half a
lifetime of Quaker service, through which he had come to focus his
attention on "the social application of religious faith." He had grown
up on a farm in Kansas, studied at Penn College and at Hartford
Theological Seminary, had been pastor of a Friends Meeting in Toronto, and secretary of the Young Friends Movement. At the time
when he was called to the A.F.S.C. he was professor of Bible at
Earlham College.

He first appears in Rufus Jones's correspondence in 1912, in a letter
from John Hoyland, a young English Friend who was then in the
United States. With the help and encouragement of Rufus Jones, a
team of young Friends, including John Hoyland, Corder Catchpool,
Elizabeth Fox Howard and others, had come from England and with
a group of young American Friends were visiting meetings over
the country in the interests of Quaker unity. John Hoyland met Clarence Pickett at Hartford, where he was then studying, and at once
conceived a plan to get him to England that summer, to visit Woodbrooke and engage in young Friends activities. John Hoyland turned
to Rufus Jones for help. "Does thou think it [i.e. money for passage]
could be raised anywhere?" he inquired. Rufus Jones responded by
calling on the generous and dependable T. Wistar Brown, and after
that Clarence Pickett was one of the many younger men who were

drawn into Rufus Jones's orbit and whose lives later showed the contagion of his spirit.

From 1929 until Rufus Jones's death, he and Clarence Pickett were to be closely associated in the work of the A.F.S.C. Again and again the two went together to confer quietly with people in key positions, to ask for aid in opening new services in sensitive situations, or, on the other hand, to be asked if the Committee could undertake some venture in areas of human relations where only a body known to be impartial and compassionate would be received. In 1931 at the suggestion of Herbert Hoover, then President of the United States, the Committee undertook the feeding of undernourished and tuberculosis children of miners in the coal fields of West Virginia and Pennsylvania, beginning with the sum of $225,000 which Mr. Hoover made available to them.

The lifting of the burden of the regular sessions of the Board and the Executive Committee of the A.F.S.C. in 1928 set Rufus Jones free for other enterprises. He gave three important series of lectures: the "New Era" Lectures at the University of Southern California School of Religion, in 1929, which were published under the title: SOME EXPONENTS OF MYSTICAL RELIGION, a course of lectures to the School of Religion in Athens, the same year, and the William Belden Noble Lectures at Harvard in the spring of 1931. In preparation for the latter, he took a semester's sabbatical leave and went to London, where he and Elizabeth Jones worked for three months in the British Museum on the great religious movements of the Commonwealth period. These lectures formed the basis of a book, MYSTICISM AND DEMOCRACY IN THE ENGLISH COMMONWEALTH, which bore the dedication:

"To my wife, Elizabeth B. Jones, whose cooperative help in the work of research involved in these chapters was invaluable, I dedicate this book with affectionate appreciation."

When the research for this book had been completed, they went to Greece to visit a Friends Center in Salonica, where English Friends were helping refugees, and to spend three weeks in Athens, where Rufus Jones gave five lectures on "The Nature of Religion and Man's Approach to It."

Christmas that year they spent in Assisi, and on the last day of 1929, Rufus Jones made a pilgrimage to La Verna, the mountain where St. Francis received the Stigmata, climbing through snow for the last three miles of the way. Though he had, in his younger days, been inclined to regard the stigmatization of St. Francis as an experience more psychic than spiritual, he was now, when he saw the lonely cave and stood on the narrow crevice of rock where St. Francis prayed, deeply stirred by the place and its story.

They were at home again in Haverford for the opening of the second semester in February 1930. Late in June of that year there came a telegram from John D. Rockefeller Jr. asking Rufus Jones to confer with him about "an important matter."

Rufus Jones and John D. Rockefeller Jr. had been friends for several years. Every summer Rufus Jones went to Mt. Desert, to preach at the Union Church in Northeast Harbor and since 1922 also at the little Congregational Church at Seal Harbor. Frequently he stayed with the Rockefellers at the Eyrie, high on the hill above the sea. One year when the Rockefellers were obliged to be away at the time of his coming, he visited their young sons instead, to the genuine enjoyment of both sides.

The important matter which Mr. Rockefeller now had to put before his friend had grown out of a conference in Jerusalem in the spring of 1928, which Rufus Jones had not been able to attend but for which he had written a paper that had made a profound impression.

The International Missionary Council, made up of representatives of churches and missions all over the world, had met at Jerusalem to discuss the problems of spreading Christianity in the modern world. For the first time at such a meeting questions of race relations, economic factors and other social issues were taken into account. For the first time a good deal of attention was given to the consideration of the relationship of the Christian life with the non-Christian systems, and other religions appeared in the novel light of possible allies instead of enemies to be overcome and exterminated.

In his paper, persuasive, vigorous, flickering with humor, fresh, yet scholarly, critical yet encouraging, which was read at the meeting, Rufus Jones set forth his theme boldly in the first sentence:

"No student of the deeper problems of life can fail to see that the greatest rival of Christianity in the world today is not Mohammedanism or Buddhism or Hinduism or Confucianism but a world-wide secular way of life and interpretation of the nature of things."

After tracing the historical development of the drift away from Christianity, he called on Christian leaders to welcome joyously as from God all newly discovered truth. As the early Christian church was enriched by the weaving in of Platonism and the medieval Church by Aquinas's synthesis of Aristotelian thought, so, he declared, we must have today "a fresh and living interpretation of all discovered and verified truth, through science or history." He pointed to the rejection by Oriental students of a missionary doctrine that refused to recognize scientific discoveries and taught what was to them out-worn superstition and emphasized the devastating effect on the secular-minded everywhere of the Christian's failure to "live the life about which we talk and preach." The conclusion which he found "easy to draw" was that Christian leaders must be much more carefully chosen and effectively trained, so that the message which is "the eternally precious treasure" may reach a generation that actually, though often unconsciously, is hungering for it.

Following this meeting in Jerusalem, Dr. John R. Mott, who had been its chairman, made a trip around the world visiting the principal mission fields, and in January 1930, at the invitation of Mr. Rockefeller, he addressed a group of leading Baptist laymen in New York. Out of this, with Mr. Rockefeller's encouragement and support, came the plan to make an independent, intensive study of foreign missions. Laymen of six other denominations, Congregational, Methodist, Episcopal, Presbyterian, United Presbyterian, and Reformed Church, were invited to join in the project, which now consisted of a fact-finding inquiry by technical experts, to be followed by an appraisal of the facts by fifteen commissioners, who would spend the greater part of a year visiting India, Burma, China and Japan, meeting the principal missionaries and drawing up a report and recommendations.

When Rufus Jones was asked to be a member of the appraisal group, he declined. It would mean a year away from Haverford and the time of his retirement was drawing near. "I have only two more years to teach at Haverford," he wrote to John R. Mott, "and my life is tremendously bound up with these men. Each year here means more than the one before did and I have found through my work here an amazing open door into lives and thoughts of students everywhere and my interpretation of life and of God is ripening up in just the way I want it to do. The break of a year out of the two precious ones left for this kind of work seems hardly the right thing for me to do, and those who are closest to me feel this almost more strongly than I do. An intellectual task of spiritual interpretation does seem clearly laid on me and I hesitate to go away and leave it."

A compromise was suggested. Would Rufus Jones go for half the time? His wife and daughter were invited to accompany him. "I have never been able to convey to you," wrote John R. Mott, "the position of leadership you won among the forces of the world-wide mission of Christianity through your paper for the Jerusalem meeting."

On the basis of a half year Rufus Jones accepted.

It was characteristic of him and of his way of going about things that he at once turned an appraising eye on the state of religion in America. "I felt it wrong," he said, "to go out and study the Orient without first considering the condition of Christianity at home."

He gathered around himself a little council of religious leaders, including such men as Charles Gilkie, Henry Sloan Coffin, Henry Hodgkin, Douglas Horton, and Arthur Lee Kinsolving, on whom he could call for help and advice. Some of them were also members of the Fellowship for Christian Cooperation, a rather short-lived organization of which Rufus Jones was president and to which he gave much time and thought between the years of 1930 and 1935. The question he asked them all was, "What seem to you to be the most striking and difficult intellectual and practical obstacles to the revival and spread of Christian faith in the world of this present generation?"

At a meeting in New York in January, 1931, it was decided that Rufus Jones should write, and John D. Rockefeller Jr. would subsidize, a "restatement for the present day of the fundamental content and program of the Christian religion." By the following November this statement was ready, and at a conference in Haverford his advisory council criticized it and made suggestions for changes. Under the title A PREFACE TO CHRISTIAN FAITH IN A NEW AGE it was published the following year. Though it was primarily addressed, not to the general reader, but to ministers and concerned laymen in the church, it was chosen as the May selection of the Religious Book of the Month Club.

Leaving Howard Brinton to carry on his classes at Haverford and taking with him forty term-papers to read and return, as well as the proofs of A PREFACE TO CHRISTIAN FAITH to correct, Rufus Jones, with Elizabeth and Mary, departed from Haverford on January 10, 1932. They sailed on the 15th from San Francisco on the *President Grant*. A telegram signed by Clarence Pickett gave them an encouraging send-off:

STAFF OF AMERICAN FRIENDS SERVICE COMMITTEE EXTENDS GREETINGS TO JONES FAMILY ON THEIR DEPARTURE PRAYS FOR THEIR SAFETY AND BELIEVES THAT THEIR WISDOM AND PROPHETIC SPIRIT TOGETHER WITH HUMOR AND NATIVE BUOY-

ANCE WILL MEAN MUCH TO DELEGATION AND TO FUTURE OF
MISSIONS OUR AFFECTIONS GO WITH YOU.

The three-week voyage was marked by the loss of Rufus Jones's
sixty-ninth birthday on the international date-line, by rough seas,
and by radio reports, meager but ominous, of Japanese military
activity in China.

During the previous September Japanese troops had begun the
invasion of Manchuria. On the 28th of January they had attacked
Shanghai.

Under a cold and cloudy sky the *President Grant* docked at Shanghai. The harbor was full of cruisers and gunboats of various countries.
The Joneses did not go ashore but friends came aboard and told them
the news. Part of the International Settlement had been occupied by
the Japanese; the native quarter, Chapei, had been bombed and destroyed, with great loss of life; many of their Chinese acquaintances
had lost everything. Two hundred new passengers, both westerners
and Chinese, eager to get away from Shanghai, crowded onto the
ship. Between the time that they went up the Whangpoo River one
day and came down the next, the Japanese had shelled the town and
fort of Woosung, situated at the point where the Whangpoo emptied
into the Yangtse. "Today as we came down," wrote Elizabeth Jones
to her family, "we saw the houses that had been hit and the fires still
burning that had started."

Wondering what the Commission would be able to accomplish
under these conditions, the Joneses reached Hong Kong two days
later and went directly to Canton to stay with William and Catherine
Cadbury. Within a few days the rest of the Commission, who had
been working their way up through India and Burma since October,
reached Hong Kong, and Rufus Jones joined them there at the Peninsula Hotel, Kowloon.

It was a distinguished group of people whom he met. Dr. William
Ernest Hocking, of the Harvard Philosophy Department, was the
chairman. There were two college presidents, Dr. Clarence A. Barbour
of Brown and Dr. Arlo A. Brown of Drew, and a vice-president, Dr.
Frederic C. Woodward of the University of Chicago; two medical
college deans, Dr. Henry S. Houghton of the University of Iowa
and Dr. Charles Phillips Emerson of the University of Illinois;
an agricultural economist, Dr. Henry C. Taylor; three leading
business men, Mr. Albert L. Scott of New York, Mr. Harper Sibley
of Rochester, Mr. Edgar L. Betts of Troy; and the pastor of the Brick

Presbyterian Church in New York, Dr. William Pierson Merrill. Mrs. Harper Sibley and Mrs. Hocking were there as leaders in religion and education in their own right, and Miss Ruth F. Woodsmall of the International Y.W.C.A. was the third woman member.

The first meeting with Rufus Jones was a stirring occasion. Ten leading Chinese and ten foremost missionaries had been invited to a conference with the commissioners, and Rufus Jones spoke to the whole group. Dr. Hocking remembers vividly the lift and the fresh enthusiasm that Rufus Jones, with his humor and that native buoyancy which the A.F.S.C. so much prized, brought to people who were ready to catch their second wind.

The method of procedure was to hold group conferences in the larger cities with representative bodies of missionaries, Christian nationals, and non-Christians; then to disperse for more intimate conversations and interviews, as well as visits to the missions themselves. The group was organized in nine committees. Rufus Jones served on the committees on the Mission and Indigenous Church, on Higher Education and on Literature.

For nearly four weeks Elizabeth and Mary Hoxie Jones stayed with the Cadburys in Canton, joining in the activities of Lingnan, including a Quaker wedding and the making of garments for refugees from Shanghai, while the Commission, extending their time in the south of China until the situation in the north should be clarified, visited missionary undertakings in the neighborhood of Canton. Rufus Jones with two others took an eight-day trip up the coast by steamer, stopping at Swatow, Amoy and Foochow, all missionary centers and important coastal cities. It was, he said afterwards, the most interesting single trip of the entire mission.

After a truce was effected in Shanghai, the entire group returned to that city and made their headquarters for the next two weeks at the Cathay Hotel, in the International Settlement. Now they saw the destruction and the suffering that had been wrought by the attack of the previous month.

"Three hundred thousand people lived in Chapei," wrote Rufus Jones, "and hardly a single home is left standing . . . Not often does one see more widespread signs of sheer, stark tragedy, unrelieved by any good that can come out of it . . . I am pledged to fight this thing [i.e. war] until I die."

Some of the group, including Rufus Jones, went to Nanking and Hangchow, with the risk that the return might be cut off. They got back safely, however, and reported that a section of the Lytton Commission had been in Hangchow. The Lytton Commission, which consisted of five men, an Englishman, a Frenchman, an American, an Italian, and a German, headed by Lord Lytton, had been sent by the League of Nations to investigate the Japanese action in Manchuria and Shanghai. Though they were entirely an investigating group with no power to make a settlement, the Chinese, burning with resentment toward Japan, were indignant with their failure to act.

The Laymen's Commission left Shanghai on the 26th of March and went to Peking for the last stage of their work in China. Here an attack of bronchitis which he had not been able to shake off took Rufus Jones to the Union Medical College Hospital, kept him there for a week, and prevented him from joining those members who went on to Japan via Dairen, Mukden and Korea. This time during their stay in Peking Elizabeth Jones and Mary managed to see the Great Wall, on a brilliantly beautiful day.

The divided group travelled to Japan by different routes and met in Nara late in April, to spend the first ten days working on the report on China. They stayed in the Nara Hotel, and had at least some free time for visiting places of interest in that fascinating ancient town. A rumor reached the National Christian Council of Japan that some of the members of the Laymen's Commission were talking to Buddhists and Shintoists, a dangerous waste of time, from the Council's point of view. Their letter of protest arrived on the day that Rufus Jones and Dr. Hocking had an invitation to take part in an evening of Zazen (meditation) in a Zen Buddhist monastery. Dr. Hocking asked Rufus Jones what they should do, and Rufus Jones replied with, in Dr. Hocking's words, "beautiful quietude and humor," "We'll spend the evening with our Buddhist brethren." They enjoyed a rare and deeply moving opportunity, and added the knowledge of experience to a theoretical understanding of Rudolph Otto's distinction between mysticism of the self and mysticism of the deity.

In Tokyo in May the Joneses were given a "tempura party" by the local Bryn Mawr graduates. In another room of the restaurant Charlie Chaplin was being similarly feted. "We were invited to see him between courses," wrote Rufus Jones to Marion Edwards Park of Bryn Mawr, "and were quite entertained by him. I told him that whatever distinction he might have he could never be a Bryn Mawr graduate! This [sic] Japanese Bryn Mawr women are very fine quality and they are full of good humor."

From Tokyo they sailed on a Japanese ship to Honolulu, where the Commission spent two weeks "blocking out our report and untangling our minds."

Those two weeks of work in a glorious setting of beach and sunshine required from all the group the most intense labor, forebearance, understanding and vision. They represented not only a variety of vocations and interests but a wide spread in religious belief. Determined though they were to produce a report which should satisfy everyone, some of them were disturbed by what they felt to be the secular and liberal attitudes of some of the others. Their decision not to water down the final statements but to include differing views added much to the value of the report and was at least partly due to Rufus Jones's gift for seizing and expressing the essentials of a conviction. Dr. Hocking, who as chairman had the steering to do, testifies warmly to Rufus Jones's help in outlining the report, in writing certain parts of it, and in drawing the group together. Every part of it had to be re-written several times, but when the Commission met again in Rockland, Maine, for two weeks in August, they were able to unite on a final draft.

In September, after a further, briefer meeting at Lake Mohonk, Rufus Jones wrote to Henry Cadbury, then in Holland, that the report was finished and being printed. "It is quite an epoch-making piece of work, and will," he prophesied, "rattle dry bones for years to come." A quarter of a century later some of the bones are still rattling.

Entitled RE-THINKING MISSIONS, the report appeared in book form in November. After describing the inception of the Inquiry, its composition, its history, and the different points of view which it represented, the report set forth the questions which it asked and for which it had sought answers. "The first and most searching question, whether these missions should in our judgment any longer go on," they answered unhesitatingly and emphatically in the affirmative, but they found that "there is not alone room for change, there is necessity for change."

In a spirit of deep religious concern and earnestness, of appreciation of what had been and was being done, combined with an objective awareness of inadequacies and blind spots, the report probed sensitive areas that had never before been exposed to the surgeon's headlight and scalpel. The chapter on the Scope of the Mission, Chapter III, written by Dr. Hocking in consultation with Rufus Jones, which dealt in large part with the problem of "message" and humanitarian work, the necessity for a new kind of person "if there is to be a new social order," on the transmission of the Christian way of life by contagion,

on the desirability of "united action across denominational lines and
even across religious boundaries," showed the impress of both their
minds and the agreement they had reached in the weeks of working
together.

Chapter IV, entitled "The Mission and the Church," which was
wholly written by Rufus Jones, after paying tribute to the church
and the persons whom it had influenced, pointed out that denomina-
tionalism had been transported to the Orient and in conservative form
often unsuited to the country. In China the creators of the church
should have taken more account of family life as a unit, in Japan aes-
thetic appeal and moral and intellectual life should have had more consideration. He urged a more vital and idealistic program for the student
class, rural workers who understood rural problems and would live
among the farmers, the strengthening of the indigenous church with
independence in view, and a movement away from religion of dogma
toward a religion of life. Only persons of the highest quality, fitness
and tested ability, he concluded, should be allowed to go as missionaries to other lands.

Other chapters dealt with the different kinds of missionary work,
educational, medical, agricultural, and so forth, with administration,
reorganization at the home base, and supplied a summary of conclusions and recommendations.

The book made an immediate sensation, and controversy raged
around it.

"A unique book, a great book," Pearl Buck declared in the *Christian
Century* and Henry W. Luce, Professor of Chinese at Hartford Theological Seminary, Kennedy School of Missions, wrote to Rufus Jones,
"I think it's the greatest church document in a decade—perhaps in
many decades."

Months of discussion followed, in the religious and secular press,
in mission boards, in church and lay groups of all kinds. To most
people it appeared sane, forward-looking, fresh, hopeful and realistic.
To others it seemed to be an attack on their most cherished beliefs
and a dastardly attempt to destroy the missionary movement altogether. The controversy centered about the first three chapters, which
set forth basic Christian beliefs, and on the part which dealt with the
training and qualifications of missionaries and called for a raising of the
standard of both. To many missionaries this appeared to be personal,
wounding criticism. The recommendation that church government
and finances be turned over as quickly as possible to the indigenous

churches seemed to many a blow at the whole missionary apparatus.

Two of the most influential and beloved leaders in the missionary movement, Dr. Robert E. Speer and Dr. E. Stanley Jones, came out very strongly in opposition to the report and carried many with them.

So strongly did the conservative elements feel that the Southern Baptist Theological Seminary, Louisville, Kentucky, which had asked Rufus Jones to deliver its Norton Lectures in 1933, wrote to him and withdrew the invitation. It was the unanimous opinion of his faculty, the chairman of the Committee explained regretfully, that it would expose the Seminary to criticism to have a speaker so prominently associated with a report which could only be understood as recommending the abandonment of the missionary enterprise as a Christian undertaking.

Undismayed, however, Rufus Jones was writing a few weeks later to a correspondent, "I am not at all disturbed over the attacks on the Report of our Commission . . . The young people all over the country are thrilled with it, and the more intelligent persons in all denominations are strongly in favor of it. It will take five or six years probably before it will make a real impression on the churches. But 43,000 copies have been sold and they have been read by many people."

Besides the books already mentioned, Rufus Jones wrote four other books in the six years between his trips to the Orient: THE NEW QUEST, a book on prayer and worship, on life and immortality; GEORGE FOX, SEEKER AND FRIEND; THE TRAIL OF LIFE IN COLLEGE, the continuation of his spiritual autobiography, which took him, actually, beyond college to his experience at Dieu-le-fit and his later meeting with John Wilhelm Rowntree. When he was searching for a title to continue the thought of FINDING THE TRAIL OF LIFE, his daughter suggested, "You might call this one 'Lost in the Underbrush'." The fourth book, PATHWAYS TO THE REALITY OF GOD, was one of the most important of his books. Beginning with the premise that "the universe involves and implies a Mind operating through its processes," it explored the pathways of evolution, history, philosophy, and daily experience, as well as others well trodden by the man whose faith is secure. He had to an extraordinary degree the gift of making God real to people. "I have thought of you as one of the few men who really believed in God," had written, wistfully, some years earlier a man who wanted him to speak at a conference of ministers. "Can you not come and help us to believe and teach us how to believe?" PATHWAYS

TO THE REALITY OF GOD met a wide response and went into seven printings in the first two months after it was published in 1931.

Another important enterprise in which Rufus Jones had a hand during these busy years just before his retirement from Haverford was the launching of the American Woodbrooke. Pendle Hill, a Quaker graduate school for religious and social studies, was, however, no mere copy of the older English school. It had from the beginning its own character and flavor. Built in part upon the resources of an earlier, similar attempt, the Woolman School in Swarthmore, it was established in a suburb of Philadelphia by a group of Quakers belonging to both Philadelphia yearly meetings. Rufus Jones participated in the early planning of it, he was a member of the first board, his old friend Henry T. Hodgkin was its first director, and he himself in 1930-31, the opening year, and 1932, after his return from the Orient, gave a course on the History of Christian Thought.

In the autumn of 1932, after having served a six-year term, he was elected a "life-trustee" of Brown University, Providence. Associated with him on the Board were Clarence A. Barbour, president of the University, and Albert L. Scott, with both of whom he had worked closely over the Laymen's Commission.

Midwife to the Soul

A SEVENTIETH birthday is no longer a time "to be old, to take in sail," but it does mark a pause between the closing of one period and the opening of another. It is a time of summation and of concentration, an opportunity for one's friends to express their awareness of what one's life has meant and is meaning. Rufus Jones's seventieth birthday brought him a sunburst of love and appreciation from all over the world. More than two hundred and fifty letters, some of them signed by many names, carried greetings from all quarters of Quakerdom, from the world of education, from Maine villages, from former school and college mates and former students, from missionaries, from a host of friends who had come to know him through his books.

"Please accept my very best wishes," wrote Dean Inge, "and thanks for all that I owe to your books, which have helped to convince me that when I am kicked out of the Church of England for heresy I may find a congenial spiritual home in the Society of Friends."

"You have made a good start, boy, now keep it up," came a hail from "Cousin Genie" in South China, the widow of Richard Jones; "seventy is lots of fun, eighty is better and ninety the best of all."

There were articles about him in the American Friends papers, in the London *Friend*, in *The Guardian*, Madras, India. Sir George Newman, describing the partnership between Rufus Jones and John Wilhelm Rowntree, which resulted in the development of the Summer School movement, the establishment of Woodbrooke, the Swarthmore lectures and the great Quaker History, wrote, "Out of that partnership too was to come a modern interpretation of the very meaning and universality of spirit of the Quaker Faith as one of the dynamic forms of mystical religion, the religion of life. . . . The eloquence, insight, understanding and sympathy of this most friendly man," he concluded, "have always been vitalized and enlightened by a rich and fertile humor of a large and expanding humanity, which whatever the calendar may say have kept him always young."

In Philadelphia his birthday was celebrated by a dinner given by the Friends Social Union at the Down Town Club, at which four hundred were present. George Walton, headmaster of George School, was the genial toastmaster, and among the speakers were Marion Edwards Park of Bryn Mawr, and George A. Barton, that old and dear friend whose rejection of Quakerism had caused pain and sorrow and estrangement. A warm letter from President Hoover was read.

In October of the same year Haverford College celebrated its hundredth birthday, and during the previous summer Rufus Jones had written its history. He worked every day in the little log cabin study which he had built overlooking China Lake, out of earshot of the cottage, where there were always guests and much coming and going. For reference he had Allen Thomas's earlier history of the college and the notes of the research which his daughter had done for him in the office files and the library during the spring. The rest of it was in his head. He had been a Junior in college at the time of the fiftieth anniversary celebration; for most of the second fifty years he had lived on the campus, had been himself part of the warp and woof of the fabric created there. He wrote, as he always did, in longhand. Contrary to what many people have assumed, his hand moved slowly, not rapidly, over the paper, as if giving time for his thoughts to order and arrange themselves, so that there were few erasures and corrections.

The book was published in the fall: HAVERFORD COLLEGE: A HISTORY AND AN INTERPRETATION. There is inevitably something parochial about a college history, but there was nothing dull or sterilely academic about this one. It was told largely in terms of the men who had made the college, and the great figures—Rufus King of Baltimore, Thomas and Pliny Chase, Isaac Sharpless, Francis B. Gummere, Theodore Richards of the class of 1885, who "pursued chemistry as though his life depended on his discovery of its central secret" and who was rewarded with the Nobel Prize in 1914—all live in its pages. There is, necessarily, one large and glaring omission, Rufus Jones himself.

He was by no means missing from the centennial celebration, which lasted three days in early October. He spoke at the Old Graduates' dinner on October sixth; on the seventh he spoke on the steps of Founders' Hall on "The Spiritual History of Haverford" and lectured in Philosophy Four, to all who cared to visit his class, on "The Great Philosopher of Ephesus"; at the Convocation, at which James Rowland Angell, president of Yale and William Mather Lewis of Lafayette spoke, he made the prayer. Honorary degrees were awarded to Henry J. Cadbury, Cecil K. Drinker, and Christopher Morley. On Sunday, Rufus Jones spoke at the special Friends Meeting which was held for the visitors.

The year 1933-34 was his last year of teaching. He had actually reached the usual retiring age in 1928, but the college had urged him to continue, and he had been glad to do so. Now, though he was seventy, the college still pressed him to go on, but he had made the decision to resign in June, 1934. "He was determined," his daughter says, "to stop his work before the college authorities reached the point of wishing that he would."

He had taught at Haverford for forty-one years, as instructor, associate professor, and professor. He had taught, but not all of them every year, Psychology, History of Philosophy, Ethics, Biblical Literature, History of Christian Thought.

Teaching was to him "that rare profession which Socrates called the *midwife to the soul*." He would never for a moment be content with a definition of education that limited it to the development of intellectual content or capacity. It was the weakness of higher institutions of learning, he maintained, that they put their emphasis on information, forgetting that their primary purpose "is to make moral and spiritual persons." You can't expect, he declared, such influence to emanate from chapel alone; it should be part of the fiber of college life. All who teach in a college should be *"reverent interpreters of truth*, persons who feel a genuine concern for the moral and spiritual *effect* of their work upon the making of the lives which pass under their hands."

Though his educational purpose was Socratic, his method was not. He did not seek by gradual and often apparently oblique questioning to draw the ideas he sought to establish out of the students themselves. He lectured, with varying amounts of time for discussion afterwards. His lectures, though prepared with care beforehand, were "something more than a douche of words, sprayed out through a speaking tube." He sought to make them like St. Francis's sermons in the style of a

man conversing, and his Maine drawl and his Maine stories sent home
many a point that might otherwise have slid into oblivion. A few
students have said that he made his explanations "too clear," to the
point of over-simplification of subtle philosophical theories; a very few
have complained that the lectures were "canned" or that they were sermons rather than lectures; the vast majority remember him as a vivid
and absorbing teacher.

He had a characteristic way of leaning back and folding his hands
over his stomach, which grew larger with the increasing years, and
twiddling his thumbs to emphasize a point. "When a boy jumps off
the roof of a barn," he would declare, his eyes twinkling and his
thumbs revolving, "he isn't defying the law of gravity, he's *illustrating*
it!"

"Rufus's classes are a delight," one student wrote to his father in that
last year before he retired. "His peculiar drawl is delightful, the stories
he tells to illustrate his points so whimsical that the class rolls in the
aisles with splitting sides, and the personal conceptions of life which
he works into even the dryest philosopher are extremely satisfying.
He makes us love men even like Parmenides and Diogenes and men
more unpromising I can hardly imagine . . . The Philosophers, I feel,
when they talk are too much like the economists, except a rare few
like 'Woofus' who realise that 'character is higher than intellect', that
'thinking is the functionary'. Why does he have to be retiring at the
end of *this* year?"

It was a source of pride to him that in his forty years of teaching at
Haverford he never lost a class because of being late. The students
had to wait for five minutes after the hour for a tardy professor;
after that they got a "time-cut." Though Rufus Jones might, if he
knew that he would have to be a few minutes late, tell them so beforehand, he never inadvertently missed the hour.

The first course that he gave at Haverford was a course in Psychology, and for a number of years it was required for Juniors. The
textbook was William James's PRINCIPLES OF PSYCHOLOGY, and Howard Comfort, son of William Wistar Comfort, the President, says, "He
taught William James himself, with the tacit assumption that here was
a great mind and a great spirit whom the students would not know
unless he [Rufus] pushed them through James's book."

In the early days of his teaching, when Psychology was still a fairly
new subject, Rufus Jones felt an enthusiasm for it that he lost when the
attempt was made to turn it into an exact science and the major em-

phasis was laid upon abnormal psychology. Throughout his teaching of Psychology he had little use for psycho-physiology, abnormal psychology, or for experiments with rats and mazes. One lecture sufficed for "The Physiological Basis of Psychology" before he went on to more congenial topics like Time, Memory, Imagination, Volition, the Subconscious and so forth. "I was soon impressed with the fact that Psychology tended to shake the student awake if he had not already found himself. It opened many new approaches to life. It gave fresh insights into the significance of what was going on within the man himself. He began to see what it meant to be 'captain of his own soul' and he wondered whether he might be. The formation of habits, laws of memory, importance of imagination, control of instincts, possibilities of freedom, these and hosts of kindred problems, caught him where he lived and aroused the keenest interest in him, though of course it was not universally so."

When psychology moved into the laboratory and "body-facts" were substituted for "mind-facts," then, he felt, psychology became a "subtler branch of physiology," and the development of Behaviorism not only changed the character of psychology but invaded the field of ethics and threatened to turn it into a kind of anthropology. "I was always convinced," he said, "that the right way of approach to all these deeper problems of life was to begin by asking, humbly and modestly as Plato and Kant did, what kind of a mind is implied in a person who possesses knowledge of what may be called 'truth', who loves, enjoys and appreciates the beautiful and good for their own sake and who has inherent capacity in his being to transcend the given, to live beyond everything that is presented to the senses, and, in some measure to help to create, that is, to make *real*, the world of these ideal visions. That was my way of approach in my college lectures, during these years."

His course in the History of Philosophy centered around Plato in the first semester and Kant in the second. The notes for his lectures are still extant. They consist of twelve lectures on the Greek philosophers and one on Plotinus and Neo-Platonism; one each on Bacon, Descartes, Hobbes, the Cambridge Platonists, Spinoza, Locke, Leibnitz, Berkeley, Hume, Fichte, Hegel, Schelling, Bergson, Emerson, Rationalism, Pragmatism, with eighteen papers on Kant. Nietzsche and Schopenhauer he omitted altogether. He gave his students what he considered good for them, he made it all crystal clear, he left them in no doubt what his own convictions were.

Philosophy he defined as "a rational, logical, systematic search for truth," but he started with the reality of the religious experience, not with the sceptic's blank question. The "testimony of the soul" was for him forever valid. His professional contacts outside Haverford were not with the philosophy departments of other universities but with the theological schools, and he wrote, not for the philosophical periodicals but for the Friends journals, the *Christian Century*, the *Homiletic Review* and the *Harvard Theological Review*. "He was not a meta-physician either," William Wistar Comfort said of him, "but if phi-losophy means a guide of life, he was a religious philosopher, for he had found a Guide for himself and for thousands of others." Many a student of his might have said, as one of them did, "I will never forget the day in our philosophy class while studying Kant's work that I suddenly for the first time received a perception of the real meaning of faith."

For a number of years he taught Freshman Bible, and he at least, he declared, "learned a lot about the Bible!" In the early 1900's there were still students to whom his liberal point of view was a hazard. Sigmund Spaeth, the well known music critic, tells how, the strictly brought up son of a Lutheran minister, he heard Rufus Jones remark mildly that the story of the flood need not be taken literally, and was so shocked that he burst into tears. "He spoke to me afterwards, very kindly and comfortingly, saying that he did not want to upset any-body's faith and that I had a perfect right to interpret Genesis as I liked."

Concern for the faith of a Roman Catholic student, who was a Sophomore during Rufus Jones's last year of teaching, was responsible for a revealing incident.

"It was announced," writes Daniel Coogan, Jr. "that he would teach Philosophy 2b, Development of Christian Thought, during the second semester, and naturally there was a rush to get in the class, since it was known that it would be his last semester of teaching. When he learned that I was one of those eager to enter his course he wrote me the following letter, which I have treasured ever since as evidence of great understanding and charity and good will:

1.23.1934

Dear Coogan,

I have a concern that you should consider carefully whether it is wise for you to take Phil. 2b this semester. I shall have to deal in the course with move-ments that are considered by your Church as heretical and I must naturally study the Reformation, including Luther and Calvin. I always expect to be impartial but such movements are not usually studied by Roman Catholics from the Quaker point of view and it might be disturbing to you. I should like to talk it over with you, but my feeling is that you would not be happy in that work.

Sincerely your friend,

Rufus M. Jones

Of course, I accepted his invitation to talk it over and I was able to convince him that my faith was sufficiently strong to hold up under his teaching. I took the course, wrote a paper on the Council of Trent and the Counter-Reformation, and came away from it richer, wiser, and more intensely and devotedly Catholic than I had been before. Indeed I may say that at Haverford as an undergraduate I had the unique (perhaps even paradoxical) experience of a strengthening and deepening of religious conviction within the Catholic framework which has resulted in a lifelong commitment to and devout interest in Catholicism; Rufus Jones by word and example contributed profoundly to this, and I shall always be grateful to him."

For thirty-three years, from 1901, he taught the course in Ethics that was required of all Seniors. It was here perhaps that he was at his best. The basis of moral freedom, the reality of the moral experience, the significance of beauty, the capacity to live "beyond the edge of what now *is*" and strive for what ought to be, the difference between happiness and pleasure: these were some of the topics that his students remember him talking about.

"Realization is the secret of life," he said in his farewell lecture to one class, "and the key to it. Each occasion is what it is and it opens out a more yet.

"Adjustment," he continued, "is no adequate test of moral height."

"The only thing he ever warned us *against*," remembers Howard Comfort, "was Joyce's *Ulysses*."

A story is told of his last class in Ethics in 1934. He came to the lecture room at the usual time, and found no one there. After a few minutes, in they came, in a body, dressed to represent the virtues and vices that they had encountered during the course, and marched in silence around the room. Rufus Jones laughed heartily. "Well, boys," he said, leaning back and twiddling his thumbs over his stomach, "I've taught this course for thirty-three years and this is the most evidence of preparation that I've seen yet!"

Those who confess freely that they can remember nothing of what he said in the classroom do remember vividly what he was. His humor, his light, his warmth, above all the conviction he gave them that it was vitally important what each student made of his life, had the power to kindle and inspire. "From my first hour in his classroom in Haverford College," said one, "he was my hero."

"I have always felt," he said himself, "that I was at my best in a classroom and there is no question that I am happiest when I am teaching a class of youth."

When he retired, Rufus Jones left his Philosophy Department in the hands of able younger associates who have since then in their turn become leaders of religious thought in the United States. Douglas V. Steere came to Haverford as assistant professor in 1928, straight from a year's study at Oriel College, Oxford, and a briefer experience at Marburg. He has remained at Haverford, succeeding Rufus Jones in the T. Wistar Brown Chair of Philosophy, writing (Prayer and Worship, and On Beginning from Within are two of many books) and travelling widely on missions of love for the A.F.S.C. D. Elton Trueblood, who came to Haverford in 1933, went on after three years to Leland Stanford, and from there to Earlham. He is well known for his Alternative to Futility, the Life We Prize, and other books. He was followed at Haverford by Thomas Kelly, who had been a student of Rufus Jones's and had kept in close touch with him from his college days. An A.F.S.C. worker in Germany, a mystic by experience, he came from teaching Philosophy at Earlham College and the University of Hawaii, to make in a few years a secure place for himself in the hearts of the college and the community. After his sudden death in 1941, his Testament of Devotion was published and has made an extraordinary appeal to seekers of all denominations.

Although Rufus Jones remained in the Haverford College catalogue as Professor Emeritus and lived in his house on the campus for his remaining years, this chapter of his life came to an end with his retirement. "There is a humorous college song about 'old Founders' bell is ringing'," writes his daughter. "But the ringing of Founders' bell is not always a matter to laugh about. It had, for forty years, called Rufus Jones across the Cricket Circle from his home to his class-room. He realized that he wanted to be out of earshot of Founders' bell when the autumn semester began in 1934." Accordingly he and Elizabeth Jones, after several weeks at South China, sailed for England on the twenty-ninth of July.

After Retirement

T HE first stop was Woodbrooke, where Rufus Jones gave three lectures on the Psychology of Religious Experience at the summer school. From there he went to Copenhagen, to address an International Conference on Religious Liberalism on "Re-thinking Religious Liberalism," a lecture subsequently published in book form.

In this lecture he reiterated the point which he so often made, that an intellectual movement must be considered in the climate of thought at the time of its inception and in relation to the historical events that gave rise to it. Liberalism, he pointed out, arose in revolt against cramping tradition and outworn dogmas; it was strongly influenced by the rationalism of the age of enlightenment. In the currents of theological thought of the early 1930's, dominated by Reinhold Niebuhr, liberalism appeared shallow, sentimental, thinly rational, over-optimistic, idealistic, unrealistic. He quoted T. S. Eliot's pronouncement, "Our present-day society is worm-eaten with liberalism."

True liberalism, however, he said, was not a set of beliefs but an attitude of mind, a spirit committed to the unceasing pursuit of truth and obedience to the enlarging vision of the soul. The new liberalism must have affirmations as well as denials. "It is not what peradventure one does not believe that matters most, but what fiery, positive faith dominates one's soul."

Berlin came next, where he acquired a German secretary, Dr. Anna Magdelina Schroeder, and started her on research on the Friends of

God of the fourteenth century, and where he conferred with the American and British Friends at the Friends Center about conditions in what was now Hitler's Germany. From there he went to Prague, where he attended a three-day International Conference of Friends, a large-sounding title for the little group of sixty who met there. Continental Quakers were still very few in numbers; most of them had joined Friends as a result of contacts with A.F.S.C. or Friends Service Council workers, and these small new meetings needed careful nurturing and encouragement and the experience of knowing themselves members of a larger body.

In September the three Joneses were together in London, for Mary was spending a year in England studying and writing. Rufus Jones preached at the City Temple. He went to Ireland for a few days to visit Friends in Dublin and Belfast, while Elizabeth Jones worked steadily at the British Museum on the fourteenth century mystics. "Today," Rufus Jones wrote to Henry Cadbury on the 20th of September, "Haverford opens and I have a tug on my heart strings, but things are in right ordering." Back to the continent they went in October, to spend the next three months. In Strasbourg he handled the precious little books written by the Friends of God, and visited the Green Isle where they had lived and worked and worshipped. In Marburg he saw again his old friends, Frau Happich, the Sippells, and Professor Otto. They returned to Berlin.

The scene in Germany was darkening. Hitler had been in power for more than a year. There were Nazi parades in all the cities and anyone who did not respond with the Hitler salute was roughly handled. Streams of Jewish people came to the Friends Center in Berlin to ask about the possibilities of emigrating to the United States.

Vienna, too, where Rufus and Elizabeth Jones were joined by Mary in November, had had a troubled year. There had been a Socialist uprising in February, which Dollfuss had crushed. The Friends Center, where Emma Cadbury, representing the A.F.S.C., worked with an English couple from the Friends Service Council, was, with the help of some two hundred young Austrian volunteers, distributing aid to 8,000 families of men killed, wounded, or imprisoned in the February fighting. An attempted Nazi putsch in July had in turn been put down with severity.

Rufus Jones went to see Chancellor Schuschnigg about relief for Vienna during the winter, if it should be necessary. While he was in Vienna he spoke on "The Quaker Attitude toward the Use of Force."

December found Rufus and Elizabeth Jones in Italy. In Florence he met Maria Sorella Minor, the Mother Superior of a Franciscan order, whom readers of Evelyn Underhill's *Letters* will recognize. Sister Maria wrote to him afterwards a letter beginning, "Frate Rufino," in which she declared, "I will always remember your visit and you." Christmas they spent in Naples, after seeing Mary off to China.

"We had a very interesting visit in the South of France," Rufus Jones wrote to Clarence Pickett in January, "where I hunted up all that remains of the old Quaker movement in that part of France. From Nîmes we went to Geneva, then back to Paris."

Two more months in England followed, where Rufus Jones lectured at various places on "Some Forces that will Remake the World," delivered the Hibbert Lecture at Cambridge, and lunched with Evelyn Underhill, before he and his wife sailed for home on the *Manhattan*, arriving in time for Elizabeth Jones to take part in Philadelphia Yearly Meeting as one of the clerks.

Rufus Jones's return to the United States, free from the confines of the class-room, opened the flood-gates of demand. He was just back from Europe, that ominous place about which the newspapers reported disturbing and conflicting news. People wanted eye-witness accounts from one who had just been there; they wanted interpretations by a wise and temperate man whom they could trust. His TRAIL OF LIFE IN THE MIDDLE YEARS, the third and last volume of his spiritual autobiography, had been published while he was away. It summed up much of his philosophy and showed how it had been forged on the anvil of his living. Yale University saluted his achievements with an honorary doctorate of divinity. Everybody wanted him to speak, to write books, articles, introductions to books, chapters in books, reviews of books, to advise them, to inspire them, to convince them that behind this nightmare world of depressions and dictatorships there was an eternally real spiritual world.

He made five commencement and baccalaureate addresses in a single week in June, before he thankfully left for South China, where he spent most of his mornings preparing lectures for the following fall and winter.

He took on the editorship of a series of books to be called "The Great Issues of Life Series." William A. Slade of the Library of Congress had conceived the idea of a number of small books by distinguished writers and scholars interpreting the fundamental aspects of Christian life and thought, to be edited by Rufus Jones and published by Macmillan. Rufus Jones was to select the men to write the books and to persuade them to do it, to write an introduction to each book, and write one of the volumes himself. The last part of the assignment proved to be the simplest part of it. For over two years his correspondence was heavy on behalf of the great issues. He found it difficult to enlist the men whom he wanted. Some of them—like Lord Tweedsmuir, whom he asked to write on "Christianity in a Changing Civilization"—were too busy; others were not drawn to the subject; still others could not reduce the material to the small compass required. Rufus Jones's own volume, THE ETERNAL GOSPEL, was published first, followed by four books by other writers before the war came to put an end to the project.

In 1938 the book for which he had done research in England and Germany on the mystics of the fourteenth century was published under the title, THE FLOWERING OF MYSTICISM. He had brought back with him a "vast collection of notes and a large addition of books" to his library, and during three busy years he had been writing the book which was to fulfill his youthful determination to make the Friends of God live again. They had occupied one chapter, and, he felt, the most important chapter, in his STUDIES IN MYSTICAL RELIGION, but the treatment had been too brief to be adequate. Further research and study, more experience in life, had changed somewhat his view of both the Friends of God and of mysticism itself. He included in the book also the English mystics of the fourteenth century, a considerable body of anonymous mystical writings and an Epilogue on the nature of mystical experience.

This was the last of his historical studies on mysticism though to the end of his life he would be writing and talking of mystical religion. His view of mysticism, steeped though he was in the writings of the mystics, great and small, through the ages, was not an academic construction or a synthesis of his readings; it had its own distinctive character. Rufus Jones was not only a student, a writer, an authority on mysticism, he was himself a mystic, living in today's world amid today's problems. The mysticism of Rufus Jones requires a chapter to itself.

The Mysticism of Rufus Jones

It was through reading Emerson in college that Rufus Jones first became aware that the religion in which he had grown up, with the dew of which he had been sprinkled from morning till night, the religion of his beloved Aunt Peace, was actually a mystical religion, a part of a great spiritual movement. By that realization and through the influence of Pliny Chase his mind was directed toward the study of mysticism from a historical viewpoint, and his first written treatment of the subject was his graduation essay, "Some Exponents of Mystical Religion."

It was, however, his own mystical experience at Dieu-le-fit which at the age of twenty-four turned him from one who had some knowledge about mysticism and who sought to know more, into one who had knowledge of mysticism through his own experience. It changed the direction of his life, provided its consuming interest, opened his understanding of the mystics of whom he was to write, and gave him an unfaltering conviction of the reality of God.

This was the first but not the only such experience in his life. Even more impressive to him was that which he had on the ship going to England when unknown to him Lowell was dying and he felt himself "surrounded as by an enfolding presence and held as though by invisible Arms," when his entire being was "fortified for the tragic news that awaited him on landing." In this experience, even more than in the earlier one, he was aware of the overwhelming love of God and of his own response to it.

He recognized also a still different kind of experience, in which there was "no single moment of invasion or uprush" but after which he discovered that new life and power had come without his knowing exactly when. Such an experience, which he called "a case of quiet mystical receptivity" occurred after his automobile accident in 1922. Though he acknowledged the exhilaration of returning health when he had thought life was ended, he was convinced that he had received also a spiritual revitalization resulting in a new level of life. He was evidently referring to this experience when he wrote in 1936, "There is a type of *organic mysticism* which is much more common than highly conscious mysticism is."

It was an experience, he said in the Introduction to W. C. Braithwaite's BEGINNINGS OF QUAKERISM, "not merely emotional, not merely intellectual, not merely volitional, through which the soul finds itself in a love-relation with the Living God. There are all possible stages and degrees of the experience of this 'relation' from simple awareness of the soul's Divine Companion to a rapt consciousness of union with the One and Only Reality."

The significant features of this experience he described many times. In the Introduction to SPIRITUAL REFORMERS he noted "the consciousness of fresh springs of life, the inauguration of a sense of mission, the flooding of the life with hope and gladness and the conviction, amounting to a certainty, that God is found as an environing and vitalizing Presence." To these he added later, the integration of the personality, "the closing of chasms and cleavages" whereby "the divided will, the divided mind, the divided heart become fused into a unity." A further characteristic of the experience is its incommunicability. In spite of the mystic's certainty that he has been in communion with God, he is unable to tell in words what he has received, and he is unable to bring back "concrete information about the nature and character of God."

Rufus Jones was firm in maintaining that mysticism was not the whole of religion. "It [religion] is essentially bound up with all the processes of the intellect and with all the deeper issues of the will as well as with these first-hand intimations of the soul's vision. The present-day revolt from doctrine is in many ways superficial. There can be no great religion without the interpretation of life, of the universe, of experience, of mind, of God. What we ought to revolt from is traditional dogma." And again, "Mystical experience is not a substitute for the moral and rational processes of every day life."

In the course of his life he defined mysticism over and over again in books and articles, in addresses, in innumerable question periods. At the end of any lecture on mysticism, he commented, some one was sure to rise and say appealingly, "Will the speaker kindly tell us in two or three plain words what mysticism really is?" The number and beauty of his definitions make a choice of a single example difficult, but one of the simplest is that given in THE TRAIL OF LIFE IN THE MIDDLE YEARS: "The essential characteristic of it is the attainment of a personal conviction by an individual that the human spirit and the divine Spirit have met, have found each other, and are in mutual and reciprocal correspondence as spirit with Spirit." The phrase "mutual and reciprocal correspondence," a favorite phrase of his, is borrowed from Clement of Alexandria, who was from his youth one of his spiritual heroes. In 1910 he published a little book of SELECTIONS FROM THE WRITINGS OF CLEMENT OF ALEXANDRIA. In his LUMINOUS TRAIL, in 1947, he repeated the definition that he gave in 1909 in his STUDIES IN MYSTICAL RELIGION and which evidently he considered the most satisfactory of his formulations: "Mysticism is the type of religion which puts the emphasis on immediate awareness of relation with God, on direct and intimate consciousness of the Divine presence. It is religion in its most acute, intense and living stage." "Mysticism may, and I think should, stand for that type of experience in which a person feels an overmastering conviction that actual contact is attained with a divine, life-giving, joy-bringing Presence," he wrote in PATHWAYS TO THE REALITY OF GOD.

Throughout his life he made a distinction between affirmative mysticism and negative mysticism. Here he parts company with many writers on the subject, to whom the negative is the classic type and indeed the only real mysticism.

The *via negativa*, as Rufus Jones saw it, called for withdrawal from the world, from all that is finite and temporal, in order to lose oneself in that which is infinite and eternal. The naughting of the self, the elimination of the I, the me, and the mine, the extirpation of all desire, the quenching of all thought, the merging of the individual personality in the divine Whole is necessary if union with the divine is to be achieved. Plotinus's often quoted phrase, "the flight of the alone to the Alone," expresses this summit experience. Ecstasy is the goal of the follower of this way.

The affirmative mysticism, to the interpretation of which Rufus Jones gave his life, was a "milder and more normal correspondence of the soul with God." The affirmation mystic, he declared in SOCIAL

LAW IN THE SPIRITUAL WORLD, "seeks union with God, but not through loss of personality." On the contrary, his personality is fulfilled in God. St. Paul's statement, "It is no longer I that live but Christ liveth in me," Rufus Jones understood as "no negation of personality but a triumphant type of immensely expanded personality." The mark of the affirmative mystic is a transformed personality, radiant, vital, filled with energy, who finds, as he said in SOCIAL LAW IN THE SPIRITUAL WORLD, obedience to the vision more important than the vision and who seeks to serve God in this world.

Ecstasy in itself he distrusted, as being related to symptoms of hysteria, auditions, bodily changes and hypnosis. Trances and ecstasies have an element of abnormality and are not the best part of mysticism. He considered it a weakness of the negation mystic that he encouraged men "to live for the rare moment of ecstasy and beatific vision, to sacrifice the chance of winning spiritual victory for the hope of receiving an ineffable illumination which would quench all further search or desire." Thirty-four years later he put it even more strongly: "I am equally convinced that the emphasis upon ecstasy which the Neoplatonic strain of thought introduced into Christian mysticism was an unfortunate and very costly contribution, and quite foreign to the mysticism of the New Testament. In fact for many interpreters ecstasy came to be thought of as the *essentia* of mysticism: No esctasy, no mystic!" He qualified this statement somewhat by making it clear that he was thinking of ecstasy chiefly as a semi-pathological state marked by an abnormal autosuggestibility and hysteria. "There is a type of ecstatic state, of inspiration and illumination, which seems to me to be a most glorious attainment and very near to the goal of life —a state of concentration, of unification, of liberation, of discovery, of heightened and intensified powers, and withal, a burst of joy, of rapture and of radiance."

The source of negative mysticism he found in the belief in a wholly transcendent God, unknowable, wholly other, abstract and characterless. He was fond of quoting in this connection the lines,

> "Whatever your mind comes at,
> I tell you flat
> God is not that!"

This God of the negation mystic, the "nameless Nothing" of Eckhart, the "Divine Dark" of Dionysius the Areopagite, the "fathomless Nothingness" of Tauler, Rufus Jones characterized as the "Abstract

Infinite." "The long struggle of man's mind with the stern compulsions of this abstract infinite is, I think, one of the major intellectual tragedies of human life . . . It is easy to see how that theory of the abstract [i.e. characterless] infinite would lead the mind of a mystic to expect his experience of God to terminate in a mental blank, an everlasting Nay."

To him God was a Concrete Infinite. He used the term for the first time in the introduction to SPIRITUAL REFORMERS and continued to employ it to the end of his life. "No ancient or medieval thinker," he wrote in TESTIMONY OF THE SOUL, "ever dealt adequately with what we have learned to call 'the concrete infinite', an infinite revealed in and through the temporal and the finite." The great symbol of the concrete infinite he finds in St. John's figure of the Vine with its many branches. "In that figure we have the suggestion of an Infinite that goes out into multitudinous manifestations and finds itself in and through its interrelated and finite branches. Perfection is not through isolation and withdrawal but through self-surrender and sacrificial limitation." In the LUMINOUS TRAIL, after interpreting John IV, 24, to mean, "God is essentially Spirit and man can join with Him in vital fellowship, for he too is spirit," he went on to say, "This report means that religion is founded on a concrete Infinite, for Spirit is a concrete Reality, not on an abstract and 'naughted' Absolute, and intercommunion is an intelligible process of Like with like."

The affirmative type of mysticism he traced first to St. John and St. Paul, who, he said, had been often disqualified as mystics by New Testament scholars who assumed that mysticism meant withdrawal from all that is finite and temporal. With the Renaissance and the recovery of New Testament models, a new type of mysticism came to birth, more Pauline and Johannine than the medieval type had been. The medieval view of God and man was broken by the new humanism, not the modern humanism of naturalistic philosophy that "reduced man to a natural creature" but the luminous humanism of Erasmus and the Renaissance thinkers, who discovered with joy the glorious potentialities of the human mind and spirit. "The focal idea of this new type of mysticism," he wrote, "is the glowing faith that there is something divine in man which under right influences and responses can become the dominant feature of a person's whole life. The favorite text of the exponents of the affirmation mysticism was that noble oracular fragment in Proverbs already quoted: 'The Spirit of man is a candle of the Lord.' This line of thought goes back for its pedigree, without much doubt, to the humanism of the Renaissance."

To this humanism, "at heart deeply Platonic and mystical," was added the Reformation's rediscovery of the primitive message of Christianity and its insistence on the responsibility of the individual in the sphere of religion. "The center of religion was no longer thought of as being an external imperial organization; it was felt to be the inner life of the individual man. This shift of attitude was like the coming of the vernal equinox and with it came a new outburst of mystical life." From the strand of mysticism of the Friends of God, the humanism of Erasmus, the inward religion of Luther's early insight, and the glowing message of the New Testament came, as Rufus Jones showed in his historical studies, the mysticism of Caspar Schwenkfeld, Hans Denck, Sebastian Franck, Sebastian Costellio, and Jacob Boehme, the spiritual reformers whom he believed to be the forerunners of the Quakers of the seventeenth century.

Thomas Traherne, the seventeenth century poet, he cited as a brilliant interpreter of affirmative mysticism, and he considered William Law its chief exponent in the eighteenth century. William Blake was, he said, the "most notable mystic" of the latter century, but in none of his books did he care to tackle the elucidation of Blake. Nor was Blake one of the many poets whom he frequently quoted.

Although he insisted upon the distinction between affirmative and negative mystics, he declared with equal emphasis that there were both affirmative and negative elements in both types of mysticism. The difference between the two types was a relative difference. "There have been no negation mystics who were not also affirmative, and there neither are nor will be any important affirmation mystics who do not tread at some point the *via negativa*,—the hard and dolorous road."

All the great mystics up to the Reformation were, he felt, negative because of the prevailing metaphysics but affirmative in their experience. Again and again he paid tribute to their lives and their personalities, to the good that they did in the world. He loved them and he wrote of them in book after book, Meister Eckhart, whom he called "the peak of the range," Plotinus, the anonymous author of the Theologia Germanica, St. Bernard of Clairvaux. Even Dionysius the Areopagite, whom he considered responsible for much of the more extreme form of negative mysticism, he spoke of as "this dear man."

This question of the classification of different types of mysticism is discussed by Thomas H. Hughes of the University of Edinburgh in his PHILOSOPHICAL BASIS OF MYSTICISM. He finds the division into Mild and Extreme Types, into Cognitive and Conative Mystics, and into Affirmative and Negative Mystics not "a sufficiently distinctive classification since it rests on a principle which is not essential to the mystical Faith." In preference he would use Rudolf Otto's Soul-mysticism and God-mysticism, or Dean Inge's Speculative, Practical, Devotional and Nature Mysticism, though these do not allow for over-lapping. The most generally accepted grouping, according to Mr. Hughes, is Philosophical, Nature, and Religious Mysticism.

Nature Mysticism is rooted in divine immanence, Philosophical mysticism in divine transcendence, Religious mysticism at its best combines the two: union with the Personal God, for transcendence and immanence are reconciled in personality.

By this classification, Rufus Jones clearly belongs with the religious mystics. God to Rufus Jones was personal in the sense that we can enter into a relationship with him. To use Martin Buber's term, He is not the God of the Philosophers, but the God of Abraham, Isaac and Jacob, to whom we can say, "O Thou!"

Beyond that, Rufus Jones's mysticism is profoundly Quaker. It is colored by the Quaker strain that has come through his home and the meeting, through his reading of Quaker sources, through his knowledge of the New Testament and the primitive Christianity to which seventeenth century Quakerism was a conscious return. Though he found immense inspiration in Plotinus, in Eckhart, Tauler, the Theologia Germanica, and Ruysbroeck, he was happiest with them when they were expressing, in other terms, ideas which were Quaker ideas; also when they moved away, he was obliged to say sadly, as he did of the author of the THEOLOGIA GERMANICA, "I go most of the way in joyous company with this dear man whom, not having seen, I love. But I cannot finally be satisfied with any system of thought which empties this world here below of present spiritual significance or which robs the life of a human personality of its glorious mission as an organ of the Life of God here and now, and which postpones the Kingdom of God to a realm where the Perfect is a One with no other."

His rejection of the negation mystic's withdrawal from the world is characteristic of Quaker thought and practice. "True godliness," wrote William Penn, "does not turn men out of the world, but enables them to live better in it and excites their endeavors to mend it." Quakers marry, engage in business, occupy themselves with a hundred activities to improve the world. In their meetings for worship and in times of private meditation, it is true, they withdraw from distractions, even the religious distractions of ritual and sacred music, but the insights which they receive at such times they return to the world to put into effect as best they can. "The history of the Society of Friends," writes Howard Brinton, "shows that acceptance of the principle of withdrawal in worship has not resulted in any attempt at final or complete withdrawal. The negative journey to the Light was invariably followed by the positive journey to the needy but good world." "Those who see God," said Rufus Jones, "must gird for service. Those who would have a closer view of the divine must seek it in a life of love and sacrifice."

George Fox was to Rufus Jones preeminently the type of the affirmation mystic. "He thought of man, raised to his full spiritual height, as an organ of the life of God. The early Friends, his followers, knew of no limits to what God could do through a man or a woman, raised by His power to stand and live in the same Spirit that the prophets and apostles were in who gave forth the Scriptures. They made conquest of their fears, they were released from a sense of danger, they became concentrated and unified spirits dedicated to the task of building the Kingdom of God according to the pattern in the Mount."

Ascetic practices, characteristic of medieval mysticism, have never been part of Quaker discipline. The testimony of temperance comes from social and moral reasons, not from a desire to mortify the flesh. Quaker simplicity in dress and speech arose out of a concern for truth and sincerity. Good food has always seemed to Friends one of the God-given pleasures of life which there is no reason to put aside except as by cutting down one's own supply one can share with those in need. Rufus Jones himself had always a healthy, human interest in food. His letters home often report on good meals he has enjoyed or bad ones he has suffered from, and lobsters and new peas were high among the joys of his summer home in Maine.

His view of mysticism was also strongly colored by the Quaker idea of the sacraments, of which a brief statement may be found in FAITH AND PRACTICE, the book of Christian discipline published by the Philadelphia Yearly Meeting. "With full appreciation of the help which has come through the outward forms to countless generations of Christians, Friends symbolize by their very lack of symbols the essentially inward nature of the sacraments. Friends testimony is not a negative protest but an affirmation of the sacramental nature of the whole of life when it is under the leading of the Spirit." The Eucharist, which Rufus Jones sometimes accepted when he was with other religious groups, was to him a moving ceremony but in no way a necessary door to communion with God. His admiration for Evelyn Underhill was tempered by his disappointment over her inability to understand the Quaker point of view on the sacraments and her insistence on the necessity of the communion service. "I have just read the proof for the American edition of Evelyn Underhill's WORSHIP," he wrote to Violet Hodgkin Holdsworth. "It is an important book, but she is quite unable to appreciate or even to understand the full meaning of Quaker worship without sacraments. I have talked with her frequently about this, but can never make her see what it means to us. She grows more high Church as she grows older and that side of her religious life overtops everything else; but she is a great soul." The affirmation mystic, Rufus Jones insisted, found God revealed in the finite. To him everything was sacramental. "Nothing now can be unimportant. There is more in the least event than the ordinary eye sees. Everywhere in the world there is stuff to be transmuted into divine material. Every situation may be turned into an occasion for winning a nearer view of God."

Perhaps the most striking difference between Rufus Jones's mysticism and that of the classical mystic, whether affirmative or negative, and at the same time the most essentially Quaker element in it, was his conviction that mysticism flourished best in groups. Preparation must be made in the individual heart but the heightened receptivity of the group waiting in silence helped many to enter into an experience of God which they would not have attained alone. There are many expressions of this fundamental Quaker principle, from Robert Barclay's statement in the seventeenth century:

"As many candles lighted and put in one place do greatly augment the light and make it more to shine forth, so when many are gathered together into the same life there is more of the glory of God and His power appears to the refreshment of each individual, for each partakes not only of the light and life raised in himself but in all the rest," to Howard Brinton's brief sentence "Quakerism is peculiar in being a group mysticism, grounded in Christian concepts."

Rufus Jones too found many ways and occasions to restate this truth. More than any other scholar he has studied and written about mystical groups; it is perhaps his most important contribution to the history of mysticism.

"Mysticism flourishes best in a group," he wrote in NEW STUDIES IN

MYSTICAL RELIGION, "and it can, if left to itself, produce out of its experience a type of organization that favors its growth and increase in depth and power."

"The great fact remains," he had said even earlier in *The American Friend*, "that there is no greater gift than the gift of listening to God, and that there is no greater spiritual power than that which comes when a whole congregation is fused and melted in silent waiting and soul-worship before the living God, when God's presence can be felt and His voice heard so distinctly that no audible words are needed."

Early Quakers, and many modern Quakers also, used the terms Light Within, Christ Within, Light of Christ, Seed of God, the Inward Teacher, That of God in every man, interchangeably. Rufus Jones seldom used the term "Christ Within." He used instead Spirit, Divine Spirit, the Spirit of Truth, the Holy Spirit, Presence, the Over-World, and Emil Boutroux's term, "the Beyond that is Within." He believed that Christ who was both human and divine had come primarily to lead people to a new experience of God. "The greatest single thing about Christ," he said in China to the eager crowds that heard him there, "is His *experience* of God and His transmission of the life of God into the lives of men." "Christ was concerned to have men's lives flooded with the consciousness of God, to have them become 'rich in God.'" "The most unique thing to my mind about the Jesus of history is, not a new ethics or a new interpretation of society or a fresh message about the Kingdom of God, important as these are, but a new and most wonderfully rich experience of God that apparently had been growing and deepening all through those silent background years."

A further question about Rufus Jones's own type of mysticism to be considered is this: Did he regard the mystical experience as open to everyone, or did he think it was a special gift or capacity determined by the individual psychic make-up or bestowed by God's favor?

There are to be found in his writings passages in which he seems to waver in his opinion or even to contradict himself wholly. "Some degree of this experience . . . is probably present in us all," he wrote in SOCIAL LAW IN THE SPIRITUAL WORLD. "Even the most prosaic of us are haunted by a Beyond." When he wrote SPIRITUAL RE-FORMERS, after long study and research on mystics who were spiritual geniuses, he seemed to change his mind. "It is an experience that is by no means universal. It is not, so far as we can see from the facts at hand, an experience which attaches to the very nature of consciousness as such, and indeed one which is bound to occur even when the human subject strains forward all the energies of his will for the adventure, or when by strict obedience to the highest laws of life known to him he *waits* for the high visitation." He goes on to describe persons "as serious and earnest and passionate as the loftiest mystical saint", who appear "impervious to divine bubblings" and he says that to make mystical experience the only way to God would be to set up an "election as rigid as that of the Calvinist system, one determined by the peculiar psychic structure of the individual."

Later, in NEW STUDIES OF MYSTICAL RELIGION, he returned to a modification of his original position. "Mysticism is a normal trend of the soul and can be cultivated," he said. The capacity for mystical experience was normal, in the sense that it was not pathological or unbalanced or evidence of a diseased mind. It was, however, he sadly conceded, not universal, in the sense that it came naturally to everybody. "Probably in the last analysis the psychical disposition of the individual himself is the crucial factor," he said. "It comes only to those who can meditate, who can stop living by clock-time and space-speed and center down into that interior hush where the human spirit touches the skirts of God."

Still later he asserted without qualification, "When I talk mysticism I mean something fundamental to the normal essential nature of the soul." And his final word, in A CALL TO WHAT IS VITAL, was: "The mystical trait—and I mean by it the consciousness of direct relation with God, existential religion—is not in any true sense confined to a small chosen list of religious geniuses, but is a feature of the democratic laity as well as of the high pulpit class that form the usual lists." In this he differs from his friend, Dean Inge, who said categorically in his CHRISTIAN MYSTICISM, "Everybody is naturally either a mystic or a legalist." He did in the Prologue to THE FLOWERING OF MYSTICISM make a half-hearted attempt to differentiate between two distinct types of men, the biological man who has no interest in the Beyond and the man for whom the walls of separation between the seen and the unseen are thinner, but he quickly concluded that the distinction is "one of degree rather than type," that the gift of "correspondence" is present in "all normally endowed persons" but rises to a higher level in those with special gifts.

The greatest mystics, Rufus Jones believed, have been religious geniuses. "They make their contribution to religion in ways similar to those in which the geniuses in other fields raise the level of human attainments and achievements." "All of the great capacities of the soul come to light best of course in persons who are geniuses." But he believed that there are far more mystics of the milder sort than is commonly supposed. "I am convinced that a great many of these so-called 'ordinary persons' have a sense of contact with spiritual forces that give their lives an extraordinary effectiveness." Indeed, he even went so far as to say that many were mystics without knowing it. "By far the larger number of mystics probably live and die without explicitly knowing they are mystics . . . They quietly manifest in acts that energies not their own and incursions of power from beyond themselves are coming through them." One of his favorite topics, which formed a chapter in his last book as well as several articles, was the mysticism of ordinary persons. Wherever he went he met people who had felt themselves "in contact with an environing Presence and supplied with new energy to live by," and among his papers are some remarkable letters from otherwise unknown people telling him of experiences they had had.

Though he believed that the capacity for such experience could be cultivated, and indeed in one place characterizes the mystic as one who "has cultivated with more strenuous care and discipline than others have done the native homing passion of the soul for the Beyond," there are no handbooks of mystical training to be found among Rufus Jones's fifty-four book titles. The classic "ladders" of ascent he considered suitable only to the few; to many these were "unreal and artificial." Though at one time he declared that it required a "training analagous to the athlete's," he was for the most part dubious about techniques and well marked roadways, "convinced that the mystic way will always remain a way of surprise and wonder."

He did nevertheless in several of his books give some hints and suggestions as to how the mystical aspirant may best pursue the serious business of his life, which is "to seek, to find, to love and to be in union with God." Though he did not use the word *purgation* he did regard the process of overcoming selfishness, of organizing the instincts and emotions, sublimating the old springs of action and energy and developing new habit tracks as primary and essential. He did not minimize the importance of concentration. "Training in concentration," he pointed out, "is the first step toward any difficult goal in life. Meditation is simply concentration in a special field."

"Preparation through appreciation of *beauty*, learning to sound the deeps of *love*, formation of purity, gentleness, tenderness of heart, freedom from harshness of judgment, absolute honesty of purpose and motive—these positive traits and qualities of life are far more important steps on the inner pathway than are artificial techniques of discipline."

The right use of great spiritual literature and the fellowship of "spiritually contagious persons" he also counted among the important aids to the deepening of the mystical capacity.

Beyond these general suggestions, which apply as much to any person who wishes to live a good life in accordance with the will of God as to him who longs to achieve mystic union, he does not go. The technique of Yoga or of Zen Buddhism, which he recognized as being "a discipline of a very high order for the control of sense, of muscles, of imagination, of wandering thoughts, of human passion," did not, he believed, achieve the end which he saw as the desirable one. "Routine, cut-and-dried systems of discipline may help to make a Stoic temper, or to prepare a climber of Mt. Everest, or"—and here he makes one catch one's breath—"to forge a mystic of the type of St. John of the Cross, but these disciplines seem to me to be too doctrinaire and too remote from life to be satisfactory ways into the heart of divine reality."

To many people any routine that could forge a mystic like St. John of the Cross would appear to leave nothing more to be desired. In another book Rufus Jones explained further what he meant about the Spanish saint. "If one wants to see a man who has climbed clear above the pleasure line and who lives in a height in which the pleasure spur is forgotten and has been left behind as though it did not exist, let him read St. John of the Cross. I admit that it sometimes seems to me as though, in leaving behind all reference to aspects of preference, of like and dislike, St. John has also left behind our human way of life and has withdrawn almost into a vacuum where exists very little of the air we mortals breathe . . . I feel a sense of hush and awe in the presence of these tremendous lovers of God" (he was writing about Fénelon and Mme Guyon as well as St. John of the Cross) "but in my critical moments I am convinced that they are endeavoring to do what cannot be done and, I am bound to add, what ought not to be done. They propose to eliminate all the springs of action which characterize us as men, to obliterate all the concrete clues from human experience which serve as practical guides for us, and to walk only by a supernatural pillar of cloud and fire from above."

A mysticism, however lofty, which left humanity behind, was foreign to Rufus Jones's thought. "I am interested," he said, "in a mysticism which brings life to its full rich goal of complete living, with radiance and joy and creative power." A mysticism, further- more, that did not find expression in creative service, remained to him incomplete. In describing John Woolman, who was to him the best expression of the ideal of Quaker mysticism, he told how Wool- man became extraordinarily tender to human need and sensitive to "every breath of wrong" which man does to man. "Here was a mysticism," he concluded, "—and it was the type to which I dedicated my life—which sought no ecstasies, no miracles of levitation, no startling phenomena, no private raptures, but whose over-mastering passion was to turn all he possessed, including his own life, 'into the channel of universal love.'"

XXIV

Great Occasions

In 1935 Rufus Jones again became chairman of the board of the A.F.S.C. He had never put aside his interest in it or ceased to give time and counsel to it, but now once more he was at the helm and must be on hand for meetings of the board and the executive committee. The A.F.S.C. was completing the work that it had done with the families of unemployed miners and was becoming increasingly involved with the problems of refugees from Germany and Austria. The Jewish Joint Distribution Committee, with which it had cooperated in the Russian feeding in 1921-22, was taking responsibility for the Jewish refugees, but there were many who were only part Jewish, who had perhaps become Christian or who professed no religion at all, who did not come within the care of the J.D.C. These were the people whom the A.F.S.C. sought to help.

In October the Five Years Meeting met again, and Rufus Jones was asked to be the presiding clerk. The entire meeting rose when he took the chair, and again at the end of the last session—a most unusual demonstration for Quakers and a signal evidence of the love and honor in which he was held. "To have lived through storms and controversy to this expression of love and unity," he wrote to Mary, "is a great consummation." *The American Friend* published a photograph of nine Friends who had been present at all the sessions from 1902 on, with Rufus Jones in the center.

In November Bryn Mawr College celebrated its fiftieth anniversary with a great meeting in Goodhart Hall. M. Carey Thomas, aged seventy-eight, came out of retirement to don her cap and gown once more and dominate the proceedings. Indeed, they became a kind of tribute to her, for she, fiery, indomitable, arrogant, brilliant, far-sighted and dedicated, had, more than anyone else, made Bryn Mawr what it was, and through Bryn Mawr had influenced the whole course of higher education for women in America.

Just a month later, Carey Thomas was dead. There was a small private service for her conducted after the manner of Friends and attended only by relatives and a few close friends—"I was at the little funeral for M. Carey Thomas yesterday," wrote Rufus Jones to Mary, "having been invited in her will to attend!"—and her ashes were buried as she desired in the cloisters of the library which she had loved. A few days later a large memorial service was held in Goodhart Hall, at which Rufus Jones, speaking for the directors, said the truest and most beautiful words that have ever been spoken of her:

"She was unmistakably a child of the Renaissance. She was in the true succession of the great spirits which that new dawn nurtured. Like them she loved beauty in all its forms. She had a passion for excellence. She had a habit of leaping frontiers. She was bent on the liberation of the mind from every kind of bondage, convention and oppression and she was a knight-errant in that chivalry."

Several years before, she had written her final estimation of him, in a letter: "In looking back over the progress of the college, it seems to me that thy understanding of college problems and thy determinedly liberal attitude, reinforced as it was by thy position as a preacher and religious worker, has been of inestimable advantage to the college . . . I want thee to know that I appreciate better than anyone else what thee has done."

At the end of the next year, Rufus Jones resigned the chairmanship of the Bryn Mawr board—though not his membership of the board itself—and was succeeded by Charles J. Rhoads, the son of the first president, Indian commissioner under Herbert Hoover, banker, concerned Friend, and wise and courtly gentleman. Of its retiring president, the Board passed a Resolution, which said in part:

"He has brought to the meetings the authority of the realist who got quickly to the questions at issue and of an idealist who refused to consider makeshift remedies. His wise counsels and his fine humor have often cleared away the fog of discussion."

His lectures during that year began with a missionary conference at Asbury Park in January, which was presided over by John R. Mott. Kagawa, the famous Japanese evangelist, was on the same program. "Kagawa and I speak tomorrow afternoon," Rufus Jones wrote to his daughter, who was spending the winter in New York, —"at least I shall speak if he finishes in time for me to follow! I know his propensities of old and I can see a long run for the money!" February saw him travelling through the middle west, speaking in Ohio, Indiana, Iowa, to "every kind of group known" with as many as eighteen meetings in a single week. "It sounds appalling, doesn't it?" he wrote to Mary. "But I have no doubt it will unroll all right as the days file by. I am keen to put in as much 'deadly work' as possible in the brief time that remains before old age rips my stitches . . . Meantime the poor old world is going 'dotty' and nothing will cure it but the grace of God running through human channels."

Earlier, on a trip to New England, he had had a somewhat unusual experience which he reported with zest to Mary: "I enjoyed my visit at Bradford College, but the chairman fainted dead away while he was introducing me! It was a novel experience to help carry him off and then to address the audience *sans* his trumpet blowing."

During that year and the next he gave the Ayer Lectures at Rochester, the Cole Lectures at Vanderbilt, and the Earl Lectures at the Pacific School of Religion. Elizabeth Jones went with him to California and while they were there they dined with the Hoovers in Palo Alto. The Ayer Lectures, expanded, appeared in book form under the title, THE TESTIMONY OF THE SOUL, the Cole Lectures, as SOME PROBLEMS OF LIFE, but the Earl Lectures, which had been entitled "Continuous Revelation," were not published. He spoke at yearly meetings across the land, at a special convocation at Columbia to celebrate the four hundredth anniversary of Erasmus's death, and gave a six-week series of lectures on Quakerism at the Race Street Meeting in Philadelphia.

His mail was enormous. "I wrote thirty letters yesterday," he reported to Mary. There were endless requests, reasonable and unreasonable. "I have the honor of addressing you on a subject of importance to myself," began one letter, but that might have accurately been the preface to nine-tenths of them. He was asked to recommend a girls' day-school in Brooklyn, "where the influence would be really good," to read and comment on a variety of manuscripts, to present copies of his books to The Theistic Endeavor

Society, to recommend books on business and public ethics, to help a
fifty-eight-year-old church member to conquer the sin of fornication,
to prepare a three-thousand word paper to be entitled "Decadence"
for "The Capital Magazine." "Would you please emphasize," specified
the editor, "the melancholy of the decadence of anything, or everything in general." Perhaps the most striking was the suggestion which
came as "a morning inspiration" to the writer, that Rufus Jones
should "invite Edward and Wallis to join the American Friends
Service Committee for the work in Spain, or one of the large groups
of refugees in France or England, it would be to Edward and Wallis
a worthy avenue of return to useful living and the hearts of critical
fellow countrymen."

When in 1936 Spain exploded into civil war, thousands of children
who themselves "were neither Nationalist nor Loyalist" became homeless and destitute. English Friends were the first to act, but the
A.F.S.C. followed soon after. It proved to be a three-year emergency
relief program, in which the A.F.S.C., assisted by contributions from
other organizations and individuals, provided milk for babies, supplementary feeding for children, mothers and old people, and distributed
clothing.

After the A.F.S.C. had been working in Spain for more than a
year Theodore Dreiser, at the suggestion of President Roosevelt,
came to see Rufus Jones at Haverford about setting up a committee
of prominent citizens to sponsor the cause of civilian relief in Spain.
They talked for about two hours, and Theodore Dreiser was deeply
impressed by Rufus Jones's "vitality and comprehensive way of looking at things."

They went together to call on various people in New York in an
attempt to enlist their support for the plan, but without success. The
joint effort had no result for the cause of Spanish relief, but during
their association Dreiser was greatly drawn to Rufus Jones as a
person. "Indeed," writes Gerhard Friedrich, "Jones was to Dreiser
a fascinating phenomenon, highly esteemed and soon so diligently
explored that his Quakerly image came to provide not only the
stimulus but also the animus, long needed to carry Dreiser's abandoned
Philadelphia Quaker novel to its completion under the title, THE
BULWARK."

When in 1943, Dreiser wrote to Rufus Jones asking for the names
of Quaker schools near Philadelphia, he added, "When I think
of you and contrast you with the average so called Christian, I am
inclined to use language that your temperament would not counte-

nance. But I still and always will hold you in my very highest esteem."

The year 1936 marked also the fruition of a cherished plan of Rufus Jones's, which had been in his mind for ten years or more. As he had travelled about Europe for the A.F.S.C. in the years following the war and then through the Orient in 1926, and as he went from college to university throughout the United States, he had become keenly aware of people who thought the Quakers had found answers to their own spiritual questions, scattered and isolated Friends who had no meeting near them, and people who were attracted to the Quaker philosophy through their touch with the work of the A.F.S.C. He felt their need and he sought a way to draw them into relationship with one another and with Friends.

In Cairo in 1926, on his way home from China, as he addressed a group of such seekers, the idea came to him of a "wider Quaker fellowship, a looser, less completely organized group than the Society itself, which these people could join." Three years later in London at a joint meeting of the Friends Service Council and the Home Service Committee, he put his thought before English Friends. "There would be no conditions of membership in this fellowship except a readiness to dedicate oneself to the way of love, and a faith that man is a candle of the Lord and can become a center of radiance, an organ of the Spirit, just where he lives," he described it. "I am not interested any more in just clinging to the Society of Friends and preserving it," he said. "We stand at a crisis and we can be bearers of the torch as our fathers were or can carefully husband a little flame and keep it from going out a little longer."

Interest and some agreement was expressed but there was no real answering enthusiasm. The danger of a two-level membership in the Society of Friends was the chief objection.

Undaunted, he followed up this presentation with an article in the *World Outlook*, London, for January, 1930, called "That Wider Fellowship," in which he called Friends to a "new spiritual adventure." The first necessity, he declared, was the "revitalization of our own membership so that we may *in fact and truth* be the living spiritual nucleus of this enlarged fellowship."

Rather ironically, since the idea never took hold in England, the name which Rufus Jones gave to the group and even the idea itself, may well have sprung from a dimly remembered report of London Yearly Meeting in 1906. Rufus Jones recorded in *The American Friend*, that " 'The Wider Fellowship' movement came again into prominence, and there was an earnest desire manifested that the great number of persons now coming under the influence of Friends through Adult Schools and in other ways might be drawn into closer fellowship."

Back in the United States he laid his concern before the Ministers and Elders of Philadelphia Yearly Meeting, with the result that the Message Committee of the A.F.S.C. held a Retreat in April at Browns Mills, New Jersey, to pursue the subject. Sixty-five people representing both branches of Philadelphia Quakerdom came, Rufus Jones enthusiastically proposed his plan, other papers were read, and a yeasty discussion followed, in which the difficulty caused by the separation between the two yearly meetings was raised and aired. No definite action was taken at this conference. Friends traditionally move slowly, and this was a new idea. Might it not have the effect of creating yet another separate body of Friends?

The seed nevertheless had been planted. The Message Committee of the A.F.S.C. grew into the Fellowship Committee, which in 1936 became the American Friends Fellowship Council, representing all Friends, the function of which was to nurture the new small independent meetings which were beginning to spring up, chiefly in college communities, across the United States. One of its duties was to be "the formation of closer relations of fellowship with religious seekers and friends of the Friends in all parts of the world."

This Council held a conference in the Florida Avenue Meetinghouse in Washington in January, 1936, at which Rufus Jones presided. He read a Letter to Seekers which he had written and which he proposed that the Fellowship Council should send out, inviting them to take part not in an organization but rather in a spontaneous reaching out and touching of hands. This letter is still used today as an invitation to all who express an interest. Rufus Jones saw the Wider Quaker Fellowship as a brotherhood, akin to the Third Order of St. Francis, "of persons who believe in a direct and immediate relation between the human soul and God, who are eager for refreshment and inspiration through times of silent communion with God and who in the faith that there are divine possibilities in all persons, would like to help promote, by the gentle forces of love and truth and friendliness, a way of life based on cooperation rather than on rivalries and contentions."

So the Wider Quaker Fellowship was born. There were no dues, no by-laws, no officers. It was held together by letters, by occasional local gatherings, by intervisitation, and by a quarterly mailing of recent Quaker literature.*

By 1937 it was reported that one hundred persons had become members, and by 1952 the number had grown to about 4000. People from Africa, South America, the Middle East, Europe, India, China, and Japan as well as from all parts of the United States, joined in the fellowship: Episcopal missionaries, students, pacifists, ministers of various denominations, rabbis, work campers, people of "Quaker background," writers, housewives.

One of the earliest members was Vida Scudder, well-known writer and distinguished member of the Wellesley College faculty. "That fellowship is a sustaining reality to me," she wrote to Rufus Jones. "I think," she added candidly, "it's in a way easier to feel near to people you don't know in the flesh than to people you do."

The Society of Friends had had in 1920 its first World Conference, held in London as soon as it had been possible after the first World War. In 1937, when the world was so plainly drifting toward a second and more terrible conflict, it was decided to hold another conference, this time in the United States. Early September was the date chosen, and Swarthmore College, outside of Philadelphia, the place. Rufus Jones was asked to preside over the meetings.

He accepted, but the Conference loomed before him as an ordeal. He wrote to Violet Holdsworth in July, "In regard to the World Conference, I sincerely hope for good results, but I have become a good deal disillusioned over 'big' conferences and large gatherings. I pin my hopes to quiet processes and small circles in which vital and transforming events take place. But, others see differently, and I respect their judgment."

He went to South China early that year. Near-by Colby College gave him an honorary doctorate of Sacred Theology, which he valued, but he had another recognition that pleased him much more. His daughter dedicated to him the history of the A.F.S.C., SWORDS INTO PLOUGHSHARES, which she had written. "The dedication," he wrote to her, "made me happier and prouder than any degree which the Universities have given me."

He developed that summer a disagreeable buzzing in his ears, which troubled him greatly, for he feared that it was an indication of an

---

* After the Second World War drove Emma Cadbury out of the Friends Center in Vienna, she took charge of this work of the Wider Quaker Fellowship, and has nurtured it ever since.

injury to the brain or a forerunner of some mental illness. Though doctors assured him that it was not serious he slept badly and was nervously wrought up and disturbed. This buzzing he never quite got rid of, but he learned to accept it.

A thousand Friends gathered in Swarthmore on the first of September, five hundred Americans and five hundred from other parts of the world, from the continent of Europe, from Africa, from India, from China and Japan. Thirteen German Friends were there. The weather was oppressively hot and air conditioning was not yet general. Nevertheless the meeting was a united, joyful, and hopeful one.

One of its high features was a broadcast by Rufus Jones, beamed by short wave to Europe, on the nature of Quakerism. A superb brief statement, summing up the Quaker philosophy and ideals, setting forth the Quaker stand on war, it brought enthusiastic letters from various parts of England, from the western isles of Scotland, from Germany. Rufus Jones's old friend, Sir George Newman, wrote to him, "It was indeed a noble exposition of the Quaker Faith and if thou hadst never told the world anything else this is sufficient— sufficient to justify thy glorious record."

Rufus Jones himself wrote an evaluation of the Conference for the London *Friend*. "Three sessions in the middle of the Conference have been dominated by these supreme issues of the modern world [i.e., problems of securing justice and making peace prevail.] The discussions have reached high levels of thought and interpretation. They have been carried on in a spirit of forbearance and much of the time in essential unity of purpose. I have never seen a large gathering handle difficult questions in better manner."

He made the same criticism that he had made of the 1920 conference: "Friends do not stand very well the deepest and severest test of their spiritual quality—their ability to worship God in spirit and in truth in large corporate gatherings. We talk and write effusively about this major business of life. We can point to glorious passages that have been produced by ready pens, but *to do the thing itself* in actual practice and experience is a rare achievement in any part of the Quaker heritage. It was never up to the ideal in this Conference, but it was at least as good as is usually the case in gatherings of this size." The silence, so precious and so necessary for Quaker worship, is usually shattered when large numbers of Friends assemble.

"The Conference was a great occasion," Rufus Jones wrote to Violet Holdsworth when it was all over, "but it 'took' about all there was in me. No more but my love!"

XXV

South Africa

R UFUS JONES'S seventy-fifth birthday, like his seventieth, was celebrated with a dinner party given by the Friends Social Union, with speeches, poems, telegrams and letters. In addition a volume called CHILDREN OF LIGHT, with chapters on Quaker subjects by leading writers among Friends, was published in his honor. In the introduction, Howard Brinton, who had become director of Pendle Hill after the death of Henry Hodgkin, paid tribute to Rufus Jones as a historian. The book was, he wrote, "a gesture of appreciation to a historian who is also a philosopher, a social reformer, and most notably a great exponent of Christian mysticism . . . In his hands history has become not a rehearsal of occurrences but a drama of souls seeking and finding fulfilment of God."

Less than a week later Rufus and Elizabeth Jones set sail for South Africa on the invitation of South African Quakers and with the support and encouragement of the Service Committee. Rufus Jones at seventy-five was in radiant health, erect, glowing, serene. Except for the persistent buzzing in his ears, the bodily ailments which had troubled him earlier had disappeared. He had found the way to carry a heavy schedule of writing, speaking and committee work and still to be unhurried, to have leisure for the people who sought him out. Part at least of his secret could be discovered in his wife. Elizabeth Jones was now sixty-seven; sunny, unruffled, with her own brand of humor, her own spiritual depths, she was ever at hand, finding missing objects, ready to go or to stay behind at need, making the home a place of refreshment and renewal.

Even so recently as 1938 people did not fly around the world in a matter of hours. When Rufus and Elizabeth Jones embarked on the *City of New York*, with the intention of going on from Africa to China and Japan and so home across the Pacific, they were setting out on a long journey, with many days at sea before them. Friends saw them go with some apprehension and a great welling up of tenderness, but they themselves set out in high spirits.

They enjoyed the life aboard ship and the people whom they met. They reached the equator after thirteen days, and the next day Rufus Jones reported with delight his first sight of the Southern Cross. On the seventeenth of February the ship put in at St. Helena, and everybody went ashore to see Napoleon's grave and Longwood, the house in which he lived out his last years.

"It was a rare day of sightseeing," wrote Rufus Jones to his daughter. "We enjoyed it much more than poor old Nap. ever did. It made me think of the rock on which Prometheus was chained."

On Stunt Night Rufus Jones gave his famous Fourth of July Oration, a parody of the old time Independence day oratory.

After a little over three weeks at sea they reached Capetown and settled down for a fortnight in a comfortable little hotel on Sea Point, with a view of Table Mountain on one side and the ocean on the other.

Their first concern was with the little group of a hundred and twenty Friends scattered among three monthly meetings centering in Capetown, Johannesburg and Port Elizabeth, who needed sympathy and encouragement in the face of the tightening racial tensions and the rising tide of public opinion so at variance with their own convictions. Rufus Jones also wanted to speak to as many college and university groups as possible and to talk with leading citizens wherever he could, to learn from them about the race situation.

On their second day in Capetown he had dinner with Senator Reinhault Jones, who represented the non-European races in Parliament, and who was to help him to arrange his speaking engagements in colleges. The next day he met General Smuts. He went to the Parliament House and sent in his card, and he and Elizabeth Jones were invited immediately to have tea with the General in his office.

Jan Christian Smuts was then sixty-eight, tall and white-haired, with a neat white beard and brilliant, searching blue eyes. He was

Minister of Justice in a Fusion cabinet and deputy Prime Minister to J.B.M. Hertzog, the leader of the Nationalist Party. Like Rufus Jones, Smuts came out of a simple farm background. Their lives had followed vastly different paths, but the basis for understanding was there. Smuts had had many friends among the English Quakers; one of his daughters had married a Friend. He had philosophical interests. At Cambridge, when he was a student there, he had written a seventy-thousand-word treatise entitled "Walt Whitman—A Study in the Evolution of Personality," in which he set forth theories which he later developed more fully in his book, HOLISM AND EVOLUTION. Though he came to it through war and politics, world peace was one of the major concerns of his later life. His pamphlet, "The League of Nations—A Practical Suggestion," published in December, 1918, was enthusiastically read by Wilson and helped to prepare the way for the Covenant; he represented South Africa at the Peace Conference and pointed out vigorously if fruitlessly the pitfalls in the Versailles Treaty; he was to take an important part in the San Francisco Conference in 1945.

"We had a delightful hour with him in extremely friendly conversation with him," wrote Rufus Jones. Smuts was saddened over the world situation, he reported, but still hopeful, though he did not think the cure would come in his life time. He felt that his life work had failed in South Africa.

"He pointed out what a snarl of complication of races and suspicions and hatred had beset this land from its beginnings to the present moment. I remarked that I thought he was going to turn from political activity to the field of philosophy in which he had shown such marked aptitude. No, he said, for better or for worse I have put my hand to this plow and I cannot turn back."

Rufus Jones found him far more sympathetic to the native races than he had expected. " 'My people, the Boers,' he said, 'have complicated the whole race situation by their intense Old Testament idea of being "a peculiar people," the one and only chosen of the Lord. They have throughout their history in South Africa proudly maintained that stern attitude and it has made them hard toward all other races and peoples and it has prevented any fair and proper treatment of other races. I have come,' he continued, 'to see that one of the most amazing things about Jesus, the supreme Figure in the entire history of the world, was the way He dealt with that claim. He swept it away and announced a gospel for the whole world—a message of universal brotherhood regardless of race or color or position. This sweep of universal inclusiveness is what cost Jesus His life. The moment He announced this superracial view He had the peculiar people set against Him and determined to destroy Him.' . . .

"I asked him if the education of the natives would not increase their race consciousness and make them much less passive and submissive . . . 'In any case the natives must be educated, and in my judgment,' he added, 'they must be educated *with* the European whites. If they are educated in segregation they will not be adapted and adjusted to the world civilization of our epoch.' . . .

"The years have softened this great man," Rufus Jones concluded. "His deeper ideals have ripened and he has taken on the vision of a prophet and he has caught much of the spirit of the Galilean."

Besides three meetings with the Capetown Friends, Rufus Jones addressed a public meeting on the Quaker way of life and philosophy of service, but only a hundred of "these strict Calvinists and High Episcopalians" came. "So far I have not met student audiences," he was writing plaintively on the first of March, but three days later he had a day packed to the brim with them. He went to Stellenbosch, near Capetown, where in the morning he spoke to the Training College for Teachers and to the Theological School, both parts of the University of Stellenbosch. In the afternoon he spoke to another Training School for Teachers in Wellington. "I got on famously at the Stellenbosch Theol. Sem." he reported delightedly to Mary, "where they wouldn't allow Stanley Jones to speak. *He* was too dangerous!"

On the way from Stellenbosch to Wellington they stopped to see the vineries which were the chief industry of that part of the Cape Province and picked grapes. The whole day, Elizabeth Jones wrote, was spent in an Afrikaans atmosphere, away from the English.

One day General Smuts gave a luncheon in their honor at the Parliament Building. Rufus Jones described the General's wife as "unique, fresh, vigorous, and very practical. When she heard I was a Quaker, she said, Then of course you are a banker, and when I said I was a philosopher, she said, Then of course you are poor!"

When Rufus Jones asked the General what chance there was of the Protectorates, Swaziland, Basutoland and Bechuanaland being brought into the Union, he replied that it would take years before it could be done.

"Then I boldly put the question: what is your judgment on the policy of absorption. He said he was convinced that it would be for the decided advantage of the *natives* in these countries. He thinks that they retrogress if left to themselves. They need white stimulus."

The following day General Smuts, as Chancellor of the University of Capetown, presided over the installation of the vice-chancellor. At the end of his speech, Rufus Jones noted with satisfaction, he said, "World peace must become the greatest of our human interests."

Rufus Jones had another visit with the statesman-general before he and Elizabeth Jones left Capetown for Johannesburg. He went to say good-by, intending just to leave his card with the secretary, but she sent it in to the General, who came out cordially and insisted that Rufus Jones have tea once more in his office. "So we sat and had a lovely visit and talk. He has been extremely nice to us all through."

Smuts expressed his opinion of Rufus Jones some years later in a letter to Margaret Gillett of Oxford. "There is something in the spirit of Rufus Jones which appeals very much to the best in me. His 'Eternal Gospel' I consider a very great book, perhaps the best on religion written in our day, and I always love to return to his simple, direct and fundamental Quaker outlook. My own world takes me far away from that simple association with life's deepest things. I live in the strife, the struggle, the noise and often the dust and dirt which form so much of our human environment and I enjoy all the more a return to that inner world of the spirit as reflected in R.J.'s thought."

On their way to the station to take the train for Johannesburg on March twelfth, they saw the newspaper headlines blazing forth Hitler's ultimatum to Austria and Schuschnigg's resignation, and they had the whole journey of nearly a thousand miles to ponder on its meaning.

"We are crushed by the news from Austria," Rufus Jones wrote to Clarence Pickett in a rare tone of despondency. "It is one of the most crashing blows that has fallen in this world of clouds and darkness and no man can see what will emerge from such desperate action. I am full of sorrow over Schuschnigg who was a brave good man trying to do his duty."

In Johannesburg, the fifty-year-old, gold-rush city six thousand feet high on the Witwatersrand plateau, they spent the next ten days. One day they went to tea with Judge and Mrs. Millin, who as Sarah Gertrude Millin, the author of GOD'S STEP-CHILDREN, was well known as South Africa's leading writer. "We had a glorious visit with Gertrude Millin, the novelist," Rufus Jones wrote enthusiastically. "Tomorrow we are to spend the day in Pretoria where I have three addresses, two big meals and probably a score of teas. It [i.e. tea] comes like April showers early and often."

A meeting with the ministers of the city, "a glorious occasion," lectures at the University of the Witwatersrand, a sermon in the leading Presbyterian Church, meetings with Johannesburg Friends, and conversations with prominent citizens, filled up the days in Johannesburg, and they were off to Durban, five hundred miles away on the coast of the Indian Ocean.

Elizabeth Jones, writing to Mary of their experiences in Durban, broke off to interpolate, "Here I stopped to find the cards of a lecture for tomorrow night, which were irrevocably lost but now are found."

From Durban they made a loop that took in Bloemfontein, Grahamstown and Port Elizabeth, and returned to Durban again. In Grahamstown they stayed with J. Sneath Thomas, the Master of Rhodes University, and his wife. The two big meetings at Rhodes provided for Rufus Jones the "peak" of his student meetings. He and the Master of Rhodes had many congenial conversations on philosophy, and F. William Fox, clerk of the Transvaal Monthly Meeting, reported to Rufus Jones afterwards, "I came up in the train with the new principal of Rhodes. What impressed him most about your visit was your profound knowledge of Paracelsus, about which he thought he knew 'about everything' as you would say!"

From Grahamstown he motored to Healdtown and Fort Hare, where he spoke to large groups of native students. His talk at the Theological Seminary and Bible Training School was translated into Bantu.

Easter was spent in Port Elizabeth, where the first General Meeting of Friends in five years was held. Otto Pietz from Germany was also there, and the three foreign Friends found that they had indeed a service to perform in raising the spirits of the dejected little group of twenty-five Friends and a few "attenders" who gathered there.

"The meetings out here are so small and feeble that the members had felt discouraged and almost [ready] to 'surrender.' But when the leaders got together with a few visitors from abroad they found new courage and went home with new born hope . . . I have seldom seen a little band so uplifted and changed in attitude and expectation."

Back in Durban, preparing to leave South Africa, Rufus Jones summed up his two months' visit for Clarence Pickett and the A.F.S.C.

Board. "We have covered 3500 miles of travel in S. Africa. We have attended all the Quaker meetings except the little one at Craddock and all the Friends there were at the General Meeting. We have personally met most of the individual Friends and twenty-eight of the 'attenders'. We have had the most happy contacts and have formed lasting friendships."

He had also visited the four universities and four of the five university colleges and lectured to them all. The only one that he had not been able to visit was that at Polchefstrom, "where they speak Afrikaans and do not like English addresses." It is probable that they would not have liked his ideas either.

His lectures covered a wide range of subjects, none of which were directly concerned with race. To the universities he spoke on: The Need for a New Emphasis in Education; Do History and Science Indicate Human Progress?; The Revealing Aspect of Great Literature; The Way of the Mystic; St. Francis of Assisi; The Heroic Period in Luther's Life; The Spiritual Aspect of Human Life (Personality). His popular addresses, which included Rotary Club luncheons, bore the titles: Some Great Adventures; New Installment of Life; Finding the Whole of Oneself; Justifiable Expectation; Life as a Fine Art; The Hero in Thy Soul.

His conclusions on South Africa inevitably bore a note of sadness. The race problem was deeper, darker and more complex than he had thought, the resources to meet and untangle it more feeble, more timid. It was not by chance that through so many of his talks ran the summons to adventure and courage. "There is widespread timidity to say the brave word or to do the manly thing," he wrote in his pocket diary . . . "The real test of Christianity is its success in bringing true unity and fellowship between the white followers of Christ and the races of color."

They left Durban on the *Barentz* on the 26th of April, for the three-week voyage to Batavia, where they were to transship for Hong Kong. Just before reaching Batavia, however, they ran into the tail end of a monsoon, which delayed them so that they lost their connection with the boat for Hong Kong. Accordingly they went on to Singapore, where they spent two or three days in the famous Raffles Hotel, waiting for the next boat for China. Late in May they reached Canton and had a brief but happy visit with Dr. William and Catharine Cadbury.

The dark and threatening clouds of aggression in Austria and of racial hatreds in South Africa had become the storms of actual war in China. When the ship entered Shanghai Harbor, where Japanese bombs had destroyed the lighthouse, it struck a rock and came very close to sinking. For a time the passengers stared death in the face, until the incoming tide lifted the crippled boat off and it limped to safety. "I don't know whether Mother has made the account of our ship's collision with Diamond Rock as harrowing as it ought to be," wrote Rufus Jones as a postscript to his wife's letter to Mary, "but it easily takes its place among the most stirring moments of one's life. When we got on deck with life jackets there rose in front not more than ten or twelve feet away a huge rock as high as the ship and we had rammed it head on and then swung round side to it with the rushing current swirling between us and it . . . I am glad to say we were favored to keep in great peace."

While they were in Shanghai the news came of Japanese air-raids on Canton, which took place just after they left. "A terrible holocaust —men, women and children. Over 100 wounded and dying brought to our hospital alone this morning," wrote William Cadbury.

Shanghai was suffering not only from the devastation of war but from an epidemic of cholera then raging. Rufus Jones, who had come primarily to survey the need and plan an A.F.S.C. relief program there, was spared no sight of the suffering. "I have been pretty well over the destroyed areas and seen enough trouble to last the rest of my life. The weather is abominable and especially so today. I came back very wet. I am kept on a constant 'go' from morning to night with two or three addresses thrown on top of the visits to scenes of desolation. I dread the time in Tokio," he added, "for it is so very difficult to know what to say to those whom we shall meet there."

The climate of thought in Japan had changed sharply from that of his last visit. During the days that he was in Tokyo, his contacts were almost entirely confined to the Japanese Friends, who were themselves in a difficult and possibly dangerous position. Pacifists, part of an international body most of whose members were English and American, they were under the suspicion of the now dominant war party. Rufus Jones, coming to them greatly troubled from China, found words of love and humility with which to speak to them.

"I have asked you to meet us here today," he said, "*not* that I might tell you what is your duty in this war, not that I might give you an easy formula of action, but rather that together we might renew the fellowship of the spirit and that we might feel the touch of a friendly hand of love."

After more than five months away he returned, a little tired, a little saddened, to his beloved refuge in South China. Whatever his travels and engagements might be, he generally managed to save for himself a quiet time at Pendle Hill, where he could watch the sunsets and the thunderstorms over China Lake and refresh himself with the beauty of nature which was to him an expression of the reality of God.

THE ETERNAL GOSPEL was published in the year 1938. He finished the writing of his scholarly and important book on the fourteenth century mystics, THE FLOWERING OF MYSTICISM, which would be published the following year. He drafted a number of speeches and wrote a dozen or more articles for periodicals. It might seem that with his trip around the world, this was enough activity for a man of seventy-five, but there loomed ahead a service more fraught with danger, more loaded with tension, more difficult yet more radically optimistic than any single action he had yet undertaken.

Mission to the Gestapo

On November 9 and 10, 1938, now known as the Day of Broken Glass, occurred an event that sent a shudder of horror and foreboding through the western world. Throughout Germany and Austria, by a prearranged and carefully planned movement officially declared spontaneous, men broke into Jewish homes, stores and synagogues, smashed the windows, looted the contents, terrified and in some cases injured the inmates, and carried off some thirty-five thousand able-bodied Jewish men to concentration camps. This outrage, while the world outside was still gasping, was followed up by proclamations forcing Jews out of their homes and jobs and denying them permission to buy necessary supplies in Gentile shops.

The A.F.S.C. in Philadelphia was instantly alert. Cables to the Quaker Centers in Berlin and Vienna accompanied anxious conferences and committee meetings in the quiet offices at Twenty South 12th Street, and within a week a special refugee division of the Foreign Service Section was established. Clarence Pickett had been in Europe the previous summer and had seen the growing desperation of the Jews there. Reports from workers had pled with increasing urgency for affidavits for people who wanted to escape from Germany before it was too late.

The immediate fear was that the Jews would be unable to get food and that starvation would complete what violence had begun. Was a Quaker feeding program in Germany again tragically necessary?

Rufus Jones and Clarence Pickett went to Washington to talk with the State Department and with the German Ambassador, Hans Heinrich Dieckhoff, about the possibility of sending a small mission to Germany to find out what the situation actually was, to determine whether relief was needed and if it could be sent. Dieckhoff, who had been in Washington a little over a year, was not himself a member of the Nazi party, but was close to it and a propagandist for it. He received the two Friends courteously and said that he thought a mission might well go to Berlin. What was needed, he said, were plans for an orderly emigration of Jews from Germany. The State Department encouraged the idea of a Quaker feeding program and urged that the proposed delegation be sent as quickly as possible.

The two returned to Philadelphia and held quiet conversations with members of the Executive Committee and the Board. The unpredictable fury of the Nazi authorities and the extremely precarious position of the Jewish people made caution and discretion essential. It was decided to send, without any publicity at all, three representatives to Germany to observe conditions and to feel out the possibilities for alleviating the plight of the Jews.

The knowledge of the past relationship between the A.F.S.C and the German people made it seem both appropriate that such a mission should go and possible that it might find an opening not available to others. The feeding of the German children after the first World War had left a legacy of gratitude and of recognition of the reconciling nature of Quaker concern. Since those days of greatest need, moreover, there had been continuing, though much smaller, Quaker programs. In Vienna victims on both sides of recent political conflicts had been succoured. Since Friends in taking food for the body had always sought to take food for the spirit as well, there arose an unquenchable though largely unspoken hope among those who helped prepare for the mission that some opportunity might arise for reaching the Nazi leaders, who must surely be touched by the goodness and love of these three Friends. The three who were going, however, steadfastly disclaimed such extravagant purposes, maintaining only an attitude of open-minded and humble availability.

The three men chosen were Rufus Jones, D. Robert Yarnall, a "weighty" Philadelphia Friend, a manufacturer who like many others had taken time away from his business to serve the A.F.S.C. in Germany during the child-feeding, and George A. Walton, the well-known and well-loved principal of George School outside Philadelphia.

Members of the Five Years Meeting, the Arch Street Yearly Meeting and the Race Street Yearly Meeting respectively, they represented a large proportion of American Quakerdom.

Several days before they left for Germany, the three met at Clarence Pickett's house in Wallingford for a final conference. It was perhaps at this farewell meeting that Rufus Jones uttered the warning words against "illusions" about the venture which he later recorded: "Matter is no doubt stubborn but nothing in the universe is so utterly unconquerable as a mind possessed by a set of ideas that have become entrenched and sacred . . . We can almost certainly accomplish some practical things which need personal attention. Whether we can influence minds or soften hearts or make spiritual forces seem real— that remains to be seen. We shall do our best and wisest and we shall go in the strength of God."

It was a day of wind and sleet, and Mary Hoxie Jones, driving her father back to Haverford afterwards over ten skidding miles of almost invisible, ice-coated roads, felt that all the omens were bad and that an aura of doom and disaster hung over the undertaking. Rufus Jones was nearly seventy-six. He faced a December crossing of the Atlantic and a frigid reception in Berlin. The Nazis had shown themselves to be without pity and without regard for the opinion of the world beyond Germany. There seemed to her small chance that such a gentle good will mission could make the slightest impression upon those stony hearts and a rather large chance that some officially spontaneous action in a dark street might put an end to it before it so much as got started.

The three sailed unnoticed from New York on the *Queen Mary* on December second. On the ship the first day Rufus Jones met his old friend E. Stanley Jones and his wife and daughter, and it was promptly decided that the two parties should share a table in the dining-room. The conversation at table throughout the crossing was stimulating and lively, and George Walton recorded in his journal that Rufus Jones's fund of stories was inexhaustible and that he never repeated.

The second day out they worked on a memorandum, drafted by Rufus Jones, which was to be left with those whom they interviewed. George Walton, who, knowing no German, felt that he was less well-equipped than the other two for the mission, wrote in his journal: "Despite their greater knowledge they are open-minded without any fixed purpose, except to see and learn and to be Friends. Like myself they are amazed at the interest shown in our effort by those who know of it and staggered by their faith that we can do something."

A day later the degree of that interest became uncomfortably and even dangerously evident. Rufus Jones was called to the telephone by a reporter from the *Philadelphia Record*. The Associated Press had picked up a note in *The Earlhamite* that Rufus Jones had cancelled an engagement to speak at Earlham College in order to go to Germany "to see Hitler," and the *Record*, having telephoned the Jones house in Haverford in the middle of the night and got no satisfaction, made contact with Rufus Jones by radio telephone.

"The man on the *Record* tells me," he wrote to his wife, "that an article in the *Earlhamite* has let our cat out of the bag and the Associated Press is to tell of our trip and I am afraid will carry an unfortunate account of our trip. I told the *Record* to mention no names of persons to be visited for we had no fixed appointments and were waiting to see what would open. I am afraid, however, that the newspapers will do much harm to our cause."

The *Record* on Monday morning carried ribbon headlines: "Friends Society Sends Mission to Intercede for German Jews. Philadelphians Plan Plea for All Minorities. Dr. Jones Reviews Aim in Ship-to-Shore Phone Talk." The story continued in ordinary type: "Three Philadelphia leaders of the Society of Friends are en route to Europe to intervene personally with Chancellor Adolf Hitler on behalf of the persecuted Jewish and other minority groups in Germany." Their departure on Friday, it said with blithe unconcern, "was shrouded in the greatest secrecy." Rufus Jones was quoted as saying, "We are going as quietly as possible ... We don't know how high up in the German Government we will be able to go."

The reporter had had time to interview also other, unnamed Friends in Philadelphia, and was able to announce that "some members of the Society of Friends likened the expedition to Henry Ford's ill-starred Peace Ship junket in December 1915, when the motor manufacturer sought almost single-handed to end the World War."

A spate of articles and editorials followed in papers which had been scooped because they had chivalrously forborne to report what they knew for fear of damaging the mission's chances of success. The New York *Sun* recalled the mission of two Quaker servant girls to the Sultan of Turkey in 1658. The Philadelphia *Evening Bulletin* said, "In the exploratory mission to Germany of three members of the Society of Friends there arises the hope that something tangible may be accomplished for the relief of the persecuted of all religious denominations."

The striking thing about all the publicity was the interest shown in the undertaking, the hope that was so ready to spring up and the respect that clung around the Quaker name. What was in the beginning a despised and ridiculed movement and for more than a century a withdrawn and peculiar sect, now in the public eye had acquired a sort of magic which made miracles possible if not probable.

The *Queen Mary* meanwhile continued on its way across the tumbling gray winter ocean. Rufus Jones bought a "beret cap," he talked to his companions on Nietzsche and his influence on Nazi philosophy, and surprised them, well as they knew him, "by his philosophical grasp and creative power." Robert Yarnall read MEIN KAMPF and found that "the Hitler attitude toward pacifists and Jews is so condemnatory that he fears we will accomplish nothing but find official minds closed to all we know and believe in."

At Plymouth at seven-thirty in the morning of the seventh they were met by Joan Fry and a Dutch Friend, who came on board and rode with them to Cherbourg. Two London newspapers had the story of their going to see Hitler—"even worse than the *Record*," Rufus Jones commented—and English Friends were a little doubtful about this expedition. They themselves had already sent four German-speaking Friends to travel about Germany in an inconspicuous way collecting facts about the situation, and they had been able to maintain silence.

In Paris that evening the three Americans had two hours' talk at the station with the two American Quakers in the Paris Center before they took the sleeper for Berlin.

Late the next afternoon they gathered their things together in preparation for leaving the train. Rufus Jones came to the other two in consternation. "I've lost my pajamas," he said.

They helped him to hunt for them, but without success. He wanted to have a telegram sent at once to an earlier station to have a search made, but Robert Yarnall and George Walton opposed him. What would be the German reaction, what undesirable publicity might result? The train went on into Poland, they pointed out, and if the garment was still missing a wire could be sent to Warsaw from Berlin. Rufus Jones yielded, but reluctantly, for the pajamas had been made for him by Elizabeth Jones and were too precious to lose.

Arriving in Berlin they were met by a group of American, English and German Friends and taken to the Continental Hotel, where, after dinner, they had a three-hour conference with Katharine and Howard Elkinton, the A.F.S.C. workers then in Germany, Jim Lieftinck, a Dutch Friend, Hans Albrecht, the leading German Friend, and Paul Sturge of the Friends Service Council.

The next morning, when Robert Yarnall and George Walton, who shared a room, came down to breakfast, they found Rufus Jones already at the table, eating oatmeal. With his eyes on his plate, he said,

"I found them."

"Where did thee find them, Rufus?"

"I had them on."

When they had crossed the border from France into Germany early the previous morning and had been routed out for customs, he had dressed hastily, throwing his clothes on over his pajamas, and so—as he wrote home in chagrin—"did the fool thing."

This story was told over and over on their return home, when they were called upon for talks on their experience to all kinds of Quaker groups and wanted both a light note and also something to take the place of all the things that they could not say for fear of repercussions in Germany. It entered into the permanent body of Quaker folklore.

Friday the ninth was a busy day for the three. They visited the office which the Friends had opened for consultation with refugees when the number of desperate people seeking help and advice grew too large for the Center itself to handle. They sat in on a meeting of the secretariat and heard discussions of the problems of relief and emigration, the possibility of starting retreats for older people and children. They heard distressing tales of the tens of thousands of Jewish men in the three great concentration camps of Buchenwald, Dachau and Sachsenhausen.

After lunch they visited a Jewish leader, Dr. Wilfred Israel, who lived in a big house off the Tiergarten. Sitting in his pleasant drawing room amid his books and objets-d'art, they heard from this slender, polished, youthful-looking old man the story they were to hear again and again: there was no pressing need for food-relief; emigration was vital, before all the Jews should be destroyed. Dr. Israel himself, sitting there in normal, civilized surroundings, expected to be shot within ten days.

From Dr. Israel they went to the American Embassy nearby. Hugh Wilson, the ambassador, had been recalled to Washington in November and Prentiss B. Gilbert was chargé d'affaires. They talked with him about ways to approach the German government. Dr. Freitag, chief of American Affairs in the Foreign Office, was, they thought, the one to open doors for them and they wanted an introduction to him. Gilbert, however, was evasive. Raymond B. Geist, the consul-general, was ill at home that day and they were unable to see him. They returned to their hotel with a feeling of frustration.

At a meeting in Rufus Jones's room that evening, they talked again with the Elkintons, Paul Sturge, Roger Carter, another English Friend, and Hans Albrecht. Speedy emigration on a large scale, they were now convinced, was the important thing. The magnitude of this problem must have been heavy on their hearts as this discouraging day came to an end.

By the Quakers in Berlin they were called affectionately "the three wise men," but were not told why. In fact, they did not know until they were back again in Philadelphia, that *Der Angriff*, Goebbels's newspaper, had published an article about them with that title, in which it had said:

"Surely these three Quaker figures are wise men who, no doubt, this time too hail from the East, or at least regard it as their spiritual home. So we will offer myrrh and incense for them, but of course after our own fashion. We hope they will make themselves known when they are here. Then we will know, you see, when to begin to quake—quake duly before the Quakers from the U.S.A. . . . They are to investigate us, for bad things are told in Pennsylvania about Germans who relieve poor Jewish millionaires of a little of their swindled money. If three quaking men were only content with making observations! But they are going the limit. They want to formulate plans for curing us and ameliorating the situation in Germany. Don't expect us to take them seriously. We can't help it but we must laugh, even if in this case it is ever so honorable a sect."

Although that article was kept from them, they read in *Der Angriff* on their first Sunday morning a scathing attack on "Der Gesellshaft der Freunde," which depressed them greatly until it became clear that the Freunde in question were a society of the Masonic Order and had nothing at all to do with Quakers.

The next morning they telephoned to the Foreign Office and asked for an appointment. They were told that they would receive an answer soon, but no answer came. Impatient, they got into a taxi, and, going directly to the Foreign Office, asked for Dr. Freitag. Told at first that he was in, they waited for a time, only to have the attendant return to say, "Sorry, Dr. Freitag is not here." They were further discouraged by the fact that they saw Dr. Dieckhoff (who had returned to Germany after the American ambassador was recalled to Washington) in the hall, but the German pretended not to see them and turned away to avoid speaking.

After they had returned to the Friends Center they received a telephone call explaining that they had not been able to see Dr. Freitag because they had not been introduced by the American Embassy and suggesting that they see instead the head of the Bureau of Jewish Affairs in the Department of the Interior.

By Monday morning Raymond Geist had recovered from his illness and met them with a keen, practical, competent interest that lifted their hopes. He believed their mission to be important, but, he said, they must have a plan. Hitler, he told them, was impossible to see, Goebbels extremely doubtful, but it was conceivable that they might be able to meet the head of the Gestapo. He—Geist—was ready to help them, but they must work up something more definite.

Back they went, therefore, to wrestle with this problem of emigration, which was so very much larger and thornier than the problem of food relief. Rufus Jones wrote to Clarence Pickett:

"I therefore worked out an extensive plan for Quakers to take the lead as a neutral agency to secure from the chief authorities a fundamental arrangement for the migration of all the Jews who are in a condition to go to other lands. There are 35,000 Jewish men in concentration camps and very ominous signs of trouble in the near future. We proposed to find out what conditions of financial resources could be proposed for their exit. We read our entire document to Mr. Geist —Consul-General—and received his enthusiastic support for it and his promise to open doors for us to present it. Before bringing it to the German authorities I felt sure that I ought to inform Myron Taylor of the project."

Myron C. Taylor had been chairman of the Conference on International Refugees that had met at Evian the previous summer and established a permanent Intergovernmental Committee on Refugees with headquarters in London.

"I sent him a letter Sunday by Paul Sturge who sat with us as we developed the plan . . . He called up from London last night to say that Taylor was not happy over it. I at once called him up. He said he wanted us to go ahead but I felt that he thought we were running into his job. I thereupon decided to go across and talk it out with him

... This plan of ours is the only approach to those higher up. Dykoff [Dieckhoff] is annoyed that we came over. Our main track is not through the foreign office but straight up with a proposal that will interest them."

On the fourteenth, "Here I am in London," he wrote.

He had no trouble in seeing both Mr. Taylor and Mr. Rublee, who was American chairman of the Committee, and he learned from them that Dr. Hjalmar Schacht, President of the Reichsbank, was then in London to discuss with the Committee a proposal for setting up a fund on which Jews emigrating from Germany might draw for their new start in life. Myron Taylor's report of the negotiations with Dr. Schacht gave Rufus Jones encouragement, and he was also cheered by the suggestion that the visit of the three Friends "may have hastened the action." Schacht himself, in his autobiography, CONFESSIONS OF "THE OLD WIZARD," makes no mention of the Quaker mission, but he does say, "Hitler himself seemed ill at ease in face of the world-wide repercussions aroused by the bestiality of November 9" and that to his surprise Hitler made no objection to his attempt to put his plan into practice. Whether or not the publicized arrival of the "three wise men" added a feather weight to the delicate balance, Rufus Jones left London on the sixteenth with the blessing of the Intergovernmental Committee and the promise of an appointment with Schacht the following Monday in Berlin.

"We shall likely see Goerring [sic] though that is not certain," he wrote. "The English Friends are most thankful for our coming and they have received me here with striking enthusiasm . . . The Friends House is full of Refugees and it is rather a frantic scene."

It was pouring rain in London and he had no umbrella. Wet through, he made the winter crossing of the Channel to the Hook and then spent hours on an icy train to Berlin, which was in the grip of the worst December storm in eighty years. Sneezing and coughing, he went to bed with a hot water bottle as soon as he arrived, and remained in bed all of Sunday the eighteenth.

While Rufus Jones was in London Robert Yarnall and George Walton had had a number of interviews and conferences which filled in the details of the dark picture whose outlines were already clear. Everyone with whom they talked reiterated that the pressing need was emigration.

A tall, brisk man in the Foreign Office whom they managed to see and who had had eight years experience in the consular service in the United States, told them flatly: " 'We have no *colonies*, nowhere to send the Jews, while there are many outside places where they can be sent in addition to Palestine, which is too small . . . We know we cannot get rid of all of them, but putting pressure on is the only way we can get any action.' . . . He said that the Evian Conference did nothing of importance and the new permanent Intergovernmental Committee has presented no plan except 'Give Jews some money when they emigrate. But we cannot do this on account of the *Devise*. [Foreign Exchange]'." His own solution was a Jewish state of 15,000,-000, "perhaps in South Africa," and a large fund to be raised in the United States to help with emigration.

Wherever they turned they found the implacable decision stated coldly and without shame. The Jews must go. Germany would have them no longer. It was up to the outside world to receive and help them. Germany would do nothing and certainly would not allow Jewish property to be taken out of the country.

From Vienna, where he spent two days, Robert Yarnall brought back the same report: the carefully planned uprising on November tenth, the terror of the Jewish people, the anguished cries for help to emigrate.

On Monday the nineteenth, which was bitterly cold and snowy, Rufus Jones, still suffering from a bad bronchial cold, got out of bed and the three, taking with them a written statement in German and English, went to the American Consulate to claim Raymond Geist's promised help in seeing the Gestapo.

Mr. Geist—"if ever there was a good man he was one," said Rufus Jones—made a telephone call and then, abruptly deciding that direct action was necessary, jumped into a taxi and disappeared. For twenty-five minutes they waited, aware of what George Walton called "a quiet throng of intense humanity" around them that had come there seeking help. Suddenly the call came from Geist to join him at the Gestapo.

When the taxi stopped in front of the huge grim building they were escorted by six black-shirted soldiers with helmets and guns to the great iron doors, where they were given tickets, and were told, Rufus Jones remembered, "that we did not need them to get in but we should need them to get out!"

"We went through seven corridors, each one opening into an un-covered square, and then climbed five flights of stairs to a top room where Raymond Geist met us and said, 'I have done it. Two chief

officers of the Gestapo have been delegated to hear your plans and to
get a decision on your project.' "

Reinhard Heydrich was Himmler's immediate subordinate and the
real head of the Secret State Police, known and feared as "the Hang-
man." He had been in charge of the concentration camp at Dachau
from 1934 and had taken part in the "Blood Purge" of the same year.
In 1942 he would be assassinated in Czechoslovakia and the Lidice
massacre would follow on the charge that the town had harbored
his murderers.

The room into which the three Friends were escorted this Monday
morning was a large corner room furnished with a "round table, glass
top, modern design, big chairs." Heydrich himself was not there, but
they could hear his voice through the folding doors between this
room and the adjoining one. They interviewed instead his two associates, Standatenführer Dr. Erlinger and Regierungerat Dr. Lischka.
George Walton described the "dramatis personae" of the scene:

"Rufus, clear, positive, brief, daring

Geist, crusty, clever, direct, a magic open sesame

Lischka, tall, quick, earnest, responsive, partly bald, punctilious."

Rufus Jones, nine years later, called Erlinger and Lischka "hard-
faced, iron-natured men." He gave them the statement prepared for
the purpose and asked them to read it.

"We have come to Germany at this present time," they read in
the German translation, "to see whether there might be any service
which American Quakers could render, and to use every opportunity
open to us to understand the present situation. Those whom we are to
meet and with whom we are to consult should clearly understand that
we have had close and friendly relations with the German people
throughout the entire post-war period. We represent no governments,
or international organizations, no parties, no sects, and we have no
interest in propaganda in any form. We have always been concerned
over the conditions of the Peace Treaty and in spirit opposed to these
conditions.

"We came to Germany in the time of the blockade; organized and
directed the feeding of German children, reaching at the peak no less
than a million two hundred thousand children per day. We were
first to arrive in Vienna after the war where we brought in coal for
the fires in the hospitals. After the different revolutions in Austria, we
gave relief to the families of those who suffered most in these colli-
sions, always having permission from the existing government to do

so. And at the time of the 'Anschluss' we were distributing food to a number of Nazi families.

"In all this work we have kept entirely free of party lines or party spirit. We have not used any propaganda or aimed to make converts to our own views. We have simply, quietly, and in a friendly spirit endeavored to make life possible for those who were suffering. We do not ask who is to blame for the trouble which may exist or what has produced the sad situation. Our task is to support and save life and to suffer with those who are suffering.

"We have come now in the same spirit as in the past and we believe that all Germans who remember the past and who are familiar with our ways and methods and spirit will know that we do not come to judge or criticize or to push ourselves in, but to inquire in the most friendly manner whether there is anything we can do to promote life and human welfare and to relieve suffering."

After the reading of this paper, Robert Yarnall wrote in his diary, "We discuss freely our progress to date in relief matters and the question of quicker emigration, possibility of transient camps, etc. They ask us for a definite plan, but we explained why we cannot give it. We finally asked if we might proceed along the lines suggested of relief through Jewish organizations and working through Inter-government Committee London and America on plans for faster emigration."

The two Nazis then went out to consult Heydrich, and the Friends were left in the room to wait. "During this awesome period," wrote Rufus Jones, "we bowed our heads and entered upon a time of deep quiet meditation and prayer—the only Quaker meeting ever held in the Gestapo! It proved to have been rightly ordered. The two men returned at the announced time and the leader said, 'Everything you have asked for is granted.' I said, 'That is splendid. We should like to have the report in writing.' 'No,' the leader said, 'the Gestapo does not give its decisions in writing.' 'What will be the evidence then?' 'Every word,' he said, 'that has been spoken in this room has been recorded by a mechanism and this decision will be in the record.' We were glad then that we had kept the period of hush and quiet and had uttered no words for the record! The leader then said, 'I shall tele-graph tonight to every police station in Germany that the Quakers are given full permission to investigate the sufferings of Jews and to bring such relief as they see necessary.' "

Robert Yarnall recorded that the complete authority to proceed, which Lischka brought from Heydrich, included permission for Quaker representatives to move freely in Germany and Austria in making and carrying out plans for non-Aryan relief if needed and for emigration.

Two more days remained to them in Berlin. On the afternoon of the twentieth they had their meeting with Hjalmar Horace Greeley Schacht, president of the Reichsbank in the Weimar Republic and again under Hitler, who had dared to oppose Hitler to his face, and who would, in 1943 take part in the unsuccessful plot against him. He explained to them the plan for financial relief of emigrating Jews which he had presented to the Intergovernmental Committee, and which he has described in his autobiography in the following terms:

"The whole of the property of Jews in Germany shall be brought into a trust company who will administer it according to law. This trust company shall be governed by an international committee, on which the Jews are also represented. On the basis of this property held in trust by way of security the committee will issue a loan in the international market amounting to, say, one to one and a half billion Reichsmarks. This loan carries an interest of about five per cent and is repayable by annual installments over a period of twenty to twenty-five years. The German government guarantees the transfer of interests and repayment installments in dollars so that the loan can be issued as a dollar loan. Jews all over the world will be urged to subscribe . . . Out of the dollar proceeds of this loan every Jew wishing to emigrate will receive a certain sum which will facilitate his reception in another country and serve as a foundation on which to build a new life."

If 50,000 Jews a year could be taken by other countries, he said, it would settle the problem; those who then remained in Germany might have some sort of decent life. "Then he said, 'Be quick, for nobody knows what happens in this country tomorrow.' "

Advising the Friends to cooperate with the Intergovernmental Committee and to use their own resources for help with feeding and in training camps, he said, "Emigration is too big for charity."

He had, he told them, been given authority to present his plan in London, now he would seek authority to go ahead with it. But exactly one month later Hitler dismissed him from the Reichsbank, and nothing more was heard of his plan.

On December twenty-second the three Friends left Berlin and two days later sailed on the *Franconia*, with a shipload of refugees.

They were back in Philadelphia after Christmas, within a month of their departure. There arose a clamor about them, to know what they had seen, what they thought of the situation, what they had accomplished.

In immediate, practical terms, they had got permission for two Quaker commissioners to go to Germany to oversee the disbursement of Quaker relief funds, to help especially the non-synagogue Jews who did not come within the scope of other organizations, to assist with the emigration of individuals. "Workers in our Berlin Center," writes Clarence Pickett, "found they had a new freedom in making emigration arrangements for Jewish families and in bringing relief. This short reprieve meant the difference between life and death to some families, at least."

In the light of subsequent history, it seems unlikely that the Nazi hearts were touched by the unexpected encounter with a different way of life, though Rufus Jones to the end of his days believed that there had been a softening and a moment of vision. What is perhaps of lasting significance is the sheer fact that three Friends—modern, practical men—faced enormous forces of evil and directly and quietly offered an alternative, the way of love.

The Vital Cell

T HE Philadelphia Award, conceived and endowed by Edward W. Bok in 1921, is given each year to a Philadelphian "for service best calculated to advance the best interests of the community." The presentation takes place before a large audience in the Academy of Music, and throughout the program of speeches and music suspense is maintained until the climax, when the secret is revealed.

On February 20, 1939, Dr. Joseph Fort Newton, rector of the Church of St. Luke and the Epiphany, spun out the mystification. The award was going, he said, "to a great business man, a mighty captain of industry, the leader of a business utterly unique, and yet it should have had its origin in the City of Brotherly Love . . . There are two kinds of businesses at least. There is a little business that uses men to make money . . . The really big business represented by the winner of this Award uses money to make men and when they are broken to mend them."

When the scrolls and the old medallions and the $10,000 were presented to Rufus M. Jones and Clarence E. Pickett, Chairman and Executive Secretary of the American Friends Service Committee, the audience "arose in one vast wave to applaud and cheer." Seldom had the award aroused such whole-hearted enthusiasm and approval.

During the war that moved inexorably upon the world in 1939 Rufus Jones's part in the Service Committee was different from his role in the first World War. The instrument of healing which he had done so much to create was tested and ready, and though the demands made upon it and the conditions of fulfilling them differed from those of its early days, the organization was flexible and sturdy enough to cope with them. Civilian Public Service for conscientious objectors, assistance to college age students in the Japanese relocation camps, refugee problems, distribution of food to children in unoccupied France, cooperation with English Friends in the work of the Friends Ambulance Unit in China, aid to famine-stricken India with funds supplied by the agency called American Relief for India: these were the chief activities of the Committee during the war years. Rufus Jones and Clarence Pickett together made an unceasing attempt to send food to the children in occupied France, in Belgium and Holland, but the stand of the allied governments was that aid sent to these countries would be diverted to the use of the Germans and so would undermine the efficiency of the war effort. As there was not sufficient public support for the humanitarian point of view, they were up against a stone wall. In 1944 Rufus Jones resigned the chairmanship of the A.F.S.C. to become again Honorary Chairman, while Henry J. Cadbury again succeeded him in active leadership.

In the main, in the second World War, Rufus Jones's part was that of an elder statesman. His energy, amazing for a man of his years, was given to the task of encouragement and inspiration, to holding before people's eyes constantly the necessity to look beyond the present dark time of war to the peace which must be carefully prepared for, to remember the unsuspected forces of good in areas of hate, to keep alive "vital cells" of love and understanding and faith, to get ready for the part that a revitalized Quakerism might play in the exhaustion and devastation of war's aftermath. The titles of some of his seventy-odd articles published in more than twenty-five different journals during these years suggest the lines of his thought: "Back to the Springs and Sources of Life"; "What can Americans do for Humanity Today?"; "Dedicated to a Better Way"; "Seeing in the Dark"; "A Call to Persons of Good Will"; "Begin with the Church"; "Are We Ready?"; "Thou Shalt not Hate." Among the seven books which he wrote at this time were, SPIRIT IN MAN, THE VITAL CELL, which was the published form of his William Penn address to the two Philadelphia Yearly Meetings in 1941, NEW EYES FOR INVISIBLES, THE RADIANT LIFE.

More than ever, if possible, he was in demand for lectures, for

sermons, for addresses. He gave five lectures in "Ministers' Week"
at Southern Methodist University in Dallas; he gave the West Lectures
at Stanford University in Palo Alto, which became the basis for his
book SPIRIT IN MAN: in 1942 he went from a program of twenty
meetings in a single week at Seattle to a series of addresses in the
south, at Raleigh, Orlando, and St. Petersburg. He spoke in successive years at the famous Chicago "Sunday Evening Club." He gave
the Ingersoll Lecture on the Immortality of Man at Harvard. With
Herbert Hoover he spoke at a meeting at Carnegie Hall in New York
to plead for the feeding of the children of Europe. A year later
he had the sad duty of speaking at the funeral of Mrs. Hoover at
St. Bartholomew's Church, New York. He preached the sermon
at the united Thanksgiving service of the churches of Bryn Mawr.
In addition he spoke to Quaker groups too numerous to mention.

Much of what he wrote and said was the interpretation of the
Quaker position in regard to war and peace. "Peace," he stated
vigorously in A CALL TO PERSONS OF GOOD WILL, "is not a static
condition, to be attained after the defeat of those who disturb it.
On the contrary, peace is a dynamic method, by which to remove
injustices, to accomplish necessary readjustments, and to remedy
instead of aggravating the evils that have been inflicted on the world
by military aggression." "Whether in times of war or times of
peace," he wrote in a pamphlet on THE QUAKER PEACE POSITION,
"the Quaker is under peculiar obligation to assist and to forward
movements and forces which make for peace in the world and
which bind men together in ties of unity and fellowship. In time of
war, every avenue of loving service, of heroic devotion, of self-
forgetful ministry should be entered, that the Quaker may vie with
the soldier in his blood-red loyalty and devotion to his cause."

Although he believed that war is "absolutely and eternally morally
wrong" and that "with the Quaker view of life one cannot engage
in killing men, whatever may be involved in the refusal," he remained
both publicly and privately sympathetic to those whose insights
brought them to other conclusions. "He [the Quaker] must be
gentle and tenderly respectful toward all Christians who feel the
stern necessity of continuing the world-old way of settling differences
and of working out national issues," he wrote in the pamphlet mentioned above. "It is never safe to assume the role of special favorite
or sole guardian of truth, or remnant of the elect." To a correspondent
he wrote in 1943, "I do not agree with your position about war,

but I am only too conscious that only a tiny fraction of Christians in the world accept the position which I hold and I feel humble about holding it in the face of the fact that the vast majority of Christians walk a different path from mine. But absolute obedience to the clearest light one has or can get seems to me to be the priceless jewel that must never be bartered away."

He was especially pleased when he received the Theodore Roosevelt Distinguished Service Medal in October, 1942, because it was given to a pacifist in time of war. Established twenty years earlier by the Roosevelt Memorial Association, it was given annually to recognize achievements in fields of endeavor in which the former president had been interested. At the same time that Rufus Jones received his award in the field of international affairs, Henry L. Stimson, the Secretary of War, and Booth Tarkington, the novelist, were also given medals. At the award dinner, it was said of Rufus Jones:

"He is regarded as the leading spokesman of the Quaker way of life throughout the world, and has been the decisive influence in making a sect of only 120,000 members a powerful social and religious instrument. At seventy-nine he is leading the American Friends Service Committee in new ventures in practical altruism on a world scale."

Some of his writing during these years was concerned—and naturally so, as he approached and overtook his eightieth birthday— with reminiscences. In "Some Pisgah Reflections," published in the *Friends Intelligencer* in 1943, he looked back with humor and frank appraisal on his early days of teaching and editorship when "there was no such word as 'unity' in the American Quaker Dictionary." One of the most delightful of all his books A SMALL TOWN BOY, returned to the South China of his childhood and completed the picture begun in his earlier book, FINDING THE TRAIL OF LIFE. Where one depicted the inward journey, the other described the outward setting: the grocery store, the blacksmith shop, the games on summer evenings, the gang of boys, the lake, all the institutions of self-contained community and their inimitable flavor, before the in-vention of the internal combustion engine swept that old world away. Full of salty stories, nostalgic detail, and mellow wisdom, written in his clear, unhurried, spacious style, shot with shafts of illumination and insight, the book is one of the classics of American boyhood and village life.

In the war years when so many young people were dying, Rufus

Jones wrote and spoke also about immortality. The West Lectures at Stanford, which formed the basis for his book, SPIRIT IN MAN, and the Ingersoll Lecture at Harvard, "The Spell of Immortality," which became Chapter Ten in THE RADIANT LIFE, were both concerned with this subject. Recognizing the prevailing drift of contemporary thought away from the old certainties about eternal life that supported people in times of trouble and gave sanction to "noble living," he had no easy arguments for immortality. That the universe is intelligible, that it is built on moral lines, that it "can be counted on to meet and answer the hopes it has raised in the minds which it itself has produced" was a certainty for him. The moral sense in man that can look beyond what is to what ought to be, the reality of God as spirit, were to Rufus Jones sufficient basis for a conviction that our life does not end with this world, that, as he was fond of quoting, "transplanted human worth will bloom to profit otherwise." He conceded the inadequacy of the mind adapted to space-time living to conceive the nature of a life in a new form and medium and he accepted the mystery. But it was, he maintained, a mystery no greater than that "the hereditary traits of the generations behind him and his own marvellously adapted form came with the newborn child into the here over the infinitesimal bridge of a cell of protoplasm." Belief in immortality he called "a rational faith in the conservation of values," and he saw the future life as a stage not for rewards and punishments but for the completion of the drama only begun, the completion of our fragmentary being.

In April, 1943, when he was at Harvard delivering the Ingersoll Lecture he did not know that in Haverford Elizabeth Jones, then seventy-two, was suffering a coronary thrombosis. He was told as soon as the lecture was over, and he hurried home with anxiety gripping his heart. Of this illness their daughter writes: "She was an excellent patient and settled quietly into the process of recovery. She learned to find pleasure in small recreations which did not tax her strength, but her husband had little use for the crossword puzzles and detective stories with which she passed long hours. He felt sad that his wife who had worked with him in the Bodleian Library and the British Museum should allow her excellent mind to drop to so low an order of mental stimulants! He took many a trip, however, to the Haverford Library just for the sake of hunting up a crossword and he managed to wrest a good deal of enjoyment from this form of research, though he would never admit it."

By early July she had recovered enough to be moved to their

beloved Pendle Hill in South China, from where Rufus Jones wrote to Mary, who was working in the Philadelphia offices of the American Friends Service Committee, "The loons hailed us with a happy yodel almost as soon as we arrived and the mosquitoes purred a little later . . . Well, we are as happy as Darby and Joan and it will put Mother on her feet."

A little later in the month, Elizabeth Jones, with the help of the faithful Ada, was making green tomato pickles. The usual South China activities went on in spite of the war. Cousin Genie, his faithful and merry correspondent for sixty years, had died two years before, but her daughters Madeleine and Virginia still lived at Pine Rock, and every day Rufus Jones walked along the little path between the pines to chat with them. His haying days, which had continued long after he wrote to Sallie, "I have taken my degree—B. H.—that is, Bachelor of Hay-cutting," had come to an end in 1941, when he wrote, "I went out yesterday and pitched on a load of hay for Charlie Stanley, who is cutting our field. It pretty nearly laid me low. I know now that these persons who tell me that I am as young as ever are telling big lies! Once I could pitch a load of hay and not know I had done anything but *now*! Well, it is all right—I shan't pitch any more." Swimming was left to him, and walking, and enjoying lobster, the "divine manna of the Maine coast." Every morning he spent in his log cabin, writing.

Two new college presidents within Rufus Jones's orbit took office during this period. In 1940 William Wistar Comfort, Haverford's beloved president, retired and was succeeded by Felix Morley, who was the son of a former Haverford professor and one of Rufus Jones's old students, a veteran of American Friends Service Committee work in France. At Bryn Mawr two years later Marion Edwards Park retired after twenty years of distinguished service and close association with Rufus Jones and Katherine E. McBride took her place. Rufus Jones, no longer president of the Board, was still an outstanding member of it, and he took a great interest in the promising young president.

Katherine McBride, sixteen years later, a brilliant speaker, delights to remember the kindly letter that he sent her after one of her early appearances at a college function:

Jan. 29

My dear Miss McBride:
Your words about your public speaking reminded me of what Miss Thomas (M. Carey) did once for me. She called and asked me to take a ride with her.

On the way she said "I want to talk to thee (she always said "thee" to me) about thy speaking and how to improve it. It marked an epoch in my public speaking and I have never forgotten that ride! I know I cannot do as much for you, but there are one or two things I should like to say. You do not have major faults to correct. You do not halt and "err, err" as so many speakers do, and you have a good, pleasing voice, which is a great asset. I have, however, been impressed with the feeling that you stay too much on one level. It is a good level but you need occasional moments when you rise above it and lift your audience to a new level. That can be done by a brilliant touch of humor, or a burst of enthusiasm, or an effective concrete illustration of the point you are making vividly told, or by a heightening of your style. But however you do it, you must now and then shift gears and go up "on high" and take your audience to a new level. You *feel* them come up and that unconsciously puts new power into your speaking. But nothing works like constant practice, and ease and grace and power come as you go on. You have already set a good pace. It will come *nach und nach*.

Sincerely your ancient friend,
Rufus M. Jones

Travelling, writing, speaking, he weathered the war years. Tucked away in the back of a file drawer in the Haverford Library is a collection of those little blue-covered pocket diaries which the Provident Trust Company distributed each year to its depositors. Whenever a Philadelphian was asked about an engagement, out came his little blue notebook and the date was written down. Rufus Jones used his both for recording his engagements and also, as he travelled about, for jotting down ideas, quotations, stories that he heard, thoughts that came to him.

Of the stories usually just a sentence is there, enough to remind him of the rest. "I don't believe in the devil either," comes on one page, "it is like Santa Claus. It is your father." The germs of several stories in SMALL TOWN BOY, appear here: "Are you sure you got a pig?"; "I'll never forget"; "You didn't raise your grandfather from a pup."

There are many quotations, from ALICE IN WONDERLAND, from *Punch*, from Nansen, Fichte, Chesterton, the Bible, George Macdonald, and others. There are comments and questions that are obviously his own. "What is the ultimate *secret* in the life of a saint?" he wrote across two pages. In 1941 he noted the existence of people who, he wrote, "go hysterical over the critical outcome of a situation but are wholly inactive in the face of a situation bound to produce a crisis." In the same year he wrote, "A life time is not too long for two lovers to discover what love means." And, "Bernard Shaw called the U.S. a nation of villagers. Good!" Once in 1940 this man whom Haverford in its citation for an honorary doctorate had called "an impenitent optimist" and who was to all who knew him the embodiment of serenity and hope, revealed his occasional despairs when he wrote, "There is something abysmally evil about this world."

Written jerkily, as if on a moving train, is a series in 1944: "Washington is the only instance of an insane asylum run by the inmates . . . The divine unexpectedness of life . . . He couldn't possibly have said less, unless he had said more . . . Christ is already here and doth reign in the hearts of his people. G.F."

"A committee," he jotted down, "is a gathering of important people who singly can do nothing but together can decide that nothing can be done."

In 1938, the year of the visit to Germany, a trip to the middle west, scheduled for December 5th to 16th, is cancelled, and on those pages are written a number of names and addresses in Germany. "Born anew to a life of hope, I. Pet. I, 3," he wrote on one page, and on another, "We need the note of adventure, of the heroic and costly, not the twittering of birds over a volcano."

When the war came to an end in 1945, Rufus Jones was in his eighty-third year. His pocket diary for a single week in November reads:

Mon. Zen Buddhism
Tue. Mary Vaux evening
Wed. Lunch with Henry [i.e. Henry J. Cadbury] and trainees
     [workers in training for A.F.S.C. posts abroad]
Thurs. Just and Durable Peace
Fri. Ditto. Pendle Hill
Sat.
Sun. Christ Church. Sam Shoemaker.

"The Time has come," he had written on New Year's Day of that year, "to go forward."

XXVIII

The Finishing of the Work

W HEN the Five Years Meeting gathered at Richmond in 1945, the second World War was over. Rufus Jones was there as Chairman of the Business Committee, as he had been since 1912, and he delivered the Isaac T. and Lida K. Johnson Memorial Lecture, an endowed address like the Swarthmore Lecture of London or the William Penn Lecture of Philadelphia, which provided the opening and the focus of the week's sessions.

He chose as subject not something about the war or the peace or even Friends' responsibility to help war sufferers, but a theme that came out of the Quaker past and pointed toward the future. "Original Quakerism," ran the title, "a Movement Not a Sect." George Fox, he made plain, had not intended to create a new denomination but to set a fresh current flowing through all the Christian Churches. Rufus Jones saw modern Quakerism, roused by inward experience of the love of God to outward expression of the love of man through service, in a position to attempt again what George Fox had envisioned. He called on Friends to put aside the fences they had built around themselves and between the various kinds of Friends and to become once more an overflowing stream. "Whether a movement is to have its day and be 'done away' depends on the expansive scope and interior depth of its seed principle, its capacity to go on vitalizing lives. . . . We can, if we will, set our sails to the divine breezes and move away from the shallow waters out into the deeps to which God calls us."

As the second World War was vaster in destruction than the first, so the work of relief and rehabilitation was in every way larger and heavier, made more complicated by the masses of homeless and fleeing people whom war had driven out upon the roads of the world. Aid on so huge a scale could be given only by governments. UNRRA was the agent of the newly formed United Nations; occupying armies fed the conquered people whom they had beaten down to unconditional surrender. There was, however, still much to be done by the so-called non-governmental agencies, the private and independent charities, which gave aid on a personal basis. There was an especial place for the American Friends Service Committee because it had always opposed war, because its aid was given wholly on the basis of need, regardless of race, politics, or creed, and because its workers, serving on a volunteer basis, developed small, creative, personal projects which could be adopted and used on an expanded scale by others. The A.F.S.C. budget rose during the early post-war years to more than $7,000,000 and once again Rufus Jones and Herbert Hoover, Honorary Chairman of the Sub-Committee on Germany, were associated in raising money to feed German children.

At eighty-three Rufus Jones still seemed indefatigable, speaking far and wide, writing, enjoying his family and friends. Miriam Jones, the daughter of his younger brother Herbert, was now the principal of the Haverford Friends School—the latest in the long line of Joneses to leave South China and take up responsible positions in the educational world. She made her home with Rufus and Elizabeth Jones and was a second daughter to them.

As an example of the affairs in which he had a finger, I may give a personal item. Less than a year after the end of the war an American Education Mission visiting Japan to advise the Occupation about the democratization of education there, was asked by the Emperor to find an American woman to tutor his son, the Crown Prince. The American Friends Service Committee recommended me for the position. When I was interviewed by Dr. George Stoddard, the head of the Mission, he asked me if I could give Rufus Jones as a reference. I said that I thought I could. As soon as I got home I wrote and told him what I had done, and by return mail I received the following letter:

Haverford College, Haverford, Pa., 6-10-1946

My dear Elizabeth

This news in thy letter of June 7th is perfectly wonderful. I cannot think of anything more exciting and I very greatly hope the selection will come to thee. Of course I will write vigorously to Dr. Stoddard, in fact I am writing just such a letter to him today.

With all best wishes for this venture

Sincerely thy friend,

Rufus M. Jones

A little over two months later, when the choice was made and the final word had come from Japan, I wrote again to Rufus Jones, and received his answer from South China:

August 27, '46

My dear Elizabeth:

My first response as I read thy letter this morning, with its great news, was *Selah,* which is a profound pause of awe and wonder over some great new insight or discovery, and if you translate it, it means, "Just think of that"!! with two exclamation points. I need hardly say how greatly pleased I am . . . It is just right; thee is the one to do this important thing. Thee has been getting ready for it and the task has come to meet thee. Yes, we shall give our prayers for strength and guidance and we shall go on believing in thee. We expect to be back in Haverford next Second day.

Affectionately thy friend

Rufus M. Jones

It was characteristic of Rufus Jones that he should be so much interested in this venture and should respond so promptly. When in the autumn of 1947 I returned to the United States on a two-months' leave, he wrote to me:

Oct. 9

My dear Elizabeth,

Miriam has shown me thy letter. I do hope "way will open" for thee to see us. I could hardly bear not to see thee. I shall be away over this week-end, Saturday to Monday afternoon and next Thursday afternoon and evening.

Affectionately thine,

Rufus M. Jones

I went to see him. We sat in rocking chairs on the porch where for so many years he had sat to watch cricket practice, and looking out over the campus splashed with October's sun and shadows we talked of Japan and of the world.

"Yesterday," he said, "I was watching little Willie White playing. He had a wooden duck on wheels which quacked as he pulled it along the driveway. Suddenly something went wrong with the duck; the wheels stopped turning and it stopped quacking. Willie found a soft place on the grass and he lay down on his back and howled. I thought how like the world it was. Something has gone wrong with our duck; it doesn't work any more; and we lie down on the grass and howl."

Willie White was the small son of Gilbert and Anne White, who now occupied the President's house next door to Rufus Jones. In 1946 Felix Morley had resigned, and the presidency of Haverford had come to Gilbert White, a vivid and able young man, an expert in Physical Geography and Water Conservation, who had worked for the A.F.S.C. in France and in Philadelphia. Through their association in the work and councils first of the Committee and then of Haverford College, Rufus Jones and Gilbert White had become devoted friends.

In November 1947 the two Philadelphia Yearly Meetings took an important step toward healing the breach of a hundred and twenty years duration: they established a "General Meeting" to be held in the autumn of each year. Already the two bodies had united their committees on Peace, the Social Order, and Race Relations, but they were not yet ready for a common book of discipline and fused finances; the General Meeting, which would deal with reports on common interests and concerns, was seen as a move toward eventual "organic union," which, actually, did come within the next decade. Rufus Jones was asked by the Young Friends Movement to give the chief address.

He called his speech "The Great Succession of Torch Bearers." From the Friends of God of the fourteenth century, through the Spiritual Reformers of the sixteenth, he traced a line of "young torchbearers" who led to George Fox and his young Publishers of Truth, and after them to other young Friends of the eighteenth and nineteenth centuries: young Samuel Bownas, Samuel Fothergill, "a wild, unpromising youth" who developed into the man capable of guiding the Society of Friends through the crisis of the Revolution, Job Scott and others, down to John Wilhelm Rowntree and the remarkable group of young English Friends who put new life and power into the interpretation of Quakerism.

A similar theme, though expressed through different characters, ran through his book published that year: THE LUMINOUS TRAIL, which dealt with a succession of saints, canonized and uncanonized, into whose lives the spirit of Christ broke like—in one of Rufus Jones's favorite figures—"a vernal equinox." "What is the ultimate secret in the life of a saint?" he had written in his blue pocket diary;

now he answered that question in his first chapter. "I think the greatest miracle we know in our world," he said, "is the way a person who has failed, who has been like the rest of us, suddenly rises beyond himself, gets attached to the eternal reservoir of God's Grace and Truth and Power, and lets the streams of life, by a higher kind of gravitation, pour through him. When that miracle occurs we have a saint, and he is forthwith a *transmitter*." His trail led from St. Paul, through those old and dear spiritual heroes, Clement of Alexandria, Francis of Assisi, Erasmus, Hans Denck, as well as others about whom he had written less frequently. It came to an end in his own little son Lowell, in a touching chapter about that lost, golden boy, and the extent to which he felt that his own life had been "led and guided on its way" by his son. If there was something naive about the inclusion of this charming child, canonized by forty-three years of love and grief, among the giants of spiritual history, there was also something of the essence of Rufus Jones himself, for whom the word naive is as inappropriate as the word sophisticated would be; his love, humility, and unquenchable freshness of feeling are all in evidence here.

Late in the autumn of that same year the A.F.S.C. received proof that its service of love was recognized as basically a service for peace. With the Friends Service Council, with which it had worked from the beginning, it was awarded the Nobel Peace Prize. Henry J. Cadbury, as chairman of the Committee, went to Oslo to receive it on December tenth.

Gunnar John, chairman of the Nobel Committee, in his speech of award, made it clear that the prize was directed actually to all Quakers, and for a greater contribution to peace than the mere refusal to take part in war. "It is the silent help from the nameless to the nameless," he said, "which is their contribution to the promotion of brotherhood among nations . . . May we believe that there is hope of laying a foundation of peace among nations, of building up peace in man himself, so that it becomes impossible to settle disputes by use of force?"

On the same evening in New York, there was a great dinner in the ballroom of the Astor to celebrate the award. Rufus Jones sat as honored guest on the dais among such leaders as Emily Greene Balch, who had won the Nobel award the year before, other Nobel winners in chemistry, physics and medicine, several ambassadors, Trygve Lie, Secretary General of the U.N., Paul Muni, the actor, and Henry Nobel McCracken, the former president of Vassar College.

"It was an ordeal," Rufus Jones wrote to his daughter, who was in England. "There were sixteen speakers, besides a 'play' that took about 20 minutes! The dinner itself (ten dollars a plate) lasted till nine o'clock. I came on at five minutes of ten and spoke just five minutes. I am afraid I did not make much impression on the tired and blasé audience, but speaking went on till midnight. I slipped out at 10:45 and went to bed in my room in the hotel."

He was, nevertheless, "perfectly thrilled over the Nobel award and delighted that it is shared with the F.S.C." But he was, not surprisingly, beginning to be tired. Only a few days before the Nobel dinner, he had had a strenuous trip to New England. "I have just been to Phillips Exeter Academy. It snowed all Sat. evening but we held a beautiful Friends meeting, about 30 came. I had a beautiful service Sunday morning with the boys, 'best ever.' Then I went to Swampscott to the Installation of Howard Andrews. An enormous audience came and I preached my head off. At the reception 500 passed in line and vapored. I nearly fell over with fatigue and ran over my bed-time—horrors!"

He had written to his daughter the previous July, "I have lost my enthusiasm for my own birthdays but I still feel a thrill over thine." In spite of reduced enthusiasm, however, and in spite of a pain in his chest that disturbed his sleep the night before, he rose to meet the celebration of his eighty-fifth birthday with appreciation. "It has been a memorable date," he wrote to Mary Hoxie Jones, "I had 40 cards, 12 telegrams and cables, hosts of letters and many plants and flowers . . . We went to the Swarthmore Banquet which got us home at midnight. It knocked me out temporarily—never again. I am all right now. I really am old in spite of the comments about looking young. You can't fool the calendar!" He had been reading THE JAMES FAMILY by F. O. Matthiessen with great enjoyment and found it "tops." "The poor old world," he ended, "is staggering on and the franc is debased. My dear love goes to thee. Ancient Father."

Three days later he wrote again, "I have just this minute heard the awful news of the shooting of Gandhi. It must have been a crazy person for it was a Hindoo not a Moslem. But it is an awful tragedy, but now he enters an immortal career."

Just before his birthday he finished another book, "my very last," he wrote. "It has my Atlantic Monthly Article for a chapter and it is an interpretation of religion for modern scientific persons. It will produce,"—and in spite of the unfoolable calendar one hears a boyish note of satisfaction—"a stir in the dovecotes of the fundamentalists."

The *Atlantic Monthly* article which had appeared in November 1947 was entitled "What the Modern Man Can Believe," and the book was written in response to the urging of a New England Friend that he write one more book, "a book that will help the college-trained persons who have the scientific outlook to find their way back to a vital religion." It was a short book, only 143 pages, but it comprised a reaffirmation of the cherished and lived ideas of his life: that religion, unless it issues in life, is negligible; that ideas of religion, must not contradict the truth we learn in other fields; that science cannot deal with values; that the testimony of the mystics is the "laboratory evidence" of religion, that "minor mystics" are to be found everywhere, that man, unique in that he thinks and knows himself as thinking, is still in the process of development, that the Bible, in accordance with modern knowledge of it, is still "the world's greatest literature of revelation," that "every local church in Christendom ought to be a creative center of transforming life and love in its community." For the concluding chapter on prayer, he went back to one of the earliest and best of his books, THE DOUBLE SEARCH, and took passages that still expressed, though more than forty years of living had intervened, his experience in the field of prayer.

In February, in spite of what his niece, Miriam Jones, who was living with Rufus and Elizabeth Jones, called "the pain" in her reports to his daughter abroad, he went to Germantown Meeting "for another Sunday School and Meeting binge." Three days later, he wrote himself, "Wed. in the 8 inch snow storm I went to the Mental Health Luncheon and spoke and then went to the Ex. Board Meeting . . . I am glad to write Feb. 6 for it means we are moving on toward my beloved equinox!"

The electro-cardiograph and a chest x-ray revealed no changes in his heart. In February he plunged into a new public service, an attempt to bring peace through a direct appeal to the sense of the holy within two contending forces. The original idea came from a former member of the U.S. State Department.

One Sunday afternoon in February, Francis B. Sayre, formerly Assistant Secretary of State and at that time Chairman of the Trustee-ship Council of the United Nations, came with another man to call on Rufus Jones in Haverford, to talk about the dangerous situation that had developed in Palestine as the British Mandate approached its termination in May. Riots, street fighting and assassinations marked the increasing tension between Jews and Arabs, and more serious and widespread violence was feared. Mr. Sayre, seeking even a small way to halt the rising tide of war, came to suggest that Rufus Jones might organize an appeal from religious leaders in the west to religious leaders in Palestine for a Truce of God that would put an end to the fighting in the Holy City itself and from there might spread peace further.

"By the next day," Clarence Pickett tells us, "procedures were worked out in his mind and a number of people at great distance had been consulted by telephone."

Six people were invited to meet with him and Clarence Pickett at Quaker House in New York to form a plan for the appeal. Writing to Cardinal Spellman, he explained himself in these words: "You may want to know a little more of who I am. I have for thirty years been the Head of the American Friends Service Committee which has carried relief to almost all parts of the world. I have worked continually with Roman Catholic people, especially in Poland and Austria and in rural France, and I have all my life been studying and writing about Roman Catholic saints and mystics. You will find me and those who are invited sympathetic persons to work with."

Cardinal Spellman was unable to come to the meeting, but he sent a representative. The little group, which included Bishop Athenagoras of the Eastern Orthodox Church, discussed the possibilities of the appeal, the draft which Rufus Jones had drawn up, and the persons who should be asked to join in signing it. Though they were not, Clarence Pickett says in his FOR MORE THAN BREAD, "so optimistic as to believe we could bring about an over-all peace in this way, we did feel that an effort aimed at a truce in Jerusalem might be successful and that such success might in turn have some bearing on the wider reconciliation which must be achieved in time."

Rufus Jones then wrote letters explaining the appeal and its purposes to those who he hoped would join him in signing it. Cardinal Spellman did not feel that it was something in which the Roman Catholic Church could participate, but Geoffrey Francis Fisher, Archbishop of Canterbury, Eiving Bergraav, Primate of the Church of Norway, Henry Knox Sherrill, Presiding Bishop of the Protestant Episcopal Church of America, Archbishop Athenagoras

of the Eastern Orthodox Church, John R. Mott, of the International
Y.M.C.A. and Harry Emerson Fosdick, pastor emeritus of the River-
side Church, New York, signed the appeal, which read as follows:

"Those of us whose names are listed below, representing some
of the most important Christian groups all over the world, have
a profound love for the land of Palestine and for the Holy City
of Jerusalem. We devoutly wish that we could make peace and
concord prevail over the entire land, but we are representatives of
religion, not of politics or of government policies, and we can only
use persuasion, in no sense the exhibition of force.

"In the spirit of Religion and in a united love for the City which
is the mother of our religious faith and of the other religious faiths of
the Western World, we are united in asking you to establish a
'Truce of God', which means a holy area of peace and freedom from
violence, in the City of Jerusalem, until once more this whole land
which we love and cherish with devotion shall be blessed with peace."

This appeal was sent to Jerusalem on March twelfth to Rabbi Isaac
Hertzog, chief Rabbi of Palestine, and to Amin Bey Abdulhabi, head
of the Supreme Moslem Council. When no answer came, it was released to the press on Easter Sunday, March twenty-eighth. On the
same day the first reply was sent, and the cable reached Rufus Jones
on the twenty-ninth. "Heartily endorse proposal Truce of God for
City of Jerusalem—stop—My heartfelt blessing for success your
efforts. Isaac Hertzog chief Rabbi."

As the Arabs continued to maintain silence, the A.F.S.C. took steps
to follow up the appeal with personal interviews.

In New York Clarence Pickett and Elmore Jackson assistant secretary of the A.F.S.C. had two meetings with Jamel El Hussein, the
Vice-Chairman of the Arab Higher Committee, who had come to the
U.S. to participate in a special meeting of the U.N. Assembly. He
had three daughters in the Friends School at Ramallah, which Eli and
Sybil Jones had started and which Rufus Jones had more than once
visited—a circumstance which doubtless gave him some inkling of
Friends and their ways. He told Clarence Pickett that the Arab group
considered the appeal a pro-Jewish move. Though the first meeting
with Mr. Hussein was fruitless, the second one resulted in an agreement that Quaker representatives be asked to discuss the appeal directly with Rabbi Hertzog and Mr. Amin Bey Abdulhabi and also
with Dr. Khaldi, the secretary of the Arab Higher Committee and the
new Arab military commander for Jerusalem. Mr. Hussein offered

to send cables preparing the way for such interviews. Rufus Jones thereupon cabled to Rabbi Hertzog: "Only slight progress truce discussions. James Vail and Edgar Castle Quakers proceeding Beyrouth and Jerusalem from Cairo. They will contact you and Abdulhabi and Khaldi."

James Vail, who had earlier done important work for the A.F.S.C. in Germany and India, was already in Egypt; he was asked to go directly to Jerusalem, to press the appeal for the truce and to investigate the possibilities of a service project in which the A.F.S.C. might bring Arabs and Jews to work together. With him was an English educator, Edgar B. Castle, representing the Friends Service Council.

The cabled report on April twenty-sixth, after they had visited Jerusalem and returned to Cairo, gave a horrifying picture of the state to which Jerusalem had been reduced. "Saw Jerusalem disintegrating before our eyes into physical and moral chaos," it began. A second cable next day recommended refugee service for the A.F.S.C. in cooperation with the Y.M.C.A. and the Red Cross. The third day the welcome news came: AZZAM PASHA HAS JUST TOLD US ARAB LEAGUE TODAY ANNOUNCING SPONSORSHIP TRUCE OLD CITY OF JERUSALEM AND MT. OF OLIVES . . . WE HAVE ALSO PRESENTED CASE TO RELIGIOUS LEADERS JERUSALEM AND ARE HOPEFUL OF THEIR ACQUIESCENCE.

Early in May the United Nations decided to set up its own administration of Jerusalem on a temporary basis. Both Jews and Arabs united in asking that Clarence Pickett be named municipal commissioner for Jerusalem. When he declined, feeling that he was more useful in his post in the A.F.S.C., another Friend was asked for. Harold Evans of Philadelphia was appointed, and James Vail was to go with him as associate and adviser.

"The 'Truce of God' did not come to fruition as such," Mr. Sayre wrote to Rufus Jones on the nineteenth of May; "but I am sure that your efforts have not been futile. The ground work was doubtless laid for an outcome which we cannot yet see but which will be better because of what you did. Out of it has come indirectly the appointment of Harold Evans as Municipal Commissioner for Jerusalem."

Unfortunately before Harold Evans could take office, the British Mandate had ended, the state of Israel had been proclaimed and recognized, and war had broken out in earnest throughout Palestine.

Several weeks before the effort toward a Truce of God had struggled to its conclusion, Rufus Jones had suffered a coronary occlusion. He had spoken—with an effort—at Union Theological Seminary in

March. A little later in the month Bryn Mawr College had celebrated his fiftieth year on the Board of Directors with an exhibit of his books and a Directors' dinner. A move was under way to establish the Rufus Jones Chair of Philosophy and Religion at Bryn Mawr, an honor which pleased and touched him very much. He had gone to Meeting the Sunday afterwards and preached, as he usually did, and his friends had been concerned with his health. That night he was stricken. He rallied, however, and by the thirteenth of April, he was writing to a friend in England: "I am writing you from my bed, having had two weeks in the hospital and now being kept in bed at home, but I am making excellent progress and hope before long to be about as usual again."

A second attack, three days later, proved to be more serious than the first. "For three days," his daughter writes, "he was desperately ill; the family doctor sat up all one night with him and the heart specialist said only a miracle could save him. The miracle occurred. On the third morning the nurse asked Rufus Jones what kind of a night he had had and his voice rang out, with some of its old vigour, 'Splendid!' "

He had work to finish and, indomitable, he proceeded to do it. There was a review of a book on Swedenborg that he had promised to write. Laboriously, bit by bit, he wrote it. He had promised also to speak at New England Yearly Meeting in June. Three years earlier the two New England Yearly meetings had joined together after a century of separation; it meant much to Rufus Jones to be asked to speak to the joint gathering. "It is now perfectly evident," he wrote on the second of June, "that I shall not be able to attend New England Yearly Meeting, but I have been writing in bed an address for the opening Tuesday evening which I hope my daughter, Mary Hoxie, will read for me . . . The subject of the address will be 'A Call to a New Installment of the Heroic Spirit.' "

Sitting up an hour in the morning and an hour in the afternoon, he wrote at the rate of a page a day the message that he wanted to leave with the members of the New England Yearly Meeting. The original manuscript is in the Haverford files. The hand is large, open and clear as ever, but a little tremulous. There are few corrections and those are mostly insertions of words omitted as his hand tried to keep pace with his thought. An occasional typed paragraph clipped from some previous manuscript is fastened in.

He contrasted George Fox's reiterated "Be valiant for the Truth" with the unheroic atmosphere of Quakerism in his own boyhood, and recalled his own youthful determination to be a heroic Quaker. The mystical experience at Dieu-le-fit, the editorship of the *American Friend*, the work of the A.F.S.C. abroad and its work camp projects at home: these were the events in his own life that he considered significant for this address. "I believe that our next heroic effort," he wrote, "will be to recover our rural communities and bring back to full production the abandoned farm . . . The world rests upon the shoulders of common people . . . Few things in the religious world are more important than the complete recovery and return to their spiritual life of our rural meetings that have made a striking contribution to the progress of Quakerism in its earlier days."

Besides writing this address, he corrected, with the help of Elizabeth Jones, the proofs of A CALL TO WHAT IS VITAL. "His bed was strewn," his daughter writes, "with the pages of galley proof just as his study had been for the past forty years and more. He read a little each day, marking the corrections and talking them over with her, showing that his mind was as keen as ever. There were no detective stories nor crossword puzzles for him. The body might fail, but his mind must hold on to the end."

He wrote cheerful letters to his old friends. To one in England he told of his hope soon "to go downstairs where I can sit on the porch and watch the cricket games." He exchanged views of the activities of age with Vida Scudder, herself now eighty-seven.

"And now that my active responsibilities are over," wrote Miss Scudder on the eleventh of June, "I do try not to be restless, not to make people anxious about me, and to center my life in Thanksgiving and Adoration."

"I find it difficult to tell what progress I am making," he replied four days later. "I am publishing a book in the autumn which I hope will have an important influence. I am endeavoring to interpret Christianity to scientific minded people. It is a difficult and dangerous undertaking, but the book has been accepted as the Religious Book of the Month for October."

On Commencement Day he was able to go down on the porch to watch the cricket match between the Alumni and the students. On that day also, one by one, the members of the class which was having its fiftieth reunion came in to greet him, and to talk with him about old times.

During the morning of June sixteenth, he read over the typed pages of his Yearly Meeting Speech and made a few corrections. He finished the last of the galley proof of his book. After lunch he took a nap, from which he did not awake.

Long ago he had written to Sallie Coutant from Paris: "It is my great wish exceeding all others that I may feel in the last hour of my life that I have done my work and that the Great Father is satisfied with my life, so that death may be to me like falling asleep as it is for all who faithfully walk the right road."

It was a sober wish for a young man of twenty-four who had a vivid love of life, and perhaps one on which he did not dwell at length after he had written the words. At the end of the faithful road, sixty-one years later, the important part of it was the finishing of the work: to that effort over the ten weeks of pain and weakness he had given the last ounce of his strength and determination, and it had exactly sufficed.

The funeral service was held at Haverford Meeting on June twentieth, and he was buried in a corner of the little graveyard, near those old and dear friends, John Wilhelm Rowntree and Isaac Sharpless. Memorial services were held also at Twelfth Street Meeting, at South China and at Northeast Harbor, where he had preached every summer for thirty years.

There was an outpouring of love and appreciation for the life of this great and good man: tributes spoken at the services, articles in newspapers and magazines, hundreds of letters, as people, often gifted writers, attempted to express in a few words what he had been to them.

Teacher, philosopher, writer, humanitarian, religious leader: he had opened to generations of college students at Haverford and elsewhere spiritual realities in a time when the materialist and mechanistic philosophies were dominant; he had written in a genial, limpid and persuasive style, so simple that it appeared artless, books and articles on religion that went far beyond the Quaker fold and spoke to the condition of seekers everywhere; he had made a notable contribution to the history of Quakerism and to the modern literature on mysticism; he had created, as far as one man could, the American Friends Service Committee; he had led the Society of Friends, and indeed other Christians as well, through the latest of its crises, the encounter with science and the historical criticism of the Bible, which might have destroyed it; he had been the prime mover in the establishment of the Five Years

Meeting and had labored for the healing of deep and long-standing divisions among Friends; he had travelled the far reaches of the world and had made the name of Quaker honorable to many who had never heard it before. In the list of Quakers who have won fame and exerted an influence beyond the Society of Friends, he stands with William Penn, John Woolman, Elizabeth Fry, John Greenleaf Whittier.

When all that, and more, is said, there is a pause, and these achievements are quietly laid aside. Separately, or even collectively, they might have been done by others. What made them distinctive was the fact that they were done by him and bore the impress of his personality. The man that he was gave them their quality and their meaning. "I assume," he had written in THE LUMINOUS TRAIL, "that the major business we are here for in this world is to be a rightly fashioned person as an organ of the divine purpose." The core of Rufus Jones's philosophy and of his life may be found embedded in that brief, simple, profound statement.

NOTES

All letters and MSS are to be found in the Rufus Jones Collection, Haverford College Library, unless noted otherwise.

Initials have been used for names which recur frequently:

EBC—Elizabeth B. Cadbury
SHC—Sarah H. Coutant
HH—Herbert Hoover
LVH—L. Violet Hodgkin (Holdsworth)
EBJ—Elizabeth B. Jones
MHJ—Mary Hoxie Jones
RMJ—Rufus M. Jones
SCJ—Sarah Coutant Jones
JWR—John Wilhelm Rowntree
EGV—the author

Reference numbers are to page and line. The first bold-face figure is the page reference; the second, and the single bold-face figures following are line references on the same page. Thus, "**33.3** SMALL-TOWN BOY, p. 50; **37** *ibid.*" means page 33, line 3 . . . and line 37.

CHAPTER I : *South China, Maine*

17.14 Rufus M. Jones (RMJ), FINDING THE TRAIL OF LIFE (New York: The Macmillan Company, 1926), p. 20.

19.6 RMJ to Ellen Wood (July 10, 1900); **14** Mary Hoxie Jones (MHJ), RUFUS M. JONES (London: Friends Home Service Committee, 1955), p. 9; **22** RMJ, A SMALL-TOWN BOY (New York: The Macmillan Company, 1941), p. 26; **29** Florence Bussell to MHJ (July 27, 1956).

20.6 RMJ, PATHWAYS TO THE REALITY OF GOD (New York: The Macmillan

Company, 1931), p. 103; **29** RMJ to MHJ (1939); **36** Finding the Trail of Life, p. 21.

21.5 Theodore Dreiser, The Bulwark (New York: Doubleday & Company, Inc., 1946), p. 3.

22.27 RMJ, "South China's Most Distinguished Citizen" (1947), p. 3 (MS). See J. Travis Mills, John Bright and the Quakers (London: Methuēn, 1931), vol. II, p. 45, for quotations from the Journal. Of Sybil Jones, John Bright said, "She, poetical as usual and winning in her sermon but more striking in her prayer."

23.22 RMJ, "History of The American Friend," The American Friend, July 13, 1944, p. 267.

24.13 Small-Town Boy, p. 26; **24** RMJ to Elizabeth B. Cadbury (EBC), (Nov. 25, 1900); **40** Small-Town Boy, p. 32.

25.24 Lewis Finkelstein, ed., American Spiritual Autobiographies (New York: Harper & Brothers, c. 1948), pp. 122-23; **33** Finding the Trail of Life, p. 13.

26.22 RMJ, Eli and Sybil Jones (Philadelphia: Porter and Coates, 1889), p. 13.

27.39 Finding the Trail of Life, p. 44.

28.15 RMJ, "A Call to a New Installment of the Heroic Spirit" (1948); **32** Finding the Trail of Life, pp. 55-56; **40** Dreiser, op. cit., p. 19.

29.6 Loc. cit.; **12** ibid., p. 20; **17** Small-Town Boy, pp. 80-81, 86-87; **21** Dreiser, op. cit., p. 22; **39** RMJ, Address, May 19, 1946.

31.36 RMJ to MHJ (1939).

CHAPTER II : *Into the Quaker Stream*

32.5 RMJ ot MHJ (1939); **22** RMJ to E. L. Farr (July 20, 1885). Copy in Haverford Files; original at Moses Brown School, Providence, R. I.

34.3 RMJ to MHJ (March, 1942); **9** RMJ, The Luminous Trail (New York: The Macmillan Company), p. 147; **20** Commencement Address, Atlantic City Friends School, June, 1927; **32** RMJ to E. L. Farr (March, 1882); **40** RMJ to E. L. Farr (July 20, 1885).

35.12 RMJ, The Trail of Life in College (New York: The Macmillan Company, 1929), p. 21.

36.13 Logan Pearsall Smith, *Unforgotten Years* (Boston: Little, Brown & Co., 1939), p. 79; **33** RMJ to MHJ (April 11, 1948).

37.7 Frederick Strawbridge to EGV (May, 1956); **13** RMJ to MHJ (1939).

38.19 Trail of Life in College, p. 33; **36** RMJ, Haverford College: A History and an Interpretation (New York: The Macmillan Company, 1933), p. 62.

39.3 RMJ, "Quaker Outreach" (1937), p. 3; **28** Trail of Life in College, p. 133.

40.26 *The Haverfordian*, Dec. 1884, p. 34.

41.5 *Ibid.*, April, 1885, p. 106.

42.31 Trail of Life in College, p. 119.

CHAPTER III : *"A Grip on the Base of the World"*

44.16 RMJ to E. L. Farr (October 10, 1885).

45.14 RMJ to Sarah H. Coutant (SHC), (July 25, 1886); **16** RMJ to SHC (June 24, 1888).

46.5 MHJ, Rufus M. Jones, p. 15; **13** Lucy Hawkes Meader to MHJ (1951); **25** RMJ to SHC (July 11, 1886); **41** RMJ to SHC (July 25, 1886).

47.24 RMJ to SHC (Aug. 7, 1886).

48.2 RMJ to SHC (Aug. 26, 1886); **23** RMJ to SHC (Aug. 31, 1886); **39** RMJ to SHC (Sept. 5, 1886).

49.33 RMJ to SHC (Undated, but probably Sept. 20, 1886).

50.4 Trail of Life in College, p. 157. Identity of the Friend—Helen Graham to MHJ (July 20, 1952); **34** RMJ to SHC (Oct. 17, 1886).

51.14 RMJ, Testimony of the Soul (New York: The Macmillan Company, 1936), p. 28; **15** RMJ, New Studies in Mystical Religion (New York: The Macmillan Company, 1927), p. 20; **32** Trail of Life in College, pp. 159-60.

52.2 RMJ to SHC (Dec. 20, 1886); **13** Mary Coutant to SHC (Nov. 28, 1886); **16** RMJ to SHC (Jan. 4, 1887); **41** RMJ to SHC (Dec. 20, 1886).

53.3 RMJ to SHC (Jan. 19, 1886); **35** RMJ to SHC (April 12, 1887).

54.8 RMJ to SHC (May 25, 1887); **16** Trail of Life in College, p. 166.

55.5 RMJ to SHC (April 12, 1887); **11** RMJ to SHC (April 24, 1887); **16** RMJ to SHC (April 3, 1887); **19** RMJ to SHC (June 29, 1887); **28** RMJ to SHC (July 12, 1887); **34** Trail of Life in College, p. 81.

CHAPTER IV : *Fresh Fields*

56.8 SHC to RMJ (Sept. 5, 1887); **15** RMJ to SHC (Nov. 6, 1887); **22** SHC to RMJ (Oct. 30, 1887).

57.16 RMJ to SHC (March 10, 1888); **32** RMJ, "Whittier's Fundamental Religious Faith," in Howard H. Brinton, ed., Byways in Quaker History (Pendle Hill, Wallingford, Pa., 1944), pp. 32, 33; **34** *Ibid.*, p. 19.

58.7 SHC to RMJ (May 6, 1888); **25** SHC to RMJ (May 19, 1888); **31** SHC to RMJ (June 21, 1888); **35** RMJ to SHC (postmarked June 24, 1888).

59.13 RMJ to SHC (March 4, 1888); **31** RMJ to SHC (Oct. 10, 1887); **36** Trail of Life in College, p. 172.

60.1 Howard H. Brinton, Friends for Three Hundred Years (New York: Harper & Brothers, 1952), p. 150; **21** Arthur Hawkes to Emma Roberts (Dec. 1, 1955); **30** Nettie Burleigh to MHJ (Sept. 4, 1951).

61.19 Trail of Life in College, p. 180; **25** *Ibid.*, p. 183; **33** RMJ to SHC (Feb. 8, 1887).

62.4 RMJ to SHC (Oct. 3, 1887); **23** RMJ, The Trail of Life in the Middle Years (New York: The Macmillan Company, 1934), p. 18; **38** Brinton, Friends for Three Hundred Years, p. 193.

63.33 Isaac Sharpless to RMJ (March 25, 1893).

CHAPTER V : *A Meeting on a Mountain Top*

64.10 *Friends Review*, Aug. 24, 1893, p. 67.

65.34 *Ibid.*, April 26, 1894, pp. 388-89; **40** Agnes Brown Leach to MHJ (Feb. 1, 1951).

66.33 Trail of Life in the Middle Years, p. 52.
67.40 J. S. Bradway to RMJ (Dec. 29, 1947).
68.17 RMJ in *American Friend*, Jan. 3, 1895, p. 3; **22** *ibid.*, Nov. 19, 1896, p. 1092.
69.9 Encyclopaedia Britannica (1929). Article on Quakerism; **23** Quoted in RMJ, Later Periods of Quakerism (London: Macmillan & Co. Ltd., 1921), vol. II, p. 974.
70.20 JWR to RMJ (July 27, 1904); **22** RMJ to SCJ (May 21, 1897); **37** *American Friend*, June 7, 1897, p. 555; **41** *ibid.*, p. 556.
72.3 RMJ, John Wilhelm Rowntree (Philadelphia: Committee on Education, Friends General Conference, 1942), pamphlet, unpaged; **11** RMJ to SCJ (June 20, 1897); **36** Trail of Life in College, p. 192.
73.5 RMJ to SCJ (July 4, 1897); **9** SCJ to RMJ (June 17, 1897); **13** SCJ to RMJ (June 25, 1897); **20** RMJ to SCJ (July 7, 1897); **40** SCJ to RMJ (July 16, 1897).

CHAPTER VI : *A Time for Digging Deep*

74.6 RMJ to SCJ (Aug. 20, 1897).
75.22 RMJ to James Wood (Jan. 1, 1900); **36** Trail of Life in College, p. 183.
76.20 RMJ to SCJ (Sept. 19, 1898); **24** RMJ to SCJ (Oct. 11, 1898); **28** RMJ, "Some Pisgah Reflections," *Friends Intelligencer*, Jan. 30, 1943, p. 68.
78.1 RMJ to SCJ (Dec. 14, 1898); **28** RMJ to SCJ (Dec. 19, 1897).
79.1 Elbert Russell, History of Quakerism (New York: The Macmillan Company, 1942), p. 492; **23** Trail of Life in the Middle Years, p. 108; **33** RMJ to SCJ (Oct. 21, 1897); **39** *The Friend* (London), Nov. 12, 1897, p. 751.
80.12 RMJ to SCJ (Oct. 22, 1897); **38** London Yearly Meeting. Christian Life, Faith and Thought in the Society of Friends (London: Friends Book Centre, 1921), p. 72.
81.5 RMJ to Ellen Wood (May 29, 1900); **9** Later Periods of Quakerism, vol. II, p. 931; **16** *The Friend* (London), Sept. 5, 1924, p. 760.
82.18 Brinton, Friends for Three Hundred Years, p. 199; **40** RMJ to SCJ Sept. 10, 1898).
83.6 Trail of Life in the Middle Years, p. 120.
84.4 RMJ, A Dynamic Faith (London: Headley Brothers, 1901), p. 4; **8** *ibid.*, p. 13; **14** *ibid.*, p. 45; **17** *ibid.*, p. 57; **22** *ibid.*, p. 66; **23** *loc. cit.*; **24** *ibid*, p. 88; **30** MS, 1940.

CHAPTER VII : *The Golden Age at Harvard*

85.10 George Herbert Palmer, Autobiography of a Philosopher (Boston: Houghton Mifflin Co., 1930), pp. 52-53; **16** Ralph Barton Perry, The Thought and Character of William James (Boston: Little, Brown & Co., 1935), vol. I, p. 817; **20** George Santayana, Character and Opinion in the United States (New York: Doubleday Anchor Books, 1956), pp. 38, 39.

86.11 Transcript of RMJ's record at Harvard; **16** TRAIL OF LIFE IN THE MIDDLE YEARS, p. 6; **30** Palmer, *op. cit.*, p. 61; **33** RMJ, SOCIAL LAW IN THE SPIRITUAL WORLD (Philadelphia: The John C. Winston Co., *c.* 1904), p. 19.

87.4 RMJ, "Why I Enroll with the Mystics," in Ferm, ed., CONTEMPORARY AMERICAN THEOLOGY (New York: Round Table Press), vol. I, pp. 197-98; **8** TRAIL OF LIFE IN THE MIDDLE YEARS, p. 5; **11** Santayana, *op. cit.*, p. 60; **15** William E. Hocking, article on Royce in ENCYCLOPAEDIA BRITANNICA (1929); **19** Perry, *op. cit.*, vol. I, p. 819n; **24** "Why I Enroll," *ibid.*, vol. I, p. 198; **30** *ibid.*, p. 211; **33** RMJ to Elizabeth B. Cadbury (Dec. 13, 1900).

88.8 "Why I Enroll," *ibid.*, vol. I, p. 197; **24** TRAIL OF LIFE IN THE MIDDLE YEARS, p. 197n; **28** RMJ to EBC (Jan. 3, 1901).

89.16 Isaac Sharpless to RMJ (Feb. 12, 1901).

CHAPTER VIII : *Openings*

91.4 RMJ to EBC (Sept 12, 1900). All the letters between Elizabeth Cadbury and Rufus Jones quoted in this chapter were written between September 12, 1900 and February 17, 1902.

92.3 EBC's diaries. Yearly summaries from 1888 to 1891 speak of her longing to be a nurse—"to be a Christian nurse, such a high profession, is what I long and pray for," Dec. 29, 1890; **17** Ellen Wood to RMJ (July 11, 1900).

95.23 RMJ to JWR (Feb. 7, 1902).

97.20 JWR to RMJ (Jan. 21, 1902); **23** TRAIL OF LIFE IN THE MIDDLE YEARS, pp. 82-83; **26** RMJ to JWR (Jan. 16, 1902).

98.4 RMJ to JWR (Feb. 7, 1902); **25** *American Friend*, Nov. 6, 1902.

99.29 "Why I Enroll," *ibid.*, vol. I, p. 207.

100.21 TRAIL OF LIFE IN THE MIDDLE YEARS, p. 84; **26** LUMINOUS TRAIL, p. 163; **37** *British Friend* (London), Sept., 1903, p. 252.

101.17 *American Friend*, Sept. 17, 1903, p. 635; **30** Letter from Thomas F. Branson to RMJ (July 18, 1903).

CHAPTER IX : *"Social Law in the Spiritual World"*

102.19 SOCIAL LAW IN THE SPIRITUAL WORLD, p. 16.

103.1 TRAIL OF LIFE IN THE MIDDLE YEARS, p. 159; **31** SOCIAL LAW IN THE SPIRITUAL WORLD, p. 13; **37** *ibid.*, p. 22.

104.2 *Ibid.*, p. 230. Italics RMJ's; **8** Lecture notes; **23** SOCIAL LAW IN THE SPIRITUAL WORLD, p. 45; **34** *ibid.*, p. 135.

105.2 TESTIMONY OF THE SOUL, p. 61; **21** SOCIAL LAW IN THE SPIRITUAL WORLD, p. 171; **28** *ibid.*, p. 174; **32** *ibid.*, p. 176.

106.4 *Ibid.*, p. 176, **10** PATHWAYS TO THE REALITY OF GOD, p. 197; **26** RMJ to William Bacon Evans (Dec. 26, 1946); **34** SOCIAL LAW IN THE SPIRITUAL WORLD, p. 180.

107.8 *Ibid.*, p. 188; **24** *ibid.*, pp. 251-52; **31** RMJ, THE ETERNAL GOSPEL (New York: The Macmillan Company, 1938), p. 68; **35** RMJ, NEW

Eyes for Invisibles (New York: The Macmillan Company, 1943), p. 106.
108.2 Social Law in the Spiritual World, p. 253.
109.2 *Friend* (London), Dec. 16, 1904, p. 829; **8** RMJ to JWR (Dec. 26, 1904); **14** JWR to RMJ (Feb. 15, 1905); **30** *Friends Quarterly Examiner*, April 1907, pp. 156-57.
110.2 RMJ to George Newman (undated [1907]); **18** *Nation* (London), Aug. 8, 1908; **27** Harry E. Fosdick, The Living of These Days (New York: Harper & Brothers, 1956), p. 27; **35** Harry E. Fosdick, ed., Rufus Jones Speaks to Our Times: An Anthology (New York: The Macmillan Company, 1951), Introduction, p. v; **39** Mrs. Seth Gifford to Elizabeth B. Jones (EBJ), (1904).
111.33 MHJ, Rufus M. Jones, p. 63.

CHAPTER X : *Shaping the Course of Things*

112.5 RMJ to JWR (Jan. 10, 1905).
114.30 RMJ to EBJ (Aug. 22, 1905).
115.7 RMJ, The Double Search: Studies in Atonement and Prayer (Philadelphia: The John C. Winston Co., 1906), p. 91; A Call to What Is Vital (New York: The Macmillan Company, 1948), p. 134; **14** Double Search, p. 97; A Call to What Is Vital, p. 136; **15** Double Search, p. 101; A Call to What Is Vital, p. 139; **24** RMJ to EBJ (Sept. 1, 1905).
116.36 Report of the Conference, mimeographed.
118.7 Brinton, Friends for Three Hundred Years, p. 193; **19** *ibid.*, pp. 193-94; **28** E. Russell, *op. cit.*, p. 119.
119.5 RMJ to George Newman (Aug. 7, 1907); **23** RMJ to EBJ (June 16, 1905); **35** RMJ to EBJ (June 26, 1905).
120.4 RMJ to EBJ (June 28, 1905); **32** *American Friend*, July 13, 1905, p. 461.
121.10 RMJ to EBJ (June 12, 1905).
122.5 RMJ to EBJ (Jan. 2, 1907).
123.13 *American Friend*, June 25, 1908, p. 403; **20** R. B. Perry, Thought and Character of William James (One vol. ed.; Cambridge, Mass.: Harvard University Press, 1948), p. 329; **26** Pathways to the Reality of God, p. 209.
124.35 MHJ, Rufus M. Jones, pp. 39-40.

CHAPTER XI : *The Quaker History Begun*

126.4 *The Sheffield Telegraph*, May 7, 1909; **30** RMJ, Studies in Mystical Religion (London: Macmillan & Co., Ltd., 1909), p. xxxii; **34** RMJ, The Flowering of Mysticism (New York: The Macmillan Company, 1939), pp. 5-6.
127.10 Studies in Mystical Religion, p. 165; **25** Evelyn Underhill, Mysticism (New York: E. P. Dutton & Co., Inc.), (Pref. 1930), p. 267; **32** Studies in Mystical Religion, pp. xxix-xxx; **40** *ibid.*, p. 284n.
128.7 *Ibid.*, p. 109; **14** *ibid.*, pp. 215-16; **19** *ibid.*, p. 110; **26** *ibid.*, p. 70.

129.13 W. R. Inge to RMJ (May 20, 1908); **24** FLOWERING OF MYSTICISM, p. 27; **30** STUDIES IN MYSTICAL RELIGION, p. 7.

130.8 *Ibid.*, p. 239; **19** *ibid.*, p. 280; **27** *ibid.*, p. 296; **30** *ibid.*, p. 314; **38** *ibid.*, p. 320.

131.1 *Ibid.*, p 3.25; **3** *ibid.*, p. 327; **10** *ibid.*, p. 366; **20** *ibid.*, p. 447; **28** *ibid.*, p. 500.

132.4 Article by RMJ on Jewish Mysticism. *Harvard Theological Review*, April, 1943; **10** *The Christian Commonwealth*, Jan. 11, 1911; **13** *Daily News* (London), May 13, 1909.

CHAPTER XII : *"The Spiritual Reformers"*

133.12 Alice H. James to RMJ (Oct. 30, 1910); **23** *American Friend*, Sept. 15, 1910, p. 583.

134.12 HISTORY OF HAVERFORD COLLEGE, p. 86; **32** EBJ to her parents (June 11, 1911).

135.6 RMJ to L. Violet Hodgkin (LVH), (June 18, 1911); **18** Theodor Sippell to RMJ (Feb. 21, 1910); **35** Theodor Sippell to EGV (Marburg, May 13, 1957).

136.20 TRAIL OF LIFE IN THE MIDDLE YEARS, p. 225; **32** *American Friend*, Aug. 10, 1911, p. 499.

137.25 NEW EYES FOR INVISIBLES, p. 67; **33** RMJ to EBJ (Aug. 14, 1911).

138.3 TRAIL OF LIFE IN THE MIDDLE YEARS, p. 226; **16** John S. Hoyland to EGV (Woodbrooke, Birmingham, May 6, 1957); **32** RMJ to EBJ (Aug. 19, 1913).

139.6 RMJ to EBJ (Aug. 26, 1913); **33** Theodor Sippell to RMJ (Oct. 26, 1913; Oct. 31, 1931; Dec. 2, 1931).

140.9 RMJ, SPIRITUAL REFORMERS (London: Macmillan & Co., Ltd., 1914), p. 321; **19** *ibid.*, p. 337; **28** *ibid.*, pp. xlviii, xlix; **29** *ibid.*, p. 1; **30** *loc. cit.;* **32** *ibid.*, p. 4.

141.14 *Ibid.*, pp. 348-49; **23** Geoffrey F. Nuttall, THE HOLY SPIRIT IN PURITAN FAITH AND EXPERIENCE (Oxford: Blackwell, 1946), p. 15; **28** *ibid.*, p. 162.

142.4 Shailer Mathews to RMJ (Oct. 11, 1915); **9** Aldous Huxley to RMJ (Aug. 22, 1945).

CHAPTER XIII : *The End of an Era*

143.18 Arnold S. Rowntree (Sept. 6, 1912). MS copy of Journal.

144.2 TRAIL OF LIFE IN THE MIDDLE YEARS, p. 185.

145.5 *American Friend*, Dec. 26, 1912, p. 823; **25** TRAIL OF LIFE IN THE MIDDLE YEARS, pp. 228-29; **39** Report of the Conference at Scalby (Aug. 29, 1913).

146.33 LVH to RMJ (Dec. 13, 1915).

147.13 TRAIL OF LIFE IN THE MIDDLE YEARS, p. 221; **37** RMJ to EBJ (May 2, 1943).

148.6 D. Garsop for the Overseers (Nov. 14, 1914); **19** *Present Day Papers*, Sept., 1914, p. 247.

149.1 *Loc. cit.;* **10** RMJ to LVH (Oct. 20, 1914).

CHAPTER XIV : *Low Gear*

150.16 RMJ to EBJ (Jan. 22, 1915).
151.14 RMJ to EBJ (Feb. 4, 1915); **18** RMJ to EBJ (Feb. 5, 1915); **30** MHJ, RUFUS M. JONES, p. 43.
152.26 *Present Day Papers*, Dec., 1915, p. 351; **32** MHJ, *loc. cit.*
153.12 *Present Day Papers*, Sept., 1915, p. 264; **22** LVH to RMJ (May 31, 1915); **40** *Present Day Papers*, Aug., 1915, pp. 234-36.
154.13 RMJ to MHJ (April 4, 1948).

CHAPTER XV : *"A Service of Love in War Time"*

157.20 RMJ to LVH (July 26, 1917).
160.9 MHJ, RUFUS M. JONES, p. 51; **37** RMJ to EBJ (July 18, 1917).
162.12 Woodrow Wilson to RMJ in RMJ, SERVICE OF LOVE IN WAR TIME: AMERICAN FRIENDS RELIEF WORK IN EUROPE, 1917-1919 (New York: The Macmillan Company, 1920), p. 52; **37** Notes for a talk, 1942.
165.18 Norman Angell, AFTER ALL: THE AUTOBIOGRAPHY OF NORMAN ANGELL (New York: Farrar, Straus and Cudahy, Inc., 1952), p. 209.
166.27 SERVICE OF LOVE IN WAR TIME, p. 265; **32** *ibid.*, p. 240.
167.21 RMJ to LVH (April 17, 1921).

CHAPTER XVI : *Herbert Hoover and Friend Jones*

169.10 In all of this chapter I am greatly indebted to the Honorable Herbert Hoover for clarification of the complicated relationships between the American Relief Administration and the American Friends Service Committee, for information about the thorny problems of raising money for Russian famine relief and for permission to quote his letters to Rufus Jones.
170.17 Carolena M. Wood to Wilbur K. Thomas. Quoted in Mary Hoxie Jones, SWORDS INTO PLOUGHSHARES (New York: The Macmillan Company, 1937), pp. 77-78.
172.31 Letter in Roberts Collection, Haverford College.
174.5 RMJ to EBJ (June 13, 1921); **31** RMJ to EBJ (June 18, 1921).
175.6 RMJ to EBJ (May 26, 1921).
176.2 Wilbur K. Thomas to RMJ (Aug. 18, 1921); **26** Mr. Hoover's figures, as given to EGV (May 31, 1957).
177.39 RMJ to James Norton (Aug. 24, 1921). A.F.S.C. files, Haverford College Library.
178.7 Lewis C. Gannett to James Norton; **30** HH to RMJ (Sept. 10, 1921). A.F.S.C. files; Haverford College Library; **47** HH to RMJ (Sept. 10, 1921). A.F.S.C. files, Haverford College Library.
179.22 RMJ to HH (Sept. 16, 1921). Signed carbon copy, A.F.S.C. files, Haverford College Library; **45** HH to RMJ (Sept. 21, 1921). A.F.S.C. files, Haverford College Library.
180.12 HH to EGV (May 31, 1957).
181.35 RMJ to HH (Jan. 2, 1922). Signed carbon copy, A.F.S.C. files, Haverford College Library; **40** HH to RMJ. A.F.S.C. files, Haverford College Library.

182.17 HH to RMJ. A.F.S.C. files, Haverford College Library; **22** RMJ to HH. Signed carbon copy, A.F.S.C. files, Haverford College Library.
183.28 HH to RMJ.

CHAPTER XVII : *"Our Rufus"*

185.4 MHJ, RUFUS M. JONES, p. 53; **40** RMJ, NATURE AND AUTHORITY OF CONSCIENCE (London: Swarthmore Press, 1920), p. 73.
186.4 *Friend* (London), Aug. 20, 1920, p. 522; **10** Official Report of the Conference, p. 46.
187.8 George Newman, "House of the Four Winds," *Friends Quarterly Examiner*, Oct., 1920, p. 335; **25** *ibid.*, p. 344; **31** RMJ to LVH (Sept. 3, 1920); **35** RMJ to LVH (Sept. 11, 1920).
188.12 RMJ to MHJ (April 12, 1948).
189.37 Cornelia Meigs. WHAT MAKES A COLLEGE: A HISTORY OF BRYN MAWR (New York: The Macmillan Company, 1956), p. 82; **40** RMJ to MHJ (April, 1948).
190.15 TRAIL OF LIFE IN THE MIDDLE YEARS, p. 208; **22** *ibid.*, pp. 208-09; **26** Eleanor Little Aldrich to EGV.
191.29 RMJ to Asa Wing (May 3, 1921).
192.3 Marion E. Parks to RMJ (Jan. 24, 1922; Feb. 22, 1922; **11** Edith Finch, CAREY THOMAS OF BRYN MAWR (New York: Harper and Brothers, *c.* 1947), p. 268; RMJ to MHJ (April 2, 1948; **34** EBJ to MHJ (Oct. 22, 1922).
193.9 RMJ to LVH (July 20, 1919; **17** RMJ to LVH (April 17, 1921); **32** LATER PERIODS OF QUAKERISM, vol. II, p. 915.
194.31 Brinton, FRIENDS FOR THREE HUNDRED YEARS, p. viii; **35** *ibid.*, p. ix.
195.12 TRAIL OF LIFE IN THE MIDDLE YEARS, p. 189; **20** PATHWAYS TO THE REALITY OF GOD, p. 118; **24** ETERNAL GOSPEL, p. 79; **28** *ibid.*, p. 72; **30** RMJ, RELIGION AND LIFE (Shanghai: Association Press, 1926), p. 48; **35** PATHWAYS TO THE REALITY OF GOD, p. 119; **40** ETERNAL GOSPEL, p. 68.
196.7 LATER PERIODS OF QUAKERISM, vol. II, p. 554; **10** *loc. cit.*; **17** SOCIAL LAW IN THE SPIRITUAL WORLD, p. 75.
197.6 RMJ to Violet Hodgkin Holdsworth (LVH), (July 23, 1922); **9** RMJ, THE ABUNDANT LIFE (London: Headley, 1908), p. 31; **12** AMERICAN PULPIT SERIES (New York: Abingdon-Cokesbury Press, *c.* 1945), Bk. 8, p. 50; **16** RMJ, SPIRITUAL ENERGIES IN THE DAILY LIFE (New York: The Macmillan Company, 1922), p. 123.
198.7 RMJ to LVH (July 11, 1921).

CHAPTER XVIII : *Athens and the Holy Land*

201.24 "Why I Enroll," *ibid.*, vol. I, pp. 208-09.
202.15 RMJ to MJH (Feb. 22, 1923); **25** EBJ to MHJ (Feb. 22, 1923).
203.4 RMJ to MHJ (March 10, 1923); **9** MHJ, RUFUS M. JONES, p. 55; **17** *Friend* (London), April 13, 1923, p. 262.
204.18 RMJ to MHJ (May 23, 1923).
205.18 RMJ, THE RADIANT LIFE (New York: The Macmillan Company, 1944), p. 5.
206.5 MHJ, RUFUS M. JONES, p. 65.
207.10 RMJ to Hubert Peet (April 19, 1940).

CHAPTER XIX : *New Noises, New Calls*

209.4 RMJ to MHJ (May 30, 1926); **22** Journal, June 25, 1926; **34** *ibid.,* June 26, 1926.
210.9 *Ibid.,* July 11, 1926; **20** RMJ to Wilbur K. Thomas (July 21, 1926).
211.24 RMJ to EBJ (Aug. 10, 1926).
213.4 Commencement Address, the Atlantic City Friends School, June, 1927; **32** Journal, Sept. 3, 1926.
214.10 *Ibid.,* Sept. 7, 1926; **34** *ibid.,* Oct. 13, 1926.
215.28 *Ibid.,* Oct. 29, 1926; **38** RMJ to Charles Evans (Nov. 6, 1926).
217.17 Journal, Nov. 26, 1926.
218.4 RMJ to M. K. Gandhi (April 20, 1926). Carbon copy; **41** Signet Books, New American Library, 1954, p. 55.
220.17 Michael Coates an English Quaker whom Gandhi had known in Swaziland. RMJ corresponded with him in 1938. (RMJ to Clarence E. Pickett, April 22, 1938. Copy.)
221.40 Journal, Dec. 1, 1926.
223.2 *Ibid.,* Dec. 11, 1926; **37** RMJ, THE SHEPHERD WHO MISSED THE MANGER (New York: Doubleday & Company, Inc., 1941), pp. 4-5.

CHAPTER XX : *The Orient Again*

225.6 MHJ, SWORDS INTO PLOUGHSHARES, pp. 129-130; **21** Clarence E. Pickett, FOR MORE THAN BREAD (Boston: Little, Brown & Co., 1953), p. x.
227.3 RMJ, "What Saints and Sages See," *The Christian Century,* Jan. 12, 1930, p. 206; **35** RMJ, "Secular Civilization and the Christian Task," in International Missionary Council, *Jerusalem Meeting,* vol. I, p. 230.
228.2 *Ibid.,* p. 248; **37** RMJ to John R. Mott (Nov. 5, 1930). Carbon copy.
229.7 RMJ to Richard Roberts (Oct. 16, 1931). Carbon copy.
231.38 RMJ, "Letter from China," *Friend* (London), April 29, 1932, p. 354.
232.29 William E. Hocking to MHJ (1951).
233.31 RETHINKING MISSIONS: A LAYMEN'S INQUIRY AFTER ONE HUNDRED YEARS, by the Committee of Appraisal. William Ernest Hocking, Chairman (New York: Harper & Brothers, 1932), pp. 4-5.
234.26 *Christian Century,* Nov., 1932, p. 1434.

CHAPTER XXI : *Midwife to the Soul*

238.7 *Friend* (London), Jan. 20, 1933, pp. 48-49.
239.18 MHJ, RUFUS M. JONES, p. 60; **24** TRAIL OF LIFE IN COLLEGE, p. 11; **34** NEW STUDIES IN MYSTICAL RELIGION, p. 112; **40** TRAIL OF LIFE IN THE MIDDLE YEARS, p. 212.
240.24 David Maxfield to his father, E. L. Maxfield (Nov. 17, 1933); **37** Howard Comfort to EGV (Nov., 1956).
241.15 TRAIL OF LIFE IN THE MIDDLE YEARS, p. 154; **30** *ibid.,* pp. 161-62.
242.11 William Wistar Comfort in *The Friend* (Philadelphia), July 1, 1948; **15** F. A. Swan to RMJ, March 23, 1902; **17** RMJ, "Some Pisgah Reflections," *Friends Intelligencer,* Jan. 30, 1943, p. 69; **25** Sigmund Spaeth to EGV (July 23, 1957).

243.16 Daniel F. Coogan, Jr., to EGV (July 20, 1957); **37** Clyde E. Milner to EGV (Oct., 1955).

244.2 Dr. Frederick R. Taylor. Introduction to an Address by Rufus Jones; **5** TRAIL OF LIFE IN THE MIDDLE YEARS, p. 211; **34** MHJ, RUFUS M. JONES, p. 60.

CHAPTER XXIII : *The Mysticism of Rufus Jones*

249.22 "Why I Enroll," *ibid.*, vol. I, p. 207.

250.8 *Ibid.*, p. 209; **11** TESTIMONY OF THE SOUL, p. 21; **18** W. C. Braithwaite, THE BEGINNINGS OF QUAKERISM (London: Macmillan & Co., Ltd., 1912), Introduction, p. xxxiv; **26** TRAIL OF LIFE IN THE MIDDLE YEARS, p. 195; **30** SPIRITUAL REFORMERS, p. xxiii; **38** NEW STUDIES IN MYSTICAL RELIGION, p. 23; **39** FUNDAMENTAL ENDS OF LIFE, p. 120.

251.4 FLOWERING OF MYSTICISM, p. 251; **20** LUMINOUS TRAIL, p. 26; **24** PATHWAYS TO THE REALITY OF GOD, p. 24; **40** TESTIMONY OF THE SOUL, p. 209.

252.6 LUMINOUS TRAIL, p. 18; **12** NEW STUDIES IN MYSTICAL RELIGION, p. 49; **17** SOCIAL LAW IN THE SPIRITUAL WORLD, p. 152; **23** FLOWERING OF MYSTICISM, p. 6.

253.6 "Why I Enroll," *ibid.*, vol. I, p. 202; **18** TESTIMONY OF THE SOUL, pp. 196-97; **23** LUMINOUS TRAIL, p. 18; **29** "Why I Enroll," *ibid.*, vol. I, p. 203.

254.1 MYSTICISM AND DEMOCRACY IN THE ENGLISH COMMONWEALTH, p. 121; **9** "Why I Enroll," *ibid.*, vol. I, pp. 203-04; **28** FUNDAMENTAL ENDS OF LIFE, p. 103.

255.5 Thomas H. Hughes, PHILOSOPHIC BASIS OF MYSTICISM (Edinburgh: Clark, 1937), p. 14; **35** FLOWERING OF MYSTICISM, p. 184.

256.10 Brinton, FRIENDS FOR THREE HUNDRED YEARS, p. 64; **12** SOCIAL LAW IN THE SPIRITUAL WORLD, p. 153; **22** "Why I Enroll," *ibid.*, vol. I, p. 206.

257.1 FAITH AND PRACTICE OF THE PHILADELPHIA YEARLY MEETING (1955), p. 19; **15** RMJ to LVH (Nov. 12, 1936); **20** SOCIAL LAW IN THE SPIRITUAL WORLD, p. 153; **36** Brinton, FRIENDS FOR THREE HUNDRED YEARS, p. xiii.

258.10 *American Friend*, June 29, 1899, p. 603; **21** RELIGION AND LIFE, p. 31; **23** NEW STUDIES IN MYSTICAL RELIGION, p. 118; **28** PATHWAYS TO THE REALITY OF GOD, p. 130.

259.25 FUNDAMENTAL ENDS OF LIFE, p. 96.

260.3 SPIRITUAL REFORMERS, p. xxiv; **4** NEW STUDIES IN MYSTICAL RELIGION, p. 198; **8** *loc. cit.;* **13** FUNDAMENTAL ENDS OF LIFE, p. 115; **24** NEW STUDIES IN MYSTICAL RELIGION, p. 15; **27** SPIRITUAL REFORMERS, p. xxiiin.; **31** TESTIMONY OF THE SOUL, pp. 29-30.

261.2 *Ibid.*, pp. 30-31; **8** *ibid.*, pp. 29-30; **24** *ibid.*, p. 29.

262.3 NEW STUDIES IN MYSTICAL RELIGION, pp. 81-82; **7** TESTIMONY OF THE SOUL, p. 29.

CHAPTER XXIV : *Great Occasions*

264.23 *Alumnae Bulletin* (Bryn Mawr), Jan., 1936, p. 5; **30** M. Carey Thomas to RMJ (April 26, 1929); **40** Resolution adopted Dec. 17, 1936.

266.27 Report of Harriet B. Hubbard, Dreiser's secretary, quoted in Gerhard

Friedrich: "The Dreiser-Jones Correspondence," Friends Historical Association. *Bulletin*, Spring, 1957, p. 24; **37** *loc. cit.*

267.2 Theodore Dreiser to RMJ (April 23, 1943); **17** "Report of Rufus Jones's Remarks at a Joint Meeting of Friends Service Council and Home Service Committee, London, Oct., 1929." *American Friend*, Nov. 7, 1929, p. 825; **27** *ibid.*

268.4 *American Friend*, June 21, 1906, p. 99.

270.27 *Friend* (London), Sept. 24, 1937, p. 870; **37** *ibid.*, p. 869.

CHAPTER XXV : *South Africa*

271.12 Howard H. Brinton, ed., CHILDREN OF LIGHT (New York: The Macmillan Company, 1938), p. ix.

274.13 RMJ, Notes on meetings with General Smuts, 1938; **35** *ibid.*

275.3 *Ibid.;* **13** RMJ to MHJ (March 14, 1938); **24** Jan Smuts to Margaret Gillett (1946). Quoted by her in a letter to RMJ (Feb. 2, 1946); **34** RMJ to Clarence E. Pickett (March 13, 1938).

276.3 RMJ to MHJ (March 18, 1938); **24** F. William Fox to RMJ (April 24, 1938); **38** RMJ to Clarence E. Pickett (April 22, 1938).

278.28 RMJ to MHJ (June 8, 1938).

279.2 MS. 1938.

CHAPTER XXVI : *Mission to the Gestapo*

281.12 Pickett, *op. cit.*, p. 134.

282.14 RMJ, "Our Day in the German Gestapo," *American Friend*, July 10, 1947, p. 265.

283.17 RMJ to EBJ (Dec. 4, 1938).

284.2 Philadelphia *Evening Bulletin*, Dec. 6, 1938; **16** G. A. Walton, Journal, Dec. 6, 1938.

286.30 *Evening Bulletin*, Dec. 6, 1938; **35** "Our Day in the German Gestapo," *ibid.*, p. 266.

288.4 RMJ to Clarence E. Pickett (Dec. 13, 1938); **14** RMJ to EBJ (Dec. 16, 1938); **19** H. H. G. Schacht, CONFESSIONS OF THE "OLD WIZARD" (Boston: Houghton Mifflin & Co., 1956), pp. 351-52.

289.11 D. Robert Yarnall, "Factual notes" (Dec. 15, 1938).

290.2 "Our Day in the German Gestapo," *ibid.*, p. 266; **12** G. A. Walton, Journal, Dec. 17, 1938.

291.15 "Our Day in the German Gestapo," *ibid.*, p. 266; **39** *ibid.*, p. 267.

292.26 Schacht, *op. cit.*, p. 351-52; **30** D. R. Yarnall, "Factual notes" (Dec. 20, 1938).

293.12 Pickett, *op. cit.*, p. 137.

CHAPTER XXVII : *The Vital Cell*

296.31 RMJ, ed., THE CHURCH, THE GOSPEL AND WAR (New York: Harper & Brothers, 1946). Introduction, p. ix; **32** RMJ, THE QUAKER PEACE POSITION (Richmond, Ind.: Peace Ass'n of Friends in America), unpaged.

298.11 RADIANT LIFE, p. 111; **22** *ibid.*, p. 136; **40** MHJ, RUFUS M. JONES, p. 66.

CHAPTER XXVIII : *The Finishing of the Work*

302.22 RMJ, Original Quakerism a Movement Not a Sect (Richmond, Indiana, 1945), p. 3.
303.2 *Ibid.*, p. 24.
306.7 Luminous Trail, p. 8.
307.9 RMJ to MHJ (Dec. 11, 1947); **20** RMJ to MHJ (Dec. 3, 1947); **34** RMJ to MHJ (Jan. 27, 1948).
308.3 RMJ to MHJ (Jan. 21, 1948); **9** A Call to What Is Vital, p. 5.
309.13 *American Friend*, July 8, 1948, p. 223; **23** RMJ to Cardinal Spellman (Feb. 10, 1948). Carbon copy; **33** Pickett, *op. cit.*, p. 262.
312.12 RMJ to Corder Catchpool (April 13, 1948); **19** MHJ, Rufus M. Jones, p. 68.
313.12 MS.; **20** MHJ, Rufus M. Jones, p. 69.
314.9 RMJ to SHC (July 8, 1887).
315.14 Luminous Trail, p. 13.

BOOKS BY RUFUS M. JONES

ELI AND SYBIL JONES: Their Life and Work. Philadelphia: Porter and Coates, 1889. 316pp.

PRACTICAL CHRISTIANITY: Essays on the Practice of Religion. Philadelphia: The John C. Winston Co., 1899. 250pp.

A DYNAMIC FAITH. London: Headley Bros., 1901. 103pp.

THE MESSAGE OF QUAKERISM: Two Addresses. London: Headley Bros., 1901. 30pp.

A BOY'S RELIGION FROM MEMORY. Philadelphia: Ferris, 1902. 141pp.

SOCIAL LAW IN THE SPIRITUAL WORLD: Studies in Human and Divine Inter-relationship. Philadelphia: The John C. Winston Co., 1904. 272pp.

THE DOUBLE SEARCH: Studies in Atonement and Prayer. Philadelphia: The John C. Winston Co., 1906. 124pp.

QUAKERISM AND THE SIMPLE LIFE. London: Headley Bros., 1906. 38pp.

THE ABUNDANT LIFE. London: Headley Bros., 1908. 67pp.

QUAKERISM: A Religion of Life (Swarthmore Lecture). London: Headley Bros., 1908. 47pp.

STUDIES IN MYSTICAL RELIGION. London: Macmillan & Co., Ltd., 1909. 518pp.

SELECTIONS FROM THE WRITINGS OF CLEMENT OF ALEXANDRIA. London: Headley Bros., 1910. 86pp.

THE QUAKERS IN THE AMERICAN COLONIES. London: Macmillan & Co., Ltd., 1911. 603pp.

STORIES OF HEBREW HEROES. London: Headley Bros., 1911. 160pp.

SPIRITUAL REFORMERS IN THE SIXTEENTH AND SEVENTEENTH CENTURIES. London: Macmillan & Co., Ltd., 1914. 362pp.

THE INNER LIFE. New York: The Macmillan Company, 1916. 194pp.

ST. PAUL THE HERO. New York: The Macmillan Company, 1917. 172pp.

THE WORLD WITHIN. New York: The Macmillan Company, 1918. 172pp.

RELIGION AS REALITY, LIFE AND POWER (William Penn Lecture). Philadelphia: Jenkins, 1919. 45pp.

THE STORY OF GEORGE FOX. New York: The Macmillan Company, 1919. 169pp.

THE NATURE AND AUTHORITY OF CONSCIENCE (Swarthmore Lecture). London: Swarthmore Press, 1920. 75pp.

THE REMNANT. London: Swarthmore Press, 1920. 163pp.

A SERVICE OF LOVE IN WAR TIME: American Friends Relief Work in Europe, 1917-19. New York: The Macmillan Company, 1920. 284pp.

THE LATER PERIODS OF QUAKERISM. London: Macmillan & Co., Ltd., 1921. 1020pp. (2 vols.).

THE BOY JESUS AND HIS COMPANIONS. New York: The Macmillan Company, 1922. 189pp.

SPIRITUAL ENERGIES IN DAILY LIFE. New York: The Macmillan Company, 1922. 179pp.

THE CHURCH'S DEBT TO HERETICS. New York: George H. Doran Company, 1924. 255pp.

FUNDAMENTAL ENDS OF LIFE. New York: The Macmillan Company, 1924. 144pp.

FINDING THE TRAIL OF LIFE. New York: The Macmillan Company, 1926. 148pp.

RELIGION AND LIFE. Shanghai: Association Press, 1926. 73pp.

THE FAITH AND PRACTICE OF THE QUAKERS. London: Methuen & Co., 1927. 181pp.

NEW STUDIES IN MYSTICAL RELIGION (Ely Lectures). New York: The Macmillan Company, 1927. 205pp.

THE NEW QUEST. New York: The Macmillan Company, 1928. 202pp.

THE TRAIL OF LIFE IN COLLEGE. New York: The Macmillan Company, 1929. 201pp.

GEORGE FOX, SEEKER AND FRIEND. New York: Harper & Bros., 1930, 224pp.

SOME EXPONENTS OF MYSTICAL RELIGION. New York: Abingdon Press, 1930. 237pp.

PATHWAYS TO THE REALITY OF GOD. New York: The Macmillan Company, 1931. 253pp.

MYSTICISM AND DEMOCRACY IN THE ENGLISH COMMONWEALTH. Cambridge: Harvard University Press, 1932. 184pp.

A PREFACE TO CHRISTIAN FAITH IN A NEW AGE. New York: The Macmillan Company, 1932. 206pp.

HAVERFORD COLLEGE: A History and an Interpretation. New York: The Macmillan Company, 1933. 244pp.

THE TRAIL OF LIFE IN THE MIDDLE YEARS. New York: The Macmillan Company, 1924. 250pp.

RE-THINKING RELIGIOUS LIBERALISM. Boston: Beacon Press, 1935. 26pp.

THE TESTIMONY OF THE SOUL (Ayer Lectures). New York: The Macmillan Company, 1936. 215pp.

SOME PROBLEMS OF LIFE (Cole Lectures). Nashville: Cokesbury Press, 1937. 214pp.

THE ETERNAL GOSPEL. New York: The Macmillan Company, 1938. 235pp.

THE FLOWERING OF MYSTICISM: The Friends of God in the Fourteenth Century. New York: The Macmillan Company, 1939. 270pp.

THE SHEPHERD WHO MISSED THE MANGER. New York: Doubleday & Co., 1941. 28pp.

A SMALL-TOWN BOY. New York: The Macmillan Company, 1941. 154pp.

SPIRIT IN MAN. Stanford: Stanford University Press, 1941. 70 pp.

THE VITAL CELL (William Penn Lecture). Philadelphia: Book Committee of the Religious Society of Friends, 1941. 27pp.

NEW EYES FOR INVISIBLES. New York: The Macmillan Company, 1943. 185pp.

THE RADIANT LIFE. New York: The Macmillan Company, 1944. 154pp.

THE LUMINOUS TRAIL. New York: The Macmillan Company, 1947. 165pp.

A CALL TO WHAT IS VITAL. New York: The Macmillan Company, 1948. 143pp.

INDEX

23537